BEGINNING
ANDROID™ APPLICATION DEVELOPME

D0337852

INTRODUCTION xv

CHAPTER 1   Getting Started with Android Programming 1
CHAPTER 2   Activities and Intents. 27
CHAPTER 3   Getting to Know the Android User Interface. 81
CHAPTER 4   Designing Your User Interface Using Views. 125
CHAPTER 5   Displaying Pictures and Menus with Views. 169
CHAPTER 6   Data Persistence 203
CHAPTER 7   Content Providers 237
CHAPTER 8   Messaging and Networking. 263
CHAPTER 9   Location-Based Services 301
CHAPTER 10   Developing Android Services 331
CHAPTER 11   Publishing Android Applications. 359
APPENDIX A   Using Eclipse for Android Development 381
APPENDIX B   Using the Android Emulator. 393
APPENDIX C   Answers to Exercises 411

INDEX. 415

BEGINNING

Android™ Application Development

Wei-Meng Lee

Wiley Publishing, Inc.

Beginning Android™ Application Development

Published by
Wiley Publishing, Inc.
10475 Crosspoint Boulevard
Indianapolis, IN 46256
www.wiley.com

ISBN: 978-1-118-01711-1
ISBN: 978-1-118-08729-9 (ebk)
ISBN: 978-1-118-08749-7 (ebk)
ISBN: 978-1-118-08780-0 (ebk)

Manufactured in the United States of America

10 9 8 7 6 5 4 3 2 1

For general information on our other products and services please contact our Customer Care Department within the United States at (877) 762-2974, outside the United States at (317) 572-3993 or fax (317) 572-4002.

Wiley also publishes its books in a variety of electronic formats. Some content that appears in print may not be available in electronic books.

Library of Congress Control Number: 2011921777

To my family:

Thanks for the understanding and support while I worked on getting this book ready! I love you all!

—WEI-MENG LEE

CREDITS

ABOUT THE AUTHOR

WEI-MENG LEE is a technologist and founder of Developer Learning Solutions (www.learn2develop.net), a technology company specializing in hands-on training on the latest mobile technologies. Wei-Meng has many years of training experience, and his training courses place special emphasis on the learning-by-doing approach. This hands-on approach to learning programming makes understanding the subject much easier than reading books, tutorials, and documentation.

Wei-Meng is also the author of *Beginning iOS 4 Application Development* (Wrox), along with several other Wrox titles. You can contact Wei-Meng at weimenglee@learn2develop.net.

ABOUT THE TECHNICAL EDITOR

KUNAL MITTAL serves as an Executive Director of Technology at Sony Pictures Entertainment where he is responsible for the SOA, Identity Management, and Content Management programs. Kunal is an entrepreneur who helps startups define their technology strategy, product roadmap, and development plans. He generally works in an Advisor or Consulting CTO capacity, and serves actively in the Project Management and Technical Architect functions.

He has authored, and edited several books and articles on J2EE, Cloud Computing, and mobile technologies. He holds a Master's degree in Software Engineering and is an instrument-rated private pilot.

ACKNOWLEDGMENTS

EVERY TIME I FINISH A BOOK PROJECT, I always tell myself that this will be the last book that I ever write. That's because writing books is such a time-consuming and laborious effort. However, when you receive e-mail messages from readers who want to thank you for helping them learn a new technology, all the frustrations disappear.

Sure enough, when I finished my previous book on iOS programming, I immediately signed on to do another book — this time about Android. Although you only see the author's name on the book cover, a lot of people actually worked behind the scenes to make it possible. And now that the book is finally done, it is time to thank a number of those people.

First, a huge thanks to Ami Sullivan, my editor, who is always a pleasure to work with. I cannot believe that we have already worked on three books together in such a short duration (only one year) and this is our fourth book! When I hear that Ami is going to be my editor, I know the project is in good hands. Thanks for the guidance, Ami; and thank you for your patience during those times when it seemed like the book was never going to be finished on schedule!

I should not forget the heroes behind the scene: copy editor Luann Rouff and technical editor Kunal Mittal. They have been eagle-eye editing the book, making sure that every sentence makes sense — both grammatically as well as technically. Thanks, Luann and Kunal!

I also want to take this chance to thank my editor at `MobiForge.com`, Ruadhan O'Donoghue, who has always been very supportive of my articles. He is always receptive of my ideas and has always been understanding when my schedule falls behind. Thanks for maintaining such a great site, Ruadhan!

Last, but not least, I want to thank my parents, and my wife, Sze Wa, for all the support they have given me. They selflessly adjusted their schedules to accommodate mine when I was working on this book. My wife, as always, stayed up late with me on numerous nights as I furiously worked to meet the deadlines, and for this I am very grateful. Finally, to our lovely dog, Ookii, thanks for staying by our side. (For those readers who do not know who Ookii is, you can find two pictures of her in this book. I will leave finding them as an extra exercise for you!)

CONTENTS

INTRODUCTION   *xv*

CHAPTER 1: GETTING STARTED WITH ANDROID PROGRAMMING   **1**

What Is Android?   **2**
Android Versions   2
Features of Android   3
Architecture of Android   3
Android Devices in the Market   4
The Android Market   6
Obtaining the Required Tools   **6**
Eclipse   7
Android SDK   7
Android Development Tools (ADT)   7
Creating Android Virtual Devices (AVDs)   11
Creating Your First Android Application   14
Anatomy of an Android Application   22
Summary   **25**

CHAPTER 2: ACTIVITIES AND INTENTS   **27**

Understanding Activities   **27**
Applying Styles and Themes to Activity   32
Hiding the Activity Title   33
Displaying a Dialog Window   34
Displaying a Progress Dialog   39
Linking Activities Using Intents   **43**
Resolving Intent Filter Collision   48
Returning Results from an Intent   50
Passing Data Using an Intent Object   54
Calling Built-In Applications Using Intents   **56**
Understanding the Intent Object   64
Using Intent Filters   65
Adding Categories   71
Displaying Notifications   **73**
Summary   **78**

CHAPTER 3: GETTING TO KNOW THE ANDROID USER INTERFACE   81

Understanding the Components of a Screen   **81**

Views and ViewGroups   82

LinearLayout   83

AbsoluteLayout   87

TableLayout   89

RelativeLayout   91

FrameLayout   93

ScrollView   95

Adapting to Display Orientation   **97**

Anchoring Views   98

Resizing and Repositioning   101

Managing Changes to Screen Orientation   **104**

Persisting State Information during Changes in Configuration   108

Detecting Orientation Changes   109

Controlling the Orientation of the Activity   110

Creating the User Interface Programmatically   **111**

Listening for UI Notifications   **114**

Overriding Methods Defined in an Activity   114

Registering Events for Views   119

Summary   **122**

CHAPTER 4: DESIGNING YOUR USER INTERFACE USING VIEWS   125

Basic Views   **126**

TextView View   126

Button, ImageButton, EditText, CheckBox, ToggleButton, RadioButton, and RadioGroup Views   127

ProgressBar View   135

AutoCompleteTextView View   141

Picker Views   **144**

TimePicker View   144

Displaying the TimePicker in a Dialog Window   147

DatePicker View   149

Displaying the DatePicker View in a Dialog Window   153

List Views   **156**

ListView View   156

Customizing the ListView   159

Using the Spinner View   162

Summary   **166**

CHAPTER 5: DISPLAYING PICTURES AND MENUS WITH VIEWS — 169

Using Image Views to Display Pictures — **169**
Gallery and ImageView Views — 170
ImageSwitcher — 177
GridView — 181
Using Menus with Views — **185**
Creating the Helper Methods — 186
Options Menu — 188
Context Menu — 190
Some Additional Views — **193**
AnalogClock and DigitalClock Views — 194
WebView — 194
Summary — **200**

CHAPTER 6: DATA PERSISTENCE — 203

Saving and Loading User Preferences — **203**
Using getSharedPreferences() — 204
Using getPreferences() — 208
Persisting Data to Files — **209**
Saving to Internal Storage — 209
Saving to External Storage (SD Card) — 214
Choosing the Best Storage Option — 216
Using Static Resources — 217
Creating and Using Databases — **218**
Creating the DBAdapter Helper Class — 218
Using the Database Programmatically — 224
Adding Contacts — 224
Retrieving All the Contacts — 225
Retrieving a Single Contact — 226
Updating a Contact — 227
Deleting a Contact — 228
Upgrading the Database — 230
Pre-Creating the Database — 230
Bundling the Database with an Application — 231
Summary — **234**

CHAPTER 7: CONTENT PROVIDERS — 237

Sharing Data in Android — **237**
Using a Content Provider — **238**
Predefined Query String Constants — 243

Projections 246
Filtering 246
Sorting 247
Creating Your Own Content Providers **247**
Using the Content Provider 256
Summary **260**

CHAPTER 8: MESSAGING AND NETWORKING 263

SMS Messaging **263**
Sending SMS Messages Programmatically 264
Getting Feedback After Sending the Message 267
Sending SMS Messages Using Intent 269
Receiving SMS Messages 270
Updating an Activity from a BroadcastReceiver 273
Invoking an Activity from a BroadcastReceiver 277
Caveats and Warnings 280
Sending E-Mail **281**
Networking **284**
Downloading Binary Data 286
Downloading Text Files 288
Accessing Web Services 291
Performing Asynchronous Calls 296
Summary **297**

CHAPTER 9: LOCATION-BASED SERVICES 301

Displaying Maps **302**
Creating the Project 302
Obtaining the Maps API Key 303
Displaying the Map 305
Displaying the Zoom Control 308
Changing Views 310
Navigating to a Specific Location 312
Adding Markers 315
Getting the Location That Was Touched 318
Geocoding and Reverse Geocoding 320
Getting Location Data **322**
Monitoring a Location 327
Summary **327**

CHAPTER 10: DEVELOPING ANDROID SERVICES — 331

Creating Your Own Services — 331
Performing Long-Running Tasks in a Service — 336
Performing Repeated Tasks in a Service — 341
Executing Asynchronous Tasks on
Separate Threads Using IntentService — 343
Communicating between a Service and an Activity — 346
Binding Activities to Services — 350
Summary — 356

CHAPTER 11: PUBLISHING ANDROID APPLICATIONS — 359

Preparing for Publishing — 359
Versioning — 360
Digitally Signing Your Android Applications — 362
Deploying APK Files — 367
Using the adb.exe Tool — 367
Using a Web Server — 369
Publishing on the Android Market — 372
Creating a Developer Profile — 372
Submitting Your Apps — 373
Summary — 378

APPENDIX A: USING ECLIPSE FOR ANDROID DEVELOPMENT — 381

Getting Around in Eclipse — 381
Workspaces — 381
Package Explorer — 382
Using Projects from Other Workspaces — 383
Editors — 385
Perspectives — 387
Auto Import of Namespaces — 387
Code Completion — 388
Refactoring — 388
Debugging — 389
Setting Breakpoints — 389
Exceptions — 390

APPENDIX B: USING THE ANDROID EMULATOR — 393

Uses of the Android Emulator — 393
Installing Custom AVDs — 393

Emulating Real Devices 398
SD Card Emulation 399
Emulating Devices with Different Screen Sizes 401
Emulating Physical Capabilities 402
Sending SMS Messages to the Emulator 403
Making Phone Calls 406
Transferring Files into and out of the Emulator 407
Resetting the Emulator 409

APPENDIX C: ANSWERS TO EXERCISES 411

Chapter 1 Answers 411
Chapter 2 Answers 411
Chapter 3 Answers 412
Chapter 4 Answers 412
Chapter 5 Answers 412
Chapter 6 Answers 413
Chapter 7 Answers 413
Chapter 8 Answers 413
Chapter 9 Answers 413
Chapter 10 Answers 414
Chapter 11 Answers 414

INDEX *415*

INTRODUCTION

I FIRST STARTED PLAYING WITH THE ANDROID SDK before it was officially released as version 1.0. Back then, the tools were unpolished, the APIs in the SDK were unstable, and the documentation was sparse. Fast forward two and a half years, Android is now a formidable mobile operating system, with a following no less impressive than the iPhone. Having gone through all the growing pains of Android, I think now is the best time to start learning about Android programming — the APIs have stabilized, and the tools have improved. But one challenge remains: getting started is still an elusive goal for many. It was with this challenge in mind that I was motivated to write this book, one that could benefit beginning Android programmers and enable them to write progressively more sophisticated applications.

As a book written to help jump-start beginning Android developers, it covers the necessary topics in a linear manner so that you can build on your knowledge without being overwhelmed by the details. I adopt the philosophy that the best way to learn is by doing — hence the numerous Try It Out sections in each chapter, which first show you how to build something and then explain how everything works.

Although Android programming is a huge topic, my aim for this book is threefold: to get you started with the fundamentals, to help you understand the underlying architecture of the SDK, and to appreciate why things are done in certain ways. It is beyond the scope of any book to cover everything under the sun related to Android programming, but I am confident that after reading this book (and doing the exercises), you will be well equipped to tackle your next Android programming challenge.

WHO THIS BOOK IS FOR

This book is targeted for the beginning Android developer who wants to start developing applications using Google's Android SDK. To truly benefit from this book, you should have some background in programming and at least be familiar with object-oriented programming concepts. If you are totally new to Java — the language used for Android development — you might want to take a programming course in Java programming first, or grab one of many good books on Java programming. In my experience, if you already know C# or VB.NET, learning Java is not too much of an effort; you should be comfortable just following along with the Try It Outs.

For those totally new to programming, I know the lure of developing mobile apps and making some money is tempting. However, before attempting to try out the examples in this book, I think a better starting point would be to learn the basics of programming first.

> **NOTE** All the examples discussed in this book were written and tested using version 2.3 of the Android SDK. While every effort is made to ensure that all the tools used in this book are the latest, it is always possible that by the time you read this book, a newer version of the tools may be available. If so, some of the instructions and/or screenshots may differ slightly. However, any variations should be manageable.

WHAT THIS BOOK COVERS

This book covers the fundamentals of Android programming using the Android SDK. It is divided into 11 chapters and three appendices.

Chapter 1: Getting Started with Android Programming covers the basics of the Android OS and its current state. You will learn about the features of Android devices, as well as some of the popular devices in the market. You will then learn how to download and install all the required tools to develop Android applications and then test them on the Android Emulator.

Chapter 2: Activities and Intents gets you acquainted with the two fundamental concepts in Android programming: activities and intents. Activities are the building blocks of an Android application. You will learn how to link activities together to form a complete Android application using intents, the glue to links activities and one of the unique characteristics of the Android OS.

Chapter 3: Getting to Know the Android User Interface covers the various components that make up the UI of an Android application. You will learn about the various layouts you can use to build the UI of your application, and the numerous events that are associated with the UI when users interact with the application.

Chapter 4: Designing Your User Interface Using Views walks you through the various basic views you can use to build your Android UI. You will learn three main groups of views: basic views, picker views, and list views.

Chapter 5: Displaying Pictures and Menus with Views continues the exploration of views. Here, you will learn how to display images using the various image views, as well as display options and context menus in your application. This chapter ends with some additional cool views that you can use to spice up your application.

Chapter 6: Data Persistence shows you how to save, or store, data in your Android application. In addition to learning the various techniques to store user data, you will also learn file manipulation and how to save files onto internal and external storage (SD card). In addition, you will learn how to create and use a SQLite database in your Android application.

Chapter 7: Content Providers discusses how data can be shared among different applications on an Android device. You will learn how to use a content provider and then build one yourself.

Chapter 8: Messaging and Networking explores two of the most interesting topics in mobile programming — sending SMS messages and network programming. You will learn how to programmatically send and receive SMS and e-mail messages; and how to connect to web servers to download data. Finally, you will see how Web services can be consumed in an Android application.

Chapter 9: Location-Based Services demonstrates how to build a location-based service application using Google Maps. You will also learn how to obtain geographical location data and then display the location on the map.

Chapter 10: Developing Android Services shows you how you can write applications using services. Services are background applications that run without a UI. You will learn how to run your services asynchronously on a separate thread, and how your activities can communicate with them.

Chapter 11: Publishing Android Applications discusses the various ways you can publish your Android applications when you are ready. You will also learn about the steps to publishing and selling your applications on the Android Market.

Appendix A: Using Eclipse for Android Development provides a brief overview of the many features in Eclipse.

Appendix B: Using the Android Emulator provides some tips and tricks on using the Android Emulator for testing your applications.

Appendix C: Answers to Exercises contains the solutions to the end-of-chapter exercises found in every chapter.

HOW THIS BOOK IS STRUCTURED

This book breaks down the task of learning Android programming into several smaller chunks, enabling you to digest each topic before delving into a more advanced one.

If you are a total beginner to Android programming, start with Chapter 1 first. Once you have familiarized yourself with the basics, head over to the appendixes to read more about Eclipse and the Android Emulator. When you are ready, continue with Chapter 2 and gradually move into more advanced topics.

A feature of this book is that all the code samples in each chapter are independent of those discussed in previous chapters. That way, you have the flexibility to dive into the topics that interest you and start working on the Try It Out projects.

WHAT YOU NEED TO USE THIS BOOK

All the examples in this book run on the Android Emulator (which is included as part of the Android SDK). However, to get the most out of this book, having a real Android device would be useful (though not absolutely necessary).

CONVENTIONS

To help you get the most from the text and keep track of what's happening, a number of conventions are used throughout the book.

TRY IT OUT **These Are Exercises or Examples for You to Follow**

The Try It Out sections appear once or more per chapter. These are exercises to work through as you follow the related discussion in the text.

1. They consist of a set of numbered steps.

2. Follow the steps with your copy of the project files.

How It Works

After each Try It Out, the code you've typed is explained in detail.

As for other conventions in the text:

➤ New terms and important words are *highlighted* in italics when first introduced.

➤ Keyboard combinations are treated like this: Ctrl+R.

➤ Filenames, URLs, and code within the text are treated like so: `persistence.properties`.

➤ Code is presented in two different ways:

```
We use a monofont type with no highlighting for most code examples.
```

**We use bolding to emphasize code that is of particular importance in the
present context.**

> **NOTE** *Notes, tips, hints, tricks, and asides to the current discussion look like this.*

SOURCE CODE

As you work through the examples in this book, you may choose either to type in all the code manually or to use the source code files that accompany the book. All the source code used in this book is available for download at `www.wrox.com`. When at the site, simply locate the book's title (use the Search box or one of the title lists) and click the Download Code link on the book's detail page to obtain all the source code for the book.

You'll find the filename of the project you need in a CodeNote such as this at the beginning of the Try it Out features:

code snippet filename

After you download the code, just decompress it with your favorite compression tool. Alternatively, go to the main Wrox code download page at `www.wrox.com/dynamic/books/download.aspx` to see the code available for this book and all other Wrox books.

> **NOTE** *Because many books have similar titles, you may find it easiest to search by ISBN; this book's ISBN is 978-1-118-01711-1.*

ERRATA

We make every effort to ensure that there are no errors in the text or in the code. However, no one is perfect, and mistakes do occur. If you find an error in one of our books, such as a spelling mistake or faulty piece of code, we would be very grateful for your feedback. By sending in errata, you may save another reader hours of frustration and at the same time help us provide even higher-quality information.

To find the errata page for this book, go to www.wrox.com and locate the title using the Search box or one of the title lists. Then, on the book details page, click the Book Errata link. On this page, you can view all errata that has been submitted for this book and posted by Wrox editors. A complete book list, including links to each book's errata, is also available at www.wrox.com/misc-pages/booklist.shtml.

If you don't spot "your" error on the Book Errata page, go to www.wrox.com/contact/techsupport .shtml and complete the form there to send us the error you have found. We'll check the information and, if appropriate, post a message to the book's errata page and fix the problem in subsequent editions of the book.

P2P.WROX.COM

For author and peer discussion, join the P2P forums at p2p.wrox.com. The forums are a web-based system for you to post messages relating to Wrox books and related technologies and to interact with other readers and technology users. The forums offer a subscription feature to e-mail you topics of interest of your choosing when new posts are made to the forums. Wrox authors, editors, other industry experts, and your fellow readers are present on these forums.

At p2p.wrox.com, you will find a number of different forums that will help you not only as you read this book but also as you develop your own applications. To join the forums, just follow these steps:

1. Go to p2p.wrox.com and click the Register link.
2. Read the terms of use and click Agree.
3. Complete the required information to join as well as any optional information you want to provide and click Submit.
4. You will receive an e-mail with information describing how to verify your account and complete the joining process.

> **NOTE** *You can read messages in the forums without joining P2P, but in order to post your own messages, you must join.*

After you join, you can post new messages and respond to messages that other users post. You can read messages at any time on the Web. If you want to have new messages from a particular forum e-mailed to you, click the Subscribe to This Forum icon by the forum name in the forum listing.

For more information about how to use the Wrox P2P, be sure to read the P2P FAQs for answers to questions about how the forum software works, as well as for many common questions specific to P2P and Wrox books. To read the FAQs, click the FAQ link on any P2P page.

1

Getting Started with Android Programming

WHAT YOU WILL LEARN IN THIS CHAPTER

- ➤ What is Android?
- ➤ Android versions and its feature set
- ➤ The Android architecture
- ➤ The various Android devices on the market
- ➤ The Android Market application store
- ➤ How to obtain the tools and SDK for developing Android applications
- ➤ How to develop your first Android application

Welcome! The fact that you are holding this book in your hands (or are reading it on your latest mobile device) signifies that you are interested in learning how to write applications for the Android platform — and there's no better time to do this than now! The mobile application market is exploding, and recent market research shows that Android has overtaken iPhone to occupy the second position in the U.S. smartphone market. The first place honor currently goes to Research In Motion (RIM), with Apple's iPhone taking third place. By the time you read this, chances are good that Android may have become the number one smartphone platform in the U.S., and that you may even be reading this on one of the latest Android devices.

What propelled this relatively unknown operating system, which Google bought in 2005, to its popular status today? And what features does it offer? In this chapter you will learn what Android is, and what makes it so compelling to both developers and device manufacturers alike. You will also get started with developing your first Android application, and learn how to obtain all the necessary tools and set them up. By the end of this chapter, you will be equipped with the basic knowledge you need to explore more sophisticated techniques and tricks for developing your next killer Android application.

WHAT IS ANDROID?

Android is a mobile operating system that is based on a modified version of Linux. It was originally developed by a startup of the same name, Android, Inc. In 2005, as part of its strategy to enter the mobile space, Google purchased Android and took over its development work (as well as its development team).

Google wanted Android to be open and free; hence, most of the Android code was released under the open-source Apache License, which means that anyone who wants to use Android can do so by downloading the full Android source code. Moreover, vendors (typically hardware manufacturers) can add their own proprietary extensions to Android and customize Android to differentiate their products from others. This simple development model makes Android very attractive and has thus piqued the interest of many vendors. This has been especially true for companies affected by the phenomenon of Apple's iPhone, a hugely successful product that revolutionized the smartphone industry. Such companies include Motorola and Sony Ericsson, which for many years have been developing their own mobile operating systems. When the iPhone was launched, many of these manufacturers had to scramble to find new ways of revitalizing their products. These manufacturers see Android as a solution — they will continue to design their own hardware and use Android as the operating system that powers it.

The main advantage of adopting Android is that it offers a unified approach to application development. Developers need only develop for Android, and their applications should be able to run on numerous different devices, as long as the devices are powered using Android. In the world of smartphones, applications are the most important part of the success chain. Device manufacturers therefore see Android as their best hope to challenge the onslaught of the iPhone, which already commands a large base of applications.

Android Versions

Android has gone through quite a number of updates since its first release. Table 1-1 shows the various versions of Android and their codenames.

TABLE 1-1: A Brief History of Android Versions

ANDROID VERSION	RELEASE DATE	CODENAME
1.1	9 February 2009	
1.5	30 April 2009	Cupcake
1.6	15 September 2009	Donut
2.0/2.1	26 October 2009	Eclair
2.2	20 May 2010	Froyo
2.3	6 December 2010	Gingerbread
3.0	Unconfirmed at the time of writing	Honeycomb

Features of Android

As Android is open source and freely available to manufacturers for customization, there are no fixed hardware and software configurations. However, Android itself supports the following features:

➤ **Storage** — Uses SQLite, a lightweight relational database, for data storage. Chapter 6 discusses data storage in more detail.

➤ **Connectivity** — Supports GSM/EDGE, IDEN, CDMA, EV-DO, UMTS, Bluetooth (includes A2DP and AVRCP), WiFi, LTE, and WiMAX. Chapter 8 discusses networking in more detail.

➤ **Messaging** — Supports both SMS and MMS. Chapter 8 discusses messaging in more detail.

➤ **Web browser** — Based on the open-source WebKit, together with Chrome's V8 JavaScript engine

➤ **Media support** — Includes support for the following media: H.263, H.264 (in 3GP or MP4 container), MPEG-4 SP, AMR, AMR-WB (in 3GP container), AAC, HE-AAC (in MP4 or 3GP container), MP3, MIDI, Ogg Vorbis, WAV, JPEG, PNG, GIF, and BMP

➤ **Hardware support** — Accelerometer Sensor, Camera, Digital Compass, Proximity Sensor, and GPS

➤ **Multi-touch** — Supports multi-touch screens

➤ **Multi-tasking** — Supports multi-tasking applications

➤ **Flash support** — Android 2.3 supports Flash 10.1.

➤ **Tethering** — Supports sharing of Internet connections as a wired/wireless hotspot

Architecture of Android

In order to understand how Android works, take a look at Figure 1-1, which shows the various layers that make up the Android operating system (OS).

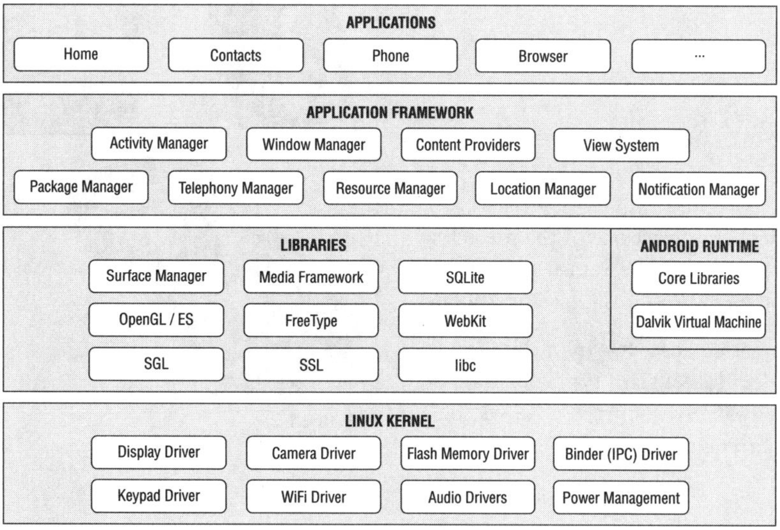

FIGURE 1-1

The Android OS is roughly divided into five sections in four main layers:

➤ **Linux kernel** — This is the kernel on which Android is based. This layer contains all the low-level device drivers for the various hardware components of an Android device.

➤ **Libraries** — These contain all the code that provides the main features of an Android OS. For example, the SQLite library provides database support so that an application can use it for data storage. The WebKit library provides functionalities for web browsing.

➤ **Android runtime** — At the same layer as the libraries, the Android runtime provides a set of core libraries that enable developers to write Android apps using the Java programming language. The Android runtime also includes the Dalvik virtual machine, which enables every Android application to run in its own process, with its own instance of the Dalvik virtual machine (Android applications are compiled into the Dalvik executables). Dalvik is a specialized virtual machine designed specifically for Android and optimized for battery-powered mobile devices with limited memory and CPU.

➤ **Application framework** — Exposes the various capabilities of the Android OS to application developers so that they can make use of them in their applications.

➤ **Applications** — At this top layer, you will find applications that ship with the Android device (such as Phone, Contacts, Browser, etc.), as well as applications that you download and install from the Android Market. Any applications that you write are located at this layer.

Android Devices in the Market

Android devices come in all shapes and sizes. As of late November 2010, the Android OS can be seen powering the following types of devices:

➤ Smartphones

➤ Tablets

➤ E-reader devices

➤ Netbooks

➤ MP4 players

➤ Internet TVs

Chances are good that you own at least one of the preceding devices. Figure 1-2 shows (clockwise) the Samsung Galaxy S, the HTC Desire HD, and the LG Optimus One smartphones.

Another popular category of devices that manufacturers are rushing out is the *tablet*. Tablet sizes typically start at seven inches, measured diagonally. Figure 1-3 shows the Samsung Galaxy Tab and the Dell Streak, which is a five-inch phone tablet.

FIGURE 1-2

Besides smartphones and tablets, Android is also beginning to appear in dedicated devices, such as e-book readers. Figure 1-4 shows the Barnes and Noble's NOOKcolor, which is a color e-Book reader running the Android OS.

FIGURE 1-3   **FIGURE 1-4**

In addition to these popular mobile devices, Android is also slowly finding its way into your living room. People of Lava, a Swedish company, has developed an Android-based TV, call the Scandinavia Android TV (see Figure 1-5).

Google has also ventured into a proprietary smart TV platform based on Android and co-developed with companies such as Intel, Sony, and Logitech. Figure 1-6 shows Sony's Google TV.

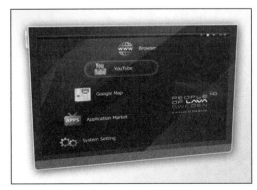

FIGURE 1-5   **FIGURE 1-6**

The Android Market

As mentioned earlier, one of the main factors determining the success of a smartphone platform is the applications that support it. It is clear from the success of the iPhone that applications play a very vital role in determining whether a new platform swims or sinks. In addition, making these applications accessible to the general user is extremely important.

As such, in August 2008, Google announced the Android Market, an online application store for Android devices, and made it available to users in October 2008. Using the Market application that is preinstalled on their Android device, users can simply download third-party applications directly onto their devices. Both paid and free applications are supported on the Android Market, though paid applications are available only to users in certain countries due to legal issues.

Similarly, in some countries, users can buy paid applications from the Android Market, but developers cannot sell in that country. As an example, at the time of writing, users in India can buy apps from the Android Market, but developers in India cannot sell apps on the Android Market. The reverse may also be true; for example, users in South Korea cannot buy apps, but developers in South Korea can sell apps on the Android Market.

Chapter 11 discusses more about the Android Market and how you can sell your own applications in it.

OBTAINING THE REQUIRED TOOLS

Now that you know what Android is and its feature set, you are probably anxious to get your hands dirty and start writing some applications! Before you write your first app, however, you need to download the required tools and SDKs.

For Android development, you can use a Mac, a Windows PC, or a Linux machine. All the tools needed are free and can be downloaded from the Web. Most of the examples provided in this book should work fine with the Android emulator, with the exception of a few examples that require access to the hardware. For this book, I will be using a Windows 7 computer to demonstrate all the code samples. If you are using a Mac or Linux computer, the screenshots should look similar; some minor differences may be present, but you should be able to follow along without problems.

So, let the fun begin!

JAVA JDK

The Android SDK makes use of the Java SE Development Kit (JDK). Hence, if your computer does not have the JDK installed, you should start by downloading the JDK from www.oracle.com/technetwork/java/javase/downloads/index.html and installing it prior to moving to the next section.

Eclipse

The first step towards developing any applications is obtaining the integrated development environment (IDE). In the case of Android, the recommended IDE is Eclipse, a multi-language software development environment featuring an extensible plug-in system. It can be used to develop various types of applications, using languages such as Java, Ada, C, C++, COBOL, Python, etc.

For Android development, you should download the Eclipse IDE for Java EE Developers (`www.eclipse.org/downloads/packages/eclipse-ide-java-ee-developers/heliossr1`). Six editions are available: Windows (32 and 64-bit), Mac OS X (Cocoa 32 and 64), and Linux (32 and 64-bit). Simply select the relevant one for your operating system. All the examples in this book were tested using the 32-bit version of Eclipse for Windows.

Once the Eclipse IDE is downloaded, unzip its content (the `eclipse` folder) into a folder, say `C:\Android\`. Figure 1-7 shows the content of the `eclipse` folder.

Android SDK

The next important piece of software you need to download is, of course, the Android SDK. The Android SDK contains a debugger, libraries, an emulator, documentation, sample code, and tutorials.

You can download the Android SDK from `http://developer.android.com/sdk/index.html`.

FIGURE 1-7

Once the SDK is downloaded, unzip its content (the `android-sdk-windows` folder) into the `C:\Android\` folder, or whatever name you have given to the folder you just created.

Android Development Tools (ADT)

The Android Development Tools (ADT) plug-in for Eclipse is an extension to the Eclipse IDE that supports the creation and debugging of Android applications. Using the ADT, you will be able to do the following in Eclipse:

➤ Create new Android application projects.

➤ Access the tools for accessing your Android emulators and devices.

➤ Compile and debug Android applications.

➤ Export Android applications into Android Packages (APK).

➤ Create digital certificates for code-signing your APK.

To install the ADT, first launch Eclipse by double-clicking on the `eclipse.exe` file located in the `eclipse` folder.

When Eclipse is first started, you will be prompted for a folder to use as your workspace. In Eclipse, a workspace is a folder where you store all your projects. Take the default suggested and click OK.

Once Eclipse is up and running, select the Help ➪ Install New Software... menu item (see Figure 1-8).

In the Install window that appears, type **http://dl-ssl.google.com/android/eclipse** in the text box (see Figure 1-9) and click Add....

After a while, you will see the Developer Tools item appear in the middle of the window (see Figure 1-10). Expand it, and it will reveal its content: Android DDMS, Android Development Tools, and Android Hierarchy Viewer. Check all of them and click Next.

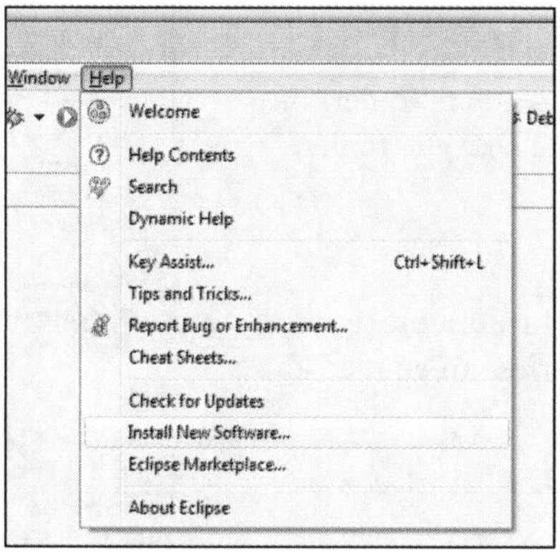

FIGURE 1-8

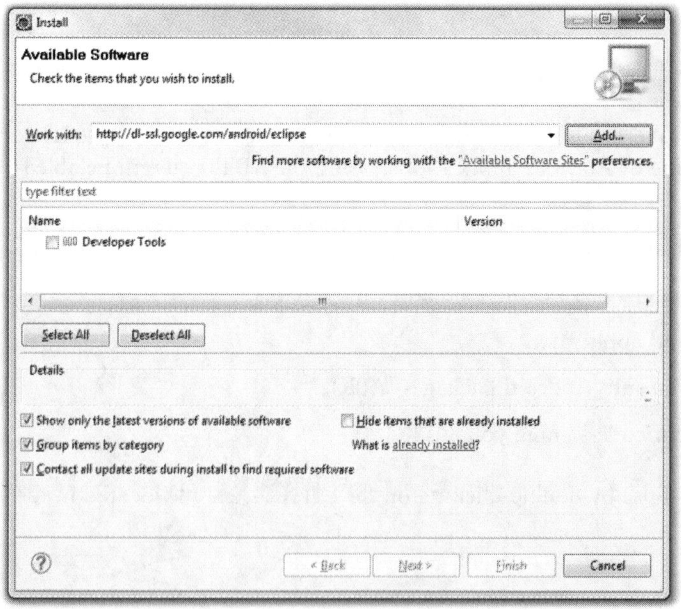

FIGURE 1-9

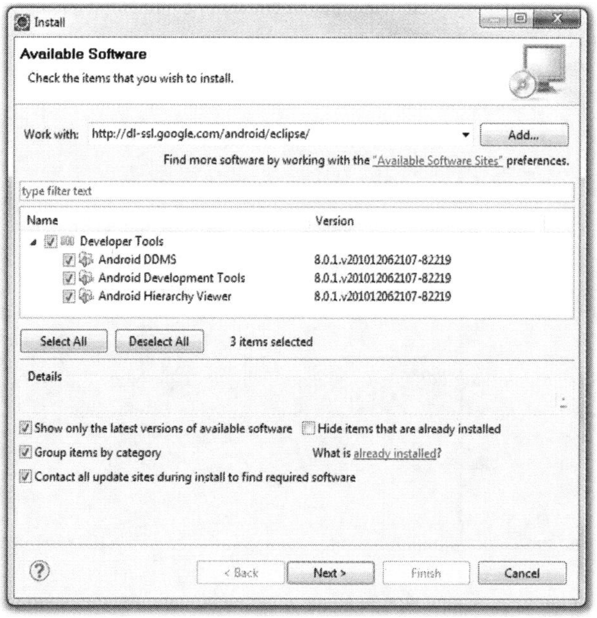

FIGURE 1-10

When you see the installation details, as shown in Figure 1-11, click Next.

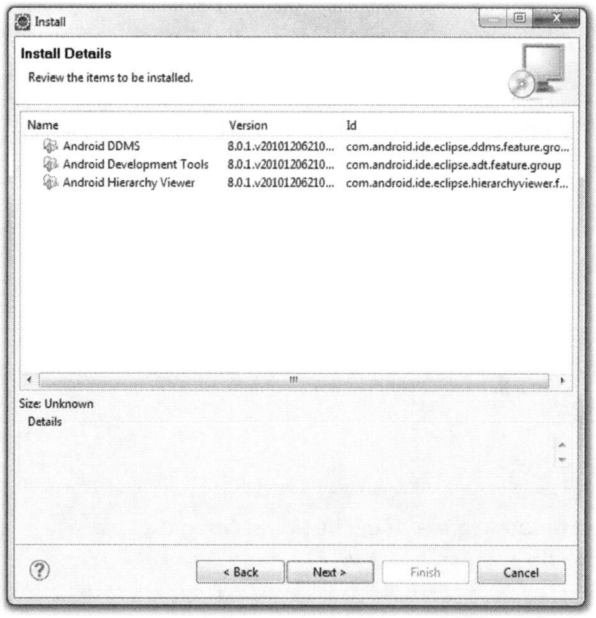

FIGURE 1-11

You will be asked to review the licenses for the tools. Check the option to accept the license agreements (see Figure 1-12). Click Finish to continue.

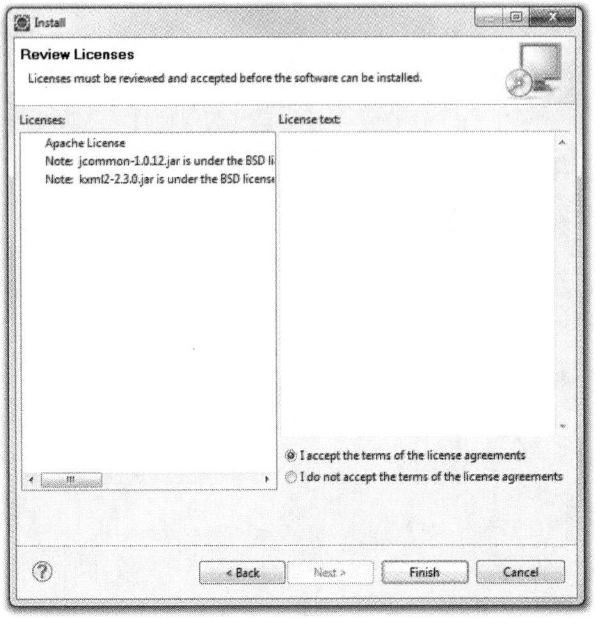

FIGURE 1-12

Eclipse will now proceed to download the tools from the Internet and install them (see Figure 1-13). This will take some time, so be patient.

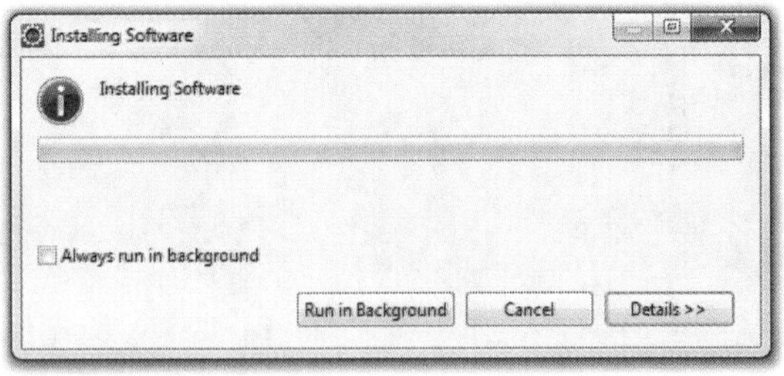

FIGURE 1-13

> **NOTE** If you have any problems downloading the ADT, check out Google's help at http://developer.android.com/sdk/eclipse-adt.html#installing.

Once the ADT is installed, you will be prompted to restart Eclipse. After doing so, go to Window ⇨ Preferences (see Figure 1-14).

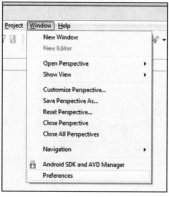

FIGURE 1-14

In the Preferences window that appears, select Android. You will see an error message saying that the SDK has not been set up (see Figure 1-15). Click OK to dismiss it.

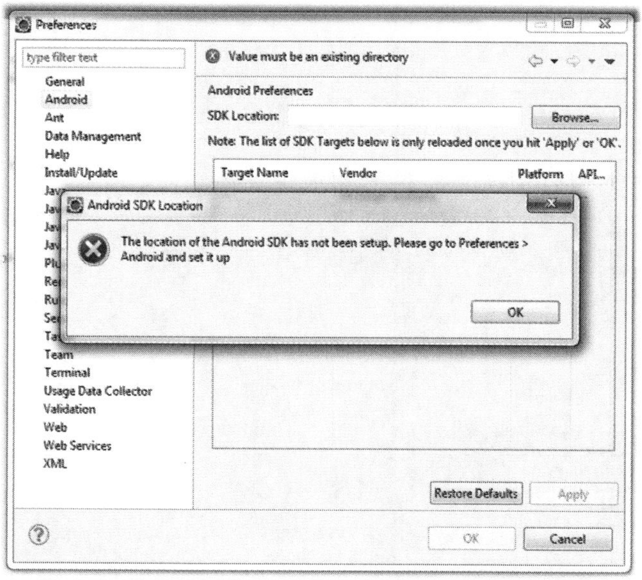

FIGURE 1-15

Enter the location of the Android SDK folder. In this example, it would be `C:\Android\android-sdk-windows`. Click OK.

Creating Android Virtual Devices (AVDs)

The next step is to create AVD to be used for testing your Android applications. AVD stands for Android Virtual Devices. An AVD is an emulator instance that enables you to model an actual device.

Each AVD consists of a hardware profile, a mapping to a system image, as well as emulated storage, such as a secure digital (SD) card.

You can create as many AVDs as you want in order to test your applications with several different configurations. This testing is important to confirm the behavior of your application when it is run on different devices with varying capabilities.

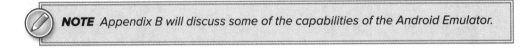

NOTE *Appendix B will discuss some of the capabilities of the Android Emulator.*

To create an AVD, go to Windows ➪ Android SDK and AVD Manager.

Select the Available packages option in the left pane and expand the package name shown in the right pane. Figure 1-16 shows the various packages available for you to create AVDs to emulate the different versions of an Android device.

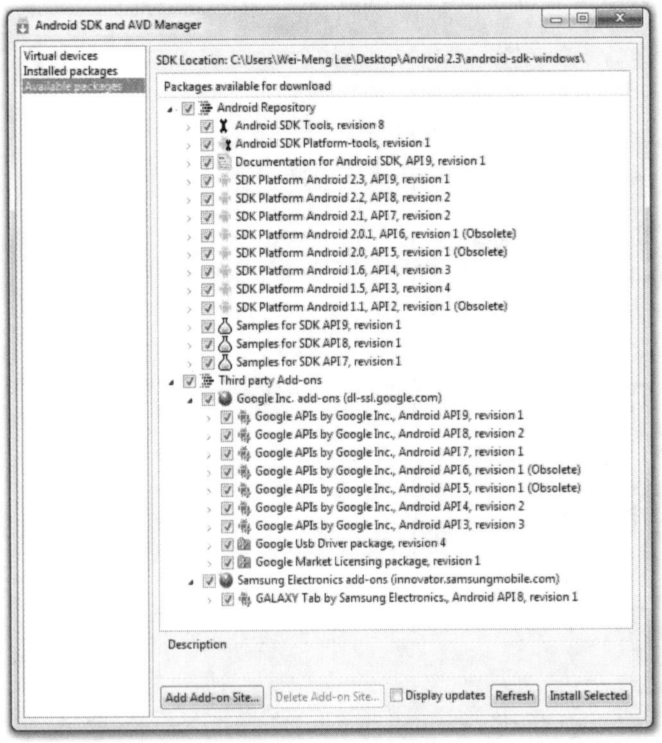

FIGURE 1-16

Check the relevant tools, documentation, and platforms you need for your project.

Once you have selected the items you want, click the Install Selected button to download them. Because it takes a while to download from Google's server, it is a good idea to download only whatever you need immediately, and download the rest when you have more time.

> **NOTE** *For a start, you should at least select the latest SDK platform. At the time of writing, the latest SDK platform is SDK Platform Android 2.3, API 9, revision 1.*

Each version of the Android OS is identified by an API level number. For example, Android 2.3 is level 9 (API 9), while Android 2.2 is level 8 (API 8), and so on. For each level, two platforms are available. For example, level 9 offers the following:

➤ SDK Platform Android 2.3

➤ Google APIs by Google Inc.

The key difference between the two is that the Google APIs platform contains the Google Maps library. Therefore, if the application you are writing requires Google Maps, you need to create an AVD using the Google APIs platform (more on this in Chapter 9, "Location Based Services."

Click the Virtual Devices item in the left pane of the window. Then click the New... button located in the right pane of the window.

In the Create new Android Virtual Device (AVD) window, enter the items as shown in Figure 1-17. Click the Create AVD button when you are done.

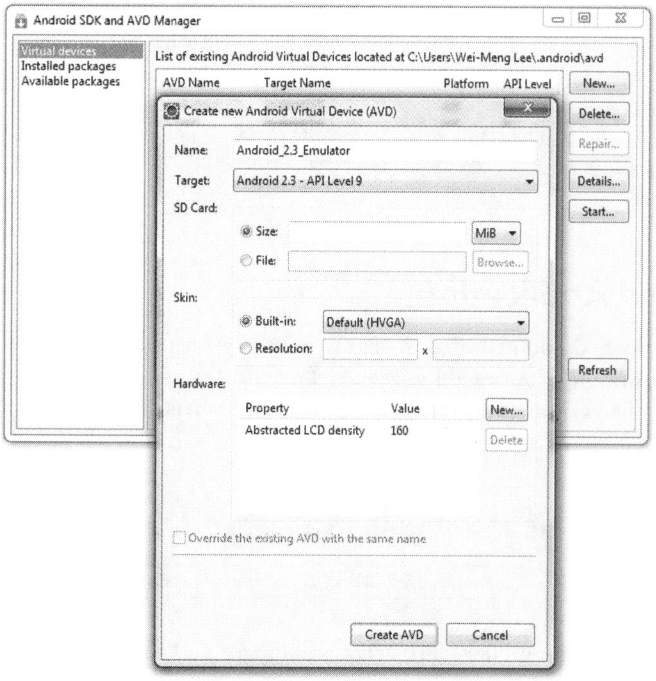

FIGURE 1-17

In this case, you have created an AVD (put simply, an Android emulator) that emulates an Android device running version 2.3 of the OS. In addition to what you have created, you also have the option to emulate the device with an SD card and different screen densities and resolutions.

> **NOTE** *Appendix B explains how to emulate the different types of Android devices.*

It is preferable to create a few AVDs with different API levels so that your application can be tested on different devices. The example shown in Figure 1-18 shows the many AVDs created to test your applications on a wide variety of different Android platforms.

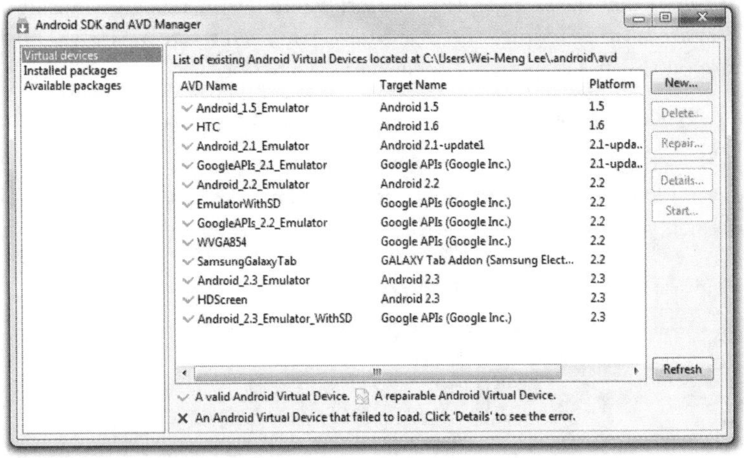

FIGURE 1-18

Creating Your First Android Application

With all the tools and the SDK downloaded and installed, it is now time to start your engine! As in all programming books, the first example uses the ubiquitous Hello World application. This will enable you to have a detailed look at the various components that make up an Android project.

So, without any further ado, let's dive straight in!

TRY IT OUT Creating Your First Android Application

codefile HelloWorld.zip available for download at Wrox.com

1. Using Eclipse, create a new project by selecting File ⇨ Project... (see Figure 1-19).

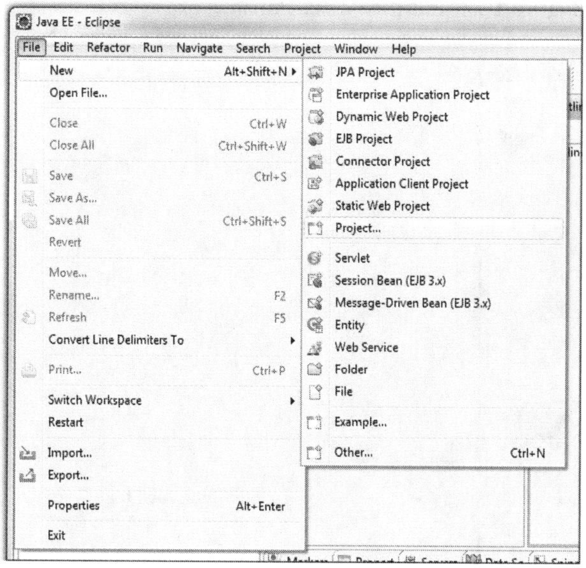

FIGURE 1-19

> **NOTE** *After you have created your first Android application, subsequent Android projects can be created by selecting File ➪ New ➪ Android Project.*

2. Expand the Android folder and select Android Project (see Figure 1-20).

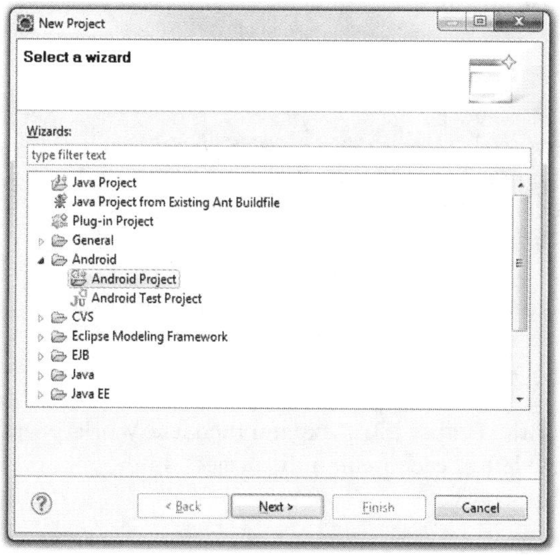

FIGURE 1-20

3. Name the Android project as shown in Figure 1-21 and then click Finish.

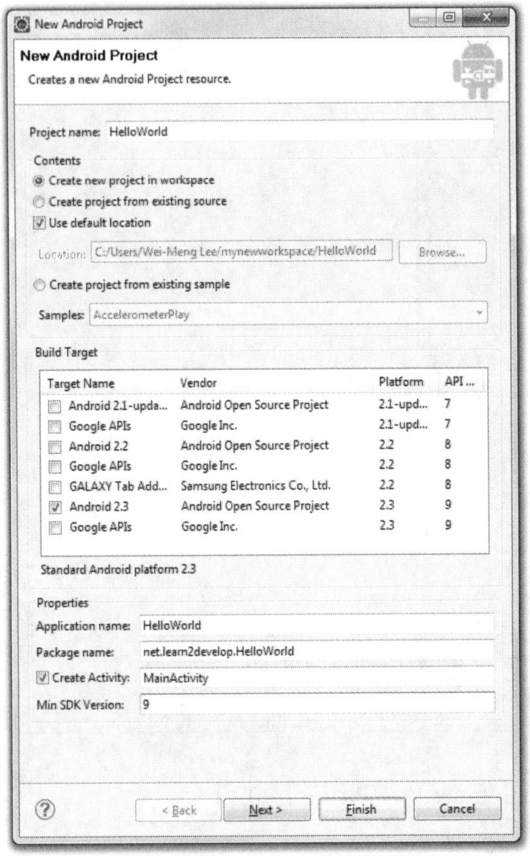

FIGURE 1-21

> **NOTE** You need to have at least a period (.) in the package name. The recommended convention for the package name is to use your domain name in reverse order, followed by the project name. For example, my company's domain name is `learn2develop.net`, hence my package name would be `net.learn2develop.HelloWorld`.

4. The Eclipse IDE should now look like Figure 1-22.

5. In the Package Explorer (located on the left of the Eclipse IDE), expand the HelloWorld project by clicking on the various arrows displayed to the left of each item in the project. In the `res/layout` folder, double-click the `main.xml` file (see Figure 1-23).

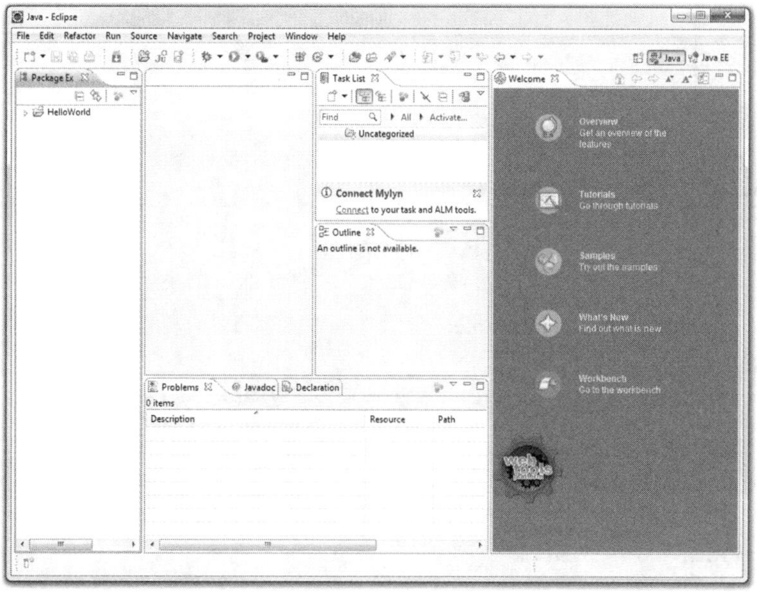

FIGURE 1-22

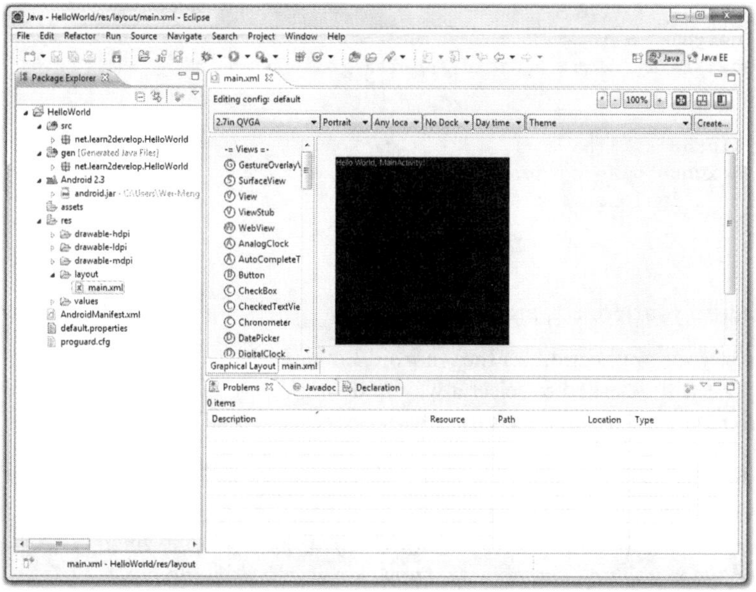

FIGURE 1-23

6. The `main.xml` file defines the user interface (UI) of your application. The default view is the Layout view, which lays out the activity graphically. To modify the UI, click the `main.xml` tab located at the bottom (see Figure 1-24).

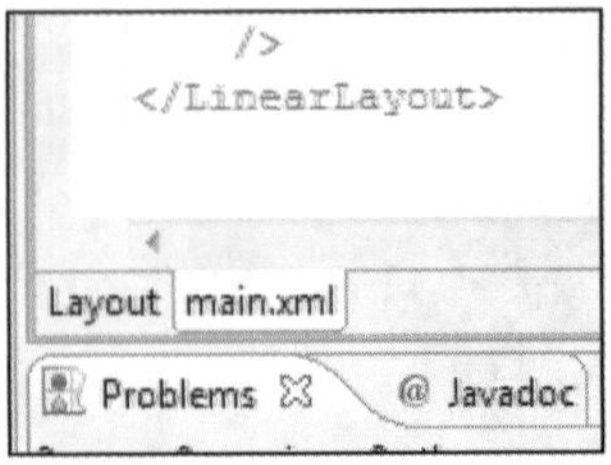

FIGURE 1-24

7. Add the following code in bold to the `main.xml` file:

```xml
<?xml version="1.0" encoding="utf-8"?>
<LinearLayout xmlns:android="http://schemas.android.com/apk/res/android"
    android:orientation="vertical"
    android:layout_width="fill_parent"
    android:layout_height="fill_parent" >

<TextView
    android:layout_width="fill_parent"
    android:layout_height="wrap_content"
    android:text="@string/hello" />

<TextView
    android:layout_width="fill_parent"
    android:layout_height="wrap_content"
    android:text="This is my first Android Application!" />

<Button
    android:layout_width="fill_parent"
    android:layout_height="wrap_content"
    android:text="And this is a clickable button!" />

</LinearLayout>
```

8. To save the changes made to your project, press Ctrl+s.

9. You are now ready to test your application on the Android Emulator. Select the project name in Eclipse and press F11. You will be asked to select a way to debug the application. Select Android Application as shown in Figure 1-25 and click OK.

> **NOTE** Some Eclipse installations have an irritating bug: After creating a new project, Eclipse reports that it contains errors when you try to debug the application. This happens even when you have not modified any files or folders in the project. To solve this problem, simply delete the `R.java` file located under the `gen/net` `.learn2develop.HelloWorld` folder; Eclipse will automatically generate a new `R.java` file for you. Once this is done, the project shouldn't contain any errors.

FIGURE 1-25

10. The Android Emulator will now be started (if the emulator is locked, you need to slide the unlock button to unlock it first). Figure 1-26 shows the application running on the Android Emulator.

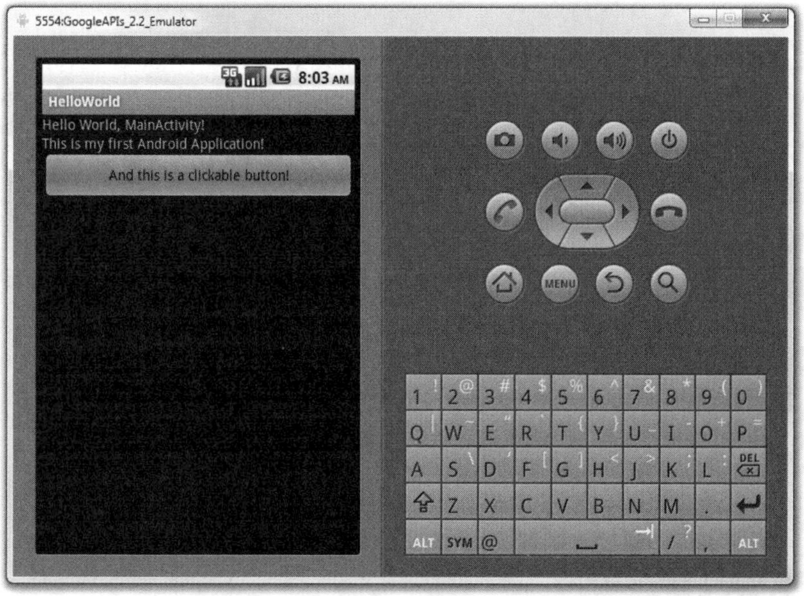

FIGURE 1-26

11. Click the Home button (the house icon in the lower-left corner above the keyboard) so that it now shows the Home screen (see Figure 1-27).

FIGURE 1-27

12. Click the application Launcher icon to display the list of applications installed on the device. Note that the HelloWorld application is now installed in the application launcher (see Figure 1-28).

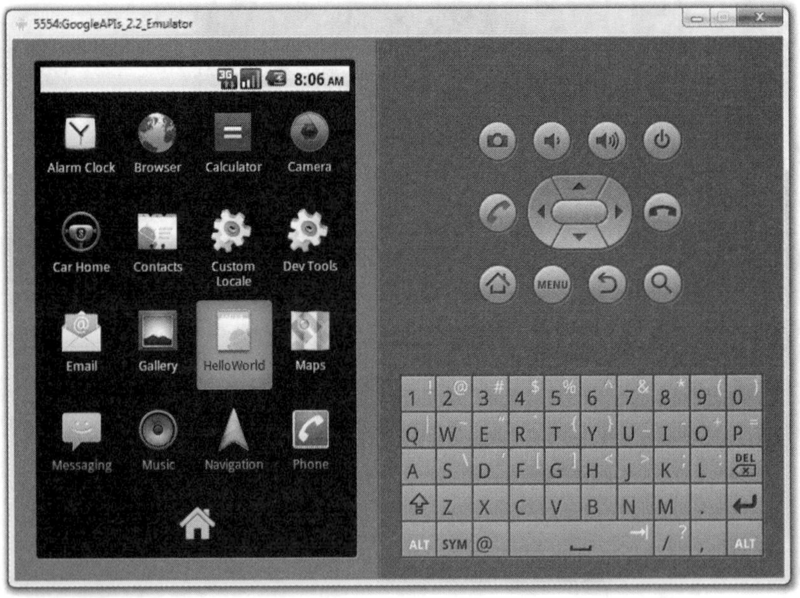

FIGURE 1-28

WHICH AVD WILL BE USED TO TEST YOUR APPLICATION?

Recall that earlier you created a few AVDs using the AVD Manager. So which one will be launched by Eclipse when you run an Android application? Eclipse will check the target that you specified (when you created a new project), comparing it against the list of AVDs that you have created. The first one that matches will be launched to run your application.

If you have more than one suitable AVD running prior to debugging the application, Eclipse will display the Android Device Chooser window, which enables you to select the desired emulator/device to debug the application (see Figure 1-29).

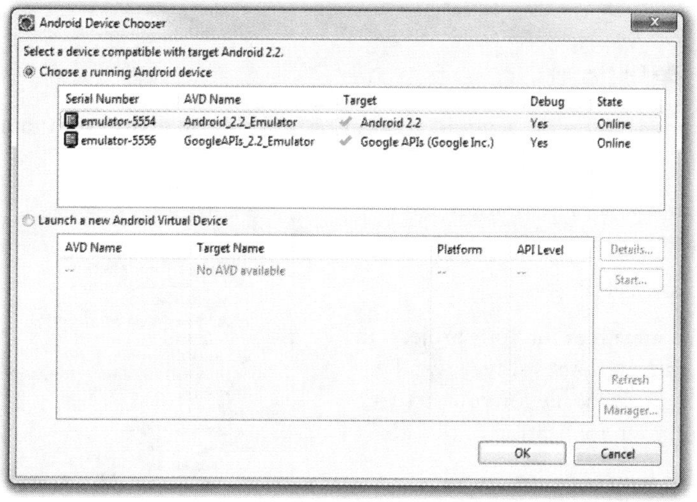

FIGURE 1-29

How It Works

To create an Android project using Eclipse, you need to supply the information shown in Table 1-2.

TABLE 1-2: Project Files Created by Default

PROPERTIES	DESCRIPTION
Project name	The name of the project
Application name	A user-friendly name for your application
Package name	The name of the package. You should use a reverse domain name for this.
Create Activity	The name of the first activity in your application
Min SDK Version	The minimum version of the SDK that your project is targeting

In Android, an Activity is a window that contains the user interface of your applications. An application can have zero or more activities; in this example, the application contains one activity: `MainActivity`. This `MainActivity` is the entry point of the application, which is displayed when the application is started. Chapter 2 discusses activities in more detail.

In this simple example, you modified the `main.xml` file to display the string "This is my first Android Application!" and a button. The `main.xml` file contains the user interface of the activity, which is displayed when `MainActivity` is loaded.

When you debug the application on the Android Emulator, the application is automatically installed on the emulator. And that's it — you have developed your first Android application!

The next section unravels how all the various files in your Android project work together to make your application come alive.

Anatomy of an Android Application

Now that you have created your first Hello World Android application, it is time to dissect the innards of the Android project and examine all the parts that make everything work.

First, note the various files that make up an Android project in the Package Explorer in Eclipse (see Figure 1-30).

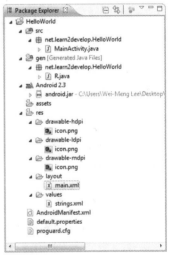

The various folders and their files are as follows:

➤ `src` — Contains the `.java` source files for your project. In this example, there is one file, `MainActivity.java`. The `MainActivity.java` file is the source file for your activity. You will write the code for your application in this file.

➤ `Android 2.3 library` — This item contains one file, `android.jar`, which contains all the class libraries needed for an Android application.

➤ `gen` — Contains the `R.java` file, a compiler-generated file that references all the resources found in your project. You should not modify this file.

➤ `assets` — This folder contains all the assets used by your application, such as HTML, text files, databases, etc.

FIGURE 1-30

➤ `res` — This folder contains all the resources used in your application. It also contains a few other subfolders: `drawable-<resolution>`, `layout`, and `values`. Chapter 3 talks more about how you can support devices with different screen resolutions and densities.

➤ `AndroidManifest.xml` — This is the manifest file for your Android application. Here you specify the permissions needed by your application, as well as other features (such as intent-filters, receivers, etc.). Chapter 2 discusses the use of the `AndroidManifest.xml` file in more details.

The `main.xml` file defines the user interface for your activity. Observe the following in bold:

```
<TextView
    android:layout_width="fill_parent"
    android:layout_height="wrap_content"
    android:text="@string/hello" />
```

The `@string` in this case refers to the `strings.xml` file located in the `res/values` folder. Hence, `@string/hello` refers to the `hello` string defined in the `strings.xml` file, which is "Hello World, MainActivity!":

```
<?xml version="1.0" encoding="utf-8"?>
<resources>
    <string name="hello">Hello World, MainActivity!</string>
    <string name="app_name">HelloWorld</string>
</resources>
```

It is recommended that you store all the string constants in your application in this `strings.xml` file and reference these strings using the `@string` identifier. That way, if you ever need to localize your application to another language, all you need to do is replace the strings stored in the `strings.xml` file with the targeted language and recompile your application.

Observe the content of the `AndroidManifest.xml` file:

```
<?xml version="1.0" encoding="utf-8"?>
<manifest xmlns:android="http://schemas.android.com/apk/res/android"
    package="net.learn2develop.HelloWorld"
    android:versionCode="1"
    android:versionName="1.0">
    <application android:icon="@drawable/icon" android:label="@string/app_name">
        <activity android:name=".MainActivity"
            android:label="@string/app_name">
            <intent-filter>
                <action android:name="android.intent.action.MAIN" />
                <category android:name="android.intent.category.LAUNCHER" />
            </intent-filter>
        </activity>
    </application>
    <uses-sdk android:minSdkVersion="9" />
</manifest>
```

The `AndroidManifest.xml` file contains detailed information about the application:

➤   It defines the package name of the application as `net.learn2develop.HelloWorld`.

➤   The version code of the application is 1. This value is used to identify the version number of your application. It can be used to programmatically determine whether an application needs to be upgraded.

➤   The version name of the application is 1.0. This string value is mainly used for display to the user. You should use the format: *<major>.<minor>.<point>* for this value.

➤   The application uses the image named `icon.png` located in the `drawable` folder.

➤ The name of this application is the string named `app_name` defined in the `strings.xml` file.

➤ There is one activity in the application represented by the `MainActivity.java` file. The label displayed for this activity is the same as the application name.

➤ Within the definition for this activity, there is an element named `<intent-filter>`:

  ➤ The action for the intent filter is named `android.intent.action.MAIN` to indicate that this activity serves as the entry point for the application.

  ➤ The category for the intent-filter is named `android.intent.category.LAUNCHER` to indicate that the application can be launched from the device's Launcher icon. Chapter 2 discusses intents in more details.

➤ Finally, the `android:minSdkVersion` attribute of the `<uses-sdk>` element specifies the minimum version of the OS on which the application will run.

As you add more files and folders to your project, Eclipse will automatically generate the content of `R.java`, which at the moment contains the following:

```
package net.learn2develop.HelloWorld;

public final class R {
    public static final class attr {
    }
    public static final class drawable {
        public static final int icon=0x7f020000;
    }
    public static final class layout {
        public static final int main=0x7f030000;
    }
    public static final class string {
        public static final int app_name=0x7f040001;
        public static final int hello=0x7f040000;
    }
}
```

You are not supposed to modify the content of the `R.java` file; Eclipse automatically generates the content for you when you modify your project.

> **NOTE** If you delete `R.java` manually, Eclipse will regenerate it for you immediately. Note that in order for Eclipse to generate the `R.java` file for you, the project must not contain any errors. If you realize that Eclipse has not regenerated `R.java` after you have deleted it, check your project again. The code may contain syntax errors, or your XML files (such as `AndroidManifest.xml`, `main.xml`, etc.) may not be well-formed.

Finally, the code that connects the activity to the UI (`main.xml`) is the `setContentView()` method, which is in the `MainActivity.java` file:

```
package net.learn2develop.HelloWorld;

import android.app.Activity;
import android.os.Bundle;

public class MainActivity extends Activity {
    /** Called when the activity is first created. */
    @Override
    public void onCreate(Bundle savedInstanceState) {
        super.onCreate(savedInstanceState);
        setContentView(R.layout.main);
    }
}
```

Here, `R.layout.main` refers to the `main.xml` file located in the `res/layout` folder. As you add additional XML files to the `res/layout` folder, the filenames will automatically be generated in the `R.java` file. The `onCreate()` method is one of many methods that are fired when an activity is loaded. Chapter 2 discusses the life cycle of an activity in more detail.

SUMMARY

This chapter has provided a brief overview of Android, and highlighted some of its capabilities. If you have followed the sections on downloading the tools and SDK, you should now have a working system — one that is capable of developing more interesting Android applications other than the Hello World application. In the next chapter, you will learn about the concepts of activities and intents, and the very important roles they play in Android.

EXERCISES

1. What is an AVD?

2. What is the difference between the `android:versionCode` and `android:versionName` attributes in the `AndroidManifest.xml` file?

3. What is the use of the `strings.xml` file?

Answers to the Exercises can be found in Appendix C.

▶ **WHAT YOU LEARNED IN THIS CHAPTER**

TOPIC	KEY CONCEPTS
Android OS	Android is an open-source mobile operating system based on the Linux operating system. It is available to anyone who wants to adapt it to run on their own devices.
Languages used for Android application development	You use the Java programming language to develop Android applications. Written applications are compiled into Dalvik executables, which are then run on top of the Dalvik Virtual Machine.
Android Market	The Android Market hosts all the various Android applications written by third-party developers.
Tools for Android Application Development	Eclipse IDE, Android SDK, and the ADT
Activity	An activity is represented by a screen in your Android application. Each application can have zero or more activities.
The Android manifest file	The `AndroidManifest.xml` file contains detailed configuration information for your application. As your application gets more sophisticated, you will modify this file, and you will see the different information you can add to this file as you progress through the chapters.

2

Activities and Intents

WHAT YOU WILL LEARN IN THIS CHAPTER

- ➤ What activities are
- ➤ How to apply styles and themes to activities
- ➤ How to display activities as dialog windows
- ➤ Understanding the concept of intents
- ➤ How to use the `Intent` object to link activities
- ➤ How intent filters help you to selectively connect to other activities
- ➤ How to display alerts to the user using notifications

In Chapter 1, you learned that an activity is a window that contains the user interface of your applications. An application can have zero or more activities. Typically, applications have one or more activities, and the main aim of an activity is to interact with the user. From the moment an activity appears on the screen to the moment it is hidden, it goes through a number of stages, known as an activity's life cycle. Understanding the life cycle of an activity is vital to ensuring that your application works correctly. In this chapter, you will learn more about how activities work and the things that you need to take note of when designing your Android application.

Apart from activities, another unique concept in Android is that of an intent. An intent is basically the "glue" that enables different activities from different applications to work together seamlessly, ensuring that tasks can be performed as though they all belong to one single application. In the second part of this chapter, you will learn more about this very important concept and how you can use it to call built-in applications such as the Browser, Phone, Maps, and more.

UNDERSTANDING ACTIVITIES

This chapter begins by looking at how to create an activity. To create an activity, you create a Java class that extends the `Activity` base class:

```
package net.learn2develop.Activities;
```

```
import android.app.Activity;
import android.os.Bundle;

public class MainActivity extends Activity {
    /** Called when the activity is first created. */
    @Override
    public void onCreate(Bundle savedInstanceState) {
        super.onCreate(savedInstanceState);
        setContentView(R.layout.main);
    }
}
```

Your activity class would then load its UI component using the XML file defined in your `res/layout` folder. In this example, you would load the UI from the `main.xml` file:

```
setContentView(R.layout.main);
```

Every activity you have in your application must be declared in your `AndroidManifest.xml` file, like this:

```
<?xml version="1.0" encoding="utf-8"?>
<manifest xmlns:android="http://schemas.android.com/apk/res/android"
    package="net.learn2develop.Activities"
    android:versionCode="1"
    android:versionName="1.0">
    <application android:icon="@drawable/icon"
        android:label="@string/app_name">
        <activity android:name=".MainActivity"
                android:label="@string/app_name">
            <intent-filter>
                <action android:name="android.intent.action.MAIN" />
                <category
                    android:name="android.intent.category.LAUNCHER" />
            </intent-filter>
        </activity>
    </application>
    <uses-sdk android:minSdkVersion="9" />
</manifest>
```

The `Activity` base class defines a series of events that governs the life cycle of an activity. The `Activity` class defines the following events:

➤   `onCreate()` — Called when the activity is first created

➤   `onStart()` — Called when the activity becomes visible to the user

➤   `onResume()` — Called when the activity starts interacting with the user

➤   `onPause()` — Called when the current activity is being paused and the previous activity is being resumed

➤   `onStop()` — Called when the activity is no longer visible to the user

➤   `onDestroy()` — Called before the activity is destroyed by the system (either manually or by the system to conserve memory)

➤   `onRestart()` — Called when the activity has been stopped and is restarting again

By default, the activity created for you contains the `onCreate()` event. Within this event handler is the code that helps to display the UI elements of your screen.

Figure 2-1 shows the life cycle of an activity and the various stages it goes through — from when the activity is started until it ends.

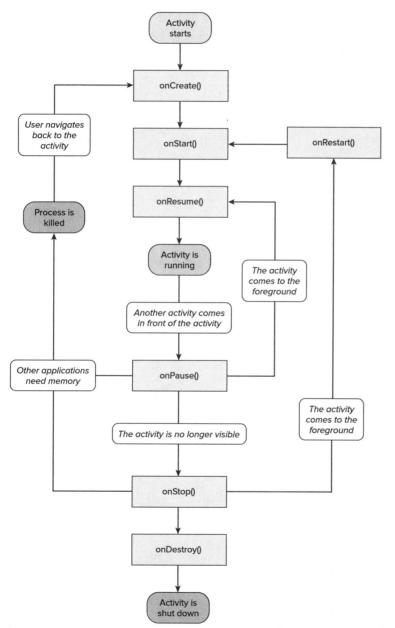

IMAGE REPRODUCED FROM WORK CREATED AND SHARED BY THE ANDROID OPEN SOURCE PROJECT AND USED ACCORDING TO TERMS DESCRIBED IN THE CREATIVE COMMONS 2.5 ATTRIBUTION LICENSE. SEE http://developer.android.com/reference/android/app/Activity.html

FIGURE 2-1

The best way to understand the various stages experienced by an activity is to create a new project, implement the various events, and then subject the activity to various user interactions.

TRY IT OUT Understanding the Life Cycle of an Activity

codefile Activities.zip available for download at Wrox.com

1. Using Eclipse, create a new Android project and name it as shown in Figure 2-2.

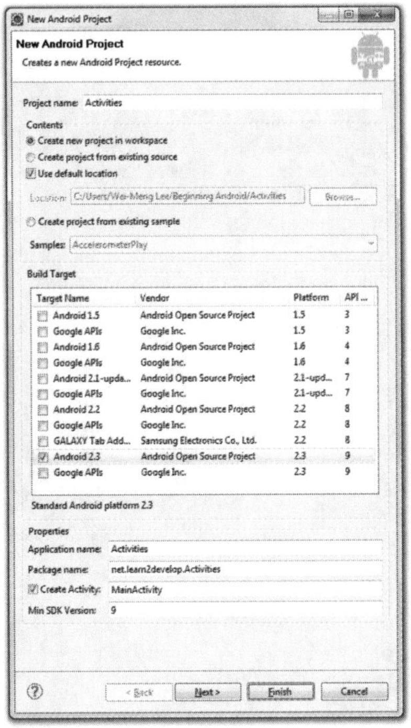

FIGURE 2-2

2. In the `MainActivity.java` file, add the following statements in bold:

```java
package net.learn2develop.Activities;

import android.app.Activity;
import android.os.Bundle;
import android.util.Log;

public class MainActivity extends Activity {
    String tag = "Events";

    /** Called when the activity is first created. */
    @Override
    public void onCreate(Bundle savedInstanceState) {
        super.onCreate(savedInstanceState);
        setContentView(R.layout.main);
        Log.d(tag, "In the onCreate() event");
```

```
    }
    public void onStart()
    {
        super.onStart();
        Log.d(tag, "In the onStart() event");
    }
    public void onRestart()
    {
        super.onRestart();
        Log.d(tag, "In the onRestart() event");
    }
    public void onResume()
    {
        super.onResume();
        Log.d(tag, "In the onResume() event");
    }
    public void onPause()
    {
        super.onPause();
        Log.d(tag, "In the onPause() event");
    }
    public void onStop()
    {
        super.onStop();
        Log.d(tag, "In the onStop() event");
    }
    public void onDestroy()
    {
        super.onDestroy();
        Log.d(tag, "In the onDestroy() event");
    }
}
```

3. Press F11 to debug the application on the Android Emulator.

4. When the activity is first loaded, you should see the following in the LogCat window (click on the Debug perspective; see also Figure 2-3):

```
12-28 13:45:28.115: DEBUG/Events(334): In the onCreate() event
12-28 13:45:28.115: DEBUG/Events(334): In the onStart() event
12-28 13:45:28.115: DEBUG/Events(334): In the onResume() event
```

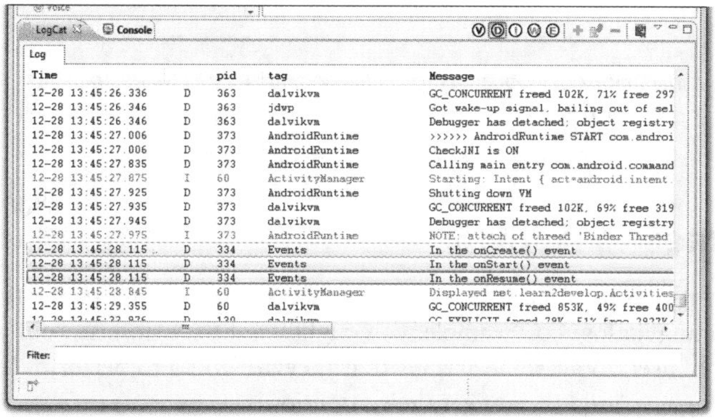

FIGURE 2-3

5. When you now press the back button on the Android Emulator, observe that the following is printed:

```
12-28 13:59:46.266: DEBUG/Events(334): In the onPause() event
12-28 13:59:46.806: DEBUG/Events(334): In the onStop() event
12-28 13:59:46.806: DEBUG/Events(334): In the onDestroy() event
```

6. Click the Home button and hold it there. Click the Activities icon and observe the following:

```
12-28 14:00:54.115: DEBUG/Events(334): In the onCreate() event
12-28 14:00:54.156: DEBUG/Events(334): In the onStart() event
12-28 14:00:54.156: DEBUG/Events(334): In the onResume() event
```

7. Press the Phone button on the Android Emulator so that the activity is pushed to the background. Observe the output in the LogCat window:

```
12-28 14:01:16.515: DEBUG/Events(334): In the onPause() event
12-28 14:01:17.135: DEBUG/Events(334): In the onStop() event
```

8. Notice that the onDestroy() event is not called, indicating that the activity is still in memory. Exit the phone dialer by pressing the Back button. The activity is now visible again. Observe the output in the LogCat window:

```
12-28 14:02:17.255: DEBUG/Events(334): In the onRestart() event
12-28 14:02:17.255: DEBUG/Events(334): In the onStart() event
12-28 14:02:17.255: DEBUG/Events(334): In the onResume() event
```

The onRestart() event is now fired, followed by the onStart() and onResume() events.

How It Works

As you can see from this simple experiment, an activity is destroyed when you press the Back button. This is crucial to know, as whatever state the activity is currently in will be lost; hence, you need to write additional code in your activity to preserve its state when it is destroyed (Chapter 3 will show you how). At this point, note that the onPause() event is called in both scenarios — when an activity is sent to the background, as well as when it is killed when the user presses the Back button.

When an activity is started, the onStart() and onResume() events are always called, regardless of whether the activity is restored from the background or newly created.

> **NOTE** *Even if an application has only one activity and the activity is killed, the application will still be running in memory.*

Applying Styles and Themes to Activity

By default, an activity occupies the entire screen. However, you can also apply a dialog theme to an activity so that it is displayed as a floating dialog. For example, you might want to customize your activity to display as a pop-up, warning the user about some actions that they are going to perform. In this case, displaying the activity as a dialog is a good way to get their attention.

To apply a dialog theme to an activity, simply modify the `<Activity>` element in the AndroidManifest.xml file by adding the `android:theme` attribute:

```xml
<?xml version="1.0" encoding="utf-8"?>
<manifest xmlns:android="http://schemas.android.com/apk/res/android"
      package="net.learn2develop.Activities"
      android:versionCode="1"
      android:versionName="1.0">
    <application android:icon="@drawable/icon"
        android:label="@string/app_name">
        <activity android:name=".MainActivity"
                android:label="@string/app_name"
                android:theme="@android:style/Theme.Dialog" >
            <intent-filter>
                <action android:name="android.intent.action.MAIN" />
                <category
                    android:name="android.intent.category.LAUNCHER" />
            </intent-filter>
        </activity>
    </application>
    <uses-sdk android:minSdkVersion="9" />
</manifest>
```

Doing so will make the activity appear as a dialog, as shown in Figure 2-4.

Hiding the Activity Title

You can also hide the title of an activity if desired (such as when you just want to display a status update to the user). To do so, use the `requestWindowFeature()` method and pass it the `Window.FEATURE_NO_TITLE` constant, like this:

```java
package net.learn2develop.Activities;

import android.app.Activity;
import android.os.Bundle;
import android.util.Log;

import android.view.Window;

public class MainActivity extends Activity {
    String tag = "Events";

    /** Called when the activity is first created. */
    @Override
    public void onCreate(Bundle savedInstanceState) {
        super.onCreate(savedInstanceState);

        //---hides the title bar---
        requestWindowFeature(Window.FEATURE_NO_TITLE);

        setContentView(R.layout.main);
        Log.d(tag, "In the onCreate() event");
    }
}
```

This will hide the title bar, as shown in Figure 2-5.

FIGURE 2-4

FIGURE 2-5

Displaying a Dialog Window

There are times where you need to display a dialog window to get a confirmation from the user. In this case, you can override the onCreateDialog() protected method defined in the base Activity class to display a dialog window. The following Try It Out shows you how.

TRY IT OUT   Displaying a Dialog Window Using an Activity

codefile Dialog.zip available for download at Wrox.com

1.   Using Eclipse, create a new Android project and name it Dialog.

2.   Add the following statements in bold to the main.xml file:

```xml
<?xml version="1.0" encoding="utf-8"?>
<LinearLayout xmlns:android="http://schemas.android.com/apk/res/android"
    android:orientation="vertical"
    android:layout_width="fill_parent"
    android:layout_height="fill_parent" >
<TextView
    android:layout_width="fill_parent"
    android:layout_height="wrap_content"
    android:text="@string/hello" />
<Button
    android:id="@+id/btn_dialog"
    android:layout_width="fill_parent"
    android:layout_height="wrap_content"
    android:text="Click to display a dialog" />
</LinearLayout>
```

3. Add the following statements in bold to the `MainActivity.java` file:

```java
package net.learn2develop.Dialog;

import android.app.Activity;
import android.os.Bundle;
import android.app.AlertDialog;
import android.app.Dialog;
import android.content.DialogInterface;
import android.view.View;
import android.widget.Button;
import android.widget.Toast;

public class MainActivity extends Activity {
    CharSequence[] items = { "Google", "Apple", "Microsoft" };
    boolean[] itemsChecked = new boolean [items.length];

    /** Called when the activity is first created. */
    @Override
    public void onCreate(Bundle savedInstanceState) {
        super.onCreate(savedInstanceState);
        setContentView(R.layout.main);

        Button btn = (Button) findViewById(R.id.btn_dialog);
        btn.setOnClickListener(new View.OnClickListener() {
            public void onClick(View v) {
                showDialog(0);
            }
        });
    }

    @Override
    protected Dialog onCreateDialog(int id) {
        switch (id) {
        case 0:
            return new AlertDialog.Builder(this)
            .setIcon(R.drawable.icon)
            .setTitle("This is a dialog with some simple text...")
            .setPositiveButton("OK", new
                DialogInterface.OnClickListener() {
                public void onClick(DialogInterface dialog,
                int whichButton)
                {
                    Toast.makeText(getBaseContext(),
                        "OK clicked!", Toast.LENGTH_SHORT).show();
                }
            })
            .setNegativeButton("Cancel", new
                DialogInterface.OnClickListener() {
                public void onClick(DialogInterface dialog,
                    int whichButton)
                {
                    Toast.makeText(getBaseContext(),
                        "Cancel clicked!", Toast.LENGTH_SHORT).show();
                }
            })
```

```
            .setMultiChoiceItems(items, itemsChecked, new
                DialogInterface.OnMultiChoiceClickListener() {
                    @Override
                    public void onClick(DialogInterface dialog, int which,
                    boolean isChecked) {
                        Toast.makeText(getBaseContext(),
                            items[which] + (isChecked ? " checked!":
                            " unchecked!"),
                            Toast.LENGTH_SHORT).show();
                    }
                }
            )
            .create();
        }
        return null;
    }
}
```

4. Press F11 to debug the application on the Android Emulator. Click the button to display the dialog (see Figure 2-6). Checking the various checkboxes will cause the Toast class to display the text of the item checked/unchecked. To dismiss the dialog, click the OK or Cancel button.

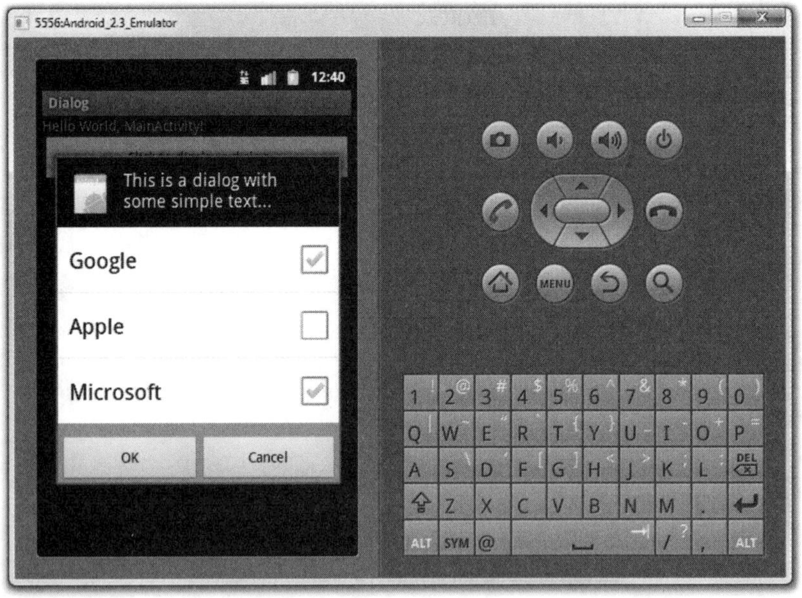

FIGURE 2-6

How It Works

To display a dialog, you first override the onCreateDialog() method in the Activity class:

```
@Override
protected Dialog onCreateDialog(int id) {
    //...
}
```

This method is called when you call the `showDialog()` method:

```
Button btn = (Button) findViewById(R.id.btn_dialog);
btn.setOnClickListener(new View.OnClickListener() {
    public void onClick(View v) {
        showDialog(0);
    }
});
```

The `onCreateDialog()` method is a callback for creating dialogs that are managed by the activity. When you call the `showDialog()` method, this callback will be invoked. The `showDialog()` method accepts an integer argument identifying a particular dialog to display.

To create a dialog, you use the `AlertDialog` class's `Builder` constructor. You set the various properties, such as icon, title, and buttons, as well as checkboxes:

```
@Override
protected Dialog onCreateDialog(int id) {
    switch (id) {
    case 0:
        return new AlertDialog.Builder(this)
        .setIcon(R.drawable.icon)
        .setTitle("This is a dialog with some simple text...")
        .setPositiveButton("OK", new
            DialogInterface.OnClickListener() {
            public void onClick(DialogInterface dialog,
            int whichButton)
            {
                Toast.makeText(getBaseContext(),
                    "OK clicked!", Toast.LENGTH_SHORT).show();
            }
        })
        .setNegativeButton("Cancel", new
            DialogInterface.OnClickListener() {
            public void onClick(DialogInterface dialog,
                int whichButton)
            {
                Toast.makeText(getBaseContext(),
                    "Cancel clicked!", Toast.LENGTH_SHORT).show();
            }
        })
        .setMultiChoiceItems(items, itemsChecked, new
            DialogInterface.OnMultiChoiceClickListener() {
                @Override
                public void onClick(DialogInterface dialog, int which,
                boolean isChecked) {
                    Toast.makeText(getBaseContext(),
                        items[which] + (isChecked ? " checked!":
                        " unchecked!"),
                        Toast.LENGTH_SHORT).show();
                }
            }
        )
        .create();
    }
    return null;
}
```

The preceding code sets two buttons: OK and Cancel, using the setPositiveButton() and setNegativeButton() methods, respectively. You also set a list of checkboxes for users to choose via the setMultiChoiceItems() method. For the setMultiChoiceItems() method, you passed in two arrays: one for the list of items to display and another to contain the value of each item to indicate if they are checked. When each item is checked, you use the Toast class to display a message (see Figure 2-7).

FIGURE 2-7

THE CONTEXT OBJECT

In Android, you will often encounter the Context class and its instances. Instances of the Context class are often used to provide reference to your application. For example, in this example, the first parameter of the Toast class takes in a Context object.

```
return new AlertDialog.Builder(this)
.setIcon(R.drawable.icon)
.setTitle("This is a dialog with some simple text...")
.setPositiveButton("OK", new
    DialogInterface.OnClickListener() {
    public void onClick(DialogInterface dialog,
    int whichButton)
    {
        Toast.makeText(getBaseContext(),
            "OK clicked!", Toast.LENGTH_SHORT).show();
    }
})
...
```

But because the Toast() class is not used directly in the activity (it is used within the AlertDialog class), you need to return an instance of the Context class by using the getBaseContext() method.

Another area where you will encounter the Context class is when creating a view dynamically in an activity. For example, you may want to dynamically create a TextView view from code. To do so, you instantiate the TextView class, like this:

```
TextView tv = new TextView(this);
```

The constructor for the TextView class takes a Context object, and because the Activity class is a subclass of Context, you can use the this keyword to represent the Context object.

Displaying a Progress Dialog

Besides the plain dialog that you created in the previous section, you can also create a *progress dialog*. A progress dialog is useful for showing the progress of some activities, such as the status of a download operation.

The following Try It Out shows you how to display a progress dialog.

TRY IT OUT Displaying a Progress Dialog Window Using an Activity

1. Using the same project created in the previous section, add the following statements in bold to the MainActivity.java file:

```java
package net.learn2develop.Dialog;

import android.app.Activity;
import android.app.AlertDialog;
import android.app.Dialog;
import android.content.DialogInterface;
import android.os.Bundle;
import android.view.View;
import android.widget.Button;
import android.widget.Toast;

import android.app.ProgressDialog;
import android.os.Handler;
import android.os.Message;

public class MainActivity extends Activity {
    CharSequence[] items = { "Google", "Apple", "Microsoft" };
    boolean[] itemsChecked = new boolean [items.length];

    private ProgressDialog _progressDialog;
    private int _progress = 0;
    private Handler _progressHandler;

    /** Called when the activity is first created. */
    @Override
    public void onCreate(Bundle savedInstanceState) {
        super.onCreate(savedInstanceState);
        setContentView(R.layout.main);

        Button btn = (Button) findViewById(R.id.btn_dialog);
        btn.setOnClickListener(new View.OnClickListener() {
            public void onClick(View v) {
                showDialog(1);
                _progress = 0;
                _progressDialog.setProgress(0);
                _progressHandler.sendEmptyMessage(0);
            }
        });

        _progressHandler = new Handler() {
```

```java
        public void handleMessage(Message msg) {
            super.handleMessage(msg);
            if (_progress >= 100) {
                _progressDialog.dismiss();
            } else {
                _progress++;
                _progressDialog.incrementProgressBy(1);
                _progressHandler.sendEmptyMessageDelayed(0, 100);
            }
        }
    };
}

@Override
protected Dialog onCreateDialog(int id) {
    switch (id) {
    case 0:
        return new AlertDialog.Builder(this)
        //...
        //...
        .create();
    case 1:
        _progressDialog = new ProgressDialog(this);
        _progressDialog.setIcon(R.drawable.icon);
        _progressDialog.setTitle("Downloading files...");
        _progressDialog.setProgressStyle(ProgressDialog.STYLE_HORIZONTAL);
        _progressDialog.setButton(DialogInterface.BUTTON_POSITIVE, "Hide", new
            DialogInterface.OnClickListener() {
            public void onClick(DialogInterface dialog,
                int whichButton)
            {
                Toast.makeText(getBaseContext(),
                    "Hide clicked!", Toast.LENGTH_SHORT).show();
            }
        });
        _progressDialog.setButton(DialogInterface.BUTTON_NEGATIVE, "Cancel", new
            DialogInterface.OnClickListener() {
            public void onClick(DialogInterface dialog,
                int whichButton)
            {
                Toast.makeText(getBaseContext(),
                    "Cancel clicked!", Toast.LENGTH_SHORT).show();
            }
        });
        return _progressDialog;
    }
    return null;
    }
}
```

2. Press F11 to debug the application on the Android Emulator. Click the button to display the progress dialog (see Figure 2-8). Observe that the progress bar will count up to 100.

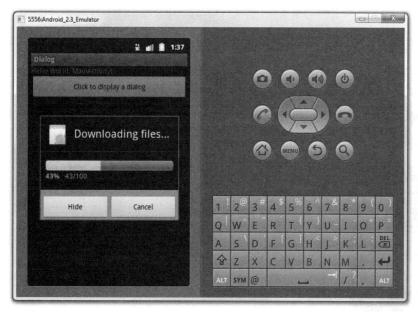

FIGURE 2-8

How It Works

To create a progress dialog, you first create an instance of the `ProgressDialog` class and set its various properties, such as icon, title, and style:

```
_progressDialog = new ProgressDialog(this);
_progressDialog.setIcon(R.drawable.icon);
_progressDialog.setTitle("Downloading files...");
_progressDialog.setProgressStyle(ProgressDialog.STYLE_HORIZONTAL);
```

You then set the two buttons that you want to display inside the progress dialog:

```
_progressDialog.setButton(DialogInterface.BUTTON_POSITIVE, "Hide", new
    DialogInterface.OnClickListener() {
    public void onClick(DialogInterface dialog,
        int whichButton)
    {
        Toast.makeText(getBaseContext(),
            "Hide clicked!", Toast.LENGTH_SHORT).show();
    }
});
_progressDialog.setButton(DialogInterface.BUTTON_NEGATIVE, "Cancel", new
    DialogInterface.OnClickListener() {
    public void onClick(DialogInterface dialog,
        int whichButton)
    {
        Toast.makeText(getBaseContext(),
            "Cancel clicked!", Toast.LENGTH_SHORT).show();
```

```
            }
        });
        return _progressDialog;
    }
```

The preceding causes a progress dialog to appear (see Figure 2-9).

FIGURE 2-9

To display the progress status in the progress dialog, you need to use a Handler object to run a background thread:

```
_progress = 0;
_progressDialog.setProgress(0);
_progressHandler.sendEmptyMessage(0);
```

The background thread counts up to 100, with each count delayed by 100 milliseconds:

```
_progressHandler = new Handler() {
    public void handleMessage(Message msg) {
        super.handleMessage(msg);
        if (_progress >= 100) {
            _progressDialog.dismiss();
        } else {
            _progress++;
            _progressDialog.incrementProgressBy(1);
            _progressHandler.sendEmptyMessageDelayed(0, 100);
        }
    }
};
```

When the count reaches 100, the progress dialog is dismissed.

LINKING ACTIVITIES USING INTENTS

An Android application can contain zero or more activities. When your application has more than one activity, you may need to navigate from one activity to another. In Android, you navigate between activities through what is known as an *intent*.

The best way to understand this very important but somewhat abstract concept in Android is to experience it firsthand and see what it helps you to achieve.

The following Try It Out shows how to add another activity to an existing project and then navigate between the two activities.

TRY IT OUT   Linking Activities with Intents

1. Using the `Activities` project created earlier, add the following statements in bold to the `AndroidManifest.xml` file:

```xml
<?xml version="1.0" encoding="utf-8"?>
<manifest xmlns:android="http://schemas.android.com/apk/res/android"
      package="net.learn2develop.Activities"
      android:versionCode="1"
      android:versionName="1.0">
    <application android:icon="@drawable/icon" android:label="@string/app_name">
        <activity android:name=".MainActivity"
                android:label="@string/app_name"
                android:theme="@android:style/Theme.Dialog" >
            <intent-filter>
                <action android:name="android.intent.action.MAIN" />
                <category android:name="android.intent.category.LAUNCHER" />
            </intent-filter>
        </activity>
        <activity android:name=".Activity2"
                android:label="Activity 2">
            <intent-filter>
                <action android:name="net.learn2develop.ACTIVITY2" />
                <category android:name="android.intent.category.DEFAULT" />
            </intent-filter>
        </activity>
    </application>
    <uses-sdk android:minSdkVersion="9" />
```

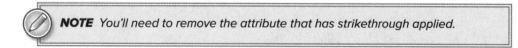

> **NOTE** *You'll need to remove the attribute that has strikethrough applied.*

2. Right click on the package name under the `src` folder and select New ⇨ Class (see Figure 2-10).

3. Name the new class file `Activity2` (see Figure 2-11) and click Finish.

4. Make a copy of the `main.xml` file by right-clicking on it and selecting `Copy`. Then, right-click on the `res/layout` folder and select `Paste`. Name the file `activity2.xml`. The `res/layout` folder will now contain the `activity2.xml` file (see Figure 2-12).

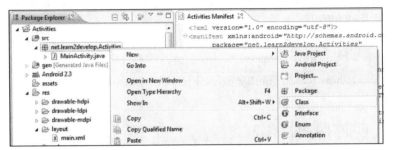

FIGURE 2-10

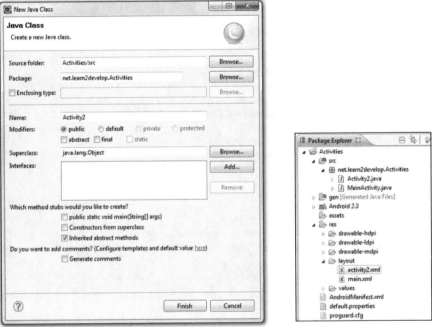

FIGURE 2-11

FIGURE 2-12

5. Modify the `activity2.xml` file as follows:

```xml
<?xml version="1.0" encoding="utf-8"?>
<LinearLayout xmlns:android="http://schemas.android.com/apk/res/android"
    android:orientation="vertical"
    android:layout_width="fill_parent"
    android:layout_height="fill_parent"
    >
```

```
<TextView
    android:layout_width="fill_parent"
    android:layout_height="wrap_content"
    android:text="This is Activity 2!"
    />
</LinearLayout>
```

6. In the `Activity2.java` file, add the following statements in bold:

```
package net.learn2develop.Activities;

import android.app.Activity;
import android.os.Bundle;

public class Activity2 extends Activity {
    @Override
    public void onCreate(Bundle savedInstanceState) {
        super.onCreate(savedInstanceState);
        setContentView(R.layout.activity2);
    }
}
```

7. Modify the `MainActivity.java` file as shown in bold:

```
package net.learn2develop.Activities;

import android.app.Activity;
import android.os.Bundle;
import android.util.Log;
import android.view.Window;

import android.view.KeyEvent;
import android.content.Intent;

public class MainActivity extends Activity {
    String tag = "Events";

    /** Called when the activity is first created. */
    @Override
    public void onCreate(Bundle savedInstanceState) {
        super.onCreate(savedInstanceState);

        //---hides the title bar---
        //requestWindowFeature(Window.FEATURE_NO_TITLE);
        setContentView(R.layout.main);
        Log.d(tag, "In the onCreate() event");
    }

    public boolean onKeyDown(int keyCode, KeyEvent event)
    {
        if (keyCode == KeyEvent.KEYCODE_DPAD_CENTER)
        {
            startActivity(new Intent("net.learn2develop.ACTIVITY2"));
```

```
        }
        return false;
    }

    public void onStart()     { //... }
    public void onRestart()    { //... }
    public void onResume()    { //... }
    public void onPause()     { //... }
    public void onStop()    { //... }
    public void onDestroy()    { //... }
}
```

8. Press F11 to debug the application on the Android Emulator. When the first activity is loaded, click the center of the directional pad (see Figure 2-13; on a real device this can be achieved by pressing down the trackball). The second activity will now be loaded.

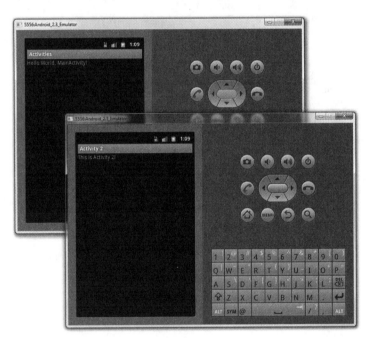

FIGURE 2-13

How It Works

As you have learned, an activity is made up of a UI component (for example, `main.xml`) and a class component (for example, `MainActivity.java`). Hence, if you want to add another activity to a project, you need to create these two components.

In the `AndroidManifest.xml` file, specifically you have added the following:

```
<activity android:name=".Activity2"
          android:label="Activity 2">
```

```
      <intent-filter>
          <action android:name="net.learn2develop.ACTIVITY2" />
          <category android:name="android.intent.category.DEFAULT" />
      </intent-filter>
  </activity>
```

Here, you have added a new activity to the application. Note the following:

➤ The name of the new activity added is "`Activity2`".

➤ The label for the activity is named "`Activity 2`".

➤ The intent filter name for the activity is "`net.learn2develop.ACTIVITY2`". Other activities that wish to call this activity will invoke it via this name. Ideally, you should use the reverse domain name of your company as the intent filter name in order to reduce the chances of another application having the same intent filter. The next section discusses what happens when two or more activities have the same intent filter.

➤ The category for the intent filter is "`android.intent.category.DEFAULT`". You need to add this to the intent filter so that this activity can be started by another activity using the `startActivity()` method (more on this shortly).

In the `MainActivity.java` file, you implemented the `onKeyDown` event handler. This event is fired whenever the user presses one of the keys on the device. When the user presses the center key on the directional pad (as represented by the `KeyEvent.KEYCODE_DPAD_CENTER` constant), you use the `startActivity()` method to display `Activity2` by creating an instance of the `Intent` class and passing it the intent filter name of `Activity2` (which is `net.learn2develop.ACTIVITY2`):

```java
public boolean onKeyDown(int keyCode, KeyEvent event)
{
    if (keyCode == KeyEvent.KEYCODE_DPAD_CENTER)
    {
        startActivity(new Intent("net.learn2develop.ACTIVITY2"));
    }
    return false;
}
```

Activities in Android can be invoked by any application running on the device. For example, you can create a new Android project and then display `Activity2` by using its `net.learn2develop.ACTIVITY2` intent filter. This is one of the fundamental concepts in Android that enables an application to invoke another easily.

If the activity that you want to invoke is defined within the same project, you can rewrite the preceding statement like this:

```java
startActivity(new Intent(this, Activity2.class));
```

However, this approach is applicable only when the activity you want to display is within the same project as the current activity.

Resolving Intent Filter Collision

In the previous section, you learned that the `<intent-filter>` element defines how your activity can be invoked by another activity. What happens if another activity (in either the same or a separate application) has the same filter name? For example, suppose your application has another activity named `Activity3`, with the following entry in the `AndroidManifest.xml` file:

```xml
<?xml version="1.0" encoding="utf-8"?>
<manifest xmlns:android="http://schemas.android.com/apk/res/android"
      package="net.learn2develop.Activities"
      android:versionCode="1"
      android:versionName="1.0">
    <application android:icon="@drawable/icon" android:label="@string/app_name">
        <activity android:name=".MainActivity"
                  android:label="@string/app_name" >
            <! -- android:theme="@android:style/Theme.Dialog" -- >
            <intent-filter>
                <action android:name="android.intent.action.MAIN" />
                <category android:name="android.intent.category.LAUNCHER" />
            </intent-filter>
        </activity>
        <activity android:name=".Activity2"
                  android:label="Activity 2">
            <intent-filter>
                <action android:name="net.learn2develop.ACTIVITY2" />
                <category android:name="android.intent.category.DEFAULT" />
            </intent-filter>
        </activity>
        <activity android:name=".Activity3"
                  android:label="Activity 3">
            <intent-filter>
                <action android:name="net.learn2develop.ACTIVITY2" />
                <category android:name="android.intent.category.DEFAULT" />
            </intent-filter>
        </activity>
    </application>
    <uses-sdk android:minSdkVersion="9" />
</manifest>
```

If you call the `startActivity()` method with the following intent, then the Android OS will display a selection as shown in Figure 2-14:

```
startActivity(new Intent("net.learn2develop.ACTIVITY2"));
```

If you check the "Use by default for this action" item and then select an activity, then the next time the intent "net.learn2develop.ACTIVITY2" is called again, it will always launch the previous activity that you have selected.

To clear away this default, go to the Settings application in Android and select Applications ➪ Manage applications and select the application name (see Figure 2-15). When the details of the application are shown, scroll down to the bottom and click the Clear defaults button.

FIGURE 2-14

FIGURE 2-15

Returning Results from an Intent

The startActivity() method invokes another activity but does not return a result to the current activity. For example, you may have an activity that prompts the user for username and password. The information entered by the user in that activity needs to be passed back to the calling activity for further processing. If you need to pass data back from an activity, you should instead use the startActivityForResult() method. The following Try It Out demonstrates this.

TRY IT OUT   Obtaining a Result from an Activity

1.   Using the same project created in the previous section, add the following statements in bold to the main.xml file:

```xml
<?xml version="1.0" encoding="utf-8"?>
<LinearLayout xmlns:android="http://schemas.android.com/apk/res/android"
    android:orientation="vertical"
    android:layout_width="fill_parent"
    android:layout_height="fill_parent" >
<TextView
    android:layout_width="fill_parent"
    android:layout_height="wrap_content"
    android:text="Please enter your name" />
<EditText
    android:id="@+id/txt_username"
    android:layout_width="fill_parent"
    android:layout_height="wrap_content" />
<Button
    android:id="@+id/btn_OK"
    android:layout_width="fill_parent"
    android:layout_height="wrap_content"
    android:text="OK" />
</LinearLayout>
```

2.   Add the following statements in bold to Activity2.java:

```java
package net.learn2develop.Activities;

import android.app.Activity;
import android.os.Bundle;

import android.content.Intent;
import android.net.Uri;
import android.view.View;
import android.widget.Button;
import android.widget.EditText;

public class Activity2 extends Activity {
    @Override
    public void onCreate(Bundle savedInstanceState) {
        super.onCreate(savedInstanceState);
        setContentView(R.layout.activity2);

        //---get the OK button---
        Button btn = (Button) findViewById(R.id.btn_OK);

        //---event handler for the OK button---
```

```java
btn.setOnClickListener(new View.OnClickListener()
{
    public void onClick(View view) {
        Intent data = new Intent();

        //---get the EditText view---
        EditText txt_username =
            (EditText) findViewById(R.id.txt_username);

        //---set the data to pass back---
        data.setData(Uri.parse(
            txt_username.getText().toString()));
        setResult(RESULT_OK, data);

        //---closes the activity---
        finish();
    }
});
    }
}
```

3. Add the following statements in bold to the `MainActivity.java` file:

```java
package net.learn2develop.Activities;

import android.app.Activity;
import android.os.Bundle;
import android.util.Log;
import android.view.Window;
import android.view.KeyEvent;
import android.widget.Toast;
import android.content.Intent;

public class MainActivity extends Activity {
    String tag = "Events";
    int request_Code = 1;

    /** Called when the activity is first created. */
    @Override
    public void onCreate(Bundle savedInstanceState) {
        super.onCreate(savedInstanceState);

        //---hides the title bar---
        //requestWindowFeature(Window.FEATURE_NO_TITLE);

        setContentView(R.layout.main);
        Log.d(tag, "In the onCreate() event");
    }

    public boolean onKeyDown(int keyCode, KeyEvent event)
    {
        if (keyCode == KeyEvent.KEYCODE_DPAD_CENTER)
        {
            //startActivity(new Intent("net.learn2develop.ACTIVITY2"));
            //startActivity(new Intent(this, Activity2.class));

            startActivityForResult(new Intent(
```

```
                    "net.learn2develop.ACTIVITY2"),
                    request_Code);
        }
        return false;
    }

    public void onActivityResult(int requestCode, int resultCode, Intent data)
    {
        if (requestCode == request_Code) {
            if (resultCode == RESULT_OK) {
                Toast.makeText(this,data.getData().toString(),
                    Toast.LENGTH_SHORT).show();
            }
        }
    }

    public void onStart()    { //... }
    public void onRestart()   { //... }
    public void onResume()    { //... }
    public void onPause()     { //... }
    public void onStop()    { //... }
    public void onDestroy()    { //... }
}
```

4. Press F11 to debug the application on the Android Emulator. When the first activity is loaded, click the center button on the directional pad. Activity2 will now be loaded. Enter your name (see Figure 2-16) and click the OK button. You will see that the first activity now displays the name you have entered using the `Toast` class.

FIGURE 2-16

How It Works

To call an activity and wait for a result to be returned from it, you need to use the `startActivityForResult()` method, like this:

```
startActivityForResult(new Intent(
    "net.learn2develop.ACTIVITY2"),
    request_Code);
```

In addition to passing in an `Intent` object, you need to pass in request code as well. The request code is simply an integer value that identifies an activity you are calling. This is needed because when an activity returns a value, you must have a way to identify it. For example, you may be calling multiple activities at the same time and some activities may not return immediately (for example, waiting for a reply from a server). When an activity returns, you need this request code to determine which activity is actually returned.

> **NOTE** If the request code is set to -1, then calling it using the `startActivityForResult()` method is equivalent to calling it using the `startActivity()` method. That is, no result will be returned.

In order for an activity to return a value to the calling activity, you use an `Intent` object to send data back via the `setData()` method:

```
Intent data = new Intent();

//---get the EditText view---
EditText txt_username =
    (EditText) findViewById(R.id.txt_username);

//---set the data to pass back---
data.setData(Uri.parse(
    txt_username.getText().toString()));
setResult(RESULT_OK, data);

//---closes the activity---
finish();
```

The `setResult()` method sets a result code (either `RESULT_OK` or `RESULT_CANCELLED`) and the data (an `Intent` object) to be returned back to the calling activity. The `finish()` method closes the activity and returns control back to the calling activity.

In the calling activity, you need to implement the `onActivityResult()` method, which is called whenever an activity returns:

```
public void onActivityResult(int requestCode, int resultCode, Intent data)
{
    if (requestCode == request_Code) {
        if (resultCode == RESULT_OK) {
            Toast.makeText(this,data.getData().toString(),
```

```
                        Toast.LENGTH_SHORT).show();
            }
        }
    }
```

Here, you check for the appropriate request code and display the result that is returned. The returned result is passed in via the `data` argument; and you obtain its details through the `getData()` method.

Passing Data Using an Intent Object

Besides returning data from an activity, it is also common to pass data to an activity. For example, in the previous example you may want to set some default text in the `EditText` view before the activity is displayed. In this case, you can use the `Intent` object to pass the data to the target activity. The following Try It Out shows you how.

TRY IT OUT   Passing Data to the Target Activity

1. Using the same project created in the previous section, add the following statements in bold to the `MainActivity.java` file:

```
public boolean onKeyDown(int keyCode, KeyEvent event)
{
    if (keyCode == KeyEvent.KEYCODE_DPAD_CENTER)
    {
        //startActivity(new Intent("net.learn2develop.ACTIVITY2"));
        //startActivity(new Intent(this, Activity2.class));
        /*
        startActivityForResult(new Intent(
            "net.learn2develop.ACTIVITY2"),
            request_Code);
        */

        Intent i = new Intent("net.learn2develop.ACTIVITY2");
        Bundle extras = new Bundle();
        extras.putString("Name", "Your name here");
        i.putExtras(extras);
        startActivityForResult(i, 1);
    }
    return false;
}
```

2. Add the following statements in bold to `Activity2.java`:

```
public void onCreate(Bundle savedInstanceState) {
    super.onCreate(savedInstanceState);
    setContentView(R.layout.activity2);

    String defaultName="";
    Bundle extras = getIntent().getExtras();
    if (extras!=null)
    {
```

```
            defaultName = extras.getString("Name");
        }
        //---get the EditText view---
        EditText txt_username =
            (EditText) findViewById(R.id.txt_username);
        txt_username.setHint(defaultName);

        //---get the OK button---
        Button btn = (Button) findViewById(R.id.btn_OK);

        //---event handler for the OK button---
        btn.setOnClickListener(new View.OnClickListener()
        {
            //...
        });
    }
```

3. Press F11 to debug the application on the Android Emulator. When you click the center button of the directional keypad, notice that the EditText view in the target activity displays the hint text (see Figure 2-17).

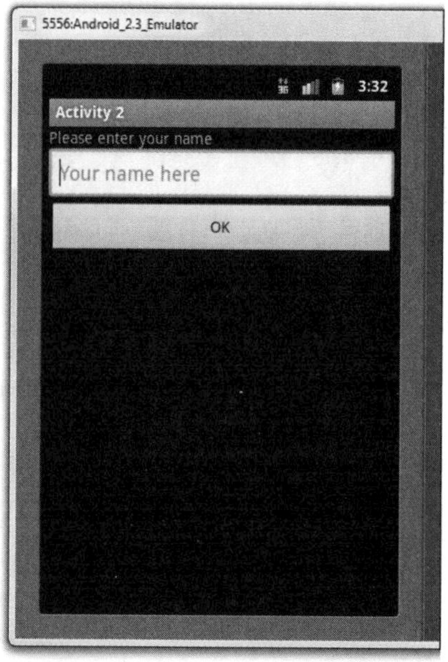

FIGURE 2-17

> **NOTE** The hint text is placeholder text that is commonly found in EditText views. It is displayed when the view is empty, and it disappears as soon as the user types something into it. It is useful for displaying hints that tell users what type of information they should enter.

How It Works

To use the `Intent` object to carry data to the target activity, you made use of a `Bundle` object:

```
Bundle extras = new Bundle();
extras.putString("Name", "Your name here");
i.putExtras(extras);
```

A `Bundle` object is basically a dictionary object that enables you to set data in key/value pairs. In this case, you created a key named `Name` and assigned it a value of "Your name here". The `Bundle` object is then added to the `Intent` object using the `putExtras()` method.

In the target activity, you first use the `getIntent()` method to obtain the intent that started the activity. You then use the `getExtras()` method to obtain the `Bundle` object:

```
Bundle extras = getIntent().getExtras();
if (extras!=null)
{
    defaultName = extras.getString("Name");
}
```

The `getString()` method retrieves the `Name` key from the `Bundle` object. The string retrieved is then assigned to the `EditText` view using the `setHint()` method:

```
//---get the EditText view---
EditText txt_username =
    (EditText) findViewById(R.id.txt_username);
txt_username.setHint(defaultName);
```

CALLING BUILT-IN APPLICATIONS USING INTENTS

Until this point, you have seen how to call activities within your own application. One of the key aspects of Android programming is using the intent to call activities from other applications. In particular, your application can call the many built-in applications that are included with an Android device. For example, if your application needs to enable a user to call a particular person saved in the Contacts application, you can simply use an `Intent` object to bring up the Contacts application, from which the user can select the person to call. This enables your application to present a consistent user experience, and enables you to avoid building another application to retrieve all the contacts in the Contacts application.

The following Try It Out demonstrates how to call some of the built-in applications commonly found on an Android device.

TRY IT OUT Calling Built-In Applications Using Intents

codefile Intents.zip available for download at Wrox.com

1. Using Eclipse, create a new Android project and name it **Intents**.

2. Add the following statements in bold to the `main.xml` file:

```xml
<?xml version="1.0" encoding="utf-8"?>
<LinearLayout xmlns:android="http://schemas.android.com/apk/res/android"
    android:orientation="vertical"
    android:layout_width="fill_parent"
    android:layout_height="fill_parent" >
<Button
    android:id="@+id/btn_webbrowser"
    android:layout_width="fill_parent"
    android:layout_height="wrap_content"
    android:text="Web Browser" />
<Button
    android:id="@+id/btn_makecalls"
    android:layout_width="fill_parent"
    android:layout_height="wrap_content"
    android:text="Make Calls" />
<Button
    android:id="@+id/btn_showMap"
    android:layout_width="fill_parent"
    android:layout_height="wrap_content"
    android:text="Show Map" />
<Button
    android:id="@+id/btn_chooseContact"
    android:layout_width="fill_parent"
    android:layout_height="wrap_content"
    android:text="Choose Contact" />
</LinearLayout>
```

3. Add the following statements in bold to the `MainActivity.java` file:

```java
package net.learn2develop.Intents;

import android.app.Activity;
import android.os.Bundle;

import android.content.Intent;
import android.net.Uri;
import android.provider.ContactsContract;
import android.view.View;
import android.view.View.OnClickListener;
import android.widget.Button;
import android.widget.Toast;

public class MainActivity extends Activity {

    Button b1, b2, b3, b4;
    int request_Code = 1;

    /** Called when the activity is first created. */
    @Override
    public void onCreate(Bundle savedInstanceState) {
        super.onCreate(savedInstanceState);
        setContentView(R.layout.main);

        //---Web browser button---
```

```java
        b1 = (Button) findViewById(R.id.btn_webbrowser);
        b1.setOnClickListener(new OnClickListener()
        {
            public void onClick(View arg0){
                Intent i = new
                    Intent(android.content.Intent.ACTION_VIEW,
                        Uri.parse("http://www.amazon.com"));
                startActivity(i);
            }
        });

        //---Make calls button---
        b2 = (Button) findViewById(R.id.btn_makecalls);
        b2.setOnClickListener(new OnClickListener()
        {
            public void onClick(View arg0){
                Intent i = new
                    Intent(android.content.Intent.ACTION_DIAL,
                    Uri.parse("tel:+651234567"));
                startActivity(i);
            }
        });

        //---Show Map button---
        b3 = (Button) findViewById(R.id.btn_showMap);
        b3.setOnClickListener(new OnClickListener()
        {
            public void onClick(View arg0){
                Intent i = new
                    Intent(android.content.Intent.ACTION_VIEW,
                    Uri.parse("geo:37.827500,-122.481670"));
                startActivity(i);
            }
        });

        //---Choose Contact button---
        b4 = (Button) findViewById(R.id.btn_chooseContact);
        b4.setOnClickListener(new OnClickListener()
        {
            public void onClick(View arg0){
                Intent i = new
                Intent(android.content.Intent.ACTION_PICK);
                i.setType(ContactsContract.Contacts.CONTENT_TYPE);
                startActivityForResult(i,request_Code);
            }
        });
    }

    public void onActivityResult(int requestCode, int resultCode, Intent data)
    {
        if (requestCode == request_Code)
        {
            if (resultCode == RESULT_OK)
            {
```

```
Toast.makeText(this,data.getData().toString(),
    Toast.LENGTH_SHORT).show();
Intent i = new Intent(
        android.content.Intent.ACTION_VIEW,
        Uri.parse(data.getData().toString()));
startActivity(i);
        }
    }
}
}
```

4. Press F11 to debug the application on the Android Emulator.

5. Click the Web Browser button to load the Browser application on the emulator (see Figure 2-18).

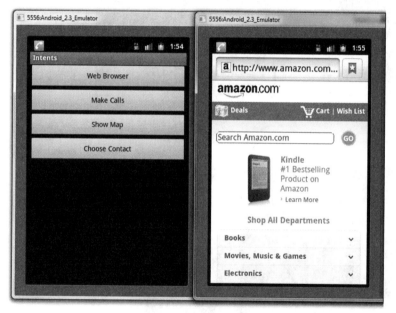

FIGURE 2-18

6. Click the Make Calls button and the Phone application will load (see Figure 2-19).

7. Similarly, to load the Maps application, shown in Figure 2-20, click the Show Map button.

 NOTE *In order to display the Maps application, you need to run the application on an AVD that supports the Google APIs.*

8. Click the Choose Contact application to show a list of contacts that you can select (see Figure 2-21). Selecting a contact will show details about that contact.

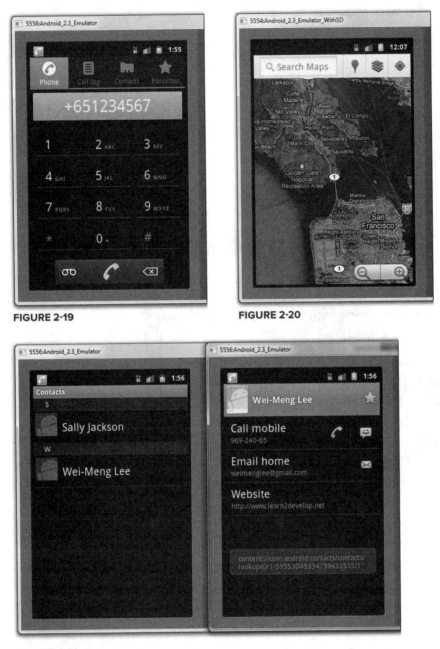

FIGURE 2-19

FIGURE 2-20

FIGURE 2-21

How It Works

In this example, you saw how you can use the `Intent` class to invoke some of the built-in applications in Android (such as Maps, Phone, Contacts, and Browser).

In Android, intents usually come in pairs: *action* and *data*. The *action* describes what is to be performed, such as editing an item, viewing the content of an item, and so on. The *data* specifies what is affected, such as a person in the Contacts database. The data is specified as an `Uri` object.

Some examples of action are as follows:

➤   `ACTION_VIEW`

➤   `ACTION_DIAL`

➤   `ACTION_PICK`

Some examples of data include the following:

➤   `http://www.google.com`

➤   `tel:+651234567`

➤   `geo:37.827500,-122.481670`

➤   `content://contacts`

> **NOTE** *The section "Using Intent Filters" will explain the type of data you can define for use in an activity.*

Collectively, the action and data pair describes the operation to be performed. For example, to dial a phone number, you would use the pair `ACTION_DIAL/tel:+651234567`. To display a list of contacts stored in your phone, you use the pair `ACTION_VIEW/content://contacts`. To pick a contact from the list of contacts, you use the pair `ACTION_PICK/content://contacts`.

In the first button, you create an `Intent` object and then pass two arguments to its constructor — the action and the data:

```
Intent i = new
    Intent(android.content.Intent.ACTION_VIEW,
        Uri.parse("http://www.amazon.com"));
startActivity(i);
```

The action here is represented by the `android.content.Intent.ACTION_VIEW` constant. You use the `parse()` method of the `Uri` class to convert an URL string into an `Uri` object.

The `android.content.Intent.ACTION_VIEW` constant actually refers to the "`android.intent.action.VIEW`" action, so the preceding could be rewritten as follows:

```
Intent i = new
    Intent("android.intent.action.VIEW",
        Uri.parse("http://www.amazon.com"));
startActivity(i);
```

The preceding code snippet can also be rewritten like this:

```
Intent i = new
    Intent("android.intent.action.VIEW");
```

```
i.setData(Uri.parse("http://www.amazon.com"));
startActivity(i);
```

Here, you set the data separately using the `setData()` method.

For the second button, you dial a specific number by passing in the telephone number in the data portion:

```
Intent i = new
    Intent(android.content.Intent.ACTION_DIAL,
        Uri.parse("tel:+651234567"));
startActivity(i);
```

In this case, the dialer will display the number to be called. The user must still press the dial button to dial the number. If you want to directly call the number without user intervention, change the action as follows:

```
Intent i = new
    Intent(android.content.Intent.ACTION_CALL,
        Uri.parse("tel:+651234567"));
startActivity(i);
```

 NOTE *If you want your application to directly call the specified number, you need to add the* `android.permission.CALL_PHONE` *permission to your application.*

If you simply want to display the dialer without specifying any number, simply omit the data portion, like this:

```
Intent i = new
    Intent(android.content.Intent.ACTION_DIAL);
startActivity(i);
```

The third button displays a map using the `ACTION_VIEW` constant:

```
Intent i = new
    Intent(android.content.Intent.ACTION_VIEW,
        Uri.parse("geo:37.827500,-122.481670"));
startActivity(i);
```

Here, instead of using "http" you use the "geo" scheme.

The fourth button invokes the Contacts application to enable the user to pick a contact. Because you are asking the user to select a contact, you need the Contacts application to return a value; in this case, you need to set the type of data to indicate what kind of data needs to be returned:

```
Intent i = new
    Intent(android.content.Intent.ACTION_PICK);
i.setType(ContactsContract.Contacts.CONTENT_TYPE);
startActivityForResult(i, request_Code);
```

If you want to view and select only those contacts with a phone number, you could set the type as follows:

```
i.setType(
    ContactsContract.CommonDataKinds.Phone.CONTENT_TYPE);
```

In this case, the contacts and their phone numbers are displayed (see Figure 2-22).

FIGURE 2-22

Because you are expecting a result from the Contacts application, you invoke it using the
`startActivityForResult()` method, passing in the `Intent` object and a request code. You need
to implement the `onActivityResult()` method in order to obtain a result from the activity:

```
public void onActivityResult(int requestCode,
int resultCode, Intent data)
{
    if (requestCode == request_Code)
    {
        if (resultCode == RESULT_OK)
          {
              Toast.makeText(this,data.getData().toString(),
                  Toast.LENGTH_SHORT).show();
              Intent i = new Intent(
                      android.content.Intent.ACTION_VIEW,
                      Uri.parse(data.getData().toString()));
              startActivity(i);
          }
    }
}
```

In the case of the Contacts application, when you choose a particular contact (using the `ACTION_PICK`
constant), an URL containing the contact selected is returned, like this:

```
content://com.android.contacts/contacts/loopup/0r1-1234567890/1
```

Obtaining this URL is not very useful unless you know what to do with it. Therefore, in this case, you can create another `Intent` object to view it:

```
Intent i = new Intent(
    android.content.Intent.ACTION_VIEW,
    Uri.parse(data.getData().toString()));
startActivity(i);
```

This will show details about the selected contact.

Understanding the Intent Object

So far, you have seen the use of the `Intent` object to call other activities. This is a good time to recap and gain a more detailed understanding of how the `Intent` object performs its magic.

First, you see that you can call another activity by passing its action to the constructor of an `Intent` object:

```
startActivity(new Intent("net.learn2develop.ACTIVITY2"));
```

The action (in this example "net.learn2develop.ACTIVITY2") is also known as the *component name*. This is used to identify the target activity/application that you want to invoke. You can also rewrite the component name by specifying the class name of the activity if it resides in your project, like this:

```
startActivity(new Intent(this, Activity2.class));
```

You can also create an `Intent` object by passing in an action constant and data, such as the following:

```
Intent i = new
    Intent(android.content.Intent.ACTION_VIEW,
        Uri.parse("http://www.amazon.com"));
startActivity(i);
```

The action portion defines what you want to do, while the data portion contains the data for the target activity to act upon. You can also pass the data to the `Intent` object using the `setData()` method:

```
Intent i = new
    Intent(android.content.Intent.ACTION_VIEW);
i.setData(Uri.parse("http://www.amazon.com"));
```

In this example, you indicate that you want to view a web page with the specified URL. The Android OS will look for all activities that are able to satisfy your request. This process is known as *intent resolution*. The next section discusses in more detail how your activities can be the target of other activities.

For some intents, there is no need to specify the data. For example, to select a contact from the Contacts application, you specify the action and then indicate the MIME type using the `setType()` method:

```
Intent i = new
    Intent(android.content.Intent.ACTION_PICK);
i.setType(ContactsContract.Contacts.CONTENT_TYPE);
```

The `setType()` method explicitly specifies the MIME data type to indicate the type of data to return. The MIME type for `ContactsContract.Contacts.CONTENT_TYPE` is `"vnd.android.cursor .dir/contact"`.

Besides specifying the action, the data, and the type, an `Intent` object can also specify a category. A category groups activities into logical units so that Android can use it for further filtering. The next section discusses categories in more details.

To summarize, an `Intent` object can contain the following information:

➤ Action

➤ Data

➤ Type

➤ Category

Using Intent Filters

Earlier, you saw how an activity can invoke another activity using the `Intent` object. In order for other activities to invoke your activity, you need to specify the action and category within the `<intent-filter>` element in the `AndroidManifest.xml` file, like this:

```
<intent-filter>
    <action android:name="net.learn2develop.ACTIVITY2" />
    <category android:name="android.intent.category.DEFAULT" />
</intent-filter>
```

This is a very simple example in which one activity calls another using the "`net.learn2develop .ACTIVITY2`" action. The following Try It Out shows you a more sophisticated example.

TRY IT OUT   Specifying Intent Filters in More Details

1.   Using the Intents project created earlier, add a new class to the project and name it **MyBrowserActivity .java**. Also add a new XML file to the `res/layout` folder and name it **browser.xml** (see Figure 2-23).

FIGURE 2-23

2. Add the following statements in bold to the `AndroidManifest.xml` file:

```xml
<?xml version="1.0" encoding="utf-8"?>
<manifest xmlns:android="http://schemas.android.com/apk/res/android"
      package="net.learn2develop.Intents"
      android:versionCode="1"
      android:versionName="1.0">
    <application android:icon="@drawable/icon" android:label="@string/app_name">
        <activity android:name=".MainActivity"
                  android:label="@string/app_name">
            <intent-filter>
                <action android:name="android.intent.action.MAIN" />
                <category android:name="android.intent.category.LAUNCHER" />
            </intent-filter>
        </activity>
        <activity android:name=".MyBrowserActivity"
                  android:label="@string/app_name">
            <intent-filter>
                <action android:name="android.intent.action.VIEW" />
                <action android:name="net.learn2develop.MyBrowser" />
                <category android:name="android.intent.category.DEFAULT" />
                <data android:scheme="http" />
            </intent-filter>
        </activity>
    </application>
    <uses-sdk android:minSdkVersion="9" />
    <uses-permission android:name="android.permission.CALL_PHONE" />
    <uses-permission android:name="android.permission.INTERNET" />
</manifest>
```

3. Add the following statements in bold to the `main.xml` file:

```xml
<?xml version="1.0" encoding="utf-8"?>
<LinearLayout xmlns:android="http://schemas.android.com/apk/res/android"
    android:orientation="vertical"
    android:layout_width="fill_parent"
    android:layout_height="fill_parent" >
<Button
    android:id="@+id/btn_webbrowser"
    android:layout_width="fill_parent"
    android:layout_height="wrap_content"
    android:text="Web Browser" />
<Button
    android:id="@+id/btn_makecalls"
    android:layout_width="fill_parent"
    android:layout_height="wrap_content"
    android:text="Make Calls" />
<Button
    android:id="@+id/btn_showMap"
    android:layout_width="fill_parent"
    android:layout_height="wrap_content"
    android:text="Show Map" />
<Button
    android:id="@+id/btn_chooseContact"
```

```
        android:layout_width="fill_parent"
        android:layout_height="wrap_content"
        android:text="Choose Contact" />
    <Button
        android:id="@+id/btn_launchMyBrowser"
        android:layout_width="fill_parent"
        android:layout_height="wrap_content"
        android:text="Launch My Browser" />
</LinearLayout>
```

4. Add the following statements in bold to the `MainActivity.java` file:

```java
package net.learn2develop.Intents;

import android.app.Activity;
import android.content.Intent;
import android.net.Uri;
import android.os.Bundle;
import android.provider.ContactsContract;
import android.view.View;
import android.view.View.OnClickListener;
import android.widget.Button;
import android.widget.Toast;

public class MainActivity extends Activity {

    Button b1, b2, b3, b4, b5;
    int request_Code = 1;

    /** Called when the activity is first created. */
    @Override
    public void onCreate(Bundle savedInstanceState) {
        super.onCreate(savedInstanceState);
        setContentView(R.layout.main);

        //---Web browser button---
        b1 = (Button) findViewById(R.id.btn_webbrowser);
        b1.setOnClickListener(new OnClickListener()
        {
            //...
        });

        //---Make calls button---
        b2 = (Button) findViewById(R.id.btn_makecalls);
        b2.setOnClickListener(new OnClickListener()
        {
            //...
        });

        //---Show Map button---
        b3 = (Button) findViewById(R.id.btn_showMap);
        b3.setOnClickListener(new OnClickListener()
        {
            //...
```

```
    });

    //---Choose Contact button---
    b4 = (Button) findViewById(R.id.btn_chooseContact);
    b4.setOnClickListener(new OnClickListener()
    {
        //...
    });

    b5 = (Button) findViewById(R.id.btn_launchMyBrowser);
    b5.setOnClickListener(new OnClickListener()
    {
        public void onClick(View arg0)
        {
        Intent i = new
            Intent("net.learn2develop.MyBrowser");
        i.setData(Uri.parse("http://www.amazon.com"));
        startActivity(i);
        }
    });
    }

    public void onActivityResult(int requestCode, int resultCode, Intent data)
    {
        //...
    }
}
```

5. Add the following statements in bold to the `browser.xml` file:

```xml
<?xml version="1.0" encoding="utf-8"?>
<LinearLayout xmlns:android="http://schemas.android.com/apk/res/android"
    android:orientation="vertical"
    android:layout_width="fill_parent"
    android:layout_height="fill_parent" >
<WebView
    android:id="@+id/WebView01"
    android:layout_width="wrap_content"
    android:layout_height="wrap_content" />
</LinearLayout>
```

6. Add the following statements in bold to the `MyBrowserActivity.java` file:

```java
package net.learn2develop.Intents;

import android.app.Activity;
import android.net.Uri;
import android.os.Bundle;
import android.webkit.WebView;
import android.webkit.WebViewClient;

public class MyBrowserActivity extends Activity {
```

```
/** Called when the activity is first created. */
@Override
public void onCreate(Bundle savedInstanceState) {
    super.onCreate(savedInstanceState);
    setContentView(R.layout.browser);

    Uri url = getIntent().getData();
    WebView webView = (WebView) findViewById(R.id.WebView01);
    webView.setWebViewClient(new Callback());
    webView.loadUrl(url.toString());
}

private class Callback extends WebViewClient {
    @Override
    public boolean shouldOverrideUrlLoading(WebView view, String url) {
        return(false);
    }
}
}
```

7. Press F11 to debug the application on the Android Emulator.

8. Click the Launch my Browser button and you should see the new activity displaying the Amazon.com web page (see Figure 2-24).

FIGURE 2-24

How It Works

In this example, you created a new activity named `MyBrowserActivity`. You first needed to declare it in the `AndroidManifest.xml` file:

```
<activity android:name=".MyBrowserActivity"
        android:label="@string/app_name">
    <intent-filter>
        <action android:name="android.intent.action.VIEW" />
        <action android:name="net.learn2develop.MyBrowser" />
        <category android:name="android.intent.category.DEFAULT" />
        <data android:scheme="http" />
    </intent-filter>
</activity>
```

In the `<intent-filter>` element, you declared it to have two actions, one category, and one data. This means that all other activities can invoke this activity using either the "`android.intent.action.VIEW`" or the "`net.learn2develop.MyBrowser`" action. For all activities that you want others to call using the `start Activity()` or `startActivityForResult()` methods, they need to have the "`android.intent.category .DEFAULT`" category. If not, your activity will not be callable by others. The `<data>` element specifies the type of data expected by the activity. In this case, it expects the data to start with the "`http://`" prefix.

The preceding intent filter could also be rewritten as follows:

```
<activity android:name=".MyBrowserActivity"
        android:label="@string/app_name">
    <intent-filter>
        <action android:name="android.intent.action.VIEW" />
        <category android:name="android.intent.category.DEFAULT" />
        <data android:scheme="http" />
    </intent-filter>
    <intent-filter>
        <action android:name="net.learn2develop.MyBrowser" />
        <category android:name="android.intent.category.DEFAULT" />
        <data android:scheme="http" />
    </intent-filter>
</activity>
```

Writing the intent filter this way makes it much more readable and logically groups the action, category, and data within an intent filter.

If you now use the `ACTION_VIEW` action with the data shown here, Android will display a selection (as shown in Figure 2-25):

```
Intent i = new
    Intent(android.content.Intent.ACTION_VIEW,
        Uri.parse("http://www.amazon.com"));
startActivity(i);
```

You can choose between using the Browser application or the Intents application that you are currently building.

FIGURE 2-25

Adding Categories

You can group your activities into categories by using the `<category>` element in the intent filter. Suppose you have added the following `<category>` element to the `AndroidManifest.xml` file:

```xml
<?xml version="1.0" encoding="utf-8"?>
<manifest xmlns:android="http://schemas.android.com/apk/res/android"
        package="net.learn2develop.Intents"
        android:versionCode="1"
        android:versionName="1.0">
    <application android:icon="@drawable/icon" android:label="@string/app_name">
        <activity android:name=".MainActivity"
                android:label="@string/app_name">
            <intent-filter>
                <action android:name="android.intent.action.MAIN" />
                <category android:name="android.intent.category.LAUNCHER" />
            </intent-filter>
        </activity>
        <activity android:name=".MyBrowserActivity"
                android:label="@string/app_name">
            <intent-filter>
                <action android:name="android.intent.action.VIEW" />
                <action android:name="net.learn2develop.MyBrowser" />
                <category android:name="android.intent.category.DEFAULT" />
                <category android:name="net.learn2develop.Apps" />
```

```
                    <data android:scheme="http" />
              </intent-filter>
          </activity>
      </application>
      <uses-sdk android:minSdkVersion="9" />
      <uses-permission android:name="android.permission.CALL_PHONE" />
      <uses-permission android:name="android.permission.INTERNET" />
  </manifest>
```

In this case, the following code will invoke the `MyBrowerActivity` activity:

```
    Intent i = new
        Intent(android.content.Intent.ACTION_VIEW,
            Uri.parse("http://www.amazon.com"));
    i.addCategory("net.learn2develop.Apps");
    startActivity(i);
```

You add the category to the `Intent` object using the `addCategory()` method. If you omit the `addCategory()` statement, the preceding code will still invoke the `MyBrowerActivity` activity because it will still match the default category `"android.intent.category.DEFAULT"`.

However, if you specify a category that does not match the category defined in the intent filter, it will not work:

```
    Intent i = new
        Intent("net.learn2develop.MyBrowser",
            Uri.parse("http://www.amazon.com"));
    //---this category does not match any in the intent-filter---
    i.addCategory("net.learn2develop.OtherApps");
    startActivity(i);
```

The preceding category ("net.learn2develop.OtherApps") does not match any in the intent filter, so a run-time exception will be raised.

If you add the preceding category in the intent filter of `MyBrowerActivity`, then the preceding code will work:

```
    <intent-filter>
        <action android:name="android.intent.action.VIEW" />
        <action android:name="net.learn2develop.MyBrowser" />
        <category android:name="android.intent.category.DEFAULT" />
        <category android:name="net.learn2develop.Apps" />
        <category android:name="net.learn2develop.OtherApps" />
        <data android:scheme="http" />
    </intent-filter>
```

You can add multiple categories to an `Intent` object; for example, the following statements add the "net.learn2develop.SomeOtherApps" category to the `Intent` object:

```
    Intent i = new
        Intent("net.learn2develop.MyBrowser",
            Uri.parse("http://www.amazon.com"));
    i.addCategory("net.learn2develop.OtherApps");
    i.addCategory("net.learn2develop.SomeOtherApps");
    startActivity(i);
```

Because the intent filter does not define the `"net.learn2develop.SomeOtherApps"` category, the preceding code will not be able to invoke the `MyBrowerActivity` activity. To fix this, you need to add the `"net.learn2develop.SomeOtherApps"` category to the intent filter again.

From this example, it is evident that when using an `Intent` object with categories, all categories added to the `Intent` object must fully match those defined in the intent filter before an activity can be invoked.

DISPLAYING NOTIFICATIONS

So far, you have been using the `Toast` class to display messages to the user. While the `Toast` class is a handy way to show users alerts, it is not persistent. It flashes on the screen for a few seconds and then disappears. If it contains important information, users may easily miss it if they are not looking at the screen.

For messages that are important, you should use a more persistent method. In this case, you should use the `NotificationManager` to display a persistent message at the top of the device, commonly known as the *status bar* (sometimes also referred to as the *notification bar*). The following Try It Out demonstrates how.

TRY IT OUT Displaying Notifications on the Status Bar

codefile Notifications.zip available for download at Wrox.com

1. Using Eclipse, create a new Android project and name it **Notifications**.

2. Add a new class file named `NotificationView.java` to the `src` folder of the project (see Figure 2-26). In addition, add a new `notification.xml` file to the `res/layout` folder as well.

FIGURE 2-26

3. Populate the `notification.xml` file as follows:

```xml
<?xml version="1.0" encoding="utf-8"?>
<LinearLayout xmlns:android="http://schemas.android.com/apk/res/android"
    android:orientation="vertical"
    android:layout_width="fill_parent"
```

```
        android:layout_height="fill_parent" >
    <TextView
        android:layout_width="fill_parent"
        android:layout_height="wrap_content"
        android:text="Here are the details for the notification..." />
    </LinearLayout>
```

4. Populate the NotificationView.java file as follows:

```
package net.learn2develop.Notifications;

import android.app.Activity;
import android.app.NotificationManager;
import android.os.Bundle;

public class NotificationView extends Activity
{
    @Override
    public void onCreate(Bundle savedInstanceState)
    {
        super.onCreate(savedInstanceState);
        setContentView(R.layout.notification);

        //---look up the notification manager service---
        NotificationManager nm = (NotificationManager)
            getSystemService(NOTIFICATION_SERVICE);

        //---cancel the notification that we started
        nm.cancel(getIntent().getExtras().getInt("notificationID"));
    }
}
```

5. Add the following statements in bold to the AndroidManifest.xml file:

```
<?xml version="1.0" encoding="utf-8"?>
<manifest xmlns:android="http://schemas.android.com/apk/res/android"
    package="net.learn2develop.Notifications"
    android:versionCode="1"
    android:versionName="1.0">
    <application android:icon="@drawable/icon" android:label="@string/app_name">
        <activity android:name=".MainActivity"
                android:label="@string/app_name">
            <intent-filter>
                <action android:name="android.intent.action.MAIN" />
                <category android:name="android.intent.category.LAUNCHER" />
            </intent-filter>
        </activity>
        <activity android:name=".NotificationView"
            android:label="Details of notification">
            <intent-filter>
                <action android:name="android.intent.action.MAIN" />
                <category android:name="android.intent.category.DEFAULT" />
            </intent-filter>
        </activity>
    </application>
    <uses-sdk android:minSdkVersion="9" />
```

```
    <uses-permission android:name="android.permission.VIBRATE" />
</manifest>
```

6. Add the following statements in bold to the `main.xml` file:

```xml
<?xml version="1.0" encoding="utf-8"?>
<LinearLayout xmlns:android="http://schemas.android.com/apk/res/android"
    android:orientation="vertical"
    android:layout_width="fill_parent"
    android:layout_height="fill_parent" >
<Button
    android:id="@+id/btn_displaynotif"
    android:layout_width="fill_parent"
    android:layout_height="wrap_content"
    android:text="Display Notification" />
</LinearLayout>
```

7. Finally, add the following statements in bold to the `MainActivity.java` file:

```java
package net.learn2develop.Notifications;

import android.app.Activity;
import android.os.Bundle;
import android.app.Notification;
import android.app.NotificationManager;
import android.app.PendingIntent;
import android.content.Intent;
import android.view.View;
import android.widget.Button;

public class MainActivity extends Activity {
    int notificationID = 1;
    /** Called when the activity is first created. */
    @Override
    public void onCreate(Bundle savedInstanceState) {
        super.onCreate(savedInstanceState);
        setContentView(R.layout.main);

        Button button = (Button) findViewById(R.id.btn_displaynotif);
        button.setOnClickListener(new Button.OnClickListener() {
            public void onClick(View v) {
                displayNotification();
            }
        });
    }

    protected void displayNotification()
    {
        //---PendingIntent to launch activity if the user selects
        // this notification---
        Intent i = new Intent(this, NotificationView.class);
        i.putExtra("notificationID", notificationID);

        PendingIntent pendingIntent =
            PendingIntent.getActivity(this, 0, i, 0);
```

```
NotificationManager nm = (NotificationManager)
    getSystemService(NOTIFICATION_SERVICE);

Notification notif = new Notification(
    R.drawable.icon,
    "Reminder: Meeting starts in 5 minutes",
    System.currentTimeMillis());

CharSequence from = "System Alarm";
CharSequence message = "Meeting with customer at 3pm...";

notif.setLatestEventInfo(this, from, message, pendingIntent);

//---100ms delay, vibrate for 250ms, pause for 100 ms and
// then vibrate for 500ms---
notif.vibrate = new long[] { 100, 250, 100, 500};
nm.notify(notificationID, notif);
    }
}
```

8. Press F11 to debug the application on the Android Emulator.

9. Click the Display Notification button (see the top left of Figure 2-27) and a notification will appear on the status bar.

10. Clicking and dragging the status bar down will reveal the notification (see the right of Figure 2-27).

11. Clicking on the notification will reveal the `NotificationView` activity. This also causes the notification to be dismissed from the status bar.

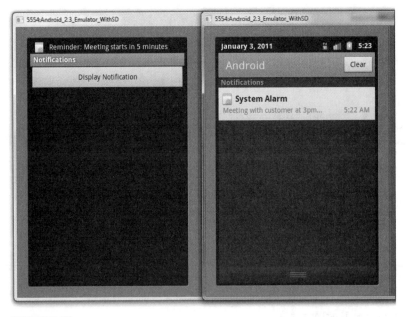

FIGURE 2-27

How It Works

To display a notification, you first created an `Intent` object to point to the `NotificationView` class:

```
//---PendingIntent to launch activity if the user selects
// this notification---
Intent i = new Intent(this, NotificationView.class);
i.putExtra("notificationID", notificationID);
```

This intent will be used to launch another activity when the user selects a notification from the list of notifications. In this example, you added a key/value pair to the `Intent` object so that you can tag the notification ID, identifying the notification to the target activity. This ID will be used to dismiss the notifications later.

You would also need to create a `PendingIntent` object. A `PendingIntent` object helps you to perform an action on your application's behalf, often at a later time, regardless of whether your application is running or not. In this case, you initialized it as follows:

```
PendingIntent pendingIntent =
    PendingIntent.getActivity(this, 0, i, 0);
```

The `getActivity()` method retrieves a `PendingIntent` object and you set it using the following arguments:

➤ context — Application context

➤ request code — Request code for the intent

➤ intent — The intent for launching the target activity

➤ flags — The flags in which the activity is to be launched

You then obtain an instance of the `NotificationManager` class and create an instance of the `Notification` class:

```
NotificationManager nm = (NotificationManager)
    getSystemService(NOTIFICATION_SERVICE);

Notification notif = new Notification(
    R.drawable.icon,
    "Reminder: Meeting starts in 5 minutes",
    System.currentTimeMillis());
```

The `Notification` class enables you to specify the notification's main information when the notification first appears on the status bar. The second argument to the `Notification` constructor sets the "ticker text" on the status bar (see Figure 2-28).

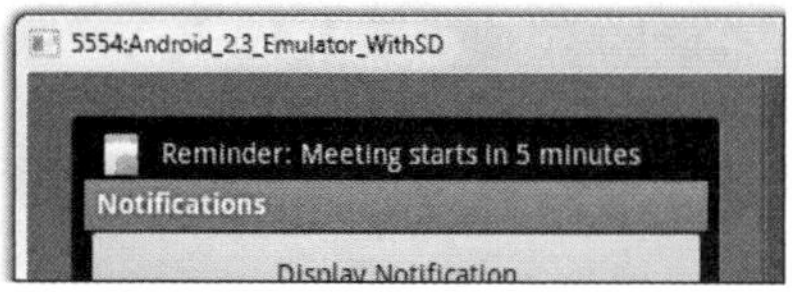

FIGURE 2-28

Next, you set the details of the notification using the `setLatestEventInfo()` method:

```
CharSequence from = "System Alarm";
CharSequence message = "Meeting with customer at 3pm...";
notif.setLatestEventInfo(this, from, message, pendingIntent);
//---100ms delay, vibrate for 250ms, pause for 100 ms and
// then vibrate for 500ms---
notif.vibrate = new long[] { 100, 250, 100, 500};
```

The preceding also sets the notification to vibrate the phone. Finally, to display the notification you use the `notify()` method:

```
nm.notify(notificationID, notif);
```

When the user clicks on the notification, the `NotificationView` activity is launched. Here, you dismiss the notification by using the `cancel()` method of the `NotificationManager` object and passing it the ID of the notification (passed in via the `Intent` object):

```
//---look up the notification manager service---
NotificationManager nm = (NotificationManager)
    getSystemService(NOTIFICATION_SERVICE);

//---cancel the notification that we started
nm.cancel(getIntent().getExtras().getInt("notificationID"));
```

SUMMARY

This chapter first provided a detailed look at how activities work and the various forms in which you can display them. You also learned how to display dialog windows using activities.

The second part of this chapter demonstrated a very important concept in Android — the intent. The intent is the "glue" that enables different activities to be connected, and is a vital concept to understand when developing for the Android platform.

EXERCISES

1. What will happen if you have two or more activities with the same intent filter action name?

2. Write the code to invoke the built-in Browser application.

3. Which components can you specify in an intent filter?

4. What is the difference between the `Toast` and `NotificationManager` class?

Answers to the Exercises can be found in Appendix C.

▶ **WHAT YOU LEARNED IN THIS CHAPTER**

TOPIC	KEY CONCEPTS
Creating an activity	All activities must be declared in the `AndroidManifest.xml` file.
Key life cycle of an activity	When an activity is started, the `onStart()` and `onResume()` events are always called.
	When an activity is killed or sent to the background, the `onPause()` event is always called.
Displaying an activity as a dialog	Use the `showDialog()` method and implement the `onCreateDialog()` method.
Intent	The "glue" that connects different activities
Intent filter	The "filter" that enables you to specify how your activities should be called
Calling an activity	Use the `startActivity()` or `startActivityForResult()` method.
Passing data to an activity	Use the `Bundle` object.
Components in an `Intent` object	An `Intent` object can contain the following: action, data, type, and category.
Displaying notifications	Use the `NotificationManager` class.
`PendingIntent` object	A `PendingIntent` object helps you to perform an action on your application's behalf, often at a later time, regardless of whether or not your application is running.

3

Getting to Know the Android User Interface

WHAT YOU WILL LEARN IN THIS CHAPTER

- ➤ The various ViewGroups you can use to lay out your views
- ➤ How to adapt to changes in screen orientation
- ➤ How to manage screen orientation changes
- ➤ How to create the UI programmatically
- ➤ How to listen for UI notifications

In Chapter 2, you learned about the `Activity` class and its life cycle. You learned that an activity is a means by which users interact with the application. However, an activity by itself does not have a presence on the screen. Instead, it has to draw the screen using *Views* and *ViewGroups*. In this chapter, you will learn the details about creating user interfaces in Android, how users interact with them. In addition, you will learn how to handle changes in screen orientation on your Android devices.

UNDERSTANDING THE COMPONENTS OF A SCREEN

In Chapter 2, you saw that the basic unit of an Android application is an *activity*. An *activity* displays the user interface of your application, which may contain widgets like buttons, labels, text boxes, and so on. Typically, you define your UI using an XML file (e.g., the `main.xml` file located in the `res/layout` folder), which may look like this:

```xml
<?xml version="1.0" encoding="utf-8"?>
<LinearLayout xmlns:android="http://schemas.android.com/apk/res/android"
    android:orientation="vertical"
```

```
        android:layout_width="fill_parent"
        android:layout_height="fill_parent"
        >
    <TextView
        android:layout_width="fill_parent"
        android:layout_height="wrap_content"
        android:text="@string/hello"
        />
    </LinearLayout>
```

During run time, you load the XML UI in the onCreate() event handler in your Activity class, using the setContentView() method of the Activity class:

```
    @Override
    public void onCreate(Bundle savedInstanceState) {
        super.onCreate(savedInstanceState);
        setContentView(R.layout.main);
    }
```

During compilation, each element in the XML file is compiled into its equivalent Android GUI class, with attributes represented by methods. The Android system then creates the UI of the activity when it is loaded.

> **NOTE** While it is always easier to build your UI using an XML file, sometimes you need to build your UI dynamically during run time (for example, when writing games). Hence, it is also possible to create your UI entirely using code. Later in this chapter you will see an example of how this can be done.

Views and ViewGroups

An activity contains Views and ViewGroups. A view is a widget that has an appearance on screen. Examples of views are buttons, labels, and text boxes. A view derives from the base class android .view.View.

> **NOTE** Chapters 4 and 5 discuss the various common views in Android.

One or more views can be grouped together into a ViewGroup. A ViewGroup (which is itself a special type of view) provides the layout in which you can order the appearance and sequence of views. Examples of ViewGroups include LinearLayout and FrameLayout. A ViewGroup derives from the base class android.view.ViewGroup.

Android supports the following ViewGroups:

➤ LinearLayout

➤ AbsoluteLayout

➤ TableLayout

➤ RelativeLayout

➤ FrameLayout

➤ ScrollView

The following sections describe each of these ViewGroups in more detail. Note that in practice it is common to combine different types of layouts to create the UI you want.

LinearLayout

The LinearLayout arranges views in a single column or a single row. Child views can be arranged either vertically or horizontally. To see how LinearLayout works, consider the following elements typically contained in the main.xml file:

```xml
<?xml version="1.0" encoding="utf-8"?>
<LinearLayout
    xmlns:android="http://schemas.android.com/apk/res/android"
    android:orientation="vertical"
    android:layout_width="fill_parent"
    android:layout_height="fill_parent"
    >
<TextView
    android:layout_width="fill_parent"
    android:layout_height="wrap_content"
    android:text="@string/hello"
    />
</LinearLayout>
```

In the main.xml file, observe that the root element is <LinearLayout> and it has a <TextView> element contained within it. The <LinearLayout> element controls the order in which the views contained within it appear.

Each View and ViewGroup has a set of common attributes, some of which are described in Table 3-1.

TABLE 3-1: Common Attributes Used in Views and ViewGroups

ATTRIBUTE	DESCRIPTION
layout_width	Specifies the width of the View or ViewGroup
layout_height	Specifies the height of the View or ViewGroup
layout_marginTop	Specifies extra space on the top side of the View or ViewGroup
layout_marginBottom	Specifies extra space on the bottom side of the View or ViewGroup
layout_marginLeft	Specifies extra space on the left side of the View or ViewGroup
layout_marginRight	Specifies extra space on the right side of the View or ViewGroup

continues

TABLE 3-1 *(continued)*

ATTRIBUTE	DESCRIPTION
layout_gravity	Specifies how child Views are positioned
layout_weight	Specifies how much of the extra space in the layout should be allocated to the View
layout_x	Specifies the x-coordinate of the View or ViewGroup
layout_y	Specifies the y-coordinate of the View or ViewGroup

> **NOTE** *Some of these attributes are applicable only when a View is in a specific ViewGroup. For example, the* layout_weight *and* layout_gravity *attributes are applicable only when a View is in either a* LinearLayout *or a* TableLayout.

For example, the width of the <TextView> element fills the entire width of its parent (which is the screen in this case) using the fill_parent constant. Its height is indicated by the wrap_content constant, which means that its height is the height of its content (in this case, the text contained within it). If you don't want to have the <TextView> view occupy the entire row, you can set its layout_width attribute to wrap_content, like this:

```
< TextView
    android:layout_width="wrap_content
    android:layout_height="wrap_content"
    android:text="@string/hello"
/>
```

This will set the width of the view to be equal to the width of the text contained within it.

Consider the following layout:

```
<?xml version="1.0" encoding="utf-8"?>
<LinearLayout xmlns:android="http://schemas.android.com/apk/res/android"
    android:orientation="vertical"
    android:layout_width="fill_parent"
    android:layout_height="fill_parent"
    >
<TextView
    android:layout_width="105dp"
    android:layout_height="wrap_content"
    android:text="@string/hello"
    />
<Button
    android:layout_width="160dp"
    android:layout_height="wrap_content"
    android:text="Button"
    />
</LinearLayout>
```

UNITS OF MEASUREMENT

When specifying the size of an element on an Android UI, you should be aware of the following units of measurement:

➤ dp — Density-independent pixel. 160dp is equivalent to one inch of physical screen size. This is the recommended unit of measurement when specifying the dimension of views in your layout. You can specify either "dp" or "dip" when referring to a density-independent pixel.

➤ sp — Scale-independent pixel. This is similar to dp and is recommended for specifying font sizes.

➤ pt — Point. A point is defined to be 1/72 of an inch, based on the physical screen size.

➤ px — Pixel. Corresponds to actual pixels on the screen. Using this unit is not recommended, as your UI may not render correctly on devices with different screen sizes.

Here, you set the width of both the TextView and Button views to an absolute value. In this case, the width for the TextView is set to 105 density-independent pixels wide, and the Button to 160 density-independent pixels wide. Figure 3-1 shows how the views look when viewed on an emulator with a resolution of 320×480.

Figure 3-2 shows how the views look when viewed on a high-resolution (480×800) emulator.

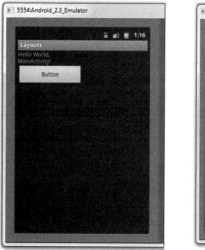

FIGURE 3-1   **FIGURE 3-2**

As you can see, in both emulators the widths of both views are the same with respect to the width of the emulator. This demonstrates the usefulness of using the dp unit, which ensures that even if the resolution of the target device is different, the size of the view relative to the device remains unchanged.

The preceding example also specifies that the orientation of the layout is vertical:

```
<LinearLayout
    xmlns:android="http://schemas.android.com/apk/res/android"
    android:orientation="vertical"
    android:layout_width="fill_parent"
    android:layout_height="fill_parent"
    >
```

The default orientation layout is horizontal, so if you omit the android:orientation attribute, the views will appear as shown in Figure 3-3.

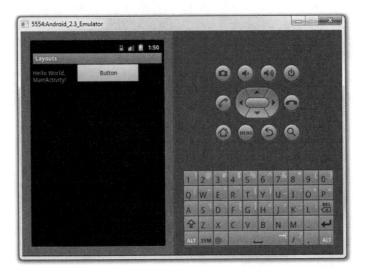

FIGURE 3-3

In LinearLayout, you can apply the layout_weight and layout_gravity attributes to views contained within it, as the following modifications to main.xml show:

```
<?xml version="1.0" encoding="utf-8"?>
<LinearLayout xmlns:android="http://schemas.android.com/apk/res/android"
    android:orientation="vertical"
    android:layout_width="fill_parent"
    android:layout_height="fill_parent"
    >
<TextView
    android:layout_width="105dp"
    android:layout_height="wrap_content"
    android:text="@string/hello"
    />
<Button
    android:layout_width="160dp"
    android:layout_height="wrap_content"
    android:text="Button"
```

```
        android:layout_gravity="right"
        android:layout_weight="0.2"
        />
    <EditText
        android:layout_width="fill_parent"
        android:layout_height="wrap_content"
        android:textSize="18sp"
        android:layout_weight="0.8"
        />
</LinearLayout>
```

Figure 3-4 shows that the button is aligned to the right of its parent (which is the `LinearLayout`) using the `layout_gravity` attribute. At the same time, you use the `layout_weight` attribute to specify the ratio in which the `Button` and `EditText` views occupy the remaining space on the screen. The total value for the `layout_weight` attribute must be equal to 1.

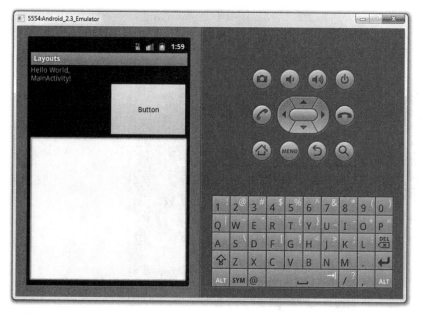

FIGURE 3-4

AbsoluteLayout

The `AbsoluteLayout` enables you to specify the exact location of its children. Consider the following UI defined in `main.xml`:

```xml
<?xml version="1.0" encoding="utf-8"?>
<AbsoluteLayout
    android:layout_width="fill_parent"
    android:layout_height="fill_parent"
    xmlns:android="http://schemas.android.com/apk/res/android"
```

```
        >
    <Button
        android:layout_width="188dp"
        android:layout_height="wrap_content"
        android:text="Button"
        android:layout_x="126px"
        android:layout_y="361px"
        />
    <Button
        android:layout_width="113dp"
        android:layout_height="wrap_content"
        android:text="Button"
        android:layout_x="12px"
        android:layout_y="361px"
        />
</AbsoluteLayout>
```

Figure 3-5 shows the two Button views located at their specified positions using the android_layout_x and android_layout_y attributes.

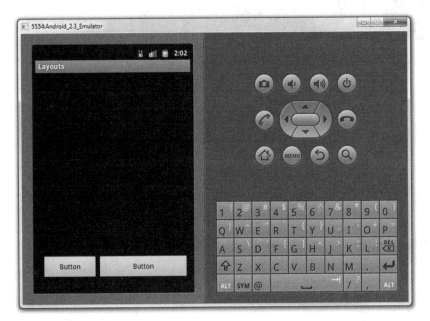

FIGURE 3-5

However, there is a problem with the AbsoluteLayout when the activity is viewed on a high-resolution screen (see Figure 3-6). For this reason, the AbsoluteLayout has been deprecated since Android 1.5 (although it is still supported in the current version). You should avoid using the AbsoluteLayout in your UI, as it is not guaranteed to be supported in future versions of Android. You should instead use the other layouts described in this chapter.

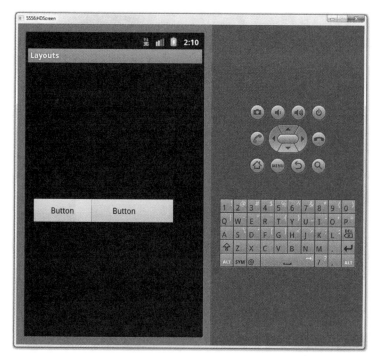

FIGURE 3-6

TableLayout

The `TableLayout` groups views into rows and columns. You use the `<TableRow>` element to designate a row in the table. Each row can contain one or more views. Each view you place within a row forms a cell. The width of each column is determined by the largest width of each cell in that column.

Consider the content of `main.xml` shown here:

```xml
<?xml version="1.0" encoding="utf-8"?>
<TableLayout
    xmlns:android="http://schemas.android.com/apk/res/android"
    android:layout_height="fill_parent"
    android:layout_width="fill_parent"
    >
    <TableRow>
        <TextView
            android:text="User Name:"
            android:width ="120px"
            />
        <EditText
            android:id="@+id/txtUserName"
            android:width="200px" />
    </TableRow>
```

```
        <TableRow>
            <TextView
                android:text="Password:"
                />
            <EditText
                android:id="@+id/txtPassword"
                android:password="true"
                />
        </TableRow>
        <TableRow>
            <TextView />
            <CheckBox android:id="@+id/chkRememberPassword"
                android:layout_width="fill_parent"
                android:layout_height="wrap_content"
                android:text="Remember Password"
                />
        </TableRow>
        <TableRow>
            <Button
                android:id="@+id/buttonSignIn"
                android:text="Log In" />
        </TableRow>
    </TableLayout>
```

Figure 3-7 shows what the preceding looks like when rendered on the Android Emulator.

Note that in the preceding example, there are two columns and four rows in the TableLayout. The cell directly under the Password TextView is populated with an <TextView/> empty element. If you don't do this, the Remember Password checkbox will appear under the Password TextView, as shown in Figure 3-8.

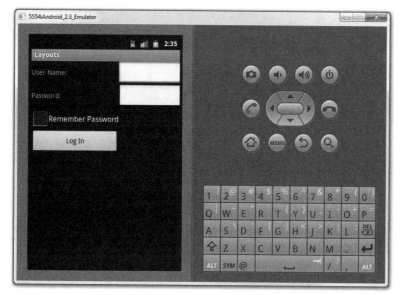

FIGURE 3-8

RelativeLayout

The RelativeLayout enables you to specify how child views are positioned relative to each other. Consider the following main.xml file:

```xml
<?xml version="1.0" encoding="utf-8"?>
<RelativeLayout
    android:id="@+id/RLayout"
    android:layout_width="fill_parent"
    android:layout_height="fill_parent"
    xmlns:android="http://schemas.android.com/apk/res/android"
    >
    <TextView
        android:id="@+id/lblComments"
        android:layout_width="wrap_content"
        android:layout_height="wrap_content"
        android:text="Comments"
        android:layout_alignParentTop="true"
        android:layout_alignParentLeft="true"
        />
    <EditText
        android:id="@+id/txtComments"
        android:layout_width="fill_parent"
        android:layout_height="170px"
        android:textSize="18sp"
        android:layout_alignLeft="@+id/lblComments"
        android:layout_below="@+id/lblComments"
        android:layout_centerHorizontal="true"
        />
    <Button
        android:id="@+id/btnSave"
```

```
            android:layout_width="125px"
            android:layout_height="wrap_content"
            android:text="Save"
            android:layout_below="@+id/txtComments"
            android:layout_alignRight="@+id/txtComments"
            />
    <Button
            android:id="@+id/btnCancel"
            android:layout_width="124px"
            android:layout_height="wrap_content"
            android:text="Cancel"
            android:layout_below="@+id/txtComments"
            android:layout_alignLeft="@+id/txtComments"
            />
</RelativeLayout>
```

Notice that each view embedded within the `RelativeLayout` has attributes that enable it to align with another view. These attributes are as follows:

➤   `layout_alignParentTop`

➤   `layout_alignParentLeft`

➤   `layout_alignLeft`

➤   `layout_alignRight`

➤   `layout_below`

➤   `layout_centerHorizontal`

The value for each of these attributes is the ID for the view that you are referencing. The preceding XML UI creates the screen shown in Figure 3-9.

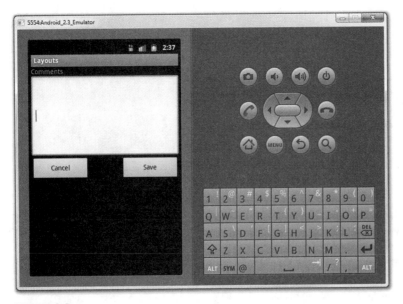

FIGURE 3-9

FrameLayout

The FrameLayout is a placeholder on screen that you can use to display a single view. Views that you add to a FrameLayout are always anchored to the top left of the layout. Consider the following content in main.xml:

```xml
<?xml version="1.0" encoding="utf-8"?>
<RelativeLayout
    android:id="@+id/RLayout"
    android:layout_width="fill_parent"
    android:layout_height="fill_parent"
    xmlns:android="http://schemas.android.com/apk/res/android"
    >
    <TextView
        android:id="@+id/lblComments"
        android:layout_width="wrap_content"
        android:layout_height="wrap_content"
        android:text="This is my lovely dog, Ookii"
        android:layout_alignParentTop="true"
        android:layout_alignParentLeft="true"
        />
    <FrameLayout
        android:layout_width="wrap_content"
        android:layout_height="wrap_content"
        android:layout_alignLeft="@+id/lblComments"
        android:layout_below="@+id/lblComments"
        android:layout_centerHorizontal="true"
        >
        <ImageView
            android:src = "@drawable/ookii"
            android:layout_width="wrap_content"
            android:layout_height="wrap_content"
            />
    </FrameLayout>
</RelativeLayout>
```

Here, you have a FrameLayout within a RelativeLayout. Within the FrameLayout, you embed an ImageView. The UI is shown in Figure 3-10.

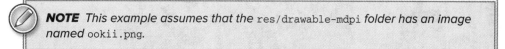

NOTE This example assumes that the res/drawable-mdpi folder has an image named ookii.png.

If you add another view (such as a Button view) within the FrameLayout, the view will overlap the previous view (see Figure 3-11):

```xml
<?xml version="1.0" encoding="utf-8"?>
<RelativeLayout
    android:id="@+id/RLayout"
    android:layout_width="fill_parent"
    android:layout_height="fill_parent"
```

```xml
    xmlns:android="http://schemas.android.com/apk/res/android"
    >
<TextView
    android:id="@+id/lblComments"
    android:layout_width="wrap_content"
    android:layout_height="wrap_content"
    android:text="This is my lovely dog, Ookii"
    android:layout_alignParentTop="true"
    android:layout_alignParentLeft="true"
    />
<FrameLayout
    android:layout_width="wrap_content"
    android:layout_height="wrap_content"
    android:layout_alignLeft="@+id/lblComments"
    android:layout_below="@+id/lblComments"
    android:layout_centerHorizontal="true"
    >
    <ImageView
        android:src = "@drawable/ookii"
        android:layout_width="wrap_content"
        android:layout_height="wrap_content"
        />
    <Button
        android:layout_width="124dp"
        android:layout_height="wrap_content"
        android:text="Print Picture"
        />
</FrameLayout>
</RelativeLayout>
```

FIGURE 3-10

FIGURE 3-11

> *NOTE* You can add multiple views to a `FrameLayout`, but each will be stacked on top of the previous one. This is useful in cases where you want to animate series of images, with only one visible at a time.

ScrollView

A `ScrollView` is a special type of `FrameLayout` in that it enables users to scroll through a list of views that occupy more space than the physical display. The `ScrollView` can contain only one child view or ViewGroup, which normally is a `LinearLayout`.

> *NOTE* Do not use a `ListView` (discussed in Chapter 4) together with the `ScrollView`. The `ListView` is designed for showing a list of related information and is optimized for dealing with large lists.

The following `main.xml` content shows a `ScrollView` containing a `LinearLayout`, which in turn contains some `Button` and `EditText` views:

```xml
<?xml version="1.0" encoding="utf-8"?>
<ScrollView
    android:layout_width="fill_parent"
```

```
        android:layout_height="fill_parent"
        xmlns:android="http://schemas.android.com/apk/res/android"
        >
    <LinearLayout
            android:layout_width="fill_parent"
            android:layout_height="wrap_content"
            android:orientation="vertical"
            >
        <Button
                android:id="@+id/button1"
                android:layout_width="fill_parent"
                android:layout_height="wrap_content"
                android:text="Button 1"
                />
        <Button
                android:id="@+id/button2"
                android:layout_width="fill_parent"
                android:layout_height="wrap_content"
                android:text="Button 2"
                />
        <Button
                android:id="@+id/button3"
                android:layout_width="fill_parent"
                android:layout_height="wrap_content"
                android:text="Button 3"
                />
        <EditText
                android:id="@+id/txt"
                android:layout_width="fill_parent"
                android:layout_height="300px"
                />
        <Button
                android:id="@+id/button4"
                android:layout_width="fill_parent"
                android:layout_height="wrap_content"
                android:text="Button 4"
                />
        <Button
                android:id="@+id/button5"
                android:layout_width="fill_parent"
                android:layout_height="wrap_content"
                android:text="Button 5"
                />
    </LinearLayout>
</ScrollView>
```

Figure 3-12 shows the ScrollView enabling the users to drag the screen upward to reveal the views located at the bottom of the screen.

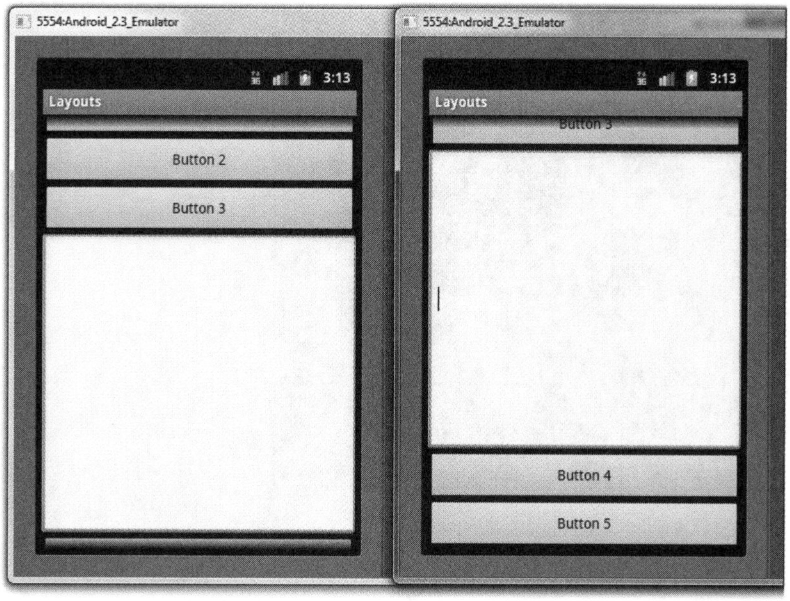

FIGURE 3-12

ADAPTING TO DISPLAY ORIENTATION

One of the key features of modern smartphones is their ability to switch screen orientation, and Android is no exception. Android supports two screen orientations: *portrait* and *landscape*. By default, when you change the display orientation of your Android device, the current activity that is displayed will automatically redraw its content in the new orientation. This is because the onCreate() event of the activity is fired whenever there is a change in display orientation.

> **NOTE** *When you change the orientation of your Android device, your current activity is actually destroyed and then re-created.*

However, when the views are redrawn, they may be drawn in their original locations (depending on the layout selected). Figure 3-13 shows one of the examples illustrated earlier displayed in both portrait and landscape mode.

As you can observe in landscape mode, a lot of empty space on the right of the screen could be used. Furthermore, any additional views at the bottom of the screen would be hidden when the screen orientation is set to landscape.

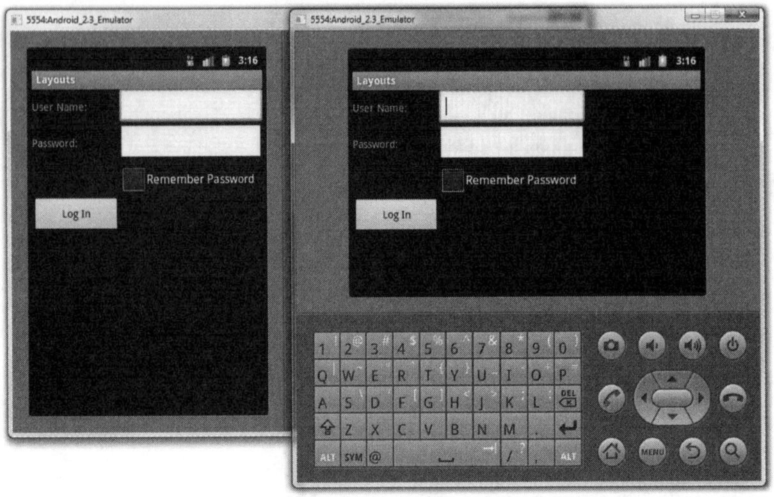

FIGURE 3-13

In general, you can employ two techniques to handle changes in screen orientation:

➤ **Anchoring** — The easiest way is to "anchor" your views to the four edges of the screen. When the screen orientation changes, the views can anchor neatly to the edges.

➤ **Resizing and repositioning** — Whereas anchoring and centralizing are simple techniques to ensure that views can handle changes in screen orientation, the ultimate technique is resizing each and every view according to the current screen orientation.

Anchoring Views

Anchoring could be easily achieved by using `RelativeLayout`. Consider the following `main.xml` containing five `Button` views embedded within the `<RelativeLayout>` element:

```xml
<?xml version="1.0" encoding="utf-8"?>
<RelativeLayout
    android:layout_width="fill_parent"
    android:layout_height="fill_parent"
    xmlns:android="http://schemas.android.com/apk/res/android"
    >
    <Button
        android:id="@+id/button1"
        android:layout_width="wrap_content"
        android:layout_height="wrap_content"
        android:text="Top Left Button"
        android:layout_alignParentLeft="true"
        android:layout_alignParentTop="true"
        />
```

```
    <Button
        android:id="@+id/button2"
        android:layout_width="wrap_content"
        android:layout_height="wrap_content"
        android:text="Top Right Button"
        android:layout_alignParentTop="true"
        android:layout_alignParentRight="true"
        />
    <Button
        android:id="@+id/button3"
        android:layout_width="wrap_content"
        android:layout_height="wrap_content"
        android:text="Bottom Left Button"
        android:layout_alignParentLeft="true"
        android:layout_alignParentBottom="true"
        />
    <Button
        android:id="@+id/button4"
        android:layout_width="wrap_content"
        android:layout_height="wrap_content"
        android:text="Bottom Right Button"
        android:layout_alignParentRight="true"
        android:layout_alignParentBottom="true"
        />
    <Button
        android:id="@+id/button5"
        android:layout_width="fill_parent"
        android:layout_height="wrap_content"
        android:text="Middle Button"
        android:layout_centerVertical="true"
        android:layout_centerHorizontal="true"
        />
</RelativeLayout>
```

Observe the following attributes found in the various `Button` views:

➤   `layout_alignParentLeft` — Aligns the view to the left of the parent view

➤   `layout_alignParentRight` — Aligns the view to the right of the parent view

➤   `layout_alignParentTop` — Aligns the view to the top of the parent view

➤   `layout_alignParentBottom` — Aligns the view to the bottom of the parent view

➤   `layout_centerVertical` — Centers the view vertically within its parent view

➤   `layout_centerHorizontal` — Centers the view horizontally within its parent view

Figure 3-14 shows the activity when viewed in portrait mode.

When the screen orientation changes to landscape mode, the four buttons are aligned to the four edges of the screen, and the center button is centered in the middle of the screen with its width fully stretched (see Figure 3-15).

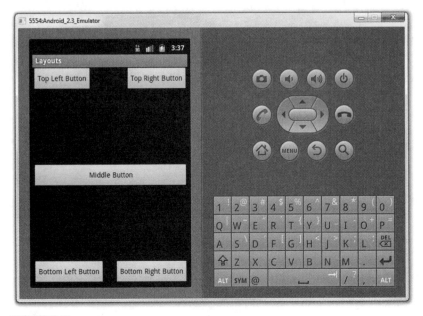

FIGURE 3-14

FIGURE 3-15

Resizing and Repositioning

Apart from anchoring your views to the four edges of the screen, an easier way to customize the UI based on screen orientation is to create a separate `res/layout` folder containing the XML files for the UI of each orientation. To support landscape mode, you can create a new folder in the `res` folder and name it as `layout-land` (representing landscape). Figure 3-16 shows the new folder containing the file `main.xml`.

FIGURE 3-16

Basically, the `main.xml` file contained within the `layout` folder defines the UI for the activity in portrait mode, whereas the `main.xml` file in the `layout-land` folder defines the UI in landscape mode.

The following shows the content of `main.xml` under the `layout` folder:

```xml
<?xml version="1.0" encoding="utf-8"?>
<RelativeLayout
    android:layout_width="fill_parent"
    android:layout_height="fill_parent"
    xmlns:android="http://schemas.android.com/apk/res/android"
    >
    <Button
        android:id="@+id/button1"
        android:layout_width="wrap_content"
        android:layout_height="wrap_content"
        android:text="Top Left Button"
        android:layout_alignParentLeft="true"
        android:layout_alignParentTop="true"
        />
    <Button
        android:id="@+id/button2"
        android:layout_width="wrap_content"
        android:layout_height="wrap_content"
        android:text="Top Right Button"
        android:layout_alignParentTop="true"
        android:layout_alignParentRight="true"
        />
    <Button
        android:id="@+id/button3"
        android:layout_width="wrap_content"
        android:layout_height="wrap_content"
        android:text="Bottom Left Button"
        android:layout_alignParentLeft="true"
        android:layout_alignParentBottom="true"
        />
    <Button
        android:id="@+id/button4"
        android:layout_width="wrap_content"
        android:layout_height="wrap_content"
        android:text="Bottom Right Button"
        android:layout_alignParentRight="true"
        android:layout_alignParentBottom="true"
        />
```

```
    <Button
        android:id="@+id/button5"
        android:layout_width="fill_parent"
        android:layout_height="wrap_content"
        android:text="Middle Button"
        android:layout_centerVertical="true"
        android:layout_centerHorizontal="true"
        />
</RelativeLayout>
```

The following shows the content of main.xml under the layout-land folder (the statements in bold are the additional views to display in landscape mode):

```
<?xml version="1.0" encoding="utf-8"?>
<RelativeLayout
    android:layout_width="fill_parent"
    android:layout_height="fill_parent"
    xmlns:android="http://schemas.android.com/apk/res/android"
    >
    <Button
        android:id="@+id/button1"
        android:layout_width="wrap_content"
        android:layout_height="wrap_content"
        android:text="Top Left Button"
        android:layout_alignParentLeft="true"
        android:layout_alignParentTop="true"
        />
    <Button
        android:id="@+id/button2"
        android:layout_width="wrap_content"
        android:layout_height="wrap_content"
        android:text="Top Right Button"
        android:layout_alignParentTop="true"
        android:layout_alignParentRight="true"
        />
    <Button
        android:id="@+id/button3"
        android:layout_width="wrap_content"
        android:layout_height="wrap_content"
        android:text="Bottom Left Button"
        android:layout_alignParentLeft="true"
        android:layout_alignParentBottom="true"
        />
    <Button
        android:id="@+id/button4"
        android:layout_width="wrap_content"
        android:layout_height="wrap_content"
        android:text="Bottom Right Button"
        android:layout_alignParentRight="true"
        android:layout_alignParentBottom="true"
        />
    <Button
        android:id="@+id/button5"
        android:layout_width="fill_parent"
```

```
            android:layout_height="wrap_content"
            android:text="Middle Button"
            android:layout_centerVertical="true"
            android:layout_centerHorizontal="true"
            />
        <Button
            android:id="@+id/button6"
            android:layout_width="180px"
            android:layout_height="wrap_content"
            android:text="Top Middle Button"
            android:layout_centerVertical="true"
            android:layout_centerHorizontal="true"
            android:layout_alignParentTop="true"
            />
        <Button
            android:id="@+id/button7"
            android:layout_width="180px"
            android:layout_height="wrap_content"
            android:text="Bottom Middle Button"
            android:layout_centerVertical="true"
            android:layout_centerHorizontal="true"
            android:layout_alignParentBottom="true"
            />
    </RelativeLayout>
```

When the activity is loaded in portrait mode, it will show five buttons, as shown in Figure 3-17.

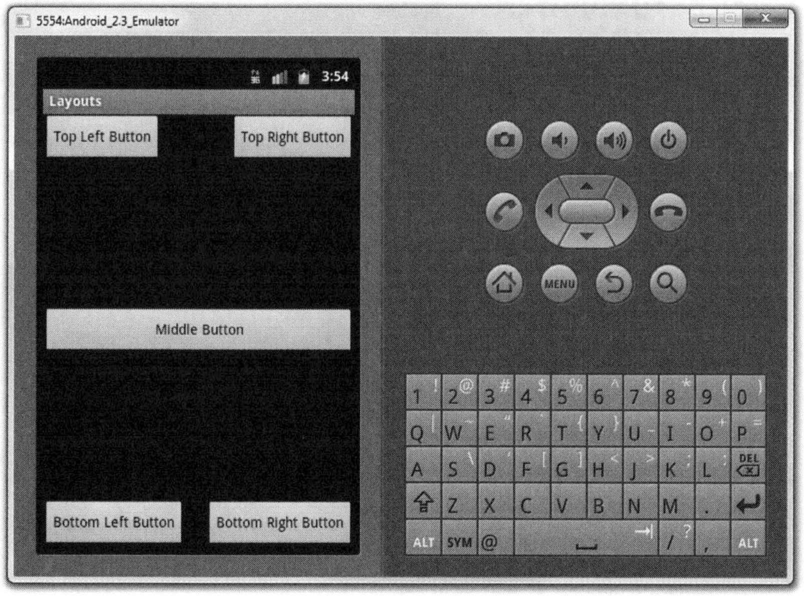

FIGURE 3-17

When the activity is loaded in landscape mode, there are now seven buttons (see Figure 3-18), proving that different XML files are loaded when the device is in a different orientation.

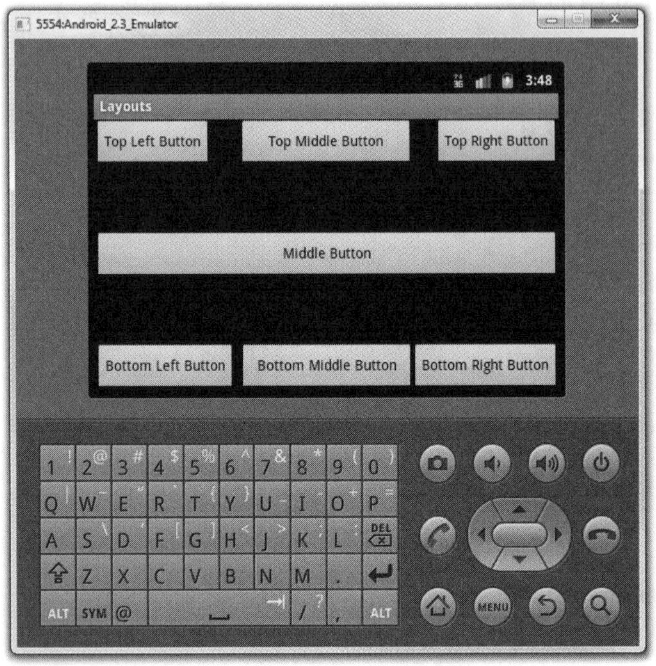

FIGURE 3-18

Using this method, when the orientation of the device changes, Android will automatically load the appropriate XML file for your activity depending on the current screen orientation.

MANAGING CHANGES TO SCREEN ORIENTATION

Now that you have looked at how to implement the two techniques for adapting to screen orientation changes, let's explore what happens to an activity's state when the device changes orientation.

The following Try It Out demonstrates the behavior of an activity when the device changes orientation.

TRY IT OUT Understanding Activity Behavior When Orientation Changes

codefile Orientations.zip available for download at Wrox.com

1. Using Eclipse, create a new Android project and name it **Orientations**.

2. Add the following statements in bold to the main.xml file:

```
<?xml version="1.0" encoding="utf-8"?>
<LinearLayout xmlns:android="http://schemas.android.com/apk/res/android"
```

```
        android:orientation="vertical"
        android:layout_width="fill_parent"
        android:layout_height="fill_parent"
        >
<EditText
    android:id="@+id/txtField1"
    android:layout_width="fill_parent"
    android:layout_height="wrap_content" />
<EditText
    android:layout_width="fill_parent"
    android:layout_height="wrap_content" />
</LinearLayout>
```

3. Add the following statements in bold to the `MainActivity.java` file:

```
package net.learn2develop.Orientations;

import android.app.Activity;
import android.os.Bundle;

import android.util.Log;

public class MainActivity extends Activity {
    /** Called when the activity is first created. */
    @Override
    public void onCreate(Bundle savedInstanceState) {
        super.onCreate(savedInstanceState);
        setContentView(R.layout.main);
        Log.d("StateInfo", "onCreate");
    }

    @Override
    public void onStart() {
        Log.d("StateInfo", "onStart");
        super.onStart();
    }

    @Override
    public void onResume() {
        Log.d("StateInfo", "onResume");
        super.onResume();
    }

    @Override
    public void onPause() {
        Log.d("StateInfo", "onPause");
        super.onPause();
    }

    @Override
    public void onStop() {
        Log.d("StateInfo", "onStop");
        super.onStop();
    }
```

```
    @Override
    public void onDestroy() {
        Log.d("StateInfo", "onDestroy");
        super.onDestroy();
    }

    @Override
    public void onRestart() {
        Log.d("StateInfo", "onRestart");
        super.onRestart();
    }
}
```

4. Press F11 to debug the application on the Android Emulator.

5. Enter some text into the two EditText views (see Figure 3-19).

6. Change the orientation of the Android Emulator by pressing Ctrl+F11. Figure 3-20 shows the emulator in landscape mode. Note that the text in the first EditText view is still visible, while the second EditText view is now empty.

7. Observe the output in the LogCat window (you need to switch to the Debug perspective in Eclipse). You should see something like this:

```
01-05 13:32:30.266: DEBUG/StateInfo(5477): onCreate
01-05 13:32:30.296: DEBUG/StateInfo(5477): onStart
01-05 13:32:30.296: DEBUG/StateInfo(5477): onResume
...
01-05 13:35:20.106: DEBUG/StateInfo(5477): onPause
01-05 13:35:20.106: DEBUG/StateInfo(5477): onStop
01-05 13:35:20.106: DEBUG/StateInfo(5477): onDestroy
01-05 13:35:20.246: DEBUG/StateInfo(5477): onCreate
01-05 13:35:20.256: DEBUG/StateInfo(5477): onStart
01-05 13:35:20.256: DEBUG/StateInfo(5477): onResume
```

How It Works

From the output shown in the LogCat window, it is apparent that when the device changes orientation, the activity is destroyed:

```
01-05 13:35:20.106: DEBUG/StateInfo(5477): onPause
01-05 13:35:20.106: DEBUG/StateInfo(5477): onStop
01-05 13:35:20.106: DEBUG/StateInfo(5477): onDestroy
```

It is then re-created:

```
01-05 13:35:20.246: DEBUG/StateInfo(5477): onCreate
01-05 13:35:20.256: DEBUG/StateInfo(5477): onStart
01-05 13:35:20.256: DEBUG/StateInfo(5477): onResume
```

It is important that you understand this behavior because you need to ensure that you take the necessary steps to preserve the state of your activity before it changes orientation. For example, you may have variables containing values needed for some calculations in the activity. For any activity, you should save whatever state you need to save in the onPause() event, which is fired every time the activity changes orientation. The following section demonstrates the different ways to save this state information.

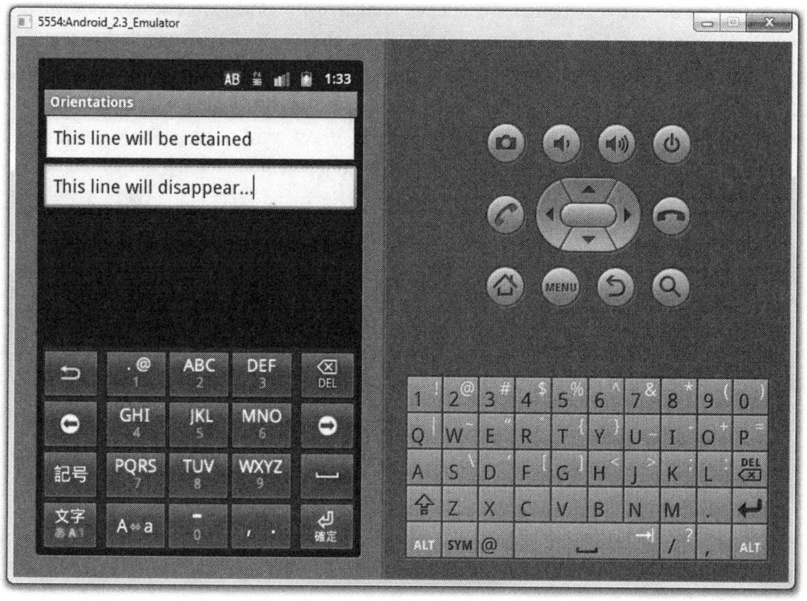

FIGURE 3-19

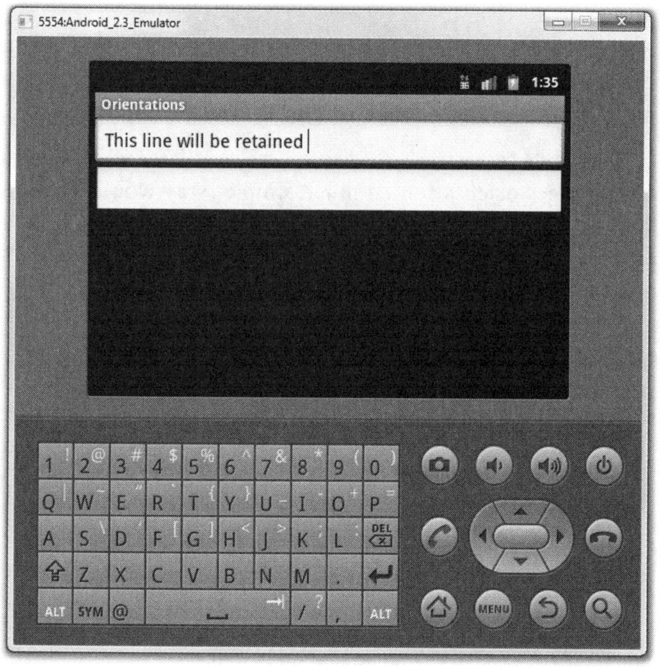

FIGURE 3-20

Another important behavior to understand is that only views that are named (via the `android:id` attribute) in an activity will have their state persisted when the activity they are contained in is destroyed. For example, the user may change orientation while entering some text into an `EditText` view. When this happens, any text inside the `EditText` view will be persisted and restored automatically when the activity is re-created. In contrast, if you do not name the `EditText` view using the `android:id` attribute, the activity will not be able to persist the text currently contained within it.

Persisting State Information during Changes in Configuration

So far, you have learned that changing screen orientation destroys an activity and re-creates it. Keep in mind that when an activity is re-created, the current state of the activity may be lost. When an activity is killed, it will fire one or more of the following two events:

➤ `onPause()` — This event is always fired whenever an activity is killed or pushed into the background.

➤ `onSaveInstanceState()` — This event is also fired whenever an activity is about to be killed or put into the background (just like the `onPause()` event). However, unlike the `onPause()` event, the `onSaveInstanceState` event is not fired when an activity is being unloaded from the stack (for example, when the user pressed the Back button), because there is no need to restore its state later.

In short, to preserve the state of an activity, you could always implement the `onPause()` event, and then use your own ways to preserve the state of your activity, such as using a database, internal or external file storage, etc.

If you simply want to preserve the state of an activity so that it can be restored later when the activity is re-created (such as when the device changes orientation), a much simpler way would be to implement the `onSaveInstanceState()` method, as it provides a `Bundle` object as an argument so that you can use it to save your activity's state. The following code shows that you can save the string `ID` into the `Bundle` object during the `onSaveInstanceState` event:

```
@Override
public void onSaveInstanceState(Bundle outState) {
    //---save whatever you need to persist---
    outState.putString("ID", "1234567890");
    super.onSaveInstanceState(outState);
}
```

When an activity is re-created, the `onCreate()` event is first fired, followed by the `onRestoreInstanceState()` event, which enables you to retrieve the state that you saved previously in the `onSaveInstanceState` event through the `Bundle` object in its argument:

```
@Override
public void onRestoreInstanceState(Bundle savedInstanceState) {
    super.onRestoreInstanceState(savedInstanceState);
    //---retrieve the information persisted earlier---
    String ID = savedInstanceState.getString("ID");
}
```

Although you can use the onSaveInstanceState() event to save state information, note the limitation that you can only save your state information into a Bundle object. If you need to save more complex data structures, then this is not an adequate solution.

Another event handler that you can use is the onRetainNonConfigurationInstance() event. This event is fired when an activity is about to be destroyed due to a *configuration change*. You can save your current data by returning it in this event, like this:

```java
@Override
public Object onRetainNonConfigurationInstance() {
    //---save whatever you want here; it takes in an Object type---
    return("Some text to preserve");
}
```

> **NOTE** *When screen orientation changes, this change is part of what is known as a* configuration change. *A* configuration change *will cause your current activity to be destroyed.*

Note that this event returns an Object type, which pretty much allows you to return any data type. To extract the saved data, you can extract it in the onCreate() event, using the getLastNonConfigurationInstance() method, like this:

```java
@Override
public void onCreate(Bundle savedInstanceState) {
    super.onCreate(savedInstanceState);
    setContentView(R.layout.main);
    Log.d("StateInfo", "onCreate");
    String str = (String) getLastNonConfigurationInstance();
}
```

Detecting Orientation Changes

Sometimes you need to know the device's current orientation during run time. To determine that, you can use the WindowManager class. The following code snippet demonstrates how you can programmatically detect the current orientation of your activity:

```java
import android.util.Log;
import android.view.Display;
import android.view.WindowManager;
//...
    public void onCreate(Bundle savedInstanceState) {
        super.onCreate(savedInstanceState);
        setContentView(R.layout.main);

        //---get the current display info---
        WindowManager wm = getWindowManager();
        Display d = wm.getDefaultDisplay();

        if (d.getWidth() > d.getHeight())
```

```
        {
            //---landscape mode---
            Log.d("Orientation", "Landscape mode");
        }
        else
        {
            //---portrait mode---
            Log.d("Orientation", "Portrait mode");
        }
    }
```

The `getDefaultDisplay()` method returns a `Display` object representing the screen of the device. You can then get its width and height and deduce the current orientation.

Controlling the Orientation of the Activity

Occasionally you might want to ensure that your application is only displayed in a certain orientation. For example, you may be writing a game that should only be viewed in landscape mode. In this case, you can programmatically force a change in orientation using the `setRequestOrientation()` method of the `Activity` class:

```
import android.content.pm.ActivityInfo;

public class MainActivity extends Activity {
    /** Called when the activity is first created. */
    @Override
    public void onCreate(Bundle savedInstanceState) {
        super.onCreate(savedInstanceState);
        setContentView(R.layout.main);
        //---change to landscape mode---
        setRequestedOrientation(ActivityInfo.SCREEN_ORIENTATION_LANDSCAPE);
    }
}
```

To change to portrait mode, use the `ActivityInfo.SCREEN_ORIENTATION_PORTRAIT` constant:

```
        setRequestedOrientation(ActivityInfo.SCREEN_ORIENTATION_PORTRAIT);
```

Besides using the `setRequestOrientation()` method, you can also use the `android:screenOrientation` attribute on the `<activity>` element in `AndroidManifest.xml` as follows to constrain the activity to a certain orientation:

```
<?xml version="1.0" encoding="utf-8"?>
<manifest xmlns:android="http://schemas.android.com/apk/res/android"
    package="net.learn2develop.Orientations"
    android:versionCode="1"
    android:versionName="1.0">
    <application android:icon="@drawable/icon" android:label="@string/app_name">
        <activity android:name=".MainActivity"
            android:label="@string/app_name"
            android:screenOrientation="landscape" >
            <intent-filter>
                <action android:name="android.intent.action.MAIN" />
                <category android:name="android.intent.category.LAUNCHER" />
            </intent-filter>
```

```
        </activity>
      </application>
      <uses-sdk android:minSdkVersion="9" />
  </manifest>
```

The preceding example constrains the activity to a certain orientation (landscape in this case) and prevents the activity from being destroyed; that is, the activity will not be destroyed and the onCreate() event will not be fired again when the orientation of the device changes.

Following are two other values that you can specify in the android:screenOrientation attribute:

➤ portrait — Portrait mode

➤ sensor — Based on the accelerometer

CREATING THE USER INTERFACE PROGRAMMATICALLY

So far, all the UIs you have seen in this chapter are created using XML. As mentioned earlier, besides using XML you can also create the UI using code. This approach is useful if your UI needs to be dynamically generated during run time. For example, suppose you are building a cinema ticket reservation system and your application will display the seats of each cinema using buttons. In this case, you would need to dynamically generate the UI based on the cinema selected by the user.

The following Try It Out demonstrates the code needed to dynamically build the UI in your activity.

TRY IT OUT Creating the UI via Code

codefile UICode.zip available for download at Wrox.com

1. Using Eclipse, create a new Android project and name it **UICode**.

2. In the MainActivity.java file, add the following statements in bold:

```
package net.learn2develop.UICode;

import android.app.Activity;
import android.os.Bundle;

import android.view.ViewGroup.LayoutParams;
import android.widget.Button;
import android.widget.LinearLayout;
import android.widget.TextView;

public class MainActivity extends Activity {
    /** Called when the activity is first created. */
    @Override
    public void onCreate(Bundle savedInstanceState) {
        super.onCreate(savedInstanceState);
        //setContentView(R.layout.main);

        //---param for views---
        LayoutParams params =
```

```
new LinearLayout.LayoutParams(
    LayoutParams.FILL_PARENT,
    LayoutParams.WRAP_CONTENT);

//---create a layout---
LinearLayout layout = new LinearLayout(this);
layout.setOrientation(LinearLayout.VERTICAL);

//---create a textview---
TextView tv = new TextView(this);
tv.setText("This is a TextView");
tv.setLayoutParams(params);

//---create a button---
Button btn = new Button(this);
btn.setText("This is a Button");
btn.setLayoutParams(params);

//---adds the textview---
layout.addView(tv);

//---adds the button---
layout.addView(btn);

//---create a layout param for the layout---
LinearLayout.LayoutParams layoutParam =
    new LinearLayout.LayoutParams(
        LayoutParams.FILL_PARENT,
        LayoutParams.WRAP_CONTENT );

this.addContentView(layout, layoutParam);
    }
}
```

3. Press F11 to debug the application on the Android Emulator. Figure 3-21 shows the activity created.

How It Works

In this example, you first commented out the setContentView() statement so that it does not load the UI from the main.xml file.

You then created a LayoutParams object to specify the layout parameter that can be used by other views (which you will create next):

```
//---param for views---
LayoutParams params =
    new LinearLayout.LayoutParams(
        LayoutParams.FILL_PARENT,
        LayoutParams.WRAP_CONTENT);
```

You also created a LinearLayout object to contain all the views in your activity:

```
//---create a layout---
LinearLayout layout = new LinearLayout(this);
layout.setOrientation(LinearLayout.VERTICAL);
```

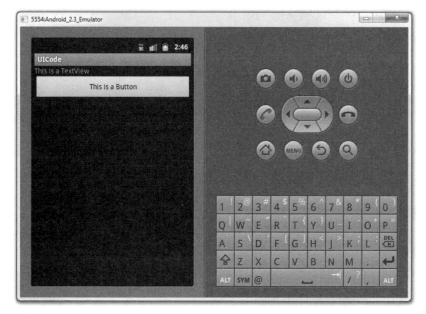

FIGURE 3-21

Next, you created a `TextView` and a `Button` view:

```
//---create a textview---
TextView tv = new TextView(this);
tv.setText("This is a TextView");
tv.setLayoutParams(params);

//---create a button---
Button btn = new Button(this);
btn.setText("This is a Button");
btn.setLayoutParams(params);
```

You then added them to the `LinearLayout` object:

```
//---adds the textview---
layout.addView(tv);

//---adds the button---
layout.addView(btn);
```

You also created a `LayoutParams` object to be used by the `LinearLayout` object:

```
//---create a layout param for the layout---
LinearLayout.LayoutParams layoutParam =
    new LinearLayout.LayoutParams(
            LayoutParams.FILL_PARENT,
            LayoutParams.WRAP_CONTENT );
```

Finally, you added the `LinearLayout` object to the activity:

```
this.addContentView(layout, layoutParam);
```

As you can see, using code to create the UI is quite a laborious affair. Hence, dynamically generate your UI using code only when necessary.

LISTENING FOR UI NOTIFICATIONS

Users interact with your UI at two levels: the activity level and the views level. At the activity level, the `Activity` class exposes methods that you can override. Some common methods that you can override in your activities include the following:

➤ `onKeyDown` — Called when a key was pressed and not handled by any of the views contained within the activity

➤ `onKeyUp` — Called when a key was released and not handled by any of the views contained within the activity

➤ `onMenuItemSelected` — Called when a panel's menu item has been selected by the user (covered in Chapter 5)

➤ `onMenuOpened` — Called when a panel's menu is opened by the user (covered in Chapter 5)

Overriding Methods Defined in an Activity

To understand how activities interact with the user, let's start off by overriding some of the methods defined in the activity's base class and learn how they are handled when the user interacts with the activity.

TRY IT OUT Overriding Activity Methods

codefile UIActivity.zip available for download at Wrox.com

1. Using Eclipse, create a new Android project and name it **UIActivity**.

2. Add the following statements in bold:

```xml
<?xml version="1.0" encoding="utf-8"?>
<LinearLayout
    android:layout_width="fill_parent"
    android:layout_height="fill_parent"
    android:orientation="vertical"
    xmlns:android="http://schemas.android.com/apk/res/android"
    >
    <TextView
        android:layout_width="214dp"
```

```
    android:layout_height="wrap_content"
    android:text="Your Name"
    />
<EditText
    android:id="@+id/txt1"
    android:layout_width="214dp"
    android:layout_height="wrap_content"
    />
<Button
    android:id="@+id/btn1"
    android:layout_width="106dp"
    android:layout_height="wrap_content"
    android:text="OK"
    />
<Button
    android:id="@+id/btn2"
    android:layout_width="106dp"
    android:layout_height="wrap_content"
    android:text="Cancel"
    />
</LinearLayout>
```

3. Add the following statements in bold to the `MainActivity.java` file:

```
package net.learn2develop.UIActivity;

import android.app.Activity;
import android.os.Bundle;

import android.view.KeyEvent;
import android.widget.Toast;

public class MainActivity extends Activity {
    /** Called when the activity is first created. */
    @Override
    public void onCreate(Bundle savedInstanceState) {
        super.onCreate(savedInstanceState);
        setContentView(R.layout.main);
    }

    @Override
    public boolean onKeyDown(int keyCode, KeyEvent event)
    {
        switch (keyCode)
        {
            case KeyEvent.KEYCODE_DPAD_CENTER:
                Toast.makeText(getBaseContext(),
                        "Center was clicked",
                        Toast.LENGTH_LONG).show();
                break;
            case KeyEvent.KEYCODE_DPAD_LEFT:
                Toast.makeText(getBaseContext(),
                        "Left arrow was clicked",
```

```
                              Toast.LENGTH_LONG).show();
                    break;
                case KeyEvent.KEYCODE_DPAD_RIGHT:
                    Toast.makeText(getBaseContext(),
                              "Right arrow was clicked",
                              Toast.LENGTH_LONG).show();
                    break;
                case KeyEvent.KEYCODE_DPAD_UP:
                    Toast.makeText(getBaseContext(),
                              "Up arrow was clicked",
                              Toast.LENGTH_LONG).show();

                    break;
                case KeyEvent.KEYCODE_DPAD_DOWN:
                    Toast.makeText(getBaseContext(),
                                "Down arrow was clicked",
                              Toast.LENGTH_LONG).show();
                    break;
            }
            return false;
        }
    }
```

4. Press F11 to debug the application on the Android Emulator.

5. When the activity is loaded, type some text into it, as shown on the left of Figure 3-22. Next, click the down arrow key on the directional pad. Observe the message shown on the screen, as shown in the black area on the right of Figure 3-22.

FIGURE 3-22

How It Works

When the activity is loaded, the cursor will be blinking in the EditText view, as it has the focus.

In the `MainActivitiy` class, you override the `onKeyDown()` method of the base `Activity` class, like this:

```
@Override
public boolean onKeyDown(int keyCode, KeyEvent event)
{
    switch (keyCode)
    {
        case KeyEvent.KEYCODE_DPAD_CENTER:
            //...
            break;
        case KeyEvent.KEYCODE_DPAD_LEFT:
            //...
            break;
        case KeyEvent.KEYCODE_DPAD_RIGHT:
            //...
            break;
        case KeyEvent.KEYCODE_DPAD_UP:
            //...
            break;
        case KeyEvent.KEYCODE_DPAD_DOWN:
            //...
            break;
    }
    return false;
}
```

In Android, whenever you press any keys on your device, the view that currently has the focus will try to handle the event generated. In this case, when the `EditText` has the focus and you press a key, the `EditText` view will handle the event and display the character you have just pressed in the view. However, if you press the up or down directional arrow key, the `EditText` view does not handle this, and instead passes the event to the activity. In this case, the `onKeyDown()` method is called. In this case, you checked the key that was pressed and displayed a message indicating the key pressed. Observe that the focus is now also transferred to the next view, which is the OK button.

Interestingly, if the `EditText` view already has some text in it and the cursor is at the end of the text (see Figure 3-23), then clicking the left arrow key does not fire the `onKeyDown()` event; it simply moves the cursor one character to the left. This is because the `EditText` view has already handled the event. If you press the right arrow key instead, then the `onKeyDown()` method will be called (because now the `EditText` view will not be handling the event). The same applies when the cursor is at the beginning of the `EditText` view. Clicking the left arrow will fire the `onKeyDown()` event, whereas clicking the right arrow will simply move the cursor one character to the right.

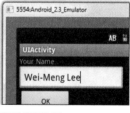

FIGURE 3-23

With the OK button in focus, press the center button in the directional pad. Observe that the message "Center was clicked" is not displayed. This is because the `Button` view itself is handling the click event. Hence the event is not caught by the `onKeyDown()` method. However, if none of the views is in focus at the moment (you can achieve this by clicking on the background of the screen), then pressing the center key will show the "Center was clicked" message (see Figure 3-24).

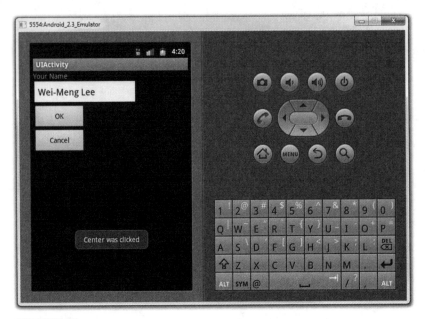

FIGURE 3-24

Note that the onKeyDown() method returns a boolean result. You should return true when you want to tell the system that you are done with the event and that the system should not proceed further with it. For example, consider the case when you return true after each key has been matched:

```
@Override
public boolean onKeyDown(int keyCode, KeyEvent event)
{
    switch (keyCode)
    {
        case KeyEvent.KEYCODE_DPAD_CENTER:
            Toast.makeText(getBaseContext(),
                    "Center was clicked",
                    Toast.LENGTH_LONG).show();
            return true;
        case KeyEvent.KEYCODE_DPAD_LEFT:
            Toast.makeText(getBaseContext(),
                    "Left arrow was clicked",
                    Toast.LENGTH_LONG).show();
            return true;
        case KeyEvent.KEYCODE_DPAD_RIGHT:
            Toast.makeText(getBaseContext(),
                    "Right arrow was clicked",
                    Toast.LENGTH_LONG).show();
            return true;
        case KeyEvent.KEYCODE_DPAD_UP:
            Toast.makeText(getBaseContext(),
                    "Up arrow was clicked",
                    Toast.LENGTH_LONG).show();
```

```
                        return true;
                    case KeyEvent.KEYCODE_DPAD_DOWN:
                        Toast.makeText(getBaseContext(),
                                "Down arrow was clicked",
                                Toast.LENGTH_LONG).show();
                        return true;
                }
                return false;
            }
```

If you test this, you will see that now you cannot navigate between the views using the arrow keys.

Registering Events for Views

Views can fire events when users interact with them. For example, when a user touches a `Button` view, you need to service the event so that the appropriate action can be performed. To do so, you need to explicitly register events for views.

Using the same example discussed in the previous section, recall that the activity has two `Button` views; therefore, you can register the button click events using an anonymous class as shown here:

```
package net.learn2develop.UIActivity;

import android.app.Activity;
import android.os.Bundle;
import android.view.KeyEvent;
import android.view.View;
import android.widget.Toast;

import android.view.View.OnClickListener;
import android.widget.Button;

public class MainActivity extends Activity {
    /** Called when the activity is first created. */
    @Override
    public void onCreate(Bundle savedInstanceState) {
        super.onCreate(savedInstanceState);
        setContentView(R.layout.main);

        //---the two buttons are wired to the same event handler---
        Button btn1 = (Button)findViewById(R.id.btn1);
        btn1.setOnClickListener(btnListener);

        Button btn2 = (Button)findViewById(R.id.btn2);
        btn2.setOnClickListener(btnListener);
    }

    //---create an anonymous class to act as a button click listener---
    private OnClickListener btnListener = new OnClickListener()
    {
        public void onClick(View v)
```

```
        {
            Toast.makeText(getBaseContext(),
                    ((Button) v).getText() + " was clicked",
                    Toast.LENGTH_LONG).show();
        }
    };

    @Override
    public boolean onKeyDown(int keyCode, KeyEvent event)
    {
        switch (keyCode)
        {
                //...
                //...
        }
        return false;
    }
}
```

If you now press either the OK button or the Cancel button, the appropriate message will be displayed (see Figure 3-25), proving that the event is wired up properly.

FIGURE 3-25

Besides defining an anonymous class for the event handler, you can also define an anonymous inner class to handle an event. The following example shows how you can handle the onFocusChange() event for the EditText view:

```
import android.widget.EditText;

public class MainActivity extends Activity {
```

```java
/** Called when the activity is first created. */
@Override
public void onCreate(Bundle savedInstanceState) {
    super.onCreate(savedInstanceState);
    setContentView(R.layout.main);

    //---the two buttons are wired to the same event handler---
    Button btn1 = (Button)findViewById(R.id.btn1);
    btn1.setOnClickListener(btnListener);

    Button btn2 = (Button)findViewById(R.id.btn2);
    btn2.setOnClickListener(btnListener);

    EditText txt1 = (EditText)findViewById(R.id.txt1);

    //---create an anonymous inner class to act as an onfocus listener---
    txt1.setOnFocusChangeListener(new View.OnFocusChangeListener()
    {
        @Override
        public void onFocusChange(View v, boolean hasFocus) {
            Toast.makeText(getBaseContext(),
                ((EditText) v).getId() + " has focus - " + hasFocus,
                Toast.LENGTH_LONG).show();
        }
    });
}
```

As shown in Figure 3-26, when the EditText view receives the focus, a message is printed on the screen.

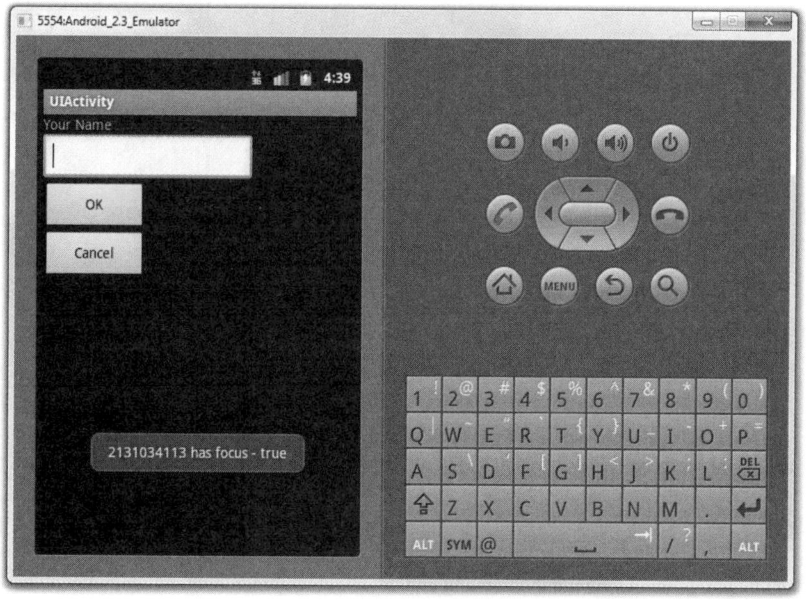

FIGURE 3-26

SUMMARY

In this chapter, you have learned how user interfaces are created in Android. You have also learned about the different layouts that you can use to position the views in your Android UI. Because Android devices support more than one screen orientation, you need to take special care to ensure that your UI can adapt to changes in screen orientation.

EXERCISES

1. What is the difference between the `dp` unit and the `px` unit? Which one should you use to specify the dimension of a view?

2. Why is the `AbsoluteLayout` not recommended for use?

3. What is the difference between the `onPause()` event and the `onSaveInstanceState()` event?

4. Name the three events you can override to save an activity's state.

Answers to Exercises can be found in Appendix C.

▶ WHAT YOU LEARNED IN THIS CHAPTER

TOPIC	KEY CONCEPTS
`LinearLayout`	Arranges views in a single column or single row
`AbsoluteLayout`	Enables you to specify the exact location of its children
`TableLayout`	Groups views into rows and columns
`RelativeLayout`	Enables you to specify how child views are positioned relative to each other
`FrameLayout`	A placeholder on screen that you can use to display a single view
`ScrollView`	A special type of `FrameLayout` in that it enables users to scroll through a list of views that occupy more space than the physical display allows
Unit of Measure	Use the `dp` for specifying the dimension of views and `sp` for font size
Two ways to adapt to changes in orientation	Anchoring, and resizing and repositioning
Using different XML files for different orientations	Use the `layout` folder for portrait UI, and `layout-land` for landscape UI.
Three ways to persist activity state	Use the `onPause()` event. Use the `onSaveInstanceState()` event. Use the `onRetainNonConfigurationInstance()` event.
Getting the dimension of the current device	Use the `WindowManager` class's `getDefaultDisplay()` method.
Constraining the activity's orientation	Use the `setRequestOrientation()` method, or the `android:screenOrientation` attribute in the `AndroidManifest.xml` file.

4

Designing Your User Interface Using Views

WHAT YOU WILL LEARN IN THIS CHAPTER

➤ How to use the basic views in Android to design your user interface

➤ How to use the picker views to display lists of items

➤ How to use the list views to display lists of items

In the previous chapter, you learned about the various layouts that you can use to position your views in an activity. You also learned about the techniques you can use to adapt to different screen resolutions and sizes. In this chapter, you will take a look at the various views that you can use to design the user interface for your applications.

In particular, you will learn about the following view groups:

➤ **Basic views** — Commonly used views such as the `TextView`, `EditText`, and `Button` views

➤ **Picker views** — Views that enable users to select from a list, such as the `TimePicker` and `DatePicker` views

➤ **List views** — Views that display a long list of items, such as the `ListView` and the `SpinnerView` views

Subsequent chapters will cover the other views not covered in this chapter, such as the date and time picker views and other views for displaying graphics, etc.

BASIC VIEWS

To get started, let's explore some of the basic views that you can use to design the UI of your Android applications:

➤ TextView

➤ EditText

➤ Button

➤ ImageButton

➤ CheckBox

➤ ToggleButton

➤ RadioButton

➤ RadioGroup

These basic views enable you to display text information, as well as perform some basic selection. The following sections explore all these views in more detail.

TextView View

When you create a new Android project, Eclipse always creates the `main.xml` file (located in the `res/layout` folder), which contains a `<TextView>` element:

```xml
<?xml version="1.0" encoding="utf-8"?>
<LinearLayout xmlns:android="http://schemas.android.com/apk/res/android"
    android:orientation="vertical"
    android:layout_width="fill_parent"
    android:layout_height="fill_parent"
    >
<TextView
    android:layout_width="fill_parent"
    android:layout_height="wrap_content"
    android:text="@string/hello"
    />
</LinearLayout>
```

The `TextView` view is used to display text to the user. This is the most basic view and one that you will frequently use when you develop Android applications. If you need to allow users to edit the text displayed, you should use the subclass of `TextView`, `EditText`, which is discussed in the next section.

> **NOTE** *In some other platforms, the* `TextView` *is commonly known as the label view. Its sole purpose is to display text on the screen.*

Button, ImageButton, EditText, CheckBox, ToggleButton, RadioButton, and RadioGroup Views

Besides the `TextView` view, which you will likely use the most often, there are some other basic controls that you will find yourself frequently using: `Button`, `ImageButton`, `EditText`, `CheckBox`, `ToggleButton`, `RadioButton`, and `RadioGroup`:

➤ `Button` — Represents a push-button widget

➤ `ImageButton` — Similar to the Button view, except that it also displays an image

➤ `EditText` — A subclass of the `TextView` view, except that it allows users to edit its text content

➤ `CheckBox` — A special type of button that has two states: checked or unchecked

➤ `RadioGroup` and `RadioButton` — The `RadioButton` has two states: either checked or unchecked. Once a `RadioButton` is checked, it cannot be unchecked. A `RadioGroup` is used to group together one or more `RadioButton` views, thereby allowing only one `RadioButton` to be checked within the `RadioGroup`.

➤ `ToggleButton` — Displays checked/unchecked states using a light indicator

The following Try It Out provides details about how these views work.

TRY IT OUT Using the Basic Views

codefile BasicViews1.zip available for download at Wrox.com

1. Using Eclipse, create an Android project and name it as shown in Figure 4-1.

> **NOTE** *For subsequent projects that you will create in this book, the various fields for the project will adopt the following values:*
>
> ➤ **Application Name:** *<project name>*
>
> ➤ **Package name:** *net.learn2develop.<project name>*
>
> ➤ **Create Activity:** *MainActivity*
>
> ➤ **Min SDK Version:** *9*

2. Modify the `main.xml` file located in the `res/layout` folder by adding the following elements shown in bold:

```xml
<?xml version="1.0" encoding="utf-8"?>
<LinearLayout xmlns:android="http://schemas.android.com/apk/res/android"
    android:orientation="vertical"
    android:layout_width="fill_parent"
```

```
    android:layout_height="fill_parent">

    <Button android:id="@+id/btnSave"
        android:layout_width="fill_parent"
        android:layout_height="wrap_content"
        android:text="Save" />

    <Button android:id="@+id/btnOpen"
        android:layout_width="wrap_content"
        android:layout_height="wrap_content"
        android:text="Open" />

    <ImageButton android:id="@+id/btnImg1"
        android:layout_width="fill_parent"
        android:layout_height="wrap_content"
        android:src="@drawable/icon" />

    <EditText android:id="@+id/txtName"
        android:layout_width="fill_parent"
        android:layout_height="wrap_content" />

    <CheckBox android:id="@+id/chkAutosave"
        android:layout_width="fill_parent"
        android:layout_height="wrap_content"
        android:text="Autosave" />

    <CheckBox android:id="@+id/star"
        style="?android:attr/starStyle"
        android:layout_width="wrap_content"
        android:layout_height="wrap_content" />

    <RadioGroup android:id="@+id/rdbGp1"
        android:layout_width="fill_parent"
        android:layout_height="wrap_content"
        android:orientation="vertical" >
        <RadioButton android:id="@+id/rdb1"
            android:layout_width="fill_parent"
            android:layout_height="wrap_content"
            android:text="Option 1" />
        <RadioButton android:id="@+id/rdb2"
            android:layout_width="fill_parent"
            android:layout_height="wrap_content"
            android:text="Option 2" />
    </RadioGroup>

    <ToggleButton android:id="@+id/toggle1"
        android:layout_width="wrap_content"
        android:layout_height="wrap_content" />

</LinearLayout>
```

3. To see the views in action, debug the project in Eclipse by selecting the project name and pressing F11. Figure 4-2 shows the various views displayed in the Android Emulator.

FIGURE 4-1

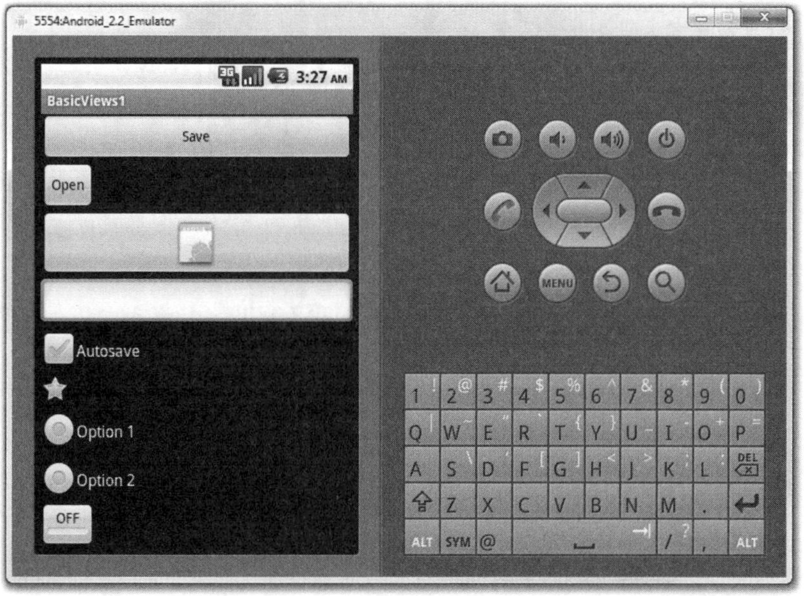

FIGURE 4-2

4.   Click on the various views and note how they vary in their look and feel. Figure 4-3 shows the following changes to the view:

➤   The first CheckBox view (Autosave) is checked.

➤   The second CheckBox View (star) is checked.

➤   The second RadioButton (Option 2) is selected.

➤   The ToggleButton is turned on.

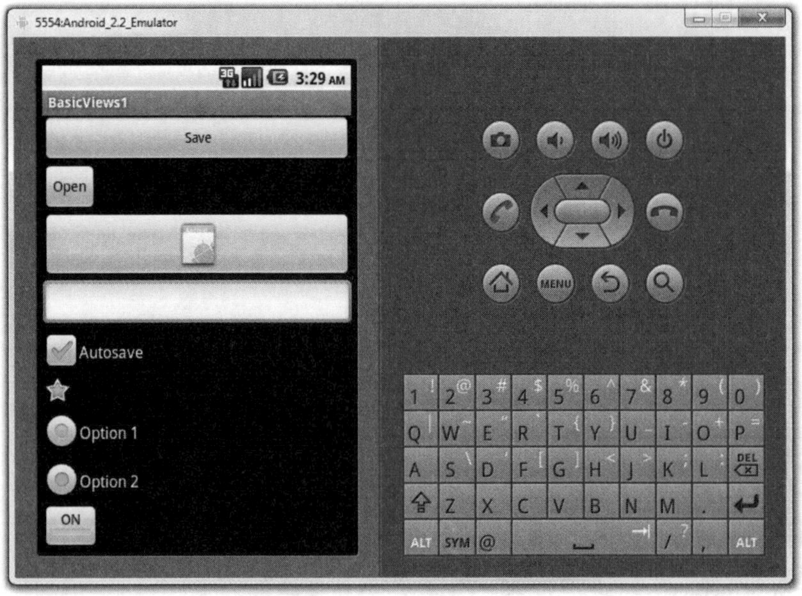

FIGURE 4-3

How It Works

So far, all the views are relatively straightforward — they are listed using the <LinearLayout> element, so they are stacked on top of each other when they are displayed in the activity.

For the first Button, the layout_width attribute is set to fill_parent so that its width occupies the entire width of the screen:

```
<Button android:id="@+id/btnSave"
    android:layout_width="fill_parent"
    android:layout_height="wrap_content"
    android:text="Save" />
```

For the second Button, the layout_width attribute is set to wrap_content so that its width will be the width of its content — specifically, the text that it is displaying (i.e.,"Open"):

```
<Button android:id="@+id/btnOpen"
    android:layout_width="wrap_content"
    android:layout_height="wrap_content"
    android:text="Open" />
```

The ImageButton displays a button with an image. The image is set through the src attribute. In this case, you simply use the image used for the application icon:

```
<ImageButton android:id="@+id/btnImg1"
    android:layout_width="fill_parent"
    android:layout_height="wrap_content"
    android:src="@drawable/icon" />
```

The EditText view displays a rectangular region where the user can enter some text. You set the layout _height to wrap_content so that if the user enters a long string of text, its height will automatically be adjusted to fit the content (see Figure 4-4).

```
<EditText android:id="@+id/txtName"
    android:layout_width="fill_parent"
    android:layout_height="wrap_content" />
```

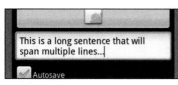

FIGURE 4-4

The CheckBox displays a checkbox that users can tap to check or uncheck it:

```
<CheckBox android:id="@+id/chkAutosave"
    android:layout_width="fill_parent"
    android:layout_height="wrap_content"
    android:text="Autosave" />
```

If you do not like the default look of the CheckBox, you can apply a style attribute to it to display it as some other image, such as a star:

```
<CheckBox android:id="@+id/star"
    style="?android:attr/starStyle"
    android:layout_width="wrap_content"
    android:layout_height="wrap_content" />
```

The format for the value of the style attribute is as follows:

```
?[package:][type:]name.
```

The RadioGroup encloses two RadioButtons. This is important because radio buttons are usually used to present multiple options to the user for selection. When a RadioButton in a RadioGroup is selected, all other RadioButtons are automatically unselected:

```
<RadioGroup android:id="@+id/rdbGp1"
    android:layout_width="fill_parent"
    android:layout_height="wrap_content"
    android:orientation="vertical" >
    <RadioButton android:id="@+id/rdb1"
        android:layout_width="fill_parent"
        android:layout_height="wrap_content"
        android:text="Option 1" />
```

```
    <RadioButton android:id="@+id/rdb2"
        android:layout_width="fill_parent"
        android:layout_height="wrap_content"
        android:text="Option 2" />
</RadioGroup>
```

Notice that the RadioButtons are listed vertically, one on top of another. If you want to list them hori-zontally, you need to change the orientation attribute to horizontal. You would also need to ensure that the layout_width attribute of the RadioButtons are set to wrap_content:

```
    <RadioGroup android:id="@+id/rdbGp1"
        android:layout_width="fill_parent"
        android:layout_height="wrap_content"
        android:orientation="horizontal" >
    <RadioButton android:id="@+id/rdb1"
        android:layout_width="wrap_content"
        android:layout_height="wrap_content"
        android:text="Option 1" />
    <RadioButton android:id="@+id/rdb2"
        android:layout_width="wrap_content"
        android:layout_height="wrap_content"
        android:text="Option 2" />
</RadioGroup>
```

Figure 4-5 shows the RadioButtons displayed horizontally.

FIGURE 4-5

The ToggleButton displays a rectangular button that users can toggle on and off by clicking it:

```
    <ToggleButton android:id="@+id/toggle1"
        android:layout_width="wrap_content"
        android:layout_height="wrap_content" />
```

One thing that has been consistent throughout this example is that each view has the id attribute set to a particular value, such as in the case of the Button:

```
    <Button android:id="@+id/btnSave"
        android:layout_width="fill_parent"
        android:layout_height="wrap_content"
        android:text="Save" />
```

The id attribute is an identifier for a view so that it may later be retrieved using the View.findViewById() or Activity.findViewById() methods.

Now that you have seen how the various views look for an activity, the following Try It Out demonstrates how you can programmatically control them

TRY IT OUT Handling View Events

1. Using the same project created in the previous Try It Out, modify the `MainActivity.java` file by adding the following statements in bold:

```
package net.learn2develop.BasicViews1;

import android.app.Activity;
import android.os.Bundle;

import android.view.View;
import android.widget.Button;
import android.widget.CheckBox;
import android.widget.RadioButton;
import android.widget.RadioGroup;
import android.widget.Toast;
import android.widget.ToggleButton;
import android.widget.RadioGroup.OnCheckedChangeListener;

public class MainActivity extends Activity {
    /** Called when the activity is first created. */
    @Override
    public void onCreate(Bundle savedInstanceState) {
        super.onCreate(savedInstanceState);
        setContentView(R.layout.main);

        //---Button view---
        Button btnOpen = (Button) findViewById(R.id.btnOpen);
        btnOpen.setOnClickListener(new View.OnClickListener() {
            public void onClick(View v) {
                DisplayToast("You have clicked the Open button");
            }
        });

        //---Button view---
        Button btnSave = (Button) findViewById(R.id.btnSave);
        btnSave.setOnClickListener(new View.OnClickListener()
        {
            public void onClick(View v) {
                DisplayToast("You have clicked the Save button");
            }
        });

        //---CheckBox---
        CheckBox checkBox = (CheckBox) findViewById(R.id.chkAutosave);
        checkBox.setOnClickListener(new View.OnClickListener()
        {
            public void onClick(View v) {
                if (((CheckBox)v).isChecked())
                    DisplayToast("CheckBox is checked");
                else
```

```
                     DisplayToast("CheckBox is unchecked");
            }
    });

    //---RadioButton---
    RadioGroup radioGroup = (RadioGroup) findViewById(R.id.rdbGp1);
    radioGroup.setOnCheckedChangeListener(new OnCheckedChangeListener()
    {
        public void onCheckedChanged(RadioGroup group, int checkedId) {
            RadioButton rb1 = (RadioButton) findViewById(R.id.rdb1);
            if (rb1.isChecked()) {
                DisplayToast("Option 1 checked!");
            } else {
                DisplayToast("Option 2 checked!");
            }
        }
    });

    //---ToggleButton---
    ToggleButton toggleButton =
        (ToggleButton) findViewById(R.id.toggle1);
    toggleButton.setOnClickListener(new View.OnClickListener()
    {
        public void onClick(View v) {
            if (((ToggleButton)v).isChecked())
                DisplayToast("Toggle button is On");
            else
                DisplayToast("Toggle button is Off");
        }
    });
}

private void DisplayToast(String msg)
{
    Toast.makeText(getBaseContext(), msg,
            Toast.LENGTH_SHORT).show();
}
}
```

2. Press F11 to debug the project on the Android Emulator.

3. Click on the various views and observe the message displayed in the Toast window.

How It Works

To handle the events fired by each view, you first have to programmatically locate the view that you created during the onCreate() event. You do so using the Activity.findViewById() method, supplying it with the ID of the view:

```
//---Button view---
Button btnOpen = (Button) findViewById(R.id.btnOpen);
```

The setOnClickListener() method registers a callback to be invoked later when the view is clicked:

```
btnOpen.setOnClickListener(new View.OnClickListener() {
```

```
            public void onClick(View v) {
                DisplayToast("You have clicked the Open button");
            }
        });
```

The onClick() method is called when the view is clicked.

For the CheckBox, to determine its state you have to typecast the argument of the onClick() method to a CheckBox and then check its isChecked() method to see if it is checked:

```
            //---CheckBox---
            CheckBox checkBox = (CheckBox) findViewById(R.id.chkAutosave);
            checkBox.setOnClickListener(new View.OnClickListener()
            {
                public void onClick(View v) {
                    if (((CheckBox)v).isChecked())
                        DisplayToast("CheckBox is checked");
                    else
                        DisplayToast("CheckBox is unchecked");
                }
            });
```

For RadioButton, you need to use the setOnCheckedChangeListener() method on the RadioGroup to register a callback to be invoked when the checked RadioButton changes in this group:

```
            //---RadioButton---
            RadioGroup radioGroup = (RadioGroup) findViewById(R.id.rdbGp1);
            radioGroup.setOnCheckedChangeListener(new OnCheckedChangeListener()
            {
                public void onCheckedChanged(RadioGroup group, int checkedId) {
                    RadioButton rb1 = (RadioButton) findViewById(R.id.rdb1);
                    if (rb1.isChecked()) {
                        DisplayToast("Option 1 checked!");
                    } else {
                        DisplayToast("Option 2 checked!");
                    }
                }
            });
```

When a RadioButton is selected, the onCheckedChanged() method is fired. Within it, you locate individual RadioButtons and then call their isChecked() method to determine which RadioButton is selected. Alternatively, the onCheckedChanged() method contains a second argument that contains a unique identifier of the RadioButton selected.

ProgressBar View

The ProgressBar view provides visual feedback of some ongoing tasks, such as when you are performing a task in the background. For example, you might be downloading some data from the Web and need to update the user about the status of the download. In this case, the ProgressBar view is a good choice for this task.

TRY IT OUT **Using the ProgressBar View**

codefile BasicViews2.zip available for download at Wrox.com

1. Using Eclipse, create an Android project and name it as **BasicViews2**.

2. Modify the `main.xml` file located in the `res/layout` folder by adding the following code in bold:

```xml
<?xml version="1.0" encoding="utf-8"?>
<LinearLayout xmlns:android="http://schemas.android.com/apk/res/android"
    android:orientation="vertical"
    android:layout_width="fill_parent"
    android:layout_height="fill_parent" >

<ProgressBar android:id="@+id/progressbar"
    android:layout_width="wrap_content"
    android:layout_height="wrap_content" />

</LinearLayout>
```

3. In the `MainActivity.java` file, add the following statements in bold:

```java
package net.learn2develop.BasicViews2;

import android.app.Activity;
import android.os.Bundle;

import android.os.Handler;
import android.widget.ProgressBar;

public class MainActivity extends Activity {

    private static int progress;
    private ProgressBar progressBar;
    private int progressStatus = 0;
    private Handler handler = new Handler();

    /** Called when the activity is first created. */
    @Override
    public void onCreate(Bundle savedInstanceState) {
        super.onCreate(savedInstanceState);
        setContentView(R.layout.main);

        progress = 0;
        progressBar = (ProgressBar) findViewById(R.id.progressbar);

        //---do some work in background thread---
        new Thread(new Runnable()
        {
            public void run()
            {
                //---do some work here---
                while (progressStatus < 10)
                {
                    progressStatus = doSomeWork();
```

```
        }

        //---hides the progress bar---
        handler.post(new Runnable()
        {
            public void run()
            {
                //---0 - VISIBLE; 4 - INVISIBLE; 8 - GONE---
                progressBar.setVisibility(8);
            }
        });
    }

    //---do some long lasting work here---
    private int doSomeWork()
    {
        try {
            //---simulate doing some work---
            Thread.sleep(500);
        } catch (InterruptedException e)
        {
            e.printStackTrace();
        }
        return ++progress;
    }
}).start();
    }
}
```

4. Press F11 to debug the project on the Android Emulator. Figure 4-6 shows the ProgressBar animating. After about five seconds, it will disappear.

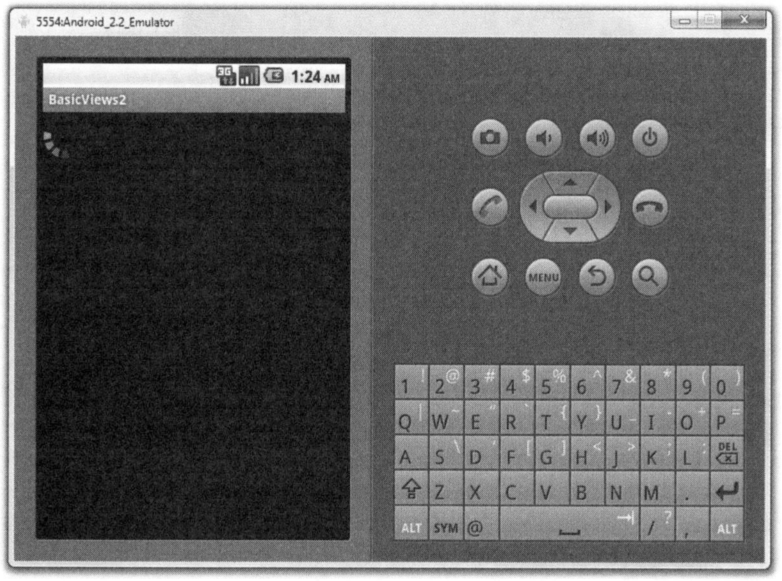

FIGURE 4-6

How It Works

The default mode of the `ProgressBar` view is indeterminate — that is, it shows a cyclic animation. This mode is useful for tasks that do not have a clear indication of when they will be completed, such as when you are sending some data to a web service and waiting for the server to respond. If you simply put the `<ProgressBar>` element in your `main.xml` file, it will display a spinning icon continuously. It is your responsibility to stop it when your background task has completed.

The code that you have added in the Java file shows how you can spin off a background thread to simulate performing some long-running tasks. To do so, you use the `Thread` class together with a `Runnable` object. The `run()` method starts the execution of the thread, which in this case calls the `doSomeWork()` method to simulate doing some work. When the simulated work is done (after about five seconds), you use a `Handler` object to send a message to the thread to dismiss the `ProgressBar`:

```java
//---do some work in background thread---
new Thread(new Runnable()
{
    public void run()
    {
        //---do some work here---
        while (progressStatus < 10)
        {
            progressStatus = doSomeWork();
        }

        //---hides the progress bar---
        handler.post(new Runnable()
        {
            public void run()
            {
                //---0 - VISIBLE; 4 - INVISIBLE; 8 - GONE---
                progressBar.setVisibility(8);
            }
        });
    }

    //---do some long lasting work here---
    private int doSomeWork()
    {
        try {
            //---simulate doing some work---
            Thread.sleep(500);
        } catch (InterruptedException e)
        {
            e.printStackTrace();
        }
        return ++progress;
    }
}).start();
```

When the task is completed, you hide the `ProgressBar` by setting its `Visibility` property to GONE (value `8`). The difference between the INVISIBLE and GONE constants is that the INVISIBLE constant simply hides the `ProgressBar` (the region occupied by the `ProgressBar` is still taking up space in the activity). The GONE constant removes the `ProgressBar` view from the activity and does not take up any space on it.

The next Try It Out shows how you can change the look of the `ProgressBar`.

TRY IT OUT Customizing the ProgressBar View

1. Using the same project created in the previous Try It Out, modify the `main.xml` file as shown here:

```xml
<?xml version="1.0" encoding="utf-8"?>
<LinearLayout xmlns:android="http://schemas.android.com/apk/res/android"
    android:orientation="vertical"
    android:layout_width="fill_parent"
    android:layout_height="fill_parent" >

<ProgressBar android:id="@+id/progressbar"
    android:layout_width="wrap_content"
    android:layout_height="wrap_content"
    style="?android:attr/progressBarStyleHorizontal" />

</LinearLayout>
```

2. Modify the `MainActivity.java` file by adding the following statements in bold:

```java
/** Called when the activity is first created. */
@Override
public void onCreate(Bundle savedInstanceState) {
    super.onCreate(savedInstanceState);
    setContentView(R.layout.main);

    progress = 0;
    progressBar = (ProgressBar) findViewById(R.id.progressbar);
    progressBar.setMax(200);

    //---do some work in background thread---
    new Thread(new Runnable()
    {
        public void run()
        {
            //---do some work here---
            while (progressStatus < 100)
            {
                progressStatus = doSomeWork();

                //---Update the progress bar---
                handler.post(new Runnable()
                {
                    public void run() {
                        progressBar.setProgress(progressStatus);
                    }
                });
            }

            //---hides the progress bar---
            handler.post(new Runnable()
            {
                public void run()
```

```
            {
                //---0 - VISIBLE; 4 - INVISIBLE; 8 - GONE---
                progressBar.setVisibility(8);
            }
        });
    }

    //---do some long lasting work here---
    private int doSomeWork()
    {
        try {
            //---simulate doing some work---
            Thread.sleep(50);
        } catch (InterruptedException e)
        {
            e.printStackTrace();
        }
        return ++progress;
    }
}).start();
}
```

3. Press F11 to debug the project on the Android Emulator.

4. Figure 4-7 shows the ProgressBar displaying the progress. The ProgressBar disappears when the progress reaches 50%.

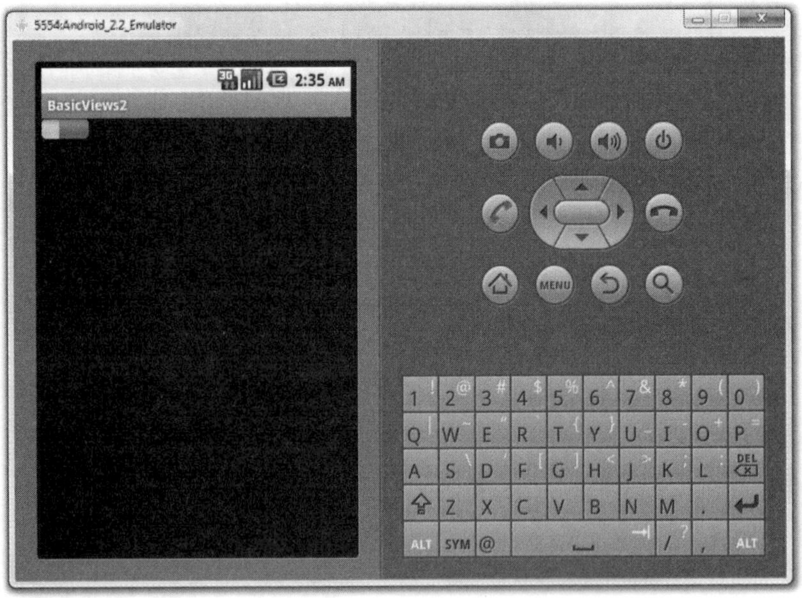

FIGURE 4-7

How It Works

To make the `ProgressBar` display horizontally, simply set its `style` attribute to `?android:attr/progress BarStyleHorizontal`:

```
<ProgressBar android:id="@+id/progressbar"
    android:layout_width="wrap_content"
    android:layout_height="wrap_content"
    style="?android:attr/progressBarStyleHorizontal" />
```

To display the progress, call its `setProgress()` method, passing in an integer indicating its progress:

```
//---Update the progress bar---
handler.post(new Runnable()
{
    public void run() {
        progressBar.setProgress(progressStatus);
    }
});
```

In this example, you set the range of the `ProgressBar` from 0 to 200 (via the `setMax()` method). Hence, the `ProgressBar` will stop and then disappear when it is halfway through (since you only continue to call the `doSomeWork()` method as long as the `progressStatus` is less than 100). To ensure that the `ProgressBar` disappears only when the progress reaches 100%, either set the maximum value to 100, or modify the `while` loop to stop when the `progressStatus` reaches 200, like this:

```
//---do some work here---
while (progressStatus < 200)
```

AutoCompleteTextView View

The `AutoCompleteTextView` is a view that is similar to `EditText` (in fact it is a subclass of `EditText`), except that it shows a list of completion suggestions automatically while the user is typing. The following Try It Out shows how to use the `AutoCompleteTextView` to automatically help users complete the text entry.

TRY IT OUT   Using the AutoCompleteTextView

codefile BasicViews3.zip available for download at Wrox.com

1.   Using Eclipse, create an Android project and name it **BasicViews3**.

2.   Modify the `main.xml` file located in the `res/layout` folder as shown here in bold:

```
<?xml version="1.0" encoding="utf-8"?>
<LinearLayout xmlns:android="http://schemas.android.com/apk/res/android"
    android:orientation="vertical"
    android:layout_width="fill_parent"
```

```
                android:layout_height="fill_parent" >

        <TextView
                android:layout_width="fill_parent"
                android:layout_height="wrap_content"
                android:text="Name of President" />

        <AutoCompleteTextView android:id="@+id/txtCountries"
                android:layout_width="fill_parent"
                android:layout_height="wrap_content" />

    </LinearLayout>
```

3. Add the following statements in bold to the `MainActivity.java` file:

```java
package net.learn2develop.BasicViews3;

import android.app.Activity;
import android.os.Bundle;

import android.widget.ArrayAdapter;
import android.widget.AutoCompleteTextView;

public class MainActivity extends Activity {
    String[] presidents = {
        "Dwight D. Eisenhower",
        "John F. Kennedy",
        "Lyndon B. Johnson",
        "Richard Nixon",
        "Gerald Ford",
        "Jimmy Carter",
        "Ronald Reagan",
        "George H. W. Bush",
        "Bill Clinton",
        "George W. Bush",
        "Barack Obama"
    };

    /** Called when the activity is first created. */
    @Override
    public void onCreate(Bundle savedInstanceState) {
        super.onCreate(savedInstanceState);
        setContentView(R.layout.main);

        ArrayAdapter<String> adapter = new ArrayAdapter<String>(this,
            android.R.layout.simple_dropdown_item_1line, presidents);

        AutoCompleteTextView textView = (AutoCompleteTextView)
            findViewById(R.id.txtCountries);

        textView.setThreshold(3);
        textView.setAdapter(adapter);
    }
}
```

4. Press F11 to debug the application on the Android Emulator. As shown in Figure 4-8, a list of matching names appears as you type into the `AutoCompleteTextView`.

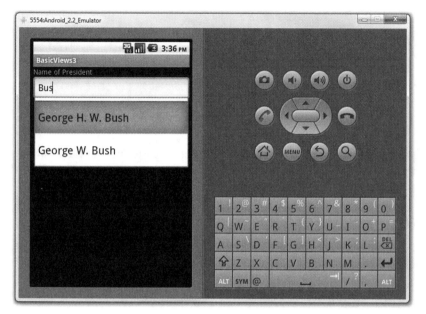

FIGURE 4-8

How It Works

In the `MainActivity` class, you first create a `String` array containing a list of presidents' names:

```
String[] presidents = {
    "Dwight D. Eisenhower",
    "John F. Kennedy",
    "Lyndon B. Johnson",
    "Richard Nixon",
    "Gerald Ford",
    "Jimmy Carter",
    "Ronald Reagan",
    "George H. W. Bush",
    "Bill Clinton",
    "George W. Bush",
    "Barack Obama"
};
```

The `ArrayAdapter` object manages the array of strings that will be displayed by the `AutoCompleteTextView`. In the preceding example, you set the `AutoCompleteTextView` to display in the `simple_dropdown_item_1line` mode:

```
ArrayAdapter<String> adapter = new ArrayAdapter<String>(this,
        android.R.layout.simple_dropdown_item_1line, presidents);
```

The `setThreshold()` method sets the minimum number of characters the user must type before the suggestions appear as a drop-down menu:

```
textView.setThreshold(3);
```

The list of suggestions to display for the `AutoCompleteTextView` is obtained from the `ArrayAdapter` object:

```
textView.setAdapter(adapter);
```

PICKER VIEWS

Selecting the date and time is one of the common tasks you need to perform in a mobile application. Android supports this functionality through the `TimePicker` and `DatePicker` views. The following sections show how to make use of these views in your activity.

TimePicker View

The `TimePicker` view enables users to select a time of the day, in either 24-hour mode or AM/PM mode. The following Try It Out shows you how to use it.

TRY IT OUT Using the TimePicker Wiew

codefile BasicViews4.zip available for download at Wrox.com

1. Using Eclipse, create an Android project and name it **BasicViews4**.

2. Modify the `main.xml` file located in the `res/layout` folder by adding the following lines in bold:

```xml
<?xml version="1.0" encoding="utf-8"?>
<LinearLayout xmlns:android="http://schemas.android.com/apk/res/android"
    android:orientation="vertical"
    android:layout_width="fill_parent"
    android:layout_height="fill_parent" >

<TimePicker android:id="@+id/timePicker"
    android:layout_width="wrap_content"
    android:layout_height="wrap_content" />

<Button android:id="@+id/btnSet"
    android:layout_width="wrap_content"
    android:layout_height="wrap_content"
    android:text="I am all set!" />

</LinearLayout>
```

3. Press F11 to debug the application on the Android Emulator. Figure 4-9 shows the `TimePicker` in action. Besides clicking on the plus (+) and minus (-) buttons, you can use the numeric keypad on the device to change the hour and minute, and click the AM button to toggle between AM and PM.

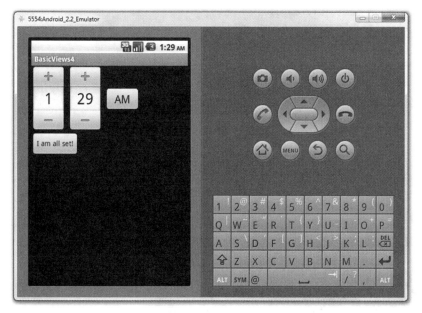

FIGURE 4-9

4. Back in Eclipse, add the following statements in bold to the `MainActivity.java` file:

```java
package net.learn2develop.BasicViews4;

import android.app.Activity;
import android.os.Bundle;

import android.view.View;
import android.widget.Button;
import android.widget.TimePicker;
import android.widget.Toast;

public class MainActivity extends Activity {
    TimePicker timePicker;

    /** Called when the activity is first created. */
    @Override
    public void onCreate(Bundle savedInstanceState) {
        super.onCreate(savedInstanceState);
        setContentView(R.layout.main);

        timePicker = (TimePicker) findViewById(R.id.timePicker);
        timePicker.setIs24HourView(true);

        //---Button view---
        Button btnOpen = (Button) findViewById(R.id.btnSet);
        btnOpen.setOnClickListener(new View.OnClickListener() {
```

```
    public void onClick(View v) {
        Toast.makeText(getBaseContext(),
            "Time selected:" +
            timePicker.getCurrentHour() +
            ":" + timePicker.getCurrentMinute(),
            Toast.LENGTH_SHORT).show();
    }
});
    }
}
```

5. Press F11 to debug the application on the Android Emulator. This time, the `TimePicker` will be displayed in the 24-hour format. Clicking the `Button` will display the time that you have set in the `TimePicker` (see Figure 4-10).

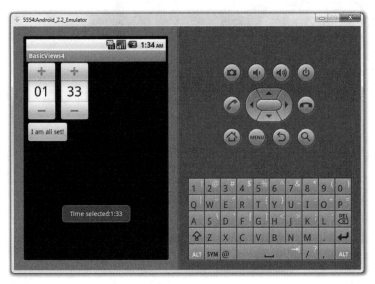

FIGURE 4-10

How It Works

The `TimePicker` displays a standard UI to enable users to set a time. By default, it displays the time in the AM/PM format. If you wish to display the time in the 24-hour format, you can use the `setIs24HourView()` method.

To programmatically get the time set by the user, use the `getCurrentHour()` and `getCurrentMinute()` methods:

```
Toast.makeText(getBaseContext(),
    "Time selected:" +
    timePicker.getCurrentHour() +
    ":" + timePicker.getCurrentMinute(),
    Toast.LENGTH_SHORT).show();
```

> **NOTE** *The* `getCurrentHour()` *method always returns the hour in 24-hour format, i.e., a value from 0 to 23.*

Displaying the TimePicker in a Dialog Window

While you can display the `TimePicker` in an activity, a better way is to display it in a dialog window, so that once the time is set, it disappears and doesn't take up any space in an activity. The following Try It Out shows how to do just that.

TRY IT OUT   Using a Dialog to Display the TimePicker View

1. Using the same project created in the previous Try It Out, modify the `MainActivity.java` file as shown here:

```
package net.learn2develop.BasicViews4;

import android.app.Activity;
import android.os.Bundle;
import android.view.View;
import android.widget.Button;
import android.widget.TimePicker;
import android.widget.Toast;

import android.app.Dialog;
import android.app.TimePickerDialog;

public class MainActivity extends Activity {
    TimePicker timePicker;

    int hour, minute;
    static final int TIME_DIALOG_ID = 0;

    /** Called when the activity is first created. */
    @Override
    public void onCreate(Bundle savedInstanceState) {
        super.onCreate(savedInstanceState);
        setContentView(R.layout.main);

        showDialog(TIME_DIALOG_ID);

        timePicker = (TimePicker) findViewById(R.id.timePicker);
        timePicker.setIs24HourView(true);

        //---Button view---
        Button btnOpen = (Button) findViewById(R.id.btnSet);
        btnOpen.setOnClickListener(new View.OnClickListener() {
            public void onClick(View v) {
                Toast.makeText(getBaseContext(),
                    "Time selected:" +
                        timePicker.getCurrentHour().toString() +
```

```
                          ":" + timePicker.getCurrentMinute().toString(),
                      Toast.LENGTH_SHORT).show();
               }
        });
    }

    @Override
    protected Dialog onCreateDialog(int id)
    {
        switch (id) {
            case TIME_DIALOG_ID:
                return new TimePickerDialog(
                    this, mTimeSetListener, hour, minute, false);
        }
        return null;
    }

    private TimePickerDialog.OnTimeSetListener mTimeSetListener =
        new TimePickerDialog.OnTimeSetListener()
        {
            public void onTimeSet(
            TimePicker view, int hourOfDay, int minuteOfHour)
            {
                hour = hourOfDay;
                minute = minuteOfHour;
                Toast.makeText(getBaseContext(),
                    "You have selected : " + hour + ":" + minute,
                    Toast.LENGTH_SHORT).show();
            }
        };
}
```

2. Press F11 to debug the application on the Android Emulator. When the activity is loaded, you can see the `TimePicker` displayed in a dialog window (see Figure 4-11). Set a time and then click the Set button. You will see the Toast window displaying the time that you just set.

How It Works

To display a dialog window, you use the `showDialog()` method, passing it an ID to identify the source of the dialog:

```
        showDialog(TIME_DIALOG_ID);
```

When the `showDialog()` method is called, the `onCreateDialog()` method will be called:

```
    @Override
    protected Dialog onCreateDialog(int id)
    {
        switch (id) {
            case TIME_DIALOG_ID:
                return new TimePickerDialog(
                    this, mTimeSetListener, hour, minute, false);
        }
        return null;
    }
```

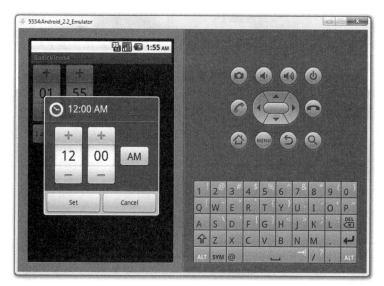

FIGURE 4-11

Here, you create a new instance of the `TimePickerDialog` class, passing it the current context, the callback, the initial hour and minute, as well as whether the `TimePicker` should be displayed in 24-hour format.

When the user clicks the Set button in the `TimePicker` dialog window, the `onTimeSet()` method will be called:

```
private TimePickerDialog.OnTimeSetListener mTimeSetListener =
    new TimePickerDialog.OnTimeSetListener()
    {
        public void onTimeSet(
        TimePicker view, int hourOfDay, int minuteOfHour)
        {
            hour = hourOfDay;
            minute = minuteOfHour;
            Toast.makeText(getBaseContext(),
                "You have selected : " + hour + ":" + minute,
                Toast.LENGTH_SHORT).show();
        }
    };
```

Here, the `onTimeSet()` method will contain the hour and minute set by the user via the `hourOfDay` and `minuteOfHour` arguments, respectively.

DatePicker View

Another view that is similar to the `TimePicker` is the `DatePicker`. Using the `DatePicker`, you can enable users to select a particular date on the activity. The following Try It Out shows you how to use the `DatePicker`.

TRY IT OUT Using the DatePicker View

1. Using the same project created in the previous Try It Out, modify the `main.xml` file as shown here:

```xml
<?xml version="1.0" encoding="utf-8"?>
<LinearLayout xmlns:android="http://schemas.android.com/apk/res/android"
    android:orientation="vertical"
    android:layout_width="fill_parent"
    android:layout_height="fill_parent" >

<DatePicker android:id="@+id/datePicker"
    android:layout_width="wrap_content"
    android:layout_height="wrap_content" />

<TimePicker android:id="@+id/timePicker"
    android:layout_width="wrap_content"
    android:layout_height="wrap_content" />

<Button android:id="@+id/btnSet"
    android:layout_width="wrap_content"
    android:layout_height="wrap_content"
    android:text="I am all set!" />

</LinearLayout>
```

2. Press F11 to debug the application on the Android Emulator. Figure 4-12 shows the `DatePicker` and `TimePicker` views.

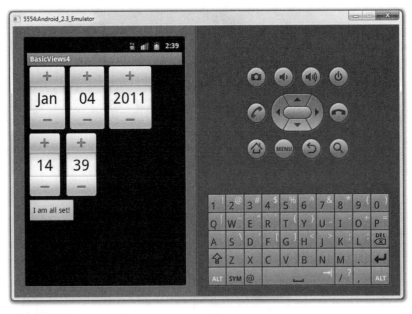

FIGURE 4-12

3. Back in Eclipse, add in the following statements in bold to the `MainActivity.java` file:

```java
package net.learn2develop.BasicViews4;

import android.app.Activity;
import android.os.Bundle;
import android.view.View;
import android.widget.Button;

import android.widget.Toast;

import android.app.Dialog;
import android.app.TimePickerDialog;

import android.widget.TimePicker;

import android.widget.DatePicker;

public class MainActivity extends Activity {
    TimePicker timePicker;
    DatePicker datePicker;

    int hour, minute;
    static final int TIME_DIALOG_ID = 0;

    /** Called when the activity is first created. */
    @Override
    public void onCreate(Bundle savedInstanceState) {
        super.onCreate(savedInstanceState);
        setContentView(R.layout.main);

        //showDialog(TIME_DIALOG_ID);

        timePicker = (TimePicker) findViewById(R.id.timePicker);
        timePicker.setIs24HourView(true);

        datePicker = (DatePicker) findViewById(R.id.datePicker);

        //---Button view---
        Button btnOpen = (Button) findViewById(R.id.btnSet);
        btnOpen.setOnClickListener(new View.OnClickListener() {
            public void onClick(View v) {
                Toast.makeText(getBaseContext(),
                        "Date selected:" + datePicker.getMonth() + 1 +
                        "/" + datePicker.getDayOfMonth() +
                        "/" + datePicker.getYear() + "\n" +
                        "Time selected:" + timePicker.getCurrentHour() +
                        ":" + timePicker.getCurrentMinute(),
                        Toast.LENGTH_SHORT).show();
            }
        });
    }

    @Override
```

```java
protected Dialog onCreateDialog(int id)
{
    switch (id) {
        case TIME_DIALOG_ID:
            return new TimePickerDialog(
                this, mTimeSetListener, hour, minute, false);
    }
    return null;
}

private TimePickerDialog.OnTimeSetListener mTimeSetListener =
    new TimePickerDialog.OnTimeSetListener()
    {
        public void onTimeSet(
        TimePicker view, int hourOfDay, int minuteOfHour)
        {
            hour = hourOfDay;
            minute = minuteOfHour;
            Toast.makeText(getBaseContext(),
                "You have selected : " + hour + ":" + minute,
                Toast.LENGTH_SHORT).show();
        }
    };
}
```

4. Press F11 to debug the application on the Android Emulator. Once the date is set, clicking the `Button` will display the date set (see Figure 4-13).

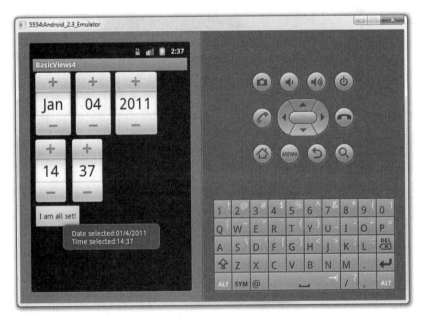

FIGURE 4-13

How It Works

Like the `TimePicker`, you call the `getMonth()`, `getDayOfMonth()`, and `getYear()` methods to get the month, day, and year, respectively:

```
"Date selected:" + datePicker.getMonth() + 1 +
"/" + datePicker.getDayOfMonth() +
"/" + datePicker.getYear() + "\n" +
```

Note that the `getMonth()` method returns 0 for January, 1 for February, and so on. Hence, you need to add a one to the result of this method to get the month number.

Displaying the DatePicker View in a Dialog Window

Like the `TimePicker`, you can also display the `DatePicker` in a dialog window. The following Try It Out shows you how.

TRY IT OUT   Using a Dialog to Display the DatePicker View

1. Using the same project created in the previous Try It Out, add the following statements in bold to the `MainActivity.java` file:

```
package net.learn2develop.BasicViews4;

import android.app.Activity;
import android.os.Bundle;

import android.view.View;
import android.widget.Button;

import android.widget.Toast;

import android.app.Dialog;
import android.app.TimePickerDialog;

import android.widget.TimePicker;
import android.widget.DatePicker;

import android.app.DatePickerDialog;
import java.util.Calendar;

public class MainActivity extends Activity {
    TimePicker timePicker;
    DatePicker datePicker;

    int hour, minute;
    int yr, month, day;

    static final int TIME_DIALOG_ID = 0;
    static final int DATE_DIALOG_ID = 1;

    /** Called when the activity is first created. */
```

```java
@Override
public void onCreate(Bundle savedInstanceState) {
    super.onCreate(savedInstanceState);
    setContentView(R.layout.main);

    //showDialog(TIME_DIALOG_ID);

    //---get the current date---
    Calendar today = Calendar.getInstance();
    yr = today.get(Calendar.YEAR);
    month = today.get(Calendar.MONTH);
    day = today.get(Calendar.DAY_OF_MONTH);
    showDialog(DATE_DIALOG_ID);

    timePicker = (TimePicker) findViewById(R.id.timePicker);
    timePicker.setIs24HourView(true);

    datePicker = (DatePicker) findViewById(R.id.datePicker);

    //---Button view---
    Button btnOpen = (Button) findViewById(R.id.btnSet);
    btnOpen.setOnClickListener(new View.OnClickListener() {
        public void onClick(View v) {
            Toast.makeText(getBaseContext(),
                    "Date selected:" + datePicker.getMonth() +
                    "/" + datePicker.getDayOfMonth() +
                    "/" + datePicker.getYear() + "\n" +
                    "Time selected:" + timePicker.getCurrentHour() +
                    ":" + timePicker.getCurrentMinute(),
                    Toast.LENGTH_SHORT).show();
        }
    });
}

@Override
protected Dialog onCreateDialog(int id)
{
    switch (id) {
        case TIME_DIALOG_ID:
            return new TimePickerDialog(
                this, mTimeSetListener, hour, minute, false);
        case DATE_DIALOG_ID:
            return new DatePickerDialog(
                this, mDateSetListener, yr, month, day);
    }
    return null;
}

private DatePickerDialog.OnDateSetListener mDateSetListener =
    new DatePickerDialog.OnDateSetListener()
    {
        public void onDateSet(
        DatePicker view, int year, int monthOfYear, int dayOfMonth)
        {
```

```
                yr = year;
                month = monthOfYear;
                day = dayOfMonth;
                Toast.makeText(getBaseContext(),
                        "You have selected : " + (month + 1) +
                        "/" + day + "/" + year,
                        Toast.LENGTH_SHORT).show();
            }
        };

    private TimePickerDialog.OnTimeSetListener mTimeSetListener =
        new TimePickerDialog.OnTimeSetListener()
        {
            public void onTimeSet(
            TimePicker view, int hourOfDay, int minuteOfHour)
            {
                hour = hourOfDay;
                minute = minuteOfHour;
                Toast.makeText(getBaseContext(),
                        "You have selected : " + hour + ":" + minute,
                        Toast.LENGTH_SHORT).show();

            }
        };
}
```

2. Press F11 to debug the application on the Android Emulator. When the activity is loaded, you can see the `DatePicker` displayed in a dialog window (see Figure 4-14). Set a date and then click the Set button. The Toast window will display the date you have just set.

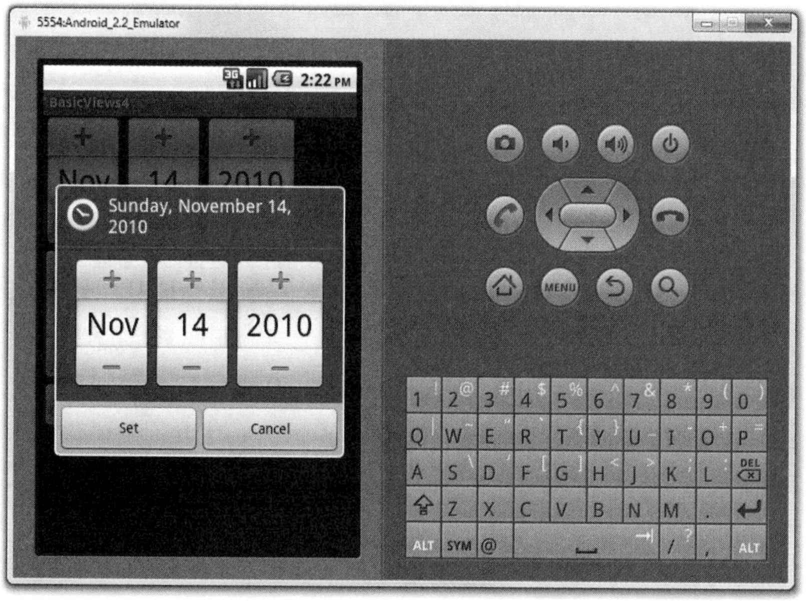

FIGURE 4-14

How It Works

The `DatePicker` works exactly like the `TimePicker`. When a date is set, it fires the `onDateSet()` method, where you can obtain the date set by the user:

```
public void onDateSet(
DatePicker view, int year, int monthOfYear, int dayOfMonth)
{
    yr = year;
    month = monthOfYear;
    day = dayOfMonth;
    Toast.makeText(getBaseContext(),
            "You have selected : " + (month + 1) +
            "/" + day + "/" + year,
            Toast.LENGTH_SHORT).show();
}
```

Note that you have to initialize the three variables — `yr`, `month`, and `day` — before showing the dialog:

```
//---get the current date---
Calendar today = Calendar.getInstance();
yr = today.get(Calendar.YEAR);
month = today.get(Calendar.MONTH);
day = today.get(Calendar.DAY_OF_MONTH);
showDialog(DATE_DIALOG_ID);
```

If you don't, you will get an illegal argument exception error during run time ("`current should be >= start and <= end`") when you create an instance of the `DatePickerDialog` class.

LIST VIEWS

List views are views that enable you to display a long list of items. In Android, there are two types of list views: `ListView` and `SpinnerView`. Both are useful for displaying long lists of items. The following Try It Outs show them in action.

ListView View

The `ListView` displays a list of items in a vertically scrolling list. The following Try It Out demonstrates how to display a list of items using the `ListView`.

TRY IT OUT Displaying a Long List of Items Using the ListView

1. Using Eclipse, create an Android project and name it **BasicView5**.

codefile BasicViews5.zip available for download at Wrox.com

2. Modify the `MainActivity.java` file by inserting the statements shown here in bold:

```java
package net.learn2develop.BasicViews5;

import android.app.Activity;
import android.os.Bundle;

import android.app.ListActivity;
import android.view.View;
import android.widget.ArrayAdapter;
import android.widget.ListView;
import android.widget.Toast;

public class MainActivity extends ListActivity {

    String[] presidents = {
        "Dwight D. Eisenhower",
        "John F. Kennedy",
        "Lyndon B. Johnson",
        "Richard Nixon",
        "Gerald Ford",
        "Jimmy Carter",
        "Ronald Reagan",
        "George H. W. Bush",
        "Bill Clinton",
        "George W. Bush",
        "Barack Obama"
    };

    /** Called when the activity is first created. */
    @Override
    public void onCreate(Bundle savedInstanceState) {
        super.onCreate(savedInstanceState);
        //setContentView(R.layout.main);

        setListAdapter(new ArrayAdapter<String>(this,
            android.R.layout.simple_list_item_1, presidents));
    }

    public void onListItemClick(
    ListView parent, View v, int position, long id)
    {
        Toast.makeText(this,
            "You have selected " + presidents[position],
            Toast.LENGTH_SHORT).show();
    }
}
```

3. Press F11 to debug the application on the Android Emulator. Figure 4-15 shows the activity displaying the list of presidents' names.

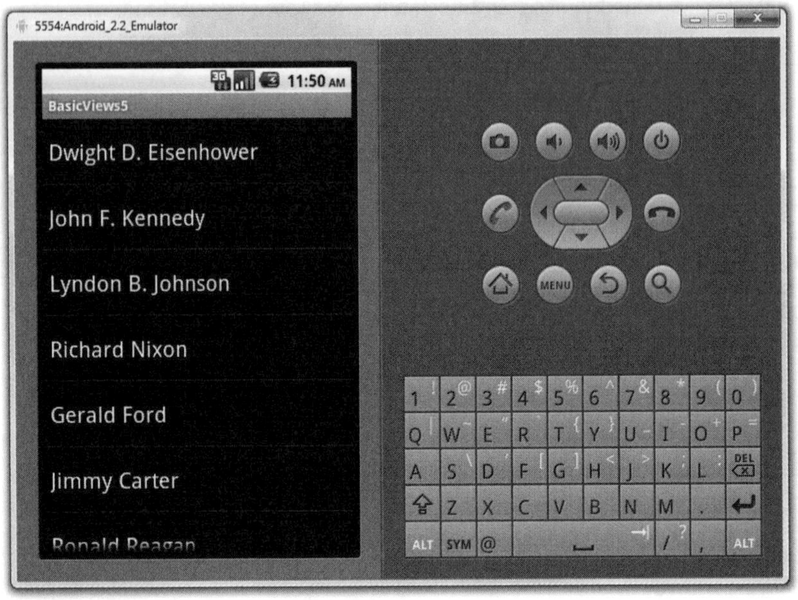

FIGURE 4-15

4. Click on an item. A message containing the item selected will be displayed.

How It Works

The first thing to notice in this example is that the `MainActivity` class extends the `ListActivity` class. The `ListActivity` class extends the `Activity` class and it displays a list of items by binding to a data source. Also, note that there is no need to modify the `main.xml` file to include the `ListView`; the `ListActivity` class itself contains a `ListView`. Hence, in the `onCreate()` method, there is no need to call the `setContentView()` method to load the UI from the `main.xml` file:

```
//---no need to call this---
//setContentView(R.layout.main);
```

In the `onCreate()` method, you use the `setListAdapter()` method to programmatically fill the entire screen of the activity with a `ListView`. The `ArrayAdapter` object manages the array of strings that will be displayed by the `ListView`. In the preceding example, you set the `ListView` to display in the `simple_list_item_1` mode:

```
setListAdapter(new ArrayAdapter<String>(this,
        android.R.layout.simple_list_item_1, presidents));
```

The `onListItemClick()` method is fired whenever an item in the `ListView` has been clicked:

```
public void onListItemClick(
ListView parent, View v, int position, long id)
```

```
    {
        Toast.makeText(this,
            "You have selected " + presidents[position],
            Toast.LENGTH_SHORT).show();
    }
```

Here, you simply display the name of the president selected using the Toast class.

Customizing the ListView

The ListView is a versatile control that you can further customize. The following Try It Out shows how you can allow multiple items in the ListView to be selected and how you can enable filtering support.

TRY IT OUT Customizing the ListView

1. Using the same project created in the previous section, add the following statements in bold to the MainActivity.java file:

```
/** Called when the activity is first created. */
@Override
public void onCreate(Bundle savedInstanceState) {
    super.onCreate(savedInstanceState);
    setContentView(R.layout.main);

    ListView lstView = getListView();
    //lstView.setChoiceMode(0); //CHOICE_MODE_NONE
    //lstView.setChoiceMode(1); //CHOICE_MODE_SINGLE
    lstView.setChoiceMode(2);   //CHOICE_MODE_MULTIPLE
    lstView.setTextFilterEnabled(true);

    setListAdapter(new ArrayAdapter<String>(this,
            android.R.layout.simple_list_item_checked, presidents));
}

public void onListItemClick(
ListView parent, View v, int position, long id)
{
    //---toggle the check displayed next to the item---
    parent.setItemChecked(position, parent.isItemChecked(position));
    Toast.makeText(this,
        "You have selected " + presidents[position],
        Toast.LENGTH_SHORT).show();
}
```

2. Press F11 to debug the application on the Android Emulator. You can now click on each item to display the check icon next to it (see Figure 4-16).

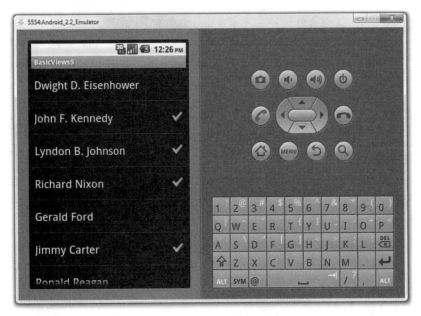

FIGURE 4-16

How It Works

To programmatically get a reference to the ListView object, you use the getListView() method, which fetches the ListActivity's list view. You need to do this so that you can programmatically modify the behavior of the ListView. In this case, you used the setChoiceMode() method to tell the ListView how it should handle a user's click. For this example, you set it to 2, which means that the user can select multiple items:

```
//lstView.setChoiceMode(0); //CHOICE_MODE_NONE
//lstView.setChoiceMode(1); //CHOICE_MODE_SINGLE
lstView.setChoiceMode(2);   //CHOICE_MODE_MULTIPLE
```

A very cool feature of the ListView is its support for filtering. When you enable filtering through the setTextFilterEnabled() method, users will be able to type on the keypad and the ListView will automatically filter to match what you have typed:

```
lstView.setTextFilterEnabled(true);
```

Figure 4-17 shows the list filtering in action. Here, all items in the list that contain the word "john" will appear in the result list.

To display the check icon displayed next to each item, use the setItemChecked() method:

```
//---toggle the check displayed next to the item---
parent.setItemChecked(position, parent.isItemChecked(position));
```

The preceding statement will toggle the check icon for each item when you click on it.

FIGURE 4-17

While this example shows that the list of presidents' names is stored in an array, in a real-life application it is recommended that you either retrieve them from a database or at least store them in the strings.xml file. The following Try It Out shows you how.

TRY IT OUT Storing Items in the strings.xml File

1. Using the same project created in the previous section, add the following lines in bold to the strings.xml file located in the res/values folder:

```xml
<?xml version="1.0" encoding="utf-8"?>
<resources>
    <string name="hello">Hello World, MainActivity!</string>
    <string name="app_name">BasicViews5</string>
    <string-array name="presidents_array">
        <item>Dwight D. Eisenhower</item>
        <item>John F. Kennedy</item>
        <item>Lyndon B. Johnson</item>
        <item>Richard Nixon</item>
        <item>Gerald Ford</item>
        <item>Jimmy Carter</item>
        <item>Ronald Reagan</item>
        <item>George H. W. Bush</item>
        <item>Bill Clinton</item>
        <item>George W. Bush</item>
        <item>Barack Obama</item>
    </string-array>
</resources>
```

2. Modify the `MainActivity.java` file as shown in bold:

```java
public class MainActivity extends ListActivity {

    String[] presidents;

    /** Called when the activity is first created. */
    @Override
    public void onCreate(Bundle savedInstanceState) {
        super.onCreate(savedInstanceState);
        setContentView(R.layout.main);

        ListView lstView = getListView();
        //lstView.setChoiceMode(0); //CHOICE_MODE_NONE
        //lstView.setChoiceMode(1); //CHOICE_MODE_SINGLE
        lstView.setChoiceMode(2);    //CHOICE_MODE_MULTIPLE
        lstView.setTextFilterEnabled(true);

        presidents =
            getResources().getStringArray(R.array.presidents_array);

        setListAdapter(new ArrayAdapter<String>(this,
                android.R.layout.simple_list_item_checked, presidents));
    }

    public void onListItemClick(
    ListView parent, View v, int position, long id)
    {
        //...
        //...
    }
};
```

3. Press F11 to debug the application on the Android Emulator. You should see the same list of names that appeared in the previous Try It Out.

How It Works

With the names now stored in the `strings.xml` file, you can retrieve it programmatically in this `MainActivity.java` file using the `getResources()` method:

```java
        presidents =
            getResources().getStringArray(R.array.presidents_array);
```

In general, you can programmatically retrieve resources bundled with your application using the `getResources()` method.

Using the Spinner View

The `ListView` displays a long list of items in an activity, but sometimes you may want your user interface to display other views, and hence you do not have the additional space for a full-screen view like the `ListView`. In such cases, you should use the `SpinnerView`. The `SpinnerView` displays one item at a time from a list and enables users to choose among them.

The following Try It Out shows how you can use the `SpinnerView` in your activity.

TRY IT OUT   Using the SpinnerView to Display an Item at a Time

1. Using Eclipse, create an Android project and name it as **BasicViews6**.

codefile BasicViews6.zip available for download at Wrox.com

2. Modify the `main.xml` file located in the `res/layout` folder as shown here:

```xml
<?xml version="1.0" encoding="utf-8"?>
<LinearLayout xmlns:android="http://schemas.android.com/apk/res/android"
    android:orientation="vertical"
    android:layout_width="fill_parent"
    android:layout_height="fill_parent"
    >

<Spinner
    android:id="@+id/spinner1"
    android:layout_width="wrap_content"
    android:layout_height="wrap_content"
    android:drawSelectorOnTop="true" />

</LinearLayout>
```

3. Add the following lines in bold to the `strings.xml` file located in the `res/values` folder:

```xml
<?xml version="1.0" encoding="utf-8"?>
<resources>
    <string name="hello">Hello World, MainActivity!</string>
    <string name="app_name">BasicViews6</string>
    <string-array name="presidents_array">
        <item>Dwight D. Eisenhower</item>
        <item>John F. Kennedy</item>
        <item>Lyndon B. Johnson</item>
        <item>Richard Nixon</item>
        <item>Gerald Ford</item>
        <item>Jimmy Carter</item>
        <item>Ronald Reagan</item>
        <item>George H. W. Bush</item>
        <item>Bill Clinton</item>
        <item>George W. Bush</item>
        <item>Barack Obama</item>
    </string-array>
</resources>
```

4. Add the following statements in bold to the `MainActivity.java` file:

```java
package net.learn2develop.BasicViews6;

import android.app.Activity;
```

```
import android.os.Bundle;

import android.view.View;
import android.widget.AdapterView;
import android.widget.AdapterView.OnItemSelectedListener;
import android.widget.ArrayAdapter;
import android.widget.Spinner;
import android.widget.Toast;

public class MainActivity extends Activity {

    String[] presidents;

    /** Called when the activity is first created. */
    @Override
    public void onCreate(Bundle savedInstanceState) {
        super.onCreate(savedInstanceState);
        setContentView(R.layout.main);

        presidents =
            getResources().getStringArray(R.array.presidents_array);
        Spinner s1 = (Spinner) findViewById(R.id.spinner1);

        ArrayAdapter<String> adapter = new ArrayAdapter<String>(this,
            android.R.layout.simple_spinner_item, presidents);

        s1.setAdapter(adapter);
        s1.setOnItemSelectedListener(new OnItemSelectedListener()
        {
            @Override
            public void onItemSelected(AdapterView<?> arg0, View arg1,
            int arg2, long arg3)
            {
                int index = arg0.getSelectedItemPosition();
                Toast.makeText(getBaseContext(),
                    "You have selected item : " + presidents[index],
                    Toast.LENGTH_SHORT).show();
            }

            @Override
            public void onNothingSelected(AdapterView<?> arg0) {}
        });
    }
}
```

5. Press F11 to debug the application on the Android Emulator. Click on the `SpinnerView` and you will see a pop-up displaying the list of presidents' names (see Figure 4-18). Clicking on an item will display a message showing you the item selected.

How It Works

The preceding example works very much like the `ListView`. One additional method you need to implement is the `onNothingSelected()` method. This method is fired when the user presses the Back button, which dismisses the list of items displayed. In this case, nothing is selected and you do not need to do anything.

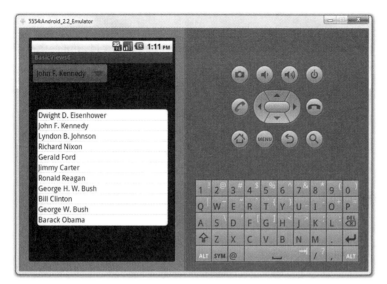

FIGURE 4-18

Instead of displaying the items in the `ArrayAdapter` as a simple list, you can also display them using radio buttons. To do so, modify the second parameter in the constructor of the `ArrayAdapter` class:

```
ArrayAdapter<String> adapter = new ArrayAdapter<String>(this,
    android.R.layout.simple_spinner_dropdown_item, presidents);
```

This will cause the items to be displayed as a list of radio buttons (see Figure 4-19).

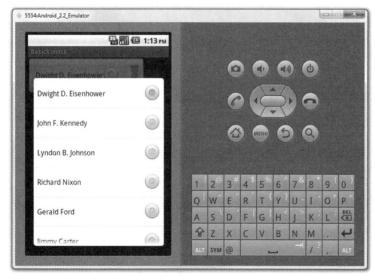

FIGURE 4-19

SUMMARY

This chapter provided a brief look at some of the commonly used views in an Android application. While it is not possible to exhaustively examine each view in detail, the views you learned about here should provide a good foundation for designing your Android application's user interface, regardless of its requirements.

EXERCISES

1. How do you programmatically determine whether a `RadioButton` is checked?

2. How do you access the string resource stored in the `strings.xml` file?

3. Write the code snippet to obtain the current date.

Answers to the Exercises can be found in Appendix C.

▶ **WHAT YOU LEARNED IN THIS CHAPTER**

TOPIC	KEY CONCEPTS
TextView	```<TextView` ` android:layout_width="fill_parent"` ` android:layout_height="wrap_content"` ` android:text="@string/hello"` ` />```
Button	```<Button android:id="@+id/btnSave"` ` android:layout_width="fill_parent"` ` android:layout_height="wrap_content"` ` android:text="Save" />```
ImageButton	```<ImageButton android:id="@+id/btnImg1"` ` android:layout_width="fill_parent"` ` android:layout_height="wrap_content"` ` android:src="@drawable/icon" />```
EditText	```<EditText android:id="@+id/txtName"` ` android:layout_width="fill_parent"` ` android:layout_height="wrap_content" />```
CheckBox	```<CheckBox android:id="@+id/chkAutosave"` ` android:layout_width="fill_parent"` ` android:layout_height="wrap_content"` ` android:text="Autosave" />```
RadioGroup and RadioButton	```<RadioGroup android:id="@+id/rdbGp1"` ` android:layout_width="fill_parent"` ` android:layout_height="wrap_content"` ` android:orientation="vertical" >` `<RadioButton android:id="@+id/rdb1"` ` android:layout_width="fill_parent"` ` android:layout_height="wrap_content"` ` android:text="Option 1" />` `<RadioButton android:id="@+id/rdb2"` ` android:layout_width="fill_parent"` ` android:layout_height="wrap_content"` ` android:text="Option 2" />` `</RadioGroup>```
ToggleButton	```<ToggleButton android:id="@+id/toggle1"` ` android:layout_width="wrap_content"` ` android:layout_height="wrap_content" />```
ProgressBar	```<ProgressBar android:id="@+id/progressbar"` ` android:layout_width="wrap_content"` ` android:layout_height="wrap_content" />```
AutoCompleteTextBox	```<AutoCompleteTextView android:id="@+id/txtCountries"` ` android:layout_width="fill_parent"` ` android:layout_height="wrap_content" />```

continues

(continued)

TOPIC	KEY CONCEPTS

TimePicker	```<TimePicker android:id="@+id/timePicker"```
	``` android:layout_width="wrap_content"```
	``` android:layout_height="wrap_content" />```

DatePicker	```<DatePicker android:id="@+id/datePicker"```
	``` android:layout_width="wrap_content"```
	``` android:layout_height="wrap_content" />```

Spinner	```<Spinner android:id="@+id/spinner1"```
	``` android:layout_width="wrap_content"```
	``` android:layout_height="wrap_content"```
	``` android:drawSelectorOnTop="true" />```

5

Displaying Pictures and Menus with Views

WHAT YOU WILL LEARN IN THIS CHAPTER

➤ How to use the `Gallery`, `ImageSwitcher`, `GridView`, and `ImageView` views to display images

➤ How to display options and context menus

➤ How to display time using the `AnalogClock` and `DigitalClock` views

➤ How to display Web content using the `WebView`

In the previous chapter, you learned about the various views that you can use to build the user interface of your Android application. In this chapter, you continue your exploration of the other views that you can use to create robust and compelling applications.

In particular, you shall turn your attention to views that enable you to display images. In addition, you will also learn how to create option and context menus in your Android application. This chapter ends with a discussion of some nice views that enable you to display the current time and Web content.

USING IMAGE VIEWS TO DISPLAY PICTURES

So far, all the views you have seen until this point are used to display text information. For displaying images, you can use the `ImageView`, `Gallery`, `ImageSwitcher`, and `GridView` views.

The following sections discuss each view in more detail.

Gallery and ImageView Views

The `Gallery` is a view that shows items (such as images) in a center-locked, horizontal scrolling list. Figure 5-1 shows how the `Gallery` view looks when it is displaying some images.

FIGURE 5-1

The following Try It Out shows you how to use the `Gallery` view to display a set of images.

TRY IT OUT Using the Gallery View

codefile Gallery.zip available for download at Wrox.com

1. Using Eclipse, create a new Android project as shown in Figure 5-2.

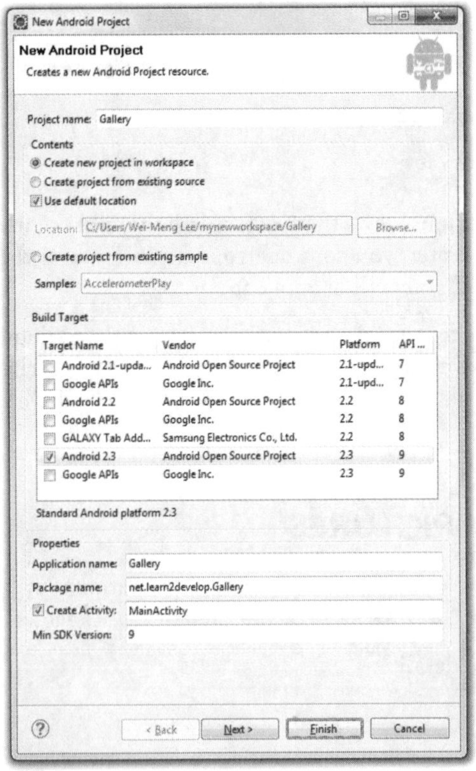

FIGURE 5-2

2. Modify the `main.xml` file as shown in bold:

```xml
<?xml version="1.0" encoding="utf-8"?>
<LinearLayout xmlns:android="http://schemas.android.com/apk/res/android"
    android:orientation="vertical"
    android:layout_width="fill_parent"
    android:layout_height="fill_parent" >

<TextView
    android:layout_width="fill_parent"
    android:layout_height="wrap_content"
    android:text="Images of San Francisco" />

<Gallery
    android:id="@+id/gallery1"
    android:layout_width="fill_parent"
    android:layout_height="wrap_content" />

<ImageView
    android:id="@+id/image1"
    android:layout_width="320px"
    android:layout_height="250px"
    android:scaleType="fitXY" />

</LinearLayout>
```

3. Right-click on the `res/values` folder and select New ➪ File. Name the file **attrs.xml**.

4. Populate the `attrs.xml` file as follows:

```xml
<?xml version="1.0" encoding="utf-8"?>
<resources>
    <declare-styleable name="Gallery1">
        <attr name="android:galleryItemBackground" />
    </declare-styleable>
</resources>
```

5. Prepare a series of images and name them **pic1.png, pic2.png**, and so on for each subsequent image (see Figure 5-3).

> **NOTE** You can download the series of images from this book's support website at www.wrox.com.

6. Drag and drop all the images into the `res/drawable-mdpi` folder (see Figure 5-4). When a dialog is displayed, check the copy option and click OK.

> **NOTE** This example assumes that this project will be tested on an AVD with medium DPI screen resolution. For a real-life project, you need to ensure that each `drawable` folder has a set of images (of different resolutions).

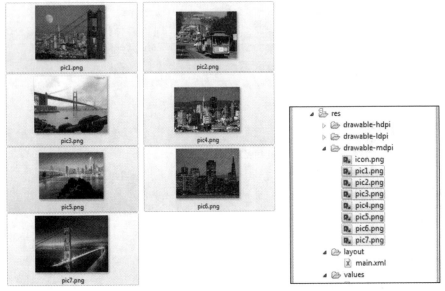

FIGURE 5-3　　　　　　　　　　　　　　　　　　　　**FIGURE 5-4**

7.　Add the following statements in bold to the `MainActivity.java` file:

```
package net.learn2develop.Gallery;

import android.app.Activity;
import android.os.Bundle;

import android.content.Context;
import android.content.res.TypedArray;
import android.view.View;
import android.view.ViewGroup;
import android.widget.AdapterView;
import android.widget.AdapterView.OnItemClickListener;
import android.widget.BaseAdapter;
import android.widget.Gallery;
import android.widget.ImageView;
import android.widget.Toast;

public class MainActivity extends Activity {
    //---the images to display---
    Integer[] imageIDs = {
            R.drawable.pic1,
            R.drawable.pic2,
            R.drawable.pic3,
            R.drawable.pic4,
            R.drawable.pic5,
            R.drawable.pic6,
            R.drawable.pic7
    };

    /** Called when the activity is first created. */
    @Override
```

```java
public void onCreate(Bundle savedInstanceState) {
    super.onCreate(savedInstanceState);
    setContentView(R.layout.main);

    Gallery gallery = (Gallery) findViewById(R.id.gallery1);

    gallery.setAdapter(new ImageAdapter(this));
    gallery.setOnItemClickListener(new OnItemClickListener()
    {
        public void onItemClick(AdapterView<?> parent, View v,
        int position, long id)
        {
            Toast.makeText(getBaseContext(),
                    "pic" + (position + 1) + " selected",
                    Toast.LENGTH_SHORT).show();
        }
    });
}

public class ImageAdapter extends BaseAdapter
{
    private Context context;
    private int itemBackground;

    public ImageAdapter(Context c)
    {
        context = c;
        //---setting the style---
        TypedArray a = obtainStyledAttributes(R.styleable.Gallery1);
        itemBackground = a.getResourceId(
            R.styleable.Gallery1_android_galleryItemBackground, 0);
        a.recycle();
    }

    //---returns the number of images---
    public int getCount() {
        return imageIDs.length;
    }

    //---returns the ID of an item---
    public Object getItem(int position) {
        return position;
    }

     //---returns the ID of an item---
    public long getItemId(int position) {
        return position;
    }

    //---returns an ImageView view---
    public View getView(int position, View convertView, ViewGroup parent) {
        ImageView imageView = new ImageView(context);
        imageView.setImageResource(imageIDs[position]);
        imageView.setScaleType(ImageView.ScaleType.FIT_XY);
        imageView.setLayoutParams(new Gallery.LayoutParams(150, 120));
        imageView.setBackgroundResource(itemBackground);
```

```
            return imageView;
        }
    }
}
```

8. Press F11 to debug the application on the Android Emulator. Figure 5-5 shows the `Gallery` view displaying the series of images.

9. You can swipe the images to view the entire series of images. Observe that as you click on an image, the `Toast` class will display its name (see Figure 5-6).

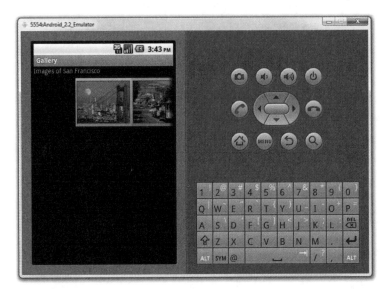

FIGURE 5-5

FIGURE 5-6

10. To display the selected image in the `ImageView`, add the following statements in bold to the `MainActivity.java` file:

```
/** Called when the activity is first created. */
@Override
public void onCreate(Bundle savedInstanceState) {
    super.onCreate(savedInstanceState);
    setContentView(R.layout.main);

    Gallery gallery = (Gallery) findViewById(R.id.gallery1);

    gallery.setAdapter(new ImageAdapter(this));
    gallery.setOnItemClickListener(new OnItemClickListener()
    {
        public void onItemClick(AdapterView<?> parent, View v,
        int position, long id)
        {
            Toast.makeText(getBaseContext(),
                    "pic" + (position + 1) + " selected",
                    Toast.LENGTH_SHORT).show();

            //---display the images selected---
            ImageView imageView = (ImageView) findViewById(R.id.image1);
            imageView.setImageResource(imageIDs[position]);
        }
    });
}
```

11. Press F11 to debug the application again. This time, you will see the image selected in the `ImageView` (see Figure 5-7).

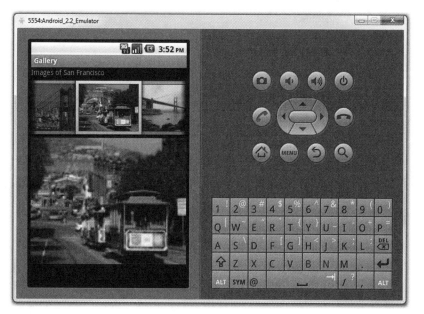

FIGURE 5-7

How It Works

You first add the `Gallery` and `ImageView` views to `main.xml`:

```
<Gallery
    android:id="@+id/gallery1"
    android:layout_width="fill_parent"
    android:layout_height="wrap_content" />

<ImageView
    android:id="@+id/image1"
    android:layout_width="320px"
    android:layout_height="250px"
    android:scaleType="fitXY" />
```

As mentioned earlier, the `Gallery` view is used to display the series of images in a horizontal scrolling list. The `ImageView` is used to display the image selected by the user.

The list of images to be displayed is stored in the `imageIDs` array:

```
//---the images to display---
Integer[] imageIDs = {
        R.drawable.pic1,
        R.drawable.pic2,
        R.drawable.pic3,
        R.drawable.pic4,
        R.drawable.pic5,
        R.drawable.pic6,
        R.drawable.pic7
};
```

You create the `ImageAdapter` class (which extends the `BaseAdapter` class) so that it can bind to the `Gallery` view with a series of `ImageView` views:

```
Gallery gallery = (Gallery) findViewById(R.id.gallery1);
gallery.setAdapter(new ImageAdapter(this));
gallery.setOnItemClickListener(new OnItemClickListener()
{
    public void onItemClick(AdapterView<?> parent, View v,
    int position, long id)
    {
        Toast.makeText(getBaseContext(),
                "pic" + (position + 1) + " selected",
                Toast.LENGTH_SHORT).show();

        //---display the images selected---
        ImageView imageView = (ImageView) findViewById(R.id.image1);
        imageView.setImageResource(imageIDs[position]);
    }
});
```

When an image in the `Gallery` view is selected (i.e., clicked), the position (0 for the first image, 1 for the second image, and so on) of the selected image is displayed and the image is displayed in the `ImageView`.

ImageSwitcher

The previous section demonstrated how to use the Gallery view together with an ImageView to display a series of thumbnail images so that when one is selected, the selected image is displayed in the ImageView. However, sometimes you don't want an image to appear abruptly when the user selects it in the Gallery view — you might, for example, want to apply some animation to the image when it transits from one image to another. In this case, you need to use the ImageSwitcher together with the Gallery view. The following Try It Out shows you how.

TRY IT OUT Using the ImageSwitcher View

codefile ImageSwitcher.zip available for download at Wrox.com

1. Using Eclipse, create a new Android project and name it as **ImageSwitcher**.

2. Modify the main.xml file by adding the following statements in bold:

```xml
<?xml version="1.0" encoding="utf-8"?>
<RelativeLayout xmlns:android="http://schemas.android.com/apk/res/android"
    android:orientation="vertical"
    android:layout_width="fill_parent"
    android:layout_height="fill_parent"
    android:background="#ff000000" >

<Gallery
    android:id="@+id/gallery1"
    android:layout_width="fill_parent"
    android:layout_height="wrap_content" />

<ImageSwitcher
    android:id="@+id/switcher1"
    android:layout_width="fill_parent"
    android:layout_height="fill_parent"
    android:layout_alignParentLeft="true"
    android:layout_alignParentRight="true"
    android:layout_alignParentBottom="true" />

</RelativeLayout>
```

3. Right-click on the res/values folder and select New ⇨ File. Name the file **attrs.xml**.

4. Populate the attrs.xml file as follows:

```xml
<?xml version="1.0" encoding="utf-8"?>
<resources>
    <declare-styleable name="Gallery1">
        <attr name="android:galleryItemBackground" />
    </declare-styleable>
</resources>
```

5. Drag and drop a series of images into the res/drawable-mdpi folder When a dialog is displayed, check the copy option and click OK.

6. Add the following bold statements to the `MainActivity.java` file:

```java
package net.learn2develop.ImageSwitcher;

import android.app.Activity;
import android.os.Bundle;

import android.content.Context;
import android.content.res.TypedArray;
import android.view.View;
import android.view.ViewGroup;
import android.view.ViewGroup.LayoutParams;
import android.view.animation.AnimationUtils;
import android.widget.BaseAdapter;
import android.widget.AdapterView;
import android.widget.AdapterView.OnItemClickListener;
import android.widget.Gallery;
import android.widget.ViewSwitcher.ViewFactory;
import android.widget.ImageSwitcher;
import android.widget.ImageView;

public class MainActivity extends Activity implements ViewFactory {
    //---the images to display---
    Integer[] imageIDs = {
            R.drawable.pic1,
            R.drawable.pic2,
            R.drawable.pic3,
            R.drawable.pic4,
            R.drawable.pic5,
            R.drawable.pic6,
            R.drawable.pic7
    };

    private ImageSwitcher imageSwitcher;

    /** Called when the activity is first created. */
    @Override
    public void onCreate(Bundle savedInstanceState) {
        super.onCreate(savedInstanceState);
        setContentView(R.layout.main);

        imageSwitcher = (ImageSwitcher) findViewById(R.id.switcher1);
        imageSwitcher.setFactory(this);
        imageSwitcher.setInAnimation(AnimationUtils.loadAnimation(this,
                android.R.anim.fade_in));
        imageSwitcher.setOutAnimation(AnimationUtils.loadAnimation(this,
                android.R.anim.fade_out));

        Gallery gallery = (Gallery) findViewById(R.id.gallery1);
        gallery.setAdapter(new ImageAdapter(this));
        gallery.setOnItemClickListener(new OnItemClickListener()
        {
            public void onItemClick(AdapterView<?> parent,
            View v, int position, long id)
            {
                imageSwitcher.setImageResource(imageIDs[position]);
```

```java
        }
    });
}

public View makeView()
{
    ImageView imageView = new ImageView(this);
    imageView.setBackgroundColor(0xFF000000);
    imageView.setScaleType(ImageView.ScaleType.FIT_CENTER);
    imageView.setLayoutParams(new
            ImageSwitcher.LayoutParams(
                    LayoutParams.FILL_PARENT,
                    LayoutParams.FILL_PARENT));
    return imageView;
}

public class ImageAdapter extends BaseAdapter
{
    private Context context;
    private int itemBackground;

    public ImageAdapter(Context c)
    {
        context = c;

        //---setting the style---
        TypedArray a = obtainStyledAttributes(R.styleable.Gallery1);
        itemBackground = a.getResourceId(
                R.styleable.Gallery1_android_galleryItemBackground, 0);
        a.recycle();
    }

    //---returns the number of images---
    public int getCount()
    {
        return imageIDs.length;
    }

    //---returns the ID of an item---
    public Object getItem(int position)
    {
        return position;
    }

    public long getItemId(int position)
    {
        return position;
    }

    //---returns an ImageView view---
    public View getView(int position, View convertView, ViewGroup parent)
    {
        ImageView imageView = new ImageView(context);

        imageView.setImageResource(imageIDs[position]);
```

```
            imageView.setScaleType(ImageView.ScaleType.FIT_XY);
            imageView.setLayoutParams(new Gallery.LayoutParams(150, 120));
            imageView.setBackgroundResource(itemBackground);

            return imageView;
        }
    }
}
```

7. Press F11 to debug the application on the Android Emulator. Figure 5-8 shows the `Gallery` and `ImageSwitcher` views, with both the collection of images as well as the image selected.

FIGURE 5-8

How It Works

The first thing you notice in this example is that the `MainActivity` not only extends `Activity`, but also implements `ViewFactory`. To use the `ImageSwitcher` view, you need to implement the `ViewFactory` interface, which creates the views for use with the `ImageSwitcher` view. For this, you need to implement the `makeView()` method:

```
public View makeView()
{
    ImageView imageView = new ImageView(this);
    imageView.setBackgroundColor(0xFF000000);
    imageView.setScaleType(ImageView.ScaleType.FIT_CENTER);
    imageView.setLayoutParams(new
            ImageSwitcher.LayoutParams(
                    LayoutParams.FILL_PARENT,
                    LayoutParams.FILL_PARENT));
    return imageView;
}
```

This method creates a new `View` to be added in the `ImageSwitcher` view.

Like the `Gallery` example in the previous section, you also implemented an `ImageAdapter` class so that it can bind to the `Gallery` view with a series of `ImageView` views.

In the `onCreate()` method, you get a reference to the `ImageSwitcher` view and set the animation, specifying how images should "fly" in and out of the view. Finally, when an image is selected from the `Gallery` view, the image is displayed in the `ImageSwitcher` view:

```
@Override
public void onCreate(Bundle savedInstanceState) {
    super.onCreate(savedInstanceState);
    setContentView(R.layout.main);

    imageSwitcher = (ImageSwitcher) findViewById(R.id.switcher1);
    imageSwitcher.setFactory(this);
    imageSwitcher.setInAnimation(AnimationUtils.loadAnimation(this,
            android.R.anim.fade_in));
    imageSwitcher.setOutAnimation(AnimationUtils.loadAnimation(this,
            android.R.anim.fade_out));

    Gallery gallery = (Gallery) findViewById(R.id.gallery1);
    gallery.setAdapter(new ImageAdapter(this));
    gallery.setOnItemClickListener(new OnItemClickListener()
    {
        public void onItemClick(AdapterView<?> parent,
        View v, int position, long id)
        {
            imageSwitcher.setImageResource(imageIDs[position]);
        }
    });
}
```

In this example, when an image is selected in the `Gallery` view, it will appear by "fading" in. When the next image is selected, the current image will fade out. If you want the image to slide in from the left and slide out to the right when another image is selected, try the following animation:

```
imageSwitcher.setInAnimation(AnimationUtils.loadAnimation(this,
        android.R.anim.slide_in_left));
imageSwitcher.setOutAnimation(AnimationUtils.loadAnimation(this,
        android.R.anim.slide_out_right));
```

Like the previous Try It Out, you also created the `ImageAdapter` class (which extends the `BaseAdapter` class) so that it can bind to the `Gallery` view with a series of `ImageView` views.

GridView

The `GridView` shows items in a two-dimensional scrolling grid. You can use the `GridView` together with an `ImageView` to display a series of images. The following Try It Out demonstrates how.

TRY IT OUT Using the GridView View

codefile Grid.zip available for download at Wrox.com

1. Using Eclipse, create a new Android project and name it **Grid**.

2. Drag and drop a series of images into the `res/drawable-mdpi` folder (see Figure 5-9). When a dialog is displayed, check the copy option and click OK.

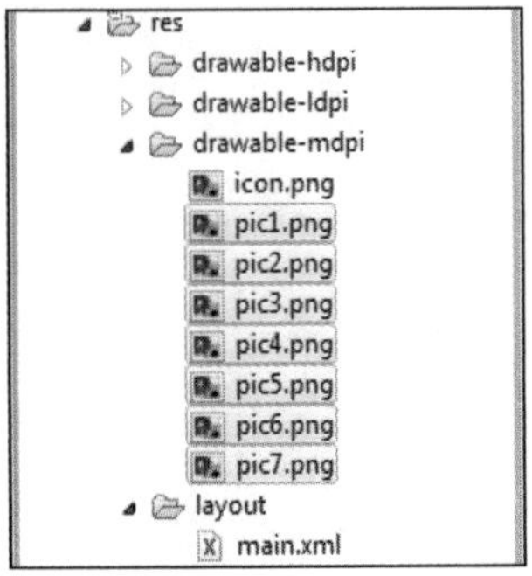

FIGURE 5-9

3. Populate the `main.xml` file with the following content:

```xml
<?xml version="1.0" encoding="utf-8"?>
<GridView xmlns:android="http://schemas.android.com/apk/res/android"
    android:id="@+id/gridview"
    android:layout_width="fill_parent"
    android:layout_height="fill_parent"
    android:numColumns="auto_fit"
    android:verticalSpacing="10dp"
    android:horizontalSpacing="10dp"
    android:columnWidth="90dp"
    android:stretchMode="columnWidth"
    android:gravity="center"
/>
```

4. Add the following statements in bold to the `MainActivity.java` file:

```java
package net.learn2develop.Grid;

import android.app.Activity;
import android.os.Bundle;

import android.content.Context;
import android.view.View;
import android.view.ViewGroup;
import android.widget.AdapterView;
import android.widget.AdapterView.OnItemClickListener;
import android.widget.BaseAdapter;
import android.widget.GridView;
import android.widget.ImageView;
import android.widget.Toast;

public class MainActivity extends Activity {
```

```java
//---the images to display---
Integer[] imageIDs = {
        R.drawable.pic1,
        R.drawable.pic2,
        R.drawable.pic3,
        R.drawable.pic4,
        R.drawable.pic5,
        R.drawable.pic6,
        R.drawable.pic7
};

/** Called when the activity is first created. */
@Override
public void onCreate(Bundle savedInstanceState) {
    super.onCreate(savedInstanceState);
    setContentView(R.layout.main);

    GridView gridView = (GridView) findViewById(R.id.gridview);
    gridView.setAdapter(new ImageAdapter(this));

    gridView.setOnItemClickListener(new OnItemClickListener()
    {
        public void onItemClick(AdapterView<?> parent,
        View v, int position, long id)
        {
            Toast.makeText(getBaseContext(),
                    "pic" + (position + 1) + " selected",
                    Toast.LENGTH_SHORT).show();
        }
    });
}

public class ImageAdapter extends BaseAdapter
{
    private Context context;

    public ImageAdapter(Context c)
    {
        context = c;
    }

    //---returns the number of images---
    public int getCount() {
        return imageIDs.length;
    }

    //---returns the ID of an item---
    public Object getItem(int position) {
        return position;
    }

    //---returns the ID of an item---
    public long getItemId(int position) {
        return position;
    }

    //---returns an ImageView view---
    public View getView(int position, View convertView,
```

```
ViewGroup parent)
{
    ImageView imageView;
    if (convertView == null) {
        imageView = new ImageView(context);
        imageView.setLayoutParams(new
            GridView.LayoutParams(85, 85));
        imageView.setScaleType(
            ImageView.ScaleType.CENTER_CROP);
        imageView.setPadding(5, 5, 5, 5);
    } else {
        imageView = (ImageView) convertView;
    }
    imageView.setImageResource(imageIDs[position]);
    return imageView;
}
}
}
```

5. Press F11 to debug the application on the Android Emulator. Figure 5-10 shows the `GridView` displaying all the images.

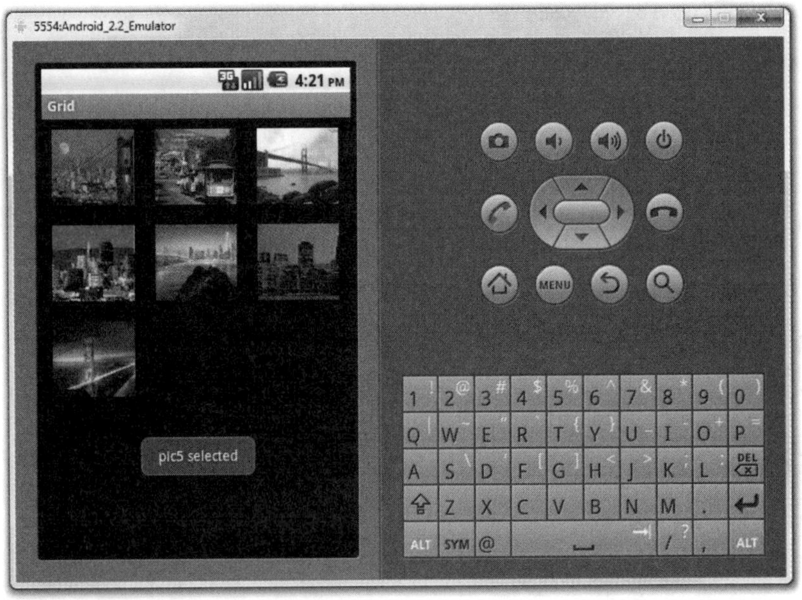

FIGURE 5-10

How It Works

Like the `Gallery` and `ImageSwitcher` example, you implement the `ImageAdapter` class and then bind it to the `GridView`:

```
GridView gridView = (GridView) findViewById(R.id.gridview);
gridView.setAdapter(new ImageAdapter(this));

gridView.setOnItemClickListener(new OnItemClickListener()
```

```
    {
        public void onItemClick(AdapterView<?> parent,
        View v, int position, long id)
        {
            Toast.makeText(getBaseContext(),
                    "pic" + (position + 1) + " selected",
                    Toast.LENGTH_SHORT).show();
        }
    });
```

When an image is selected, you display a Toast message indicating the image selected.

Within the GridView, you can specify the size of the images and how images are spaced out in the GridView by setting the padding for each image:

```
    //---returns an ImageView view---
    public View getView(int position, View convertView,
    ViewGroup parent)
    {
        ImageView imageView;
        if (convertView == null) {
            imageView = new ImageView(context);
            imageView.setLayoutParams(new
                GridView.LayoutParams(85, 85));
            imageView.setScaleType(
                ImageView.ScaleType.CENTER_CROP);
            imageView.setPadding(5, 5, 5, 5);
        } else {
            imageView = (ImageView) convertView;
        }
        imageView.setImageResource(imageIDs[position]);
        return imageView;
    }
```

USING MENUS WITH VIEWS

Menus are useful for displaying additional options that are not directly visible on the main UI of an application. There are two main types of menus in Android:

➤ **Options menu** — Displays information related to the current activity. In Android, you activate the options menu by pressing the MENU key.

➤ **Context menu** — Displays information related to a particular view on an activity. In Android, to activate a context menu you tap and hold on to it.

Figure 5-11 shows an example of an options menu in the browser application. The option menu is displayed whenever the user presses the MENU button. The menu items displayed vary according to the current activity that is running.

Figure 5-12 shows a context menu that is displayed when the user presses and holds on a hyperlink displayed on the page. The menu items displayed vary according to the component or view currently selected. To activate the context menu, the user selects an item on the screen and either taps and holds it or simply presses the center button on the directional keypad.

FIGURE 5-11   FIGURE 5-12

Creating the Helper Methods

Before you go ahead and create your options and context menus, you need to create two helper methods. One creates a list of items to show inside a menu, while the other handles the event that is fired when the user selects an item inside the menu.

TRY IT OUT Creating the Menu Helper Methods

codefile Menus.zip available for download at Wrox.com

1. Using Eclipse, create a new Android project and name it as **Menus**.

2. In the `MainActivity.java` file, add the following statements in bold:

```
package net.learn2develop.Menus;

import android.app.Activity;
import android.os.Bundle;

import android.view.Menu;
import android.view.MenuItem;
import android.widget.Button;
import android.widget.Toast;

public class MainActivity extends Activity {
    /** Called when the activity is first created. */
    @Override
    public void onCreate(Bundle savedInstanceState) {
        super.onCreate(savedInstanceState);
        setContentView(R.layout.main);
```

```
    }

    private void CreateMenu(Menu menu)
    {
        MenuItem mnu1 = menu.add(0, 0, 0, "Item 1");
        {
            mnu1.setAlphabeticShortcut('a');
            mnu1.setIcon(R.drawable.icon);
        }
        MenuItem mnu2 = menu.add(0, 1, 1, "Item 2");
        {
            mnu2.setAlphabeticShortcut('b');
            mnu2.setIcon(R.drawable.icon);
        }
        MenuItem mnu3 = menu.add(0, 2, 2, "Item 3");
        {
            mnu3.setAlphabeticShortcut('c');
            mnu3.setIcon(R.drawable.icon);
        }
        MenuItem mnu4 = menu.add(0, 3, 3, "Item 4");
        {
            mnu4.setAlphabeticShortcut('d');
        }
        menu.add(0, 3, 3, "Item 5");
        menu.add(0, 3, 3, "Item 6");
        menu.add(0, 3, 3, "Item 7");
    }

    private boolean MenuChoice(MenuItem item)
    {
        switch (item.getItemId()) {
        case 0:
            Toast.makeText(this, "You clicked on Item 1",
                Toast.LENGTH_LONG).show();
            return true;
        case 1:
            Toast.makeText(this, "You clicked on Item 2",
                Toast.LENGTH_LONG).show();
            return true;
        case 2:
            Toast.makeText(this, "You clicked on Item 3",
                Toast.LENGTH_LONG).show();
            return true;
        case 3:
            Toast.makeText(this, "You clicked on Item 4",
                Toast.LENGTH_LONG).show();
            return true;
        case 4:
            Toast.makeText(this, "You clicked on Item 5",
                Toast.LENGTH_LONG).show();
            return true;
        case 5:
            Toast.makeText(this, "You clicked on Item 6",
                Toast.LENGTH_LONG).show();
            return true;
```

```
            case 6:
                Toast.makeText(this, "You clicked on Item 7",
                    Toast.LENGTH_LONG).show();
                return true;
        }
        return false;
    }
}
```

How It Works

The preceding example creates two methods: CreateMenu() and MenuChoice(). The CreateMenu() method takes a Menu argument and adds a series of menu items to it.

To add a menu item to the menu, you create an instance of the MenuItem class and use the add() method of the Menu object.

```
MenuItem mnu1 = menu.add(0, 0, 0, "Item 1");
{
    mnu1.setAlphabeticShortcut('a');
    mnu1.setIcon(R.drawable.icon);
}
```

The four arguments of the add() method are as follows:

➤   groupId — The group identifier that the menu item should be part of. Use 0 if an item is not in a group.

➤   itemId — Unique item ID

➤   order — The order in which the item should be displayed

➤   title — The text to display for the menu item

You can use the setAlphabeticShortcut() method to assign a shortcut key to the menu item so that users can select an item by pressing a key on the keyboard. The setIcon() method sets an image to be displayed on the menu item.

The MenuChoice() method takes a MenuItem argument and checks its ID to determine the menu item that is clicked. It then displays a Toast message to let the user know which menu item was clicked.

Options Menu

You are now ready to modify the application to display the options menu when the user presses the MENU button on the Android device.

TRY IT OUT   Displaying an Options Menu

1.   Using the same project created in the previous section, add the following statements in bold to the MainActivity.java file:

```
package net.learn2develop.Menus;

import android.app.Activity;
```

```
import android.os.Bundle;
import android.view.Menu;
import android.view.MenuItem;
import android.widget.Button;
import android.widget.Toast;

public class MainActivity extends Activity {
    /** Called when the activity is first created. */
    @Override
    public void onCreate(Bundle savedInstanceState) {
        super.onCreate(savedInstanceState);
        setContentView(R.layout.main);
    }

    @Override
    public boolean onCreateOptionsMenu(Menu menu) {
        super.onCreateOptionsMenu(menu);
        CreateMenu(menu);
        return true;
    }

    @Override
    public boolean onOptionsItemSelected(MenuItem item)
    {
        return MenuChoice(item);
    }

    private void CreateMenu(Menu menu)
    {
        //...
    }

    private boolean MenuChoice(MenuItem item)
    {
        //...
    }
}
```

2. Press F11 to debug the application on the Android Emulator. Figure 5-13 shows the options menu that pops up when you click the MENU button. To select a menu item, either click on an individual item or use its shortcut key (A to D; applicable only to the first four items).

How It Works

To display the options menu for your activity, you need to override two methods in your activity: onCreateOptionsMenu() and onOptionsItemSelected(). The onCreateOptionsMenu() method is called when the MENU button is pressed. In this event, you call the CreateMenu() helper method to display the options menu. When a menu item is selected, the onOptionsItemSelected() method is called. In this case, you call the MenuChoice() method to display the menu item selected (and do whatever you want to do).

Observe the icons displayed for menu items 1, 2, and 3. Also, if the options menu has more than six items, a "More" menu item will be displayed to indicate the additional options. Figure 5-14 shows the additional menu items displayed as a list, after the user has pressed the More menu item.

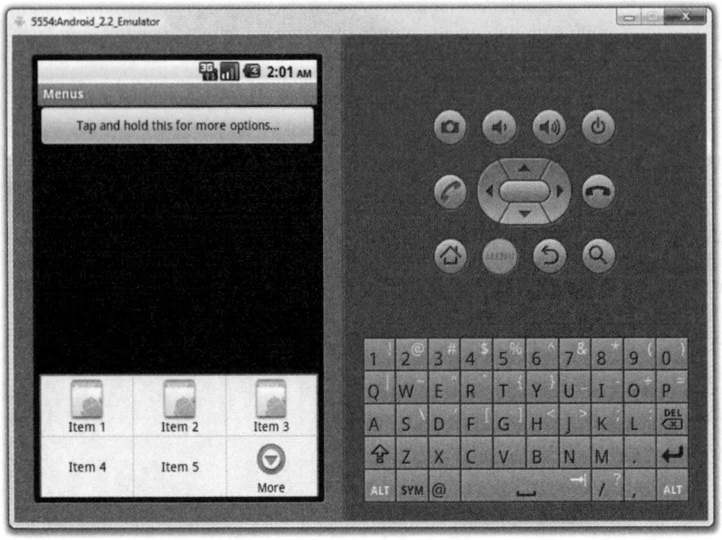

FIGURE 5-13

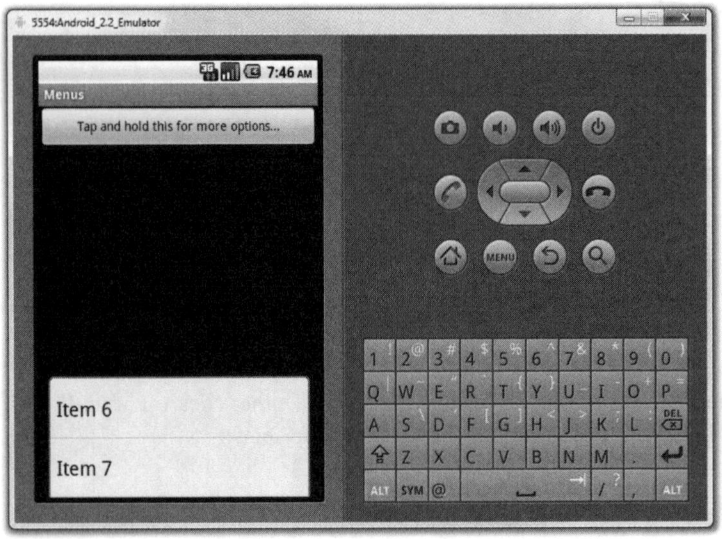

FIGURE 5-14

Context Menu

The previous section showed how the options menu is displayed when the user presses the MENU button. Besides the options menu, you can also display a context menu. A context menu is usually associated with a view on an activity, and it is displayed when the user long clicks an item. For example, if the user taps on a `Button` view and hold it for a few seconds, a context menu can be displayed.

If you want to associate a context menu with a view on an activity, you need to call the setOnCreateContextMenuListener() method of that particular view. The following Try It Out shows how you can associate a context menu with a Button view.

TRY IT OUT Displaying a Context Menu

1. Using the same project created in the previous section, add the following statements in bold to the MainActivity.java file:

```java
package net.learn2develop.Menus;

import android.app.Activity;
import android.os.Bundle;
import android.view.Menu;
import android.view.MenuItem;
import android.widget.Button;
import android.widget.Toast;

import android.view.View;
import android.view.ContextMenu;
import android.view.ContextMenu.ContextMenuInfo;

public class MainActivity extends Activity {
    /** Called when the activity is first created. */
    @Override
    public void onCreate(Bundle savedInstanceState) {
        super.onCreate(savedInstanceState);
        setContentView(R.layout.main);

        Button btn = (Button) findViewById(R.id.btn1);
        btn.setOnCreateContextMenuListener(this);
    }

    @Override
    public boolean onCreateOptionsMenu(Menu menu) {
        super.onCreateOptionsMenu(menu);
        CreateMenu(menu);
        return true;
    }

    @Override
    public boolean onOptionsItemSelected(MenuItem item)
    {
        return MenuChoice(item);
    }

    @Override
    public void onCreateContextMenu(ContextMenu menu, View view,
    ContextMenuInfo menuInfo)
    {
        super.onCreateContextMenu(menu, view, menuInfo);
        CreateMenu(menu);
    }

    @Override
```

```
public boolean onContextItemSelected(MenuItem item)
{
    return MenuChoice(item);
}

private void CreateMenu(Menu menu)
{
    //...
}

private boolean MenuChoice(MenuItem item)
{
    //...
}
}
```

2. Press F11 to debug the application on the Android Emulator. Figure 5-15 shows the context menu that is displayed when you long-click the Button view.

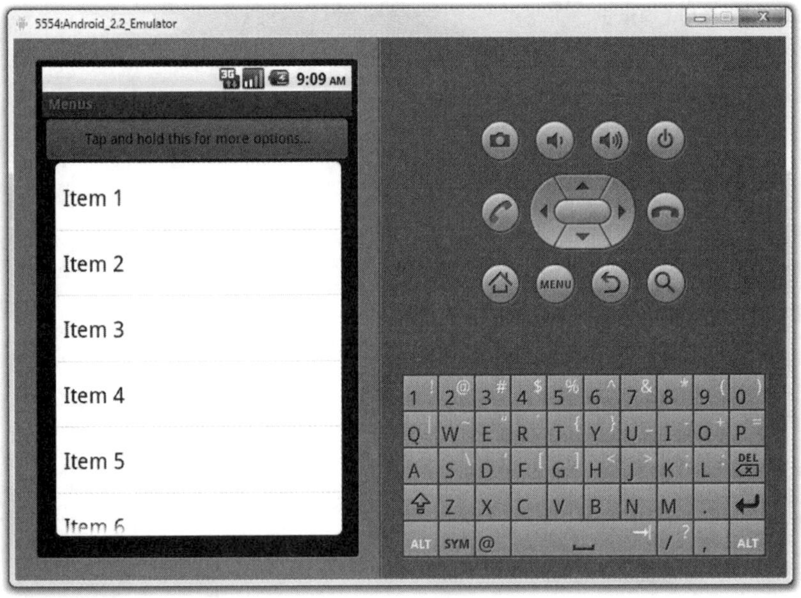

FIGURE 5-15

How It Works

In the preceding example, you call the setOnCreateContextMenuListener() method of the Button view to associate it with a context menu.

When the user long-clicks the Button view, the onCreateContextMenu() method is called. In this method, you call the CreateMenu() method to display the context menu. Similarly, when an item inside the context menu is selected, the `onContextItemSelected()` method is called, where you call the `MenuChoice()` method to display a message to the user.

Notice that the shortcut keys for the menu items do not work. To enable the shortcuts keys, you need to call the `setQuertyMode()` method of the `Menu` object, like this:

```
private void CreateMenu(Menu menu)
{
    menu.setQwertyMode(true);
    MenuItem mnu1 = menu.add(0, 0, 0, "Item 1");
    {
        mnu1.setAlphabeticShortcut('d');
        mnu1.setIcon(R.drawable.icon);
    }
    //...
}
```

Doing so will enable the shortcut key (see Figure 5-16).

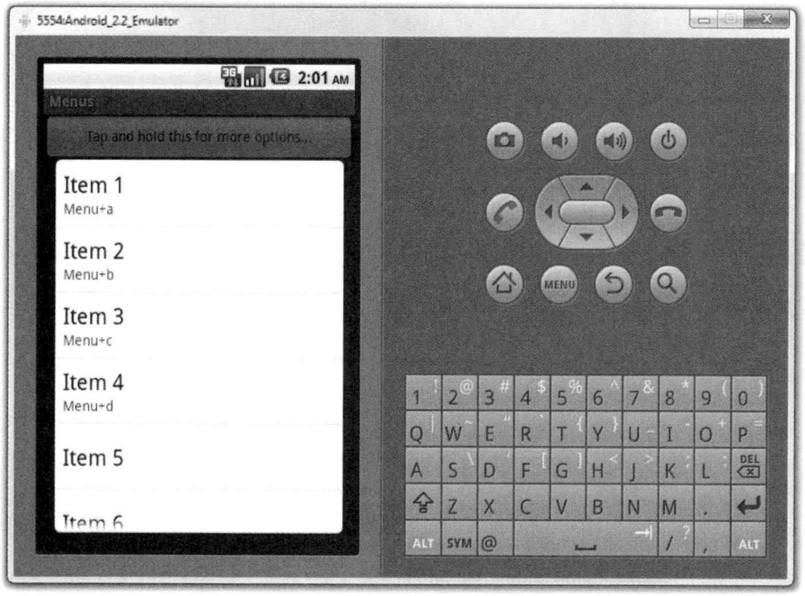

FIGURE 5-16

SOME ADDITIONAL VIEWS

Besides the standard views that you have seen up to this point, the Android SDK provides some additional views that make your applications much more interesting. In this section, you will learn more about the following views: `AnalogClock`, `DigitalClock`, and `WebView`.

AnalogClock and DigitalClock Views

The `AnalogClock` view displays an analog clock with two hands — one for minutes and one for hours. Its counterpart, the `DigitalClock` view, displays the time digitally. Both display the system time, and do not allow you to display a particular time. Hence, if you want to display the time for a particular region, you have to build your own custom views.

> **NOTE** *Creating your own custom views in Android is beyond the scope of this book. However, if you are interested in this area, take a look at Google's Android documentation on this topic at:* `http://developer.android.com/guide/topics/ui/custom-components.html.`

Using the `AnalogClock` and `DigitalClock` views are straightforward; simply declare them in your XML file (such as `main.xml`), like this:

```xml
<?xml version="1.0" encoding="utf-8"?>
<LinearLayout xmlns:android="http://schemas.android.com/apk/res/android"
    android:orientation="vertical"
    android:layout_width="fill_parent"
    android:layout_height="fill_parent"
    >
<AnalogClock
    android:layout_width="wrap_content"
    android:layout_height="wrap_content" />

<DigitalClock
    android:layout_width="wrap_content"
    android:layout_height="wrap_content" />

</LinearLayout>
```

Figure 5-17 shows the `AnalogClock` and `DigitalClock` views in action.

WebView

The `WebView` enables you to embed a web browser in your activity. This is very useful if your application needs to embed some web content, such as maps from some other providers, and so on. The following Try It Out shows how you can programmatically load the content of a web page and display it in your activity.

TRY IT OUT Using the WebView View

codefile WebView.zip available for download at Wrox.com

1. Using Eclipse, create a new Android project and name it as **WebView**.

FIGURE 5-17

2. Add the following statements to the `main.xml` file:

```xml
<?xml version="1.0" encoding="utf-8"?>
<LinearLayout xmlns:android="http://schemas.android.com/apk/res/android"
    android:orientation="vertical"
    android:layout_width="fill_parent"
    android:layout_height="fill_parent"
    >

<WebView android:id="@+id/webview1"
    android:layout_width="wrap_content"
    android:layout_height="wrap_content" />

</LinearLayout>
```

3. In the `MainActivity.java` file, add the following statements in bold:

```java
package net.learn2develop.WebView;

import android.app.Activity;
import android.os.Bundle;
import android.webkit.WebSettings;
import android.webkit.WebView;

public class MainActivity extends Activity {
    /** Called when the activity is first created. */
    @Override
    public void onCreate(Bundle savedInstanceState) {
        super.onCreate(savedInstanceState);
```

```
        setContentView(R.layout.main);

        WebView wv = (WebView) findViewById(R.id.webview1);
        WebSettings webSettings = wv.getSettings();
        webSettings.setBuiltInZoomControls(true);
        wv.loadUrl(
            "http://ecx.images-amazon.com/images/I/41HGB-W2Z8L._SL500_AA300_.jpg");
    }
}
```

4. Press F11 to debug the application on the Android Emulator. Figure 5-18 shows the content of the WebView.

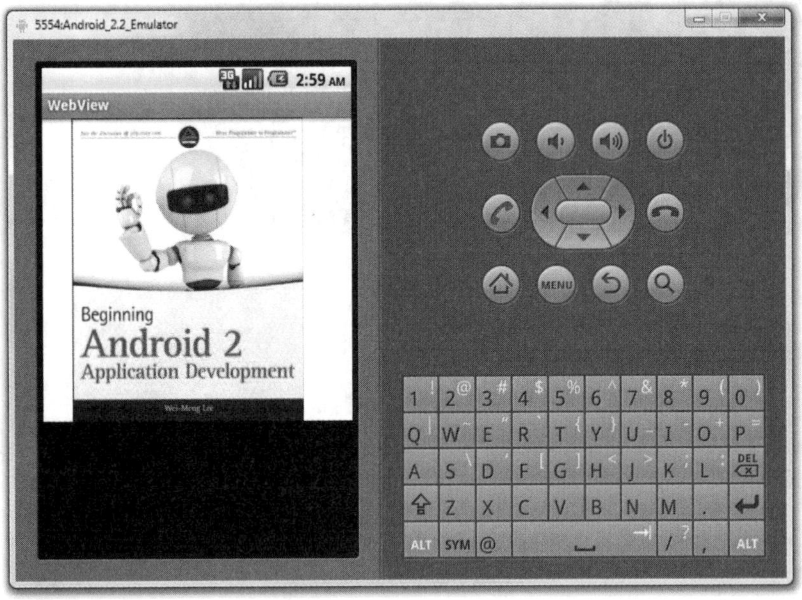

FIGURE 5-18

How It Works

To use the WebView to load a web page, you use the loadUrl() method, like this:

```
wv.loadUrl(
    "http://ecx.images-amazon.com/images/I/41HGB-W2Z8L._SL500_AA300_.jpg");
```

To display the built-in zoom controls, you need to first get the WebSettings property from the WebView and then call its setBuiltInZoomControls() method:

```
WebSettings webSettings = wv.getSettings();
webSettings.setBuiltInZoomControls(true);
```

Figure 5-19 shows the built-in zoom controls that appear when you use the mouse to click and drag the content of the WebView on the Android Emulator.

NOTE *While most Android devices support multi-touch screens, the built-in zoom controls are useful for zooming your web content when testing your application on the Android Emulator.*

Sometimes when you load a page that redirects you (such as loading www.wrox.com redirects you to www.wrox.com/wileyCDA), WebView will cause your application to launch the device's browser application to load the desired page. For example, if you ask the WebView to load www.wrox.com, Wrox.com will automatically redirect you to www.wrox.com/WileyCDA/. In this case, your application will automatically launch the device's browser application to load your page. In Figure 5-20, note the URL bar at the top of the screen.

To prevent this from happening, you need to implement the WebViewClient class and override the shouldOverrideUrlLoading() method, as shown in the following example:

FIGURE 5-19

```
package net.learn2develop.WebView;

import android.app.Activity;
import android.os.Bundle;
import android.webkit.WebSettings;
import android.webkit.WebView;
import android.webkit.WebViewClient;

public class MainActivity extends Activity {
    /** Called when the activity is first created. */
    @Override
    public void onCreate(Bundle savedInstanceState) {
        super.onCreate(savedInstanceState);
        setContentView(R.layout.main);

        WebView wv = (WebView) findViewById(R.id.webview1);
        wv.setWebViewClient(new Callback());
        WebSettings webSettings = wv.getSettings();
        webSettings.setBuiltInZoomControls(true);
        wv.loadUrl("http://www.wrox.com");
    }

    private class Callback extends WebViewClient {
        @Override
        public boolean shouldOverrideUrlLoading(WebView view, String url) {
            return(false);
        }
    }
}
```

Figure 5-21 shows the Wrox.com home page now loading correctly in the WebView.

FIGURE 5-20

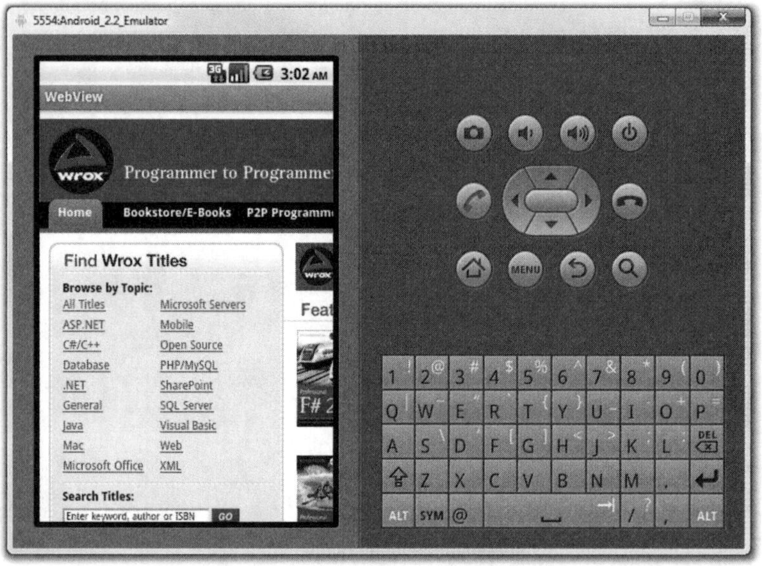

FIGURE 5-21

You can also dynamically formulate an HTML string and load it into the WebView, using the loadDataWithBaseURL() method:

```
WebView wv = (WebView) findViewById(R.id.webview1);
final String mimeType = "text/html";
final String encoding = "UTF-8";
```

```
String html = "<H1>A simple HTML page</H1><body>" +
    "<p>The quick brown fox jumps over the lazy dog</p>";
wv.loadDataWithBaseURL("", html, mimeType, encoding, "");
```

Figure 5-22 shows the content displayed by the WebView.

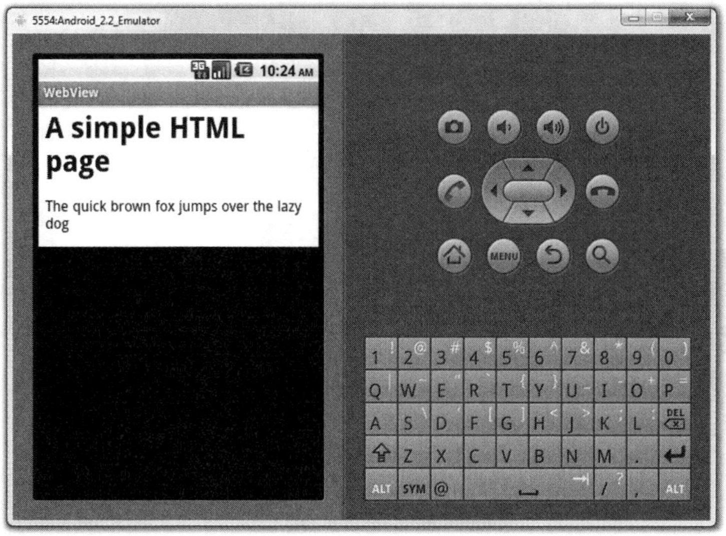

FIGURE 5-22

Alternatively, if you have an HTML file located in the assets folder (see Figure 5-23), you can also load it into the WebView using the loadUrl() method:

```
WebView wv = (WebView) findViewById(R.id.webview1);
wv.loadUrl("file:///android_asset/Index.html");
```

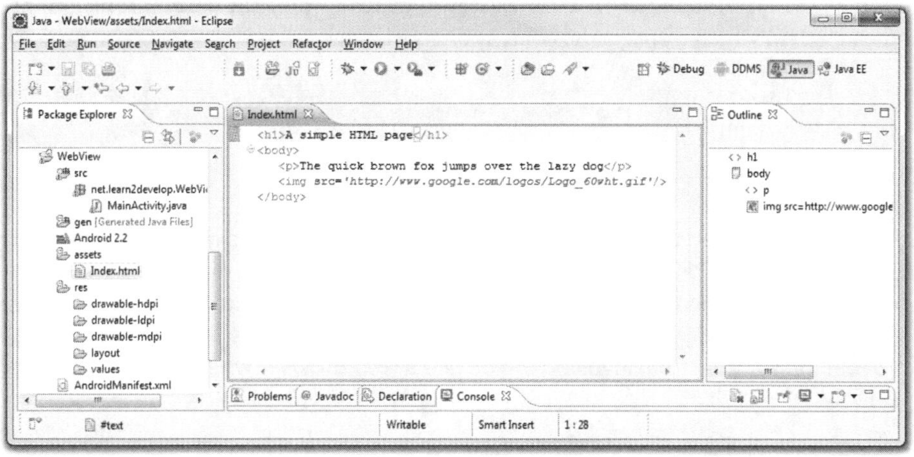

FIGURE 5-23

Figure 5-24 shows the content of the WebView.

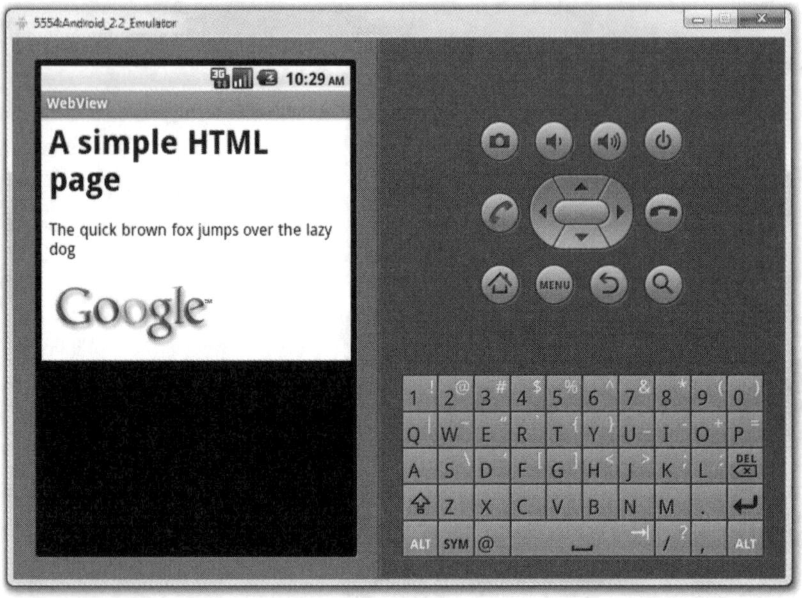

FIGURE 5-24

SUMMARY

In this chapter, you have taken a look at the various views that enable you to display images: Gallery, ImageView, ImageSwitcher, and GridView. In addition, you learned about the difference between options menus and context menus, and how to display them in your application. Finally, you learned about the AnalogClock and DigitalClock views, which display the current time graphically, as well as the WebView, which displays the content of a web page.

EXERCISES

1. What is the purpose of the ImageSwitcher?

2. Name the two methods you need to override when implementing an options menu in your activity.

3. Name the two methods you need to override when implementing a context menu in your activity.

4. How do you prevent the WebView from invoking the device's web browser when a redirection occurs in the WebView?

Answers to the Exercises can be found in Appendix C.

▶ WHAT YOU LEARNED IN THIS CHAPTER

TOPIC	KEY CONCEPTS
Use of the Gallery View	Displays a series of images in a horizontal scrolling list

Gallery	```<Gallery```
	``` android:id="@+id/gallery1"```
	``` android:layout_width="fill_parent"```
	``` android:layout_height="wrap_content" />```

ImageView	```<ImageView```
	``` android:id="@+id/image1"```
	``` android:layout_width="320px"```
	``` android:layout_height="250px"```
	``` android:scaleType="fitXY" />```

Use of the ImageSwitcher view	Performs animation when switching between images

ImageSwitcher	```<ImageSwitcher```
	``` android:id="@+id/switcher1"```
	``` android:layout_width="fill_parent"```
	``` android:layout_height="fill_parent"```
	``` android:layout_alignParentLeft="true"```
	``` android:layout_alignParentRight="true"```
	``` android:layout_alignParentBottom="true" />```

Use of the GridView	Shows items in a two-dimensional scrolling grid

GridView	```<GridView xmlns:android="http://schemas.android.com/apk/res/android"```
	``` android:id="@+id/gridview"```
	``` android:layout_width="fill_parent"```
	``` android:layout_height="fill_parent"```
	``` android:numColumns="auto_fit"```
	``` android:verticalSpacing="10dp"```
	``` android:horizontalSpacing="10dp"```
	``` android:columnWidth="90dp"```
	``` android:stretchMode="columnWidth"```
	``` android:gravity="center" />```

AnalogClock	```<AnalogClock```
	``` android:layout_width="wrap_content"```
	``` android:layout_height="wrap_content" />```

DigitalClock	```<DigitalClock```
	``` android:layout_width="wrap_content"```
	``` android:layout_height="wrap_content" />```

WebView	```<WebView android:id="@+id/webview1"```
	``` android:layout_width="wrap_content"```
	``` android:layout_height="wrap_content" />```

6

Data Persistence

WHAT YOU WILL LEARN IN THIS CHAPTER

➤ How to save simple data using the `SharedPreferences` object

➤ How to write and read files in internal and external storage

➤ How to create and use a SQLite database

In this chapter, you will learn how to persist data in your Android applications. Persisting data is an important topic in application development, as users expect to reuse the data sometime at a later stage. For Android, there are primarily three basic ways of persisting data:

A lightweight mechanism known as *shared preferences* to save small chunks of data

➤ Traditional file systems

➤ A relational database management system through the support of SQLite databases

The techniques discussed in this chapter enable applications to create and access their own private data. In the next chapter you'll learn how you can share data across applications.

SAVING AND LOADING USER PREFERENCES

Android provides the `SharedPreferences` object to help you save simple application data. For example, your application may have an option to allow users to specify the font size of the text displayed in your application. In this case, your application needs to remember the size set by the user so that the next time he or she uses the application again, your application can set the size appropriately. In order to do so, you have several options. You can save the data to a file, but you have to perform some file management routines, such as writing the data to the file, indicating how many characters to read from it, and so on. Also, if you have several pieces of information to save, such as text size, font name, preferred background color, and so on, then the task of writing to a file becomes more onerous.

An alternative to writing to a text file is to use a database, but saving simple data to a database is over-kill, both from a developer's point of view and in terms of the application's run-time performance.

Using the `SharedPreferences` object, however, you save the data you want through the use of key/value pairs — specify a key for the data you want to save, and then both it and its value will be saved automatically to an XML file for you.

Using getSharedPreferences()

To see how the `SharedPreferences` object works, the following Try It Out demonstrates how easy it is to save user data to an XML file, and then retrieve it easily via the same object.

TRY IT OUT   **Saving Data Using the SharedPreferences Object**

codefile SharedPreferences.zip available for download at Wrox.com

1.   Using Eclipse, create an Android project and name it as shown in Figure 6-1.

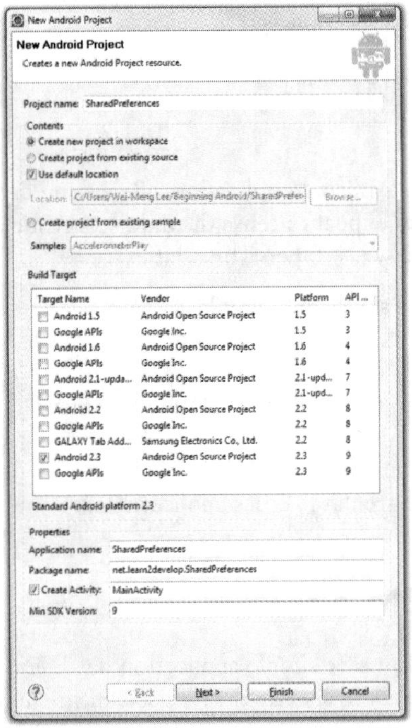

FIGURE 6-1

2.   Add the following statements in bold to the `main.xml` file:

```xml
<?xml version="1.0" encoding="utf-8"?>
<LinearLayout xmlns:android="http://schemas.android.com/apk/res/android"
    android:orientation="vertical"
```

```xml
        android:layout_width="fill_parent"
        android:layout_height="fill_parent" >
<SeekBar
    android:id="@+id/SeekBar01"
    android:layout_width="fill_parent"
    android:layout_height="wrap_content" />
<TextView
    android:id="@+id/TextView01"
    android:layout_width="fill_parent"
    android:layout_height="wrap_content"
    android:text="@string/hello" />
<EditText
    android:id="@+id/EditText01"
    android:layout_width="fill_parent"
    android:layout_height="wrap_content" />
<Button
    android:id="@+id/btnSave"
    android:text="Save"
    android:layout_width="wrap_content"
    android:layout_height="wrap_content" />
</LinearLayout>
```

3. Add the following statements in bold to the MainActivity.java file:

```java
package net.learn2develop.SharedPreferences;

import android.app.Activity;
import android.os.Bundle;

import android.content.SharedPreferences;
import android.view.View;
import android.widget.Button;
import android.widget.EditText;
import android.widget.SeekBar;
import android.widget.SeekBar.OnSeekBarChangeListener;
import android.widget.Toast;

public class MainActivity extends Activity {
    private SharedPreferences prefs;
    private String prefName = "MyPref";
    private EditText editText;
    private SeekBar seekBar;
    private Button btn;

    private static final String FONT_SIZE_KEY = "fontsize";
    private static final String TEXT_VALUE_KEY = "textvalue";

    /** Called when the activity is first created. */
    @Override
    public void onCreate(Bundle savedInstanceState) {
        super.onCreate(savedInstanceState);
        setContentView(R.layout.main);

        editText = (EditText) findViewById(R.id.EditText01);
        seekBar = (SeekBar) findViewById(R.id.SeekBar01);
```

```
        btn = (Button) findViewById(R.id.btnSave);

        btn.setOnClickListener(new View.OnClickListener() {
            public void onClick(View v) {
                //---get the SharedPreferences object---
                prefs = getSharedPreferences(prefName, MODE_PRIVATE);
                SharedPreferences.Editor editor = prefs.edit();

                //---save the values in the EditText view to preferences---
                editor.putFloat(FONT_SIZE_KEY, editText.getTextSize());
                editor.putString(TEXT_VALUE_KEY, editText.getText().toString());

                //---saves the values---
                editor.commit();

                //---display file saved message---
                Toast.makeText(getBaseContext(),
                    "Font size saved successfully!",
                    Toast.LENGTH_SHORT).show();
            }
        });

        //---load the SharedPreferences object---
        SharedPreferences prefs = getSharedPreferences(prefName, MODE_PRIVATE);

        //---set the TextView font size to the previously saved values---
        float fontSize = prefs.getFloat(FONT_SIZE_KEY, 12);

        //---init the SeekBar and EditText---
        seekBar.setProgress((int) fontSize);
        editText.setText(prefs.getString(TEXT_VALUE_KEY, ""));
        editText.setTextSize(seekBar.getProgress());

        seekBar.setOnSeekBarChangeListener(new OnSeekBarChangeListener() {
            @Override
            public void onStopTrackingTouch(SeekBar seekBar) {
            }

            @Override
            public void onStartTrackingTouch(SeekBar seekBar) {
            }

            @Override
            public void onProgressChanged(SeekBar seekBar, int progress,
                    boolean fromUser) {
                //---change the font size of the EditText---
                editText.setTextSize(progress);
            }
        });
    }
}
```

4. Press F11 to debug the application on the Android Emulator.

5. Enter some text into the EditText view and then change its font size by adjusting the SeekBar view (see Figure 6-2). Click Save.

FIGURE 6-2

6. Return to Eclipse and press F11 to debug the application on the Android Emulator again. The application now displays the same text that you entered earlier using the same font size set earlier.

How It Works

To use the SharedPreferences object, you use the getSharedPreferences() method, passing it the name of the shared preferences file (in which all the data will be saved), as well as the mode in which it should be opened:

```
private SharedPreferences prefs;
...
        //---get the SharedPreferences object---
        prefs = getSharedPreferences(prefName, MODE_PRIVATE);
        SharedPreferences.Editor editor = prefs.edit();
```

The MODE_PRIVATE constant indicates that the shared preference file can only be opened by the application that created it. The Editor class allows you to save key/value pairs to the preferences file by exposing methods such as the following:

➤ putString()

➤ putBoolean()

➤ putLong()

➤   `putInt()`

➤   `putFloat()`

When you are done saving the values, call the `commit()` method to save the changes:

```
//---save the values in the EditText view to preferences---
editor.putFloat(FONT_SIZE_KEY, editText.getTextSize());
editor.putString(TEXT_VALUE_KEY, editText.getText().toString());

//---saves the values---
editor.commit();
```

When the activity is loaded, you first obtain the `SharedPreferences` object and then retrieve all the values saved earlier:

```
//---load the SharedPreferences object---
SharedPreferences prefs = getSharedPreferences(prefName, MODE_PRIVATE);

//---set the TextView font size to the previously saved values---
float fontSize = prefs.getFloat(FONT_SIZE_KEY, 12);

//---init the SeekBar and EditText---
seekBar.setProgress((int) fontSize);
editText.setText(prefs.getString(TEXT_VALUE_KEY, ""));
editText.setTextSize(seekBar.getProgress());
```

The shared preferences file is saved as an XML file in the `/data/data/<package_name>/shared_prefs` folder (see Figure 6-3).

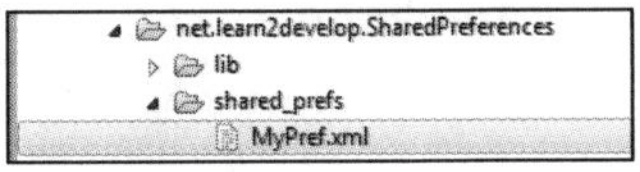

Its content is shown here (formatted for clarity):

FIGURE 6-3

```
<?xml version='1.0' encoding='utf-8' standalone='yes' ?>
<map>
    <string name="textvalue">This is so cool!</string>
    <float name="fontsize" value="75.0" />
</map>
```

Using getPreferences()

In the previous section, you used the used the `SharedPreferences` object by supplying it with a name, like this:

```
//---get the SharedPreferences object---
prefs = getSharedPreferences(prefName, MODE_PRIVATE);
```

In this case, the information saved inside the `SharedPreferences` object is visible to all the activities within the same application. However, if you don't need to share the data between activities, you can use the `getPreferences()` method, like this:

```
//---get the SharedPreferences object---
prefs = getPreferences(MODE_PRIVATE);
```

The `getPreferences()` method does not require a name, and the data saved is restricted to the activity that created it. In this case, the file-name used for the preferences file will be named after the activity that created it (see Figure 6-4).

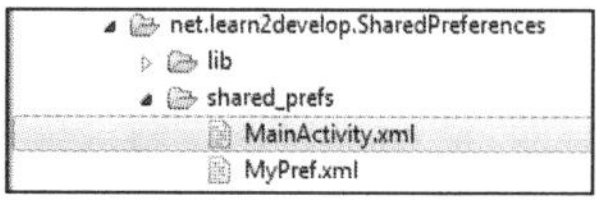

FIGURE 6-4

PERSISTING DATA TO FILES

The `SharedPreferences` object allows you to store data that could best be stored as key/value pairs, for example, data such as user ID, birthdate, gender, driving license number, etc. However, sometimes you might prefer to use the traditional file system to store your data. For example, you might want to store text of poems that you want to display in your applications. In Android, you can use the classes in the `java.io` namespace to do so.

Saving to Internal Storage

The first way to save files in your Android application is to write to the device's internal storage. The following Try It Out demonstrates how to save a string entered by the user to the device's internal storage.

TRY IT OUT Saving Data to Internal Storage

codefile Files.zip available for download at Wrox.com

1. Using Eclipse, create an Android project and name it as shown in Figure 6-5.

2. In the `main.xml` file, add the following statements in bold:

```xml
<?xml version="1.0" encoding="utf-8"?>
<LinearLayout xmlns:android="http://schemas.android.com/apk/res/android"
    android:orientation="vertical"
    android:layout_width="fill_parent"
    android:layout_height="fill_parent" >
<TextView
    android:layout_width="fill_parent"
    android:layout_height="wrap_content"
    android:text="Please enter some text"
    />
<EditText
    android:id="@+id/txtText1"
    android:layout_width="fill_parent"
    android:layout_height="wrap_content" />
<Button
    android:id="@+id/btnSave"
    android:text="Save"
    android:layout_width="fill_parent"
    android:layout_height="wrap_content" />
<Button
    android:id="@+id/btnLoad"
    android:text="Load"
    android:layout_width="fill_parent"
    android:layout_height="wrap_content" />
</LinearLayout>
```

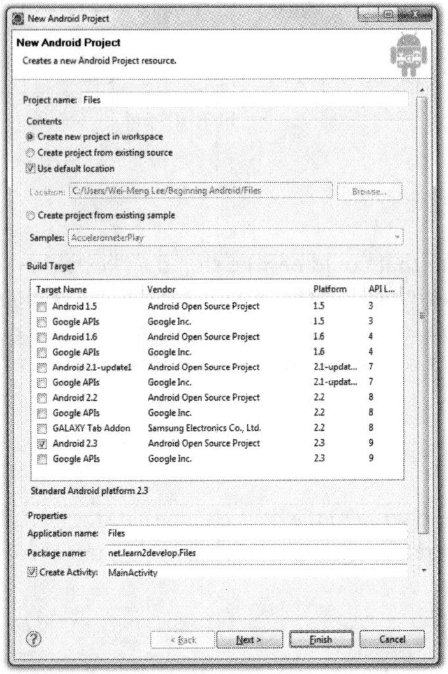

FIGURE 6-5

3. In the `MainActivity.java` file, add the following statements in bold:

```
package net.learn2develop.Files;

import android.app.Activity;
import android.view.View;

import java.io.FileInputStream;
import java.io.FileOutputStream;
import java.io.IOException;
import java.io.InputStreamReader;
import java.io.OutputStreamWriter;
import android.os.Bundle;
import android.widget.Button;
import android.widget.EditText;
import android.widget.Toast;

public class MainActivity extends Activity {
    private EditText textBox;
    private static final int READ_BLOCK_SIZE = 100;

    /** Called when the activity is first created. */
    @Override
    public void onCreate(Bundle savedInstanceState) {
        super.onCreate(savedInstanceState);
        setContentView(R.layout.main);

        textBox = (EditText) findViewById(R.id.txtText1);
```

```java
Button saveBtn = (Button) findViewById(R.id.btnSave);
Button loadBtn = (Button) findViewById(R.id.btnLoad);

saveBtn.setOnClickListener(new View.OnClickListener() {
    public void onClick(View v) {
        String str = textBox.getText().toString();
        try
        {
            FileOutputStream fOut =
                openFileOutput("textfile.txt",
                MODE_WORLD_READABLE);
            OutputStreamWriter osw = new
                OutputStreamWriter(fOut);

            //---write the string to the file---
            osw.write(str);
            osw.flush();
            osw.close();

            //---display file saved message---
            Toast.makeText(getBaseContext(),
                "File saved successfully!",
                Toast.LENGTH_SHORT).show();

            //---clears the EditText---
            textBox.setText("");
        }
        catch (IOException ioe)
        {
            ioe.printStackTrace();
        }
    }
});

loadBtn.setOnClickListener(new View.OnClickListener() {
    public void onClick(View v) {
        try
        {
            FileInputStream fIn =
                openFileInput("textfile.txt");
            InputStreamReader isr = new
                InputStreamReader(fIn);

            char[] inputBuffer = new char[READ_BLOCK_SIZE];
            String s = "";

            int charRead;
            while ((charRead = isr.read(inputBuffer))>0)
            {
                //---convert the chars to a String---
                String readString =
                    String.copyValueOf(inputBuffer, 0,
                    charRead);
                s += readString;

                inputBuffer = new char[READ_BLOCK_SIZE];
```

```
                            }
                            //---set the EditText to the text that has been
                            // read---
                            textBox.setText(s);

                            Toast.makeText(getBaseContext(),
                                "File loaded successfully!",
                                Toast.LENGTH_SHORT).show();
                        }
                        catch (IOException ioe) {
                            ioe.printStackTrace();
                        }
                    }
                });
            }
        }
```

4. Press F11 to debug the application on the Android Emulator.

5. Type some text into the EditText view (see Figure 6-6) and then click the Save button.

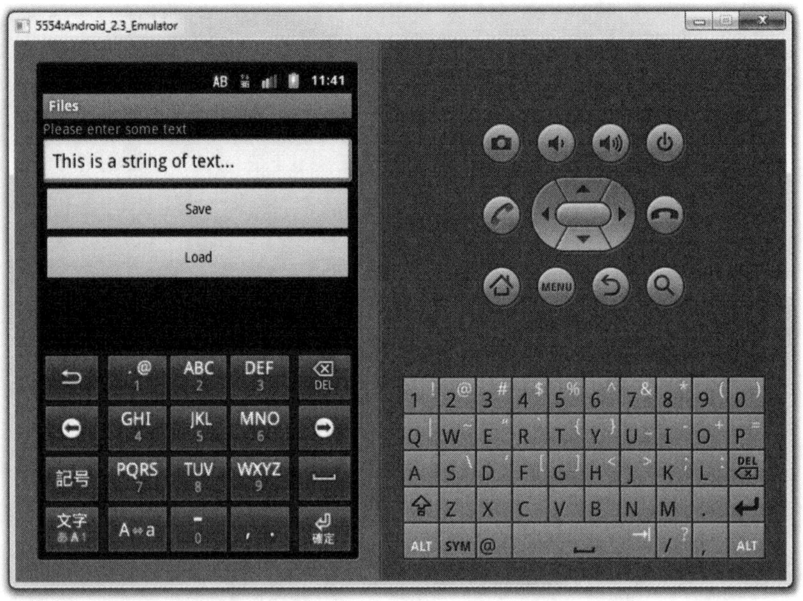

FIGURE 6-6

6. If the file is saved successfully, you will see the Toast class displaying the "File saved successfully!" message. The text in the EditText view should disappear.

7. Click the Load button and you should see the string appearing in the EditText view again. This confirms that the text is saved correctly.

How It Works

To save text into a file, you use the `FileOutputStream` class. The `openFileOutput()` method opens a named file for writing, with the mode specified. In this example, you use the `MODE_WORLD_READABLE` constant to indicate that the file is readable by all other applications:

```
FileOutputStream fOut =
    openFileOutput("textfile.txt",
    MODE_WORLD_READABLE);
```

Apart from the `MODE_WORLD_READABLE` constant, you can select from the following: `MODE_PRIVATE` (file can only be accessed by the application that created it), `MODE_APPEND` (for appending to an existing file), and `MODE_WORLD_WRITEABLE` (all other applications have write access to the file).

To convert a character stream into a byte stream, you use an instance of the `OutputStreamWriter` class, by passing it an instance of the `FileOutputStream` object:

```
OutputStreamWriter osw = new
    OutputStreamWriter(fOut);
```

You then use its `write()` method to write the string to the file. To ensure that all the bytes are written to the file, use the `flush()` method. Finally, use the `close()` method to close the file:

```
osw.write(str);
osw.flush();
osw.close();
```

To read the content of a file, you use the `FileInputStream` class, together with the `InputStreamReader` class:

```
FileInputStream fIn =
    openFileInput("textfile.txt");
InputStreamReader isr = new
    InputStreamReader(fIn);
```

As you do not know the size of the file to read, the content is read in blocks of 100 characters into a buffer (character array). The characters read are then copied into a `String` object:

```
char[] inputBuffer = new char[READ_BLOCK_SIZE];
String s = "";

int charRead;
while ((charRead = isr.read(inputBuffer))>0)
{
    //---convert the chars to a String---
    String readString =
        String.copyValueOf(inputBuffer, 0,
        charRead);
    s += readString;

    inputBuffer = new char[READ_BLOCK_SIZE];
}
```

The `read()` method of the `InputStreamReader` object reads the number of characters read and returns -1 if the end of the file is reached.

When testing this application on the Android Emulator, you can use the DDMS to verify that the application did indeed save the file into the application's `files` directory (see Figure 6-7; the actual directory is `/data/data/net.learn2develop.Files/files`)

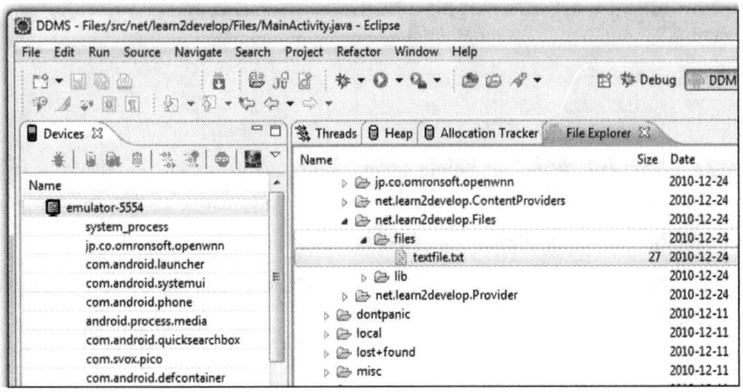

FIGURE 6-7

Saving to External Storage (SD Card)

The previous section showed how you can save your files to the internal storage of your Android device. Sometimes, it would be useful to save them to external storage (such as an SD card) because of its larger capacity, as well as the capability to share the files easily with other users (by removing the SD card and passing it to somebody else).

Using the project created in the previous section as the example, to save the text entered by the user in the SD card, modify the `onClick()` method of the Save button as shown in bold here:

```
saveBtn.setOnClickListener(new View.OnClickListener() {
    public void onClick(View v) {

        String str = textBox.getText().toString();
        try
        {
            //---SD Card Storage---
            File sdCard = Environment.getExternalStorageDirectory();
            File directory = new File (sdCard.getAbsolutePath() +
                "/MyFiles");
            directory.mkdirs();
            File file = new File(directory, "textfile.txt");
            FileOutputStream fOut = new FileOutputStream(file);

            OutputStreamWriter osw = new
            OutputStreamWriter(fOut);

            //---write the string to the file---
            osw.write(str);
            osw.flush();
```

```
            osw.close();

            //---display file saved message---
            Toast.makeText(getBaseContext(),
                "File saved successfully!",
                Toast.LENGTH_SHORT).show();

            //---clears the EditText---
            textBox.setText("");
        }
        catch (IOException ioe)
        {
            ioe.printStackTrace();
        }
    }
});
```

The preceding code uses the getExternalStorageDirectory() method to return the full path to the external storage. Typically, it should return the "/sdcard" path for a real device, and "/mnt/sdcard" for an Android Emulator. However, you should never try to hardcode the path to the SD card, as manufacturers may choose to assign a different path name to the SD card. Hence, be sure to use the getExternalStorageDirectory() method to return the full path to the SD card.

You then create a directory called MyFiles in the SD card. Finally, you save the file into this directory.

To load the file from the external storage, modify the onClick() method for the Load button:

```
loadBtn.setOnClickListener(new View.OnClickListener() {
    public void onClick(View v) {
        try
        {
            //---SD Storage---
            File sdCard = Environment.getExternalStorageDirectory();
            File directory = new File (sdCard.getAbsolutePath() +
                "/MyFiles");
            File file = new File(directory, "textfile.txt");
            FileInputStream fIn = new FileInputStream(file);
            InputStreamReader isr = new InputStreamReader(fIn);

            char[] inputBuffer = new char[READ_BLOCK_SIZE];
            String s = "";

            int charRead;
            while ((charRead = isr.read(inputBuffer))>0)
            {
                //---convert the chars to a String---
                String readString =
                    String.copyValueOf(inputBuffer, 0, charRead);
                s += readString;

                inputBuffer = new char[READ_BLOCK_SIZE];
            }
            //---set the EditText to the text that has been
            // read---
```

```
                    textBox.setText(s);

                    Toast.makeText(getBaseContext(),
                        "File loaded successfully!",
                        Toast.LENGTH_SHORT).show();
                }
                catch (IOException ioe) {
                    ioe.printStackTrace();
                }
            }
        });
```

Note that in order to write to the external storage, you need to add the WRITE_EXTERNAL_STORAGE permission in your AndroidManifest.xml file:

```xml
<?xml version="1.0" encoding="utf-8"?>
<manifest xmlns:android="http://schemas.android.com/apk/res/android"
      package="net.learn2develop.Files"
      android:versionCode="1"
      android:versionName="1.0">
    <application android:icon="@drawable/icon" android:label="@string/app_name">
        <activity android:name=".MainActivity"
                    android:label="@string/app_name">
            <intent-filter>
                <action android:name="android.intent.action.MAIN" />
                <category android:name="android.intent.category.LAUNCHER" />
            </intent-filter>
        </activity>
    </application>
    <uses-sdk android:minSdkVersion="9" />
    <uses-permission android:name="android.permission.WRITE_EXTERNAL_STORAGE">
    </uses-permission>
</manifest>
```

Choosing the Best Storage Option

And so, you have seen the few ways of saving data in your Android applications — SharedPreferences, internal storage, and external storage. Which one should you use in your applications? Here are some suggestions:

➤ If you have data that can be represented using key/value pairs, then use the SharedPreferences object. For example, if you want to store user preference data such as user name, background color, date of birth, last login date, then the SharedPreferences object is the ideal way to store these data. Moreover, you don't really have to get your hands dirty on how these data are stored; all you need is to use the SharedPreferences object to store and retrieve them.

➤ If you need to store ad-hoc data, then using the internal storage is a good option. For example, your application (such as an RSS reader) may need to download images from the Web for display. In this scenario, saving the images to internal storage is a good solution. You may also need to persist data created by the user, such as when you have a note-taking application where users can take notes and save them for later use. In all these scenarios, using the internal storage is a good choice.

➤ There are times when you need to share your application data with other users. For example, you may create an Android application that logs the coordinates of the locations that a user has been to, and you want to share all these data with other users. In this scenario, you can store your files on the SD card of the device so that users can easily transfer the data to other devices (and computers) for use later.

Using Static Resources

Besides creating and using files dynamically during run time, it is also possible to add files to your package during design time so that you can use it during run time. For example, you may want to bundle some help files with your package so that you can display some help messages when users need it. In this case, you can add the files to the res/raw folder (you need to create this folder yourself) of your package. Figure 6-8 shows the res/raw folder containing a file named textfile.txt.

FIGURE 6-8

To make use of the file in code, use the getResources() method to return a Resources object and then use its openRawResource() method to open the file contained in the res/raw folder:

```java
import java.io.InputStream;
import java.io.BufferedReader;

    /** Called when the activity is first created. */
    @Override
    public void onCreate(Bundle savedInstanceState) {
        super.onCreate(savedInstanceState);
        setContentView(R.layout.main);

        InputStream is = this.getResources().openRawResource(R.raw.textfile);
        BufferedReader br = new BufferedReader(new InputStreamReader(is));
        String str = null;
        try {
            while ((str = br.readLine()) != null) {
                Toast.makeText(getBaseContext(),
                    str, Toast.LENGTH_SHORT).show();
            }
            is.close();
            br.close();
        } catch (IOException e) {
            e.printStackTrace();
        }

        textBox = (EditText) findViewById(R.id.txtText1);
        Button saveBtn = (Button) findViewById(R.id.btnSave);
        Button loadBtn = (Button) findViewById(R.id.btnLoad);

        saveBtn.setOnClickListener(new View.OnClickListener() {
            public void onClick(View v) {
            }
        });

        loadBtn.setOnClickListener(new View.OnClickListener() {
```

```
        public void onClick(View v) {
        }
    });
}
```

The resource ID of the resource stored in the `res/raw` folder is named after its filename without its extension. For example, if the text file is `textfile.txt`, then its resource ID is `R.raw.textfile`.

CREATING AND USING DATABASES

So far, all the techniques you have seen are useful for saving simple sets of data. For saving relational data, using a database is much more efficient. For example, if you want to store the results of all the students in a school, it is much more efficient to use a database to represent them because you can use database querying to retrieve the results of the specific students. Moreover, using databases enables you to enforce data integrity by specifying the relationships between different sets of data.

Android uses the SQLite database system. The database that you create for an application is only accessible to itself; other applications will not be able to access it.

In this section, you will learn how to programmatically create a SQLite database in your Android application. For Android, the SQLite database that you create programmatically in an application is always stored in the `/data/data/<package_name>/databases` folder.

Creating the DBAdapter Helper Class

A good practice for dealing with databases is to create a helper class to encapsulate all the complexities of accessing the data so that it is transparent to the calling code. Hence, for this section, you will create a helper class called `DBAdapter` that creates, opens, closes, and uses a SQLite database.

In this example, you are going to create a database named `MyDB` containing one table named `contacts`. This table will have three columns: `_id`, `name`, and `email` (see Figure 6-9).

_id	name	email

FIGURE 6-9

TRY IT OUT   Creating the Database Helper Class

codefile Databases.zip available for download at Wrox.com

1. Using Eclipse, create an Android project and name it `Databases`.

2. Add a new class file to the project and name it `DBAdapter.java` (see Figure 6-10).

3. Add the following statements in bold to the `DBAdapter.java` file:

FIGURE 6-10

```
package net.learn2develop.Databases;

import android.content.ContentValues;
import android.content.Context;
```

```java
import android.database.Cursor;
import android.database.SQLException;
import android.database.sqlite.SQLiteDatabase;
import android.database.sqlite.SQLiteOpenHelper;
import android.util.Log;

public class DBAdapter {
    public static final String KEY_ROWID = "_id";
    public static final String KEY_NAME = "name";
    public static final String KEY_EMAIL = "email";
    private static final String TAG = "DBAdapter";

    private static final String DATABASE_NAME = "MyDB";
    private static final String DATABASE_TABLE = "contacts";
    private static final int DATABASE_VERSION = 1;

    private static final String DATABASE_CREATE =
        "create table contacts (_id integer primary key autoincrement, "
        + "name text not null, email text not null);";

    private final Context context;

    private DatabaseHelper DBHelper;
    private SQLiteDatabase db;

    public DBAdapter(Context ctx)
    {
        this.context = ctx;
        DBHelper = new DatabaseHelper(context);
    }

    private static class DatabaseHelper extends SQLiteOpenHelper
    {
        DatabaseHelper(Context context)
        {
            super(context, DATABASE_NAME, null, DATABASE_VERSION);
        }

        @Override
        public void onCreate(SQLiteDatabase db)
        {
            try {
                db.execSQL(DATABASE_CREATE);
            } catch (SQLException e) {
                e.printStackTrace();
            }
        }

        @Override
        public void onUpgrade(SQLiteDatabase db, int oldVersion, int newVersion)
        {
            Log.w(TAG, "Upgrading database from version " + oldVersion + " to "
                    + newVersion + ", which will destroy all old data");
            db.execSQL("DROP TABLE IF EXISTS contacts");
```

```
            onCreate(db);
        }
}

//---opens the database---
public DBAdapter open() throws SQLException
{
    db = DBHelper.getWritableDatabase();
    return this;
}

//---closes the database---
public void close()
{
    DBHelper.close();
}

//---insert a contact into the database---
public long insertContact(String name, String email)
{
    ContentValues initialValues = new ContentValues();
    initialValues.put(KEY_NAME, name);
    initialValues.put(KEY_EMAIL, email);
    return db.insert(DATABASE_TABLE, null, initialValues);
}

//---deletes a particular contact---
public boolean deleteContact(long rowId)
{
    return db.delete(DATABASE_TABLE, KEY_ROWID + "=" + rowId, null) > 0;
}

//---retrieves all the contacts---
public Cursor getAllContacts()
{
    return db.query(DATABASE_TABLE, new String[] {KEY_ROWID, KEY_NAME,
            KEY_EMAIL}, null, null, null, null, null);
}

//---retrieves a particular contact---
public Cursor getContact(long rowId) throws SQLException
{
    Cursor mCursor =
            db.query(true, DATABASE_TABLE, new String[] {KEY_ROWID,
            KEY_NAME, KEY_EMAIL}, KEY_ROWID + "=" + rowId, null,
            null, null, null, null);
    if (mCursor != null) {
        mCursor.moveToFirst();
    }
    return mCursor;
}

//---updates a contact---
public boolean updateContact(long rowId, String name, String email)
```

```
    {
        ContentValues args = new ContentValues();
        args.put(KEY_NAME, name);
        args.put(KEY_EMAIL, email);
        return db.update(DATABASE_TABLE, args, KEY_ROWID + "=" + rowId, null) > 0;
    }
}
```

How It Works

You first defined several constants to contain the various fields for the table that you are going to create in your database:

```
public static final String KEY_ROWID = "_id";
public static final String KEY_NAME = "name";
public static final String KEY_EMAIL = "email";
private static final String TAG = "DBAdapter";

private static final String DATABASE_NAME = "MyDB";
private static final String DATABASE_TABLE = "contacts";
private static final int DATABASE_VERSION = 1;

private static final String DATABASE_CREATE =
    "create table contacts (_id integer primary key autoincrement, "
    + "name text not null, email text not null);";
```

In particular, the DATABASE_CREATE constant contains the SQL statement for creating the contacts table within the MyDB database.

Within the DBAdapter class, you also extend the SQLiteOpenHelper class, which is a helper class in Android to manage database creation and version management. In particular, you override the onCreate() and onUpgrade() methods:

```
public class DBAdapter {
    public static final String KEY_ROWID = "_id";
    public static final String KEY_NAME = "name";
    public static final String KEY_EMAIL = "email";
    private static final String TAG = "DBAdapter";

    private static final String DATABASE_NAME = "MyDB";
    private static final String DATABASE_TABLE = "contacts";
    private static final int DATABASE_VERSION = 1;

    private static final String DATABASE_CREATE =
        "create table contacts (_id integer primary key autoincrement, "
        + "name text not null, email text not null);";

    private final Context context;

    private DatabaseHelper DBHelper;
    private SQLiteDatabase db;

    public DBAdapter(Context ctx)
    {
```

```
        this.context = ctx;
        DBHelper = new DatabaseHelper(context);
    }

    private static class DatabaseHelper extends SQLiteOpenHelper
    {
        DatabaseHelper(Context context)
        {
            super(context, DATABASE_NAME, null, DATABASE_VERSION);
        }

        @Override
        public void onCreate(SQLiteDatabase db)
        {
            try {
                db.execSQL(DATABASE_CREATE);
            } catch (SQLException e) {
                e.printStackTrace();
            }
        }

        @Override
        public void onUpgrade(SQLiteDatabase db, int oldVersion, int newVersion)
        {
            Log.w(TAG, "Upgrading database from version " + oldVersion + " to "
                    + newVersion + ", which will destroy all old data");
            db.execSQL("DROP TABLE IF EXISTS contacts");
            onCreate(db);
        }
    }
}
```

The onCreate() method creates a new database if the required database is not present. The onUpgrade() method is called when the database needs to be upgraded. This is achieved by checking the value defined in the DATABASE_VERSION constant. For this implementation of the onUpgrade() method, you simply drop the table and create it again.

You can then define the various methods for opening and closing the database, as well as the methods for adding/editing/deleting rows in the table:

```
public class DBAdapter {
//...
//...

    //---opens the database---
    public DBAdapter open() throws SQLException
    {
        db = DBHelper.getWritableDatabase();
        return this;
    }

    //---closes the database---
    public void close()
    {
```

```
        DBHelper.close();
    }

    //---insert a contact into the database---
    public long insertContact(String name, String email)
    {
        ContentValues initialValues = new ContentValues();
        initialValues.put(KEY_NAME, name);
        initialValues.put(KEY_EMAIL, email);
        return db.insert(DATABASE_TABLE, null, initialValues);
    }

    //---deletes a particular contact---
    public boolean deleteContact(long rowId)
    {
        return db.delete(DATABASE_TABLE, KEY_ROWID + "=" + rowId, null) > 0;
    }

    //---retrieves all the contacts---
    public Cursor getAllContacts()
    {
        return db.query(DATABASE_TABLE, new String[] {KEY_ROWID, KEY_NAME,
                KEY_EMAIL}, null, null, null, null, null);
    }

    //---retrieves a particular contact---
    public Cursor getContact(long rowId) throws SQLException
    {
        Cursor mCursor =
                db.query(true, DATABASE_TABLE, new String[] {KEY_ROWID,
                KEY_NAME, KEY_EMAIL}, KEY_ROWID + "=" + rowId, null,
                null, null, null, null);
        if (mCursor != null) {
            mCursor.moveToFirst();
        }
        return mCursor;
    }

    //---updates a contact---
    public boolean updateContact(long rowId, String name, String email)
    {
        ContentValues args = new ContentValues();
        args.put(KEY_NAME, name);
        args.put(KEY_EMAIL, email);
        return db.update(DATABASE_TABLE, args, KEY_ROWID + "=" + rowId, null) > 0;
    }
}
```

Notice that Android uses the Cursor class as a return value for queries. Think of the Cursor as a pointer to the result set from a database query. Using Cursor enables Android to more efficiently manage rows and columns as needed.

You use a ContentValues object to store key/value pairs. Its put() method enables you to insert keys with values of different data types.

Using the Database Programmatically

You are now ready to use the database using the helper class created in the previous section.

Adding Contacts

The following Try It Out demonstrates how you can add a contact to the table.

TRY IT OUT   Adding Contacts to a Table

1. Using the same project created earlier, add the following statements in bold to the `MainActivity`
.java file:

```
package net.learn2develop.Databases;

import android.app.Activity;
import android.os.Bundle;

public class MainActivity extends Activity {
    /** Called when the activity is first created. */
    @Override
    public void onCreate(Bundle savedInstanceState) {
        super.onCreate(savedInstanceState);
        setContentView(R.layout.main);

        DBAdapter db = new DBAdapter(this);

        //---add a contact---
        db.open();
        long id = db.insertContact("Wei-Meng Lee", "weimenglee@learn2develop.net");
        id = db.insertContact("Mary Jackson", "mary@jackson.com");
        db.close();
    }
}
```

2. Press F11 to debug the application on the Android Emulator.

How It Works

In this example, you first created an instance of the `DBAdapter` class:

```
DBAdapter db = new DBAdapter(this);
```

The `insertContact()` method returns the ID of the inserted row. If an error
occurs during the operation, it returns -1.

If you examine the file system of the Android device/emulator using DDMS,
you can see that the `MyDB` database is created under the `databases` folder (see
Figure 6-11).

FIGURE 6-11

Retrieving All the Contacts

To retrieve all the contacts in the contacts table, use the getAllContacts() method of the DBAdapter class, as the following Try It Out shows.

TRY IT OUT   Retrieving All Contacts from a Table

1. Using the same project created earlier, add the following statements in bold to the MainActivity .java file:

```
package net.learn2develop.Databases;

import android.app.Activity;
import android.os.Bundle;
import android.widget.Toast;

import android.database.Cursor;

public class MainActivity extends Activity {
    /** Called when the activity is first created. */
    @Override
    public void onCreate(Bundle savedInstanceState) {
        super.onCreate(savedInstanceState);
        setContentView(R.layout.main);

        DBAdapter db = new DBAdapter(this);

        /*
        //---add a contact---
        db.open();
        long id = db.insertContact("Wei-Meng Lee", "weimenglee@learn2develop.net");
        id = db.insertContact("Mary Jackson", "mary@jackson.com");
        db.close();
        */

        //---get all contacts---
        db.open();
        Cursor c = db.getAllContacts();
        if (c.moveToFirst())
        {
            do {
                DisplayContact(c);
            } while (c.moveToNext());
        }
        db.close();
    }

    public void DisplayContact(Cursor c)
    {
        Toast.makeText(this,
                "id: " + c.getString(0) + "\n" +
```

```
                    "Name: " + c.getString(1) + "\n" +
                    "Email:   " + c.getString(2),
                    Toast.LENGTH_LONG).show();
        }
    }
```

2. Press F11 to debug the application on the Android Emulator. Figure 6-12 shows the Toast class displaying the contacts retrieved from the database.

FIGURE 6-12

How It Works

The getAllContacts() method of the DBAdapter class retrieves all the contacts stored in the database. The result is returned as a Cursor object. To display all the contacts, you first need to call the moveToFirst() method of the Cursor object. If it succeeds (which means at least one row is available), display the details of the contact using the DisplayContact() method. To move to the next contact, call the moveToNext() method of the Cursor object.

Retrieving a Single Contact

To retrieve a single contact using its ID, call the getContact() method of the DBAdapter class, as the following Try It Out shows.

TRY IT OUT   Retrieving a Contact from a Table

1. Using the same project created earlier, add the following statements in bold to the `MainActivity` `.java` file:

```
@Override
public void onCreate(Bundle savedInstanceState) {
    super.onCreate(savedInstanceState);
    setContentView(R.layout.main);

    DBAdapter db = new DBAdapter(this);

    /*
    //---add a contact---
    //...
    */

    /*
    //---get all contacts---
    //...
    */

    //---get a contact---
    db.open();
    Cursor c = db.getContact(2);
    if (c.moveToFirst())
        DisplayContact(c);
    else
        Toast.makeText(this, "No contact found", Toast.LENGTH_LONG).show();
    db.close();
}
```

2. Press F11 to debug the application on the Android Emulator. The details of the second contact will be displayed using the `Toast` class.

How It Works

The `getContact()` method of the `DBAdapter` class retrieves a single contact using its ID. You passed in the ID of the contact; in this case, you passed in an ID of 2 to indicate that you want to retrieve the second contact:

```
Cursor c = db.getContact(2);
```

The result is returned as a `Cursor` object. If a row is returned, you display the details of the contact using the `DisplayContact()` method; otherwise, you display a message using the `Toast` class.

Updating a Contact

To update a particular contact, call the `updateContact()` method in the `DBAdapter` class by passing the ID of the contact you want to update, as the following Try It Out shows.

TRY IT OUT   Updating a Contact in a Table

1.   Using the same project created earlier, add the following statements in bold to the MainActivity
     .java file:

```
@Override
public void onCreate(Bundle savedInstanceState) {
    super.onCreate(savedInstanceState);
    setContentView(R.layout.main);

    DBAdapter db = new DBAdapter(this);

    /*
    //---add a contact---
    //...
    */

    /*
    //---get all contacts---
    //...
    */

    /*
    //...
    */

    //---update contact---
    db.open();
    if (db.updateContact(1, "Wei-Meng Lee", "weimenglee@gmail.com"))
        Toast.makeText(this, "Update successful.", Toast.LENGTH_LONG).show();
    else
        Toast.makeText(this, "Update failed.", Toast.LENGTH_LONG).show();
    db.close();
}
```

2.   Press F11 to debug the application on the Android Emulator. A message will be displayed if the
     update is successful.

How It Works

The updateContact() method in the DBAdapter class updates a contact's details by using the ID of the
contact you want to update. It returns a Boolean value, indicating whether the update was successful.

Deleting a Contact

To delete a contact, use the deleteContact() method in the DBAdapter class by passing the ID of the
contact you want to update, as the following Try It Out shows.

TRY IT OUT   Deleting a Contact from a Table

1. Using the same project created earlier, add the following statements in bold to the `MainActivity` `.java` file:

```
@Override
public void onCreate(Bundle savedInstanceState) {
    super.onCreate(savedInstanceState);
    setContentView(R.layout.main);

    DBAdapter db = new DBAdapter(this);

    /*
    //---add a contact---
    //...
    */

    /*
    //---get all contacts---
    //...
    */

    /*
    //---get a contact---
    //...
    */

    /*
    //---update contact---
    //...
    */

    //---delete a contact---
    db.open();
    if (db.deleteContact(1))
        Toast.makeText(this, "Delete successful.", Toast.LENGTH_LONG).show();
    else
        Toast.makeText(this, "Delete failed.", Toast.LENGTH_LONG).show();
    db.close();
}
```

2. Press F11 to debug the application on the Android Emulator. A message will be displayed if the deletion was successful.

How It Works

The `deleteContact()` method in the `DBAdapter` class deletes a contact using the ID of the contact you want to update. It returns a Boolean value, indicating whether the deletion was successful.

Upgrading the Database

Sometimes, after creating and using the database, you may need to add additional tables, change the schema of the database, or add columns to your tables. In this case, you need to migrate your existing data from the old database to a newer one.

To upgrade the database, change the DATABASE_VERSION constant to a value higher than the previous one. For example, if its previous value was 1, change it to 2:

```
public class DBAdapter {
    public static final String KEY_ROWID = "_id";
    public static final String KEY_NAME = "name";
    public static final String KEY_EMAIL = "email";
    private static final String TAG = "DBAdapter";

    private static final String DATABASE_NAME = "MyDB";
    private static final String DATABASE_TABLE = "contacts";
    private static final int DATABASE_VERSION = 2;
```

When you run the application one more time, you will see the following message in the LogCat window of Eclipse:

```
DBAdapter(24096): Upgrading database from version 1 to 2, which will destroy all
old data
```

In this example, for simplicity you simply drop the existing table and create a new one. In real-life, you usually back up your existing table and then copy them over to the new table.

Pre-Creating the Database

In real-life applications, sometimes it would be more efficient to pre-create the database at design time rather than run time. To pre-create a SQLite database, you can use many of the free tools available on the Internet. One such tool is the SQLite Database Browser, which is available free for the different platforms (http://sourceforge.net/projects/sqlitebrowser/).

Once you have installed the SQLite Database Browser, you can create a database visually. Figure 6-13 shows that I have created a contacts table with the fields indicated.

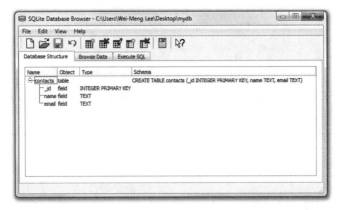

FIGURE 6-13

Populating the table with rows is also straightforward. Figure 6-14 shows how you can fill the table with data using the Browse Data tab.

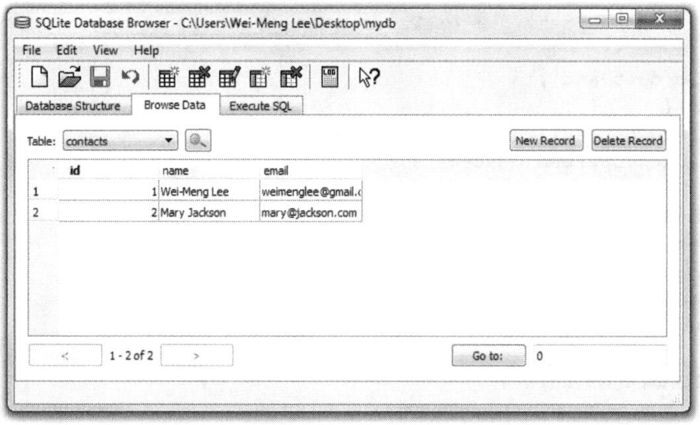

FIGURE 6-14

Bundling the Database with an Application

With the database created at design time, the next thing you should do is bundle it together with your application so that you can use it in your application. The following Try It Out shows you how.

TRY IT OUT Bundling a Database

1. Using the same project created earlier, drag and drop the SQLite database file that you have created in the previous section into the `assets` folder in your Android project in Eclipse (see Figure 6-15).

FIGURE 6-15

> **NOTE** *Note that a filename for files added to the assets folder must be in lower-case letters. As such, a filename such as* `MyDB` *is invalid, whereas* `mydb` *is fine.*

2. Add the following statements in bold to the `MainActivity.java` file:

```
@Override
```

```
public void onCreate(Bundle savedInstanceState) {
    super.onCreate(savedInstanceState);
    setContentView(R.layout.main);
    try {
        String destPath = "/data/data/" + getPackageName() +
            "/databases/MyDB";
        File f = new File(destPath);
        if (!f.exists()) {
            CopyDB( getBaseContext().getAssets().open("mydb"),
                new FileOutputStream(destPath));
        }
    } catch (FileNotFoundException e) {
        e.printStackTrace();
    } catch (IOException e) {
        e.printStackTrace();
    }

    DBAdapter db = new DBAdapter(this);

    //---get all contacts---
    db.open();
    Cursor c = db.getAllContacts();
    if (c.moveToFirst())
    {
        do {
            DisplayContact(c);
        } while (c.moveToNext());
    }
    db.close();
}

public void CopyDB(InputStream inputStream,
OutputStream outputStream)
throws IOException {
    //---copy 1K bytes at a time---
    byte[] buffer = new byte[1024];
    int length;
    while ((length = inputStream.read(buffer)) > 0) {
        outputStream.write(buffer, 0, length);
    }
    inputStream.close();
    outputStream.close();
}
```

3. Press F11 to debug the application on the Android Emulator. When the application runs, it will copy the mydb database file into the /data/data/net.learn2develop.Databases/databases/ folder with the name MyDB.

How It Works

You first defined the CopyDB() method to copy the database file from one location to another:

```
public void CopyDB(InputStream inputStream,
```

```
OutputStream outputStream)
throws IOException {
    //---copy 1K bytes at a time---
    byte[] buffer = new byte[1024];
    int length;
    while ((length = inputStream.read(buffer)) > 0) {
        outputStream.write(buffer, 0, length);
    }
    inputStream.close();
    outputStream.close();
}
```

Note that in this case you used the `InputStream` object to read from the source file, and then wrote it to the destination file using the `OutputStream` object.

When the activity is created, you copy the database file located in the `assets` folder into the `/data/data/net.learn2develop.Databases/databases/` folder on the Android device (or emulator):

```
try {
    String destPath = "/data/data/" + getPackageName() +
        "/databases/MyDB";
    File f = new File(destPath);
    if (!f.exists()) {
        CopyDB( getBaseContext().getAssets().open("mydb"),
            new FileOutputStream(destPath));
    }
} catch (FileNotFoundException e) {
    e.printStackTrace();
} catch (IOException e) {
    e.printStackTrace();
}
```

You copy the database file only if it does not exist in the destination folder. If you don't perform this check, every time the activity is created you will overwrite the database file with the one in the `assets` folder. This may not be desirable, as your application may make changes to the database file during run time, and this will wipe out all the changes you have made so far.

To ensure that the database file is indeed copied, be sure to delete the database file in your emulator (if it already existed) prior to testing the application. You can delete the database using DDMS (see Figure 6-16).

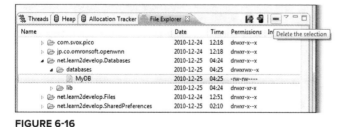

FIGURE 6-16

SUMMARY

In this chapter, you learned the different ways to save persistent data to your Android device. For simple unstructured data, using the `SharedPreferences` object is the ideal solution. If you need to store bulk data, then consider using the traditional file system. Finally, for structured data, it is more efficient to store it in a relational database management system. For this, Android provides the SQLite database, which you can access easily using the APIs exposed.

Note that for the `SharedPreferences` object and the SQLite database, the data is accessible only by the application that creates it. In other words, it is not shareable. If you need to share data among different applications, you need to create a *content provider*. Content providers are discussed in more detail in the next chapter.

EXERCISES

1. What is the difference between the `getSharedPreferences()` and `getPreferences()` methods?

2. Name the method that enables you to obtain the path of the external storage of an Android device.

3. What is the permission you need to declare when writing files to external storage?

Answers to Exercises can be found in Appendix C.

▶ WHAT YOU LEARNED IN THIS CHAPTER

TOPIC	KEY CONCEPTS
Save simple user data	Use the SharedPreferences object.
Sharing data among activities in the same application	Use the getSharedPreferences() method.
Saving data visible only to the activity that created it	Use the getPreferences() method.
Saving to file	Use the FileOutputStream and OutputStreamReader classes.
Reading from file	Use the FileInputStream and InputStreamReader classes.
Saving to external storage	Use the getExternalStorageDirectory() method to return the path to the external storage.
Accessing files in the res/raw folder	Use the openRawResource() method in the Resources object (obtained via the getResources() method).
Creating a database helper class	Extend the SQLiteOpenHelper class.

7

Content Providers

WHAT YOU WILL LEARN IN THIS CHAPTER

➤ What are content providers?

➤ How to use a content provider in Android

➤ How to create your own content provider

➤ How to use your own content provider

In the previous chapter, you learned about the various ways to persist data — using shared preferences, files, as well as SQLite databases. While using the database approach is the recommended way to save structured and complex data, sharing data is a challenge because the database is accessible to only the package that created it.

In this chapter, you will learn Android's way of sharing data through the use of *content providers*. You will learn how to use the built-in content providers, as well as implement your own content providers to share data across packages.

SHARING DATA IN ANDROID

In Android, using a content provider is the recommended way to share data across packages. Think of a content provider as a data store. How it stores its data is not relevant to the application using it; what is important is how packages can access the data stored in it using a consistent programming interface. A content provider behaves very much like a database — you can query it, edit its content, as well as add or delete its content. However, unlike a database, a content provider can use different ways to store its data. The data can be stored in a database, in files, or even over a network.

Android ships with many useful content providers, including the following:

➤ **Browser** — Stores data such as browser bookmarks, browser history, and so on

➤ **CallLog** — Stores data such as missed calls, call details, and so on

➤ **Contacts** — Stores contact details

➤ **MediaStore** — Stores media files such as audio, video and images

➤ **Settings** — Stores the device's settings and preferences

Besides the many built-in content providers, you can also create your own content providers.

To query a content provider, you specify the query string in the form of a URI, with an optional specifier for a particular row. The format of the query URI is as follows:

```
<standard_prefix>://<authority>/<data_path>/<id>
```

The various parts of the URI are as follows:

➤ The *standard prefix* for content providers is always `content://`.

➤ The *authority* specifies the name of the content provider. An example would be `contacts` for the built-in Contacts content provider. For third-party content providers, this could be the fully qualified name, such as `com.wrox.provider` or `net.learn2develop.provider`.

➤ The *data path* specifies the kind of data requested. For example, if you are getting all the contacts from the Contacts content provider, then the data path would be `people`, and the URI would look like this: `content://contacts/people`.

➤ The *id* specifies the specific record requested. For example, if you are looking for contact number 2 in the Contacts content provider, the URI would look like this: `content://contacts/people/2`.

Table 7-1 shows some examples of query strings.

TABLE 7-1: Example Query Strings

QUERY STRING	DESCRIPTION
`content://media/internal/images`	Returns a list of all the internal images on the device
`content://media/external/images`	Returns a list of all the images stored on the external storage (e.g., SD card) on the device
`content://call_log/calls`	Returns a list of all calls registered in the Call Log
`content://browser/bookmarks`	Returns a list of bookmarks stored in the browser

USING A CONTENT PROVIDER

The best way to understand content providers is to actually use one. The following Try It Out shows how you can use a content provider from within your Android application.

Using the Contacts Content Provider

codefile Provider.zip available for download at Wrox.com

1. Using Eclipse, create a new Android project and name it as shown in Figure 7-1.

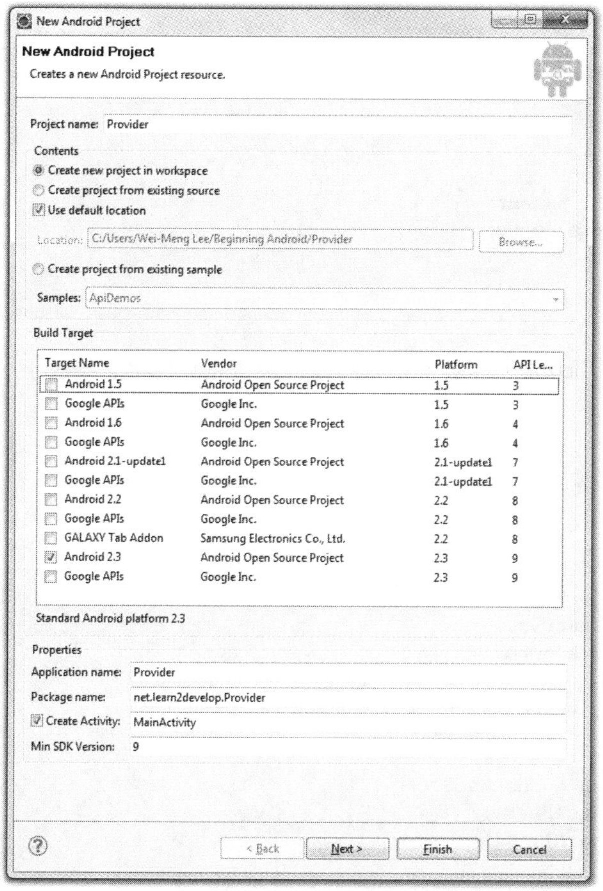

FIGURE 7-1

2. Add the following statements in bold to the `main.xml` file:

```xml
<?xml version="1.0" encoding="utf-8"?>
<LinearLayout xmlns:android="http://schemas.android.com/apk/res/android"
    android:orientation="vertical"
    android:layout_width="fill_parent"
    android:layout_height="fill_parent"
>

    <ListView
        android:id="@+id/android:list"
```

```xml
        android:layout_width="fill_parent"
        android:layout_height="wrap_content"
        android:layout_weight="1"
        android:stackFromBottom="false"
        android:transcriptMode="normal"
        />
    <TextView
        android:id="@+id/contactName"
        android:textStyle="bold"
        android:layout_width="wrap_content"
        android:layout_height="wrap_content"
        />
    <TextView
        android:id="@+id/contactID"
        android:layout_width="fill_parent"
        android:layout_height="wrap_content"
        />

</LinearLayout>
```

3. In the `MainActivity.java` class, code the following:

```java
package net.learn2develop.Provider;

import android.app.Activity;
import android.os.Bundle;

import android.app.ListActivity;
import android.database.Cursor;
import android.net.Uri;
import android.provider.ContactsContract;
import android.widget.SimpleCursorAdapter;

public class MainActivity extends ListActivity {
    /** Called when the activity is first created. */
    @Override
    public void onCreate(Bundle savedInstanceState) {
        super.onCreate(savedInstanceState);
        setContentView(R.layout.main);

        Uri allContacts = Uri.parse("content://contacts/people");

        Cursor c = managedQuery(allContacts, null, null, null, null);

        String[] columns = new String[] {
            ContactsContract.Contacts.DISPLAY_NAME,
            ContactsContract.Contacts._ID};
        int[] views = new int[] {R.id.contactName, R.id.contactID};

        SimpleCursorAdapter adapter =
            new SimpleCursorAdapter(this, R.layout.main, c, columns, views);
        this.setListAdapter(adapter);
    }
}
```

4. Add the following statements in bold to the `AndroidManifest.xml` file:

```xml
<?xml version="1.0" encoding="utf-8"?>
<manifest xmlns:android="http://schemas.android.com/apk/res/android"
    package="net.learn2develop.Provider"
    android:versionCode="1"
    android:versionName="1.0">
  <application android:icon="@drawable/icon" android:label="@string/app_name">
      <activity android:name=".MainActivity"
                android:label="@string/app_name">
          <intent-filter>
              <action android:name="android.intent.action.MAIN" />
              <category android:name="android.intent.category.LAUNCHER" />
          </intent-filter>
      </activity>
  </application>
  <uses-sdk android:minSdkVersion="7" />
  <uses-permission android:name="android.permission.READ_CONTACTS">
  </uses-permission>
</manifest>
```

5. Launch an AVD and create a few contacts in the Android Emulator (see Figure 7-2).

FIGURE 7-2

6. Press F11 to debug the application on the Android Emulator. Figure 7-3 shows the activity displaying the list of contacts you just created.

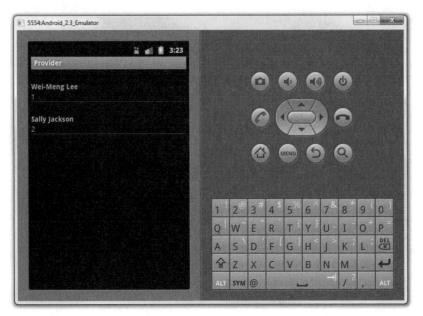

FIGURE 7-3

How It Works

In this example, you retrieved all the contacts stored in the Contacts application and displayed them in the ListView.

The managedQuery() method of the Activity class retrieves a managed cursor. A *managed cursor* handles all the work of unloading itself when the application pauses and requerying itself when the application restarts.

The statement

```
Cursor c = managedQuery(allContacts, null, null, null, null);
```

is equivalent to

```
Cursor c = getContentResolver().query(allContacts, null, null, null, null);
startManagingCursor(c); //---allows the activity to manage the Cursor's
                        // lifecyle based on the activity's lifecycle---
```

The getContentResolver() method returns a ContentResolver object, which helps to resolve a content URI with the appropriate content provider.

The SimpleCursorAdapter object maps a cursor to TextViews (or ImageViews) defined in your XML file (main.xml). It maps the data (as represented by columns) to views (as represented by views):

```
String[] columns = new String[] {
    ContactsContract.Contacts.DISPLAY_NAME,
    ContactsContract.Contacts._ID};
```

```
int[] views = new int[] {R.id.contactName, R.id.contactID};

SimpleCursorAdapter adapter =
    new SimpleCursorAdapter(this, R.layout.main, c, columns, views);
this.setListAdapter(adapter);
```

Note that in order for your application to access the Contacts application, you need to have the READ_ CONTACTS permission in your `AndroidManifest.xml` file.

Predefined Query String Constants

Besides using the query URI, you can use a list of predefined query string constants in Android to specify the URI for the different data types. For example, besides using the query `content://contacts/people`, you can rewrite the following statement

```
Uri allContacts = Uri.parse("content://contacts/people");
```

using one of the predefined constants in Android, as

```
Uri allContacts = ContactsContract.Contacts.CONTENT_URI;
```

> **NOTE** For Android 2.0 and later, to query the base Contacts records you need to use the `ContactsContract.Contacts.CONTENT_URI` URI.

Some examples of predefined query string constants are as follows:

- ➤ `Browser.BOOKMARKS_URI`
- ➤ `Browser.SEARCHES_URI`
- ➤ `CallLog.CONTENT_URI`
- ➤ `MediaStore.Images.Media.INTERNAL_CONTENT_URI`
- ➤ `MediaStore.Images.Media.EXTERNAL_CONTENT_URI`
- ➤ `Settings.CONTENT_URI`

If you want to retrieve the first contact, specify the ID of that contact, like this:

```
Uri oneContact = Uri.parse("content://contacts/people/1");
```

Alternatively, use the predefined constant together with the `withAppendedId()` method of the `ContentUris` class:

```
import android.content.ContentUris;
//...
Uri oneContact = ContentUris.withAppendedId(
    ContactsContract.Contacts.CONTENT_URI, 1);
```

Besides binding to a ListView, you can also print out the results using the `Cursor` object, as shown here:

```
package net.learn2develop.Provider;

import android.app.Activity;
import android.os.Bundle;

import android.app.ListActivity;
import android.database.Cursor;
import android.net.Uri;
import android.provider.ContactsContract;
import android.widget.SimpleCursorAdapter;

import android.util.Log;

public class MainActivity extends ListActivity {
    /** Called when the activity is first created. */
    @Override
    public void onCreate(Bundle savedInstanceState) {
        super.onCreate(savedInstanceState);
        setContentView(R.layout.main);

        Uri allContacts = ContactsContract.Contacts.CONTENT_URI;
        Cursor c = managedQuery(
            allContacts, null, null, null, null);
        String[] columns = new String[] {
            ContactsContract.Contacts.DISPLAY_NAME,
            ContactsContract.Contacts._ID};
        int[] views = new int[] {R.id.contactName, R.id.contactID};

        SimpleCursorAdapter adapter =
            new SimpleCursorAdapter(this, R.layout.main,
            c, columns, views);
        this.setListAdapter(adapter);
        PrintContacts(c);
    }

    private void PrintContacts(Cursor c)
    {
        if (c.moveToFirst()) {
            do{
            String contactID = c.getString(c.getColumnIndex(
                ContactsContract.Contacts._ID));
            String contactDisplayName =
                c.getString(c.getColumnIndex(
                    ContactsContract.Contacts.DISPLAY_NAME));
                Log.v("Content Providers", contactID + ", " +
                    contactDisplayName);
            } while (c.moveToNext());
        }
    }
}
```

> **NOTE** *If you are not familiar with how to view the LogCat window, refer to Appendix A for an quick tour of the Eclipse IDE.*

The PrintContacts() method will print out the following in the LogCat window:

```
12-13 02:40:36.825: VERBOSE/Content Providers(497):
    1, Wei-Meng Lee
12-13 02:40:36.825: VERBOSE/Content Providers(497):
    2, Sally Jackson
```

It prints out the ID and name of each contact stored in the Contacts application. In this case, you access the ContactsContract.Contacts._ID field to obtain the ID of a contact, and ContactsContract.Contacts.DISPLAY_NAME for the name of a contact. If you want to display the phone number of a contact, you need to query the content provider again, as the information is stored in another table:

```java
private void PrintContacts(Cursor c)
{
    if (c.moveToFirst()) {
        do{
            String contactID = c.getString(c.getColumnIndex(
                ContactsContract.Contacts._ID));
            String contactDisplayName =
                c.getString(c.getColumnIndex(
                    ContactsContract.Contacts.DISPLAY_NAME));
            Log.v("Content Providers", contactID + ", " +
                contactDisplayName);
            //---get phone number---
            int hasPhone =
                c.getInt(c.getColumnIndex(
                    ContactsContract.Contacts.HAS_PHONE_NUMBER));
            if (hasPhone == 1) {
                Cursor phoneCursor =
                    getContentResolver().query(
                      ContactsContract.CommonDataKinds.Phone.CONTENT_URI, null,
                      ContactsContract.CommonDataKinds.Phone.CONTACT_ID + " = " +
                      contactID, null, null);
                while (phoneCursor.moveToNext()) {
                    Log.v("Content Providers",
                      phoneCursor.getString(
                          phoneCursor.getColumnIndex(
                          ContactsContract.CommonDataKinds.Phone.NUMBER)));
                }
                phoneCursor.close();
            }
        } while (c.moveToNext());
    }
}
```

> **NOTE** *To access the phone number of a contact, you need to query against the URI stored in* `ContactsContract.CommonDataKinds.Phone.CONTENT_URI`*.*

In the preceding code snippet, you first check whether a contact has a phone number using the `ContactsContract.Contacts.HAS_PHONE_NUMBER` field. If the contact has at least a phone number, you then query the content provider again based on the ID of the contact. Once the phone number(s) are retrieved, you then iterate through them and print out the numbers. You should see something like this:

```
12-13 02:41:09.541: VERBOSE/Content Providers(546):
    1, Wei-Meng Lee
12-13 02:41:09.541: VERBOSE/Content Providers(546):
    969-240-65
12-13 02:41:09.541: VERBOSE/Content Providers(546):
    2, Sally Jackson
12-13 02:41:09.541: VERBOSE/Content Providers(546):
    345-668-43
```

Projections

The second parameter of the `managedQuery()` method controls how many columns are returned by the query; this parameter is known as the *projection*. Earlier, you specified `null`:

```
Cursor c = managedQuery(allContacts,
    null, null, null, null);
```

You can specify the exact columns to return by creating an array containing the name of the column to return, like this:

```
String[] projection = new String[]
    {ContactsContract.Contacts._ID,
     ContactsContract.Contacts.DISPLAY_NAME,
     ContactsContract.Contacts.HAS_PHONE_NUMBER};
Cursor c = managedQuery(allContacts, projection,
    null, null, null);
```

In the above case, the `_ID`, `DISPLAY_NAME`, and `HAS_PHONE_NUMBER` fields will be retrieved.

Filtering

The third and fourth parameters of the `managedQuery()` method enable you to specify a SQL WHERE clause to filter the result of the query. For example, the following statement retrieves only the people whose name ends with "Lee":

```
Cursor c = managedQuery(allContacts, projection,
    ContactsContract.Contacts.DISPLAY_NAME + " LIKE '%Lee'",
    null, null);
```

Here, the third parameter contains a SQL statement containing the name to search for ("Lee"). You can also put the search string into the fourth argument of the method, like this:

```
Cursor c = managedQuery(allContacts, projection,
    ContactsContract.Contacts.DISPLAY_NAME + " LIKE ?",
    new String[] {"%Lee"} , null);
```

Sorting

The fifth parameter of the managedQuery() method enables you to specify a SQL ORDER BY clause to sort the result of the query. For example, the following statement sorts the contact names in ascending order:

```
Cursor c = managedQuery(
    allContacts,
    projection,
    ContactsContract.Contacts.DISPLAY_NAME + " LIKE ?",
    new String[] {"%"} ,
    ContactsContract.Contacts.DISPLAY_NAME + " ASC");
```

To sort in descending order, use the DESC keyword:

```
Cursor c = managedQuery(
    allContacts,
    projection,
    ContactsContract.Contacts.DISPLAY_NAME + " LIKE ?",
    new String[] {"%"} ,
    ContactsContract.Contacts.DISPLAY_NAME + " DESC");
```

CREATING YOUR OWN CONTENT PROVIDERS

Creating your own content provider in Android is pretty simple. All you need to do is extend the abstract ContentProvider class and override the various methods defined within it.

In this section, you will learn how to create a simple content provider that stores a list of books. For ease of illustration, the content provider stores the books in a database table containing three fields, as shown in Figure 7-4.

FIGURE 7-4

The following Try It Out shows you the steps.

TRY IT OUT   Creating Your Own Content Provider

codefile ContentProviders.zip available for download at Wrox.com

1.   Using Eclipse, create a new Android project and name it as **ContentProviders**.

2. In the `src` folder of the project, add a new Java class file and name it **BooksProvider.java** (see Figure 7-5).

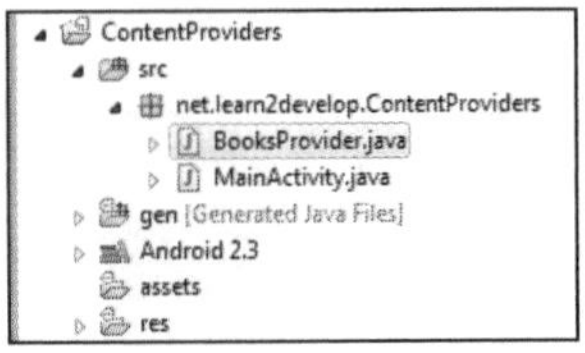

FIGURE 7-5

3. Populate the `BooksProvider.java` file as follows:

```java
package net.learn2develop.ContentProviders;

import android.content.ContentProvider;
import android.content.ContentUris;
import android.content.ContentValues;
import android.content.Context;
import android.content.UriMatcher;
import android.database.Cursor;
import android.database.SQLException;
import android.database.sqlite.SQLiteDatabase;
import android.database.sqlite.SQLiteOpenHelper;
import android.database.sqlite.SQLiteQueryBuilder;
import android.net.Uri;
import android.text.TextUtils;
import android.util.Log;

public class BooksProvider extends ContentProvider
{
    public static final String PROVIDER_NAME =
        "net.learn2develop.provider.Books";

    public static final Uri CONTENT_URI =
        Uri.parse("content://"+ PROVIDER_NAME + "/books");

    public static final String _ID = "_id";
    public static final String TITLE = "title";
    public static final String ISBN = "isbn";

    private static final int BOOKS = 1;
    private static final int BOOK_ID = 2;

    private static final UriMatcher uriMatcher;
    static{
        uriMatcher = new UriMatcher(UriMatcher.NO_MATCH);
        uriMatcher.addURI(PROVIDER_NAME, "books", BOOKS);
        uriMatcher.addURI(PROVIDER_NAME, "books/#", BOOK_ID);
    }

    //---for database use---
    private SQLiteDatabase booksDB;
```

```java
private static final String DATABASE_NAME = "Books";
private static final String DATABASE_TABLE = "titles";
private static final int DATABASE_VERSION = 1;
private static final String DATABASE_CREATE =
        "create table " + DATABASE_TABLE +
        " (_id integer primary key autoincrement, "
        + "title text not null, isbn text not null);";

private static class DatabaseHelper extends SQLiteOpenHelper
{
    DatabaseHelper(Context context) {
        super(context, DATABASE_NAME, null, DATABASE_VERSION);
    }

    @Override
    public void onCreate(SQLiteDatabase db)
    {
        db.execSQL(DATABASE_CREATE);
    }

    @Override
    public void onUpgrade(SQLiteDatabase db, int oldVersion,
    int newVersion) {
        Log.w("Content provider database",
                "Upgrading database from version " +
                oldVersion + " to " + newVersion +
                ", which will destroy all old data");
        db.execSQL("DROP TABLE IF EXISTS titles");
        onCreate(db);
    }
}
@Override
public int delete(Uri arg0, String arg1, String[] arg2) {
    // arg0 = uri
    // arg1 = selection
    // arg2 = selectionArgs
    int count=0;
    switch (uriMatcher.match(arg0)){
        case BOOKS:
            count = booksDB.delete(
                    DATABASE_TABLE,
                    arg1,
                    arg2);
            break;
        case BOOK_ID:
            String id = arg0.getPathSegments().get(1);
            count = booksDB.delete(
                    DATABASE_TABLE,
                    _ID + " = " + id +
                    (!TextUtils.isEmpty(arg1) ? " AND (" +
                            arg1 + ')' : ""),
                            arg2);
            break;
        default: throw new IllegalArgumentException("Unknown URI " + arg0);
```

```java
            }
            getContext().getContentResolver().notifyChange(arg0, null);
            return count;
        }

    @Override
    public String getType(Uri uri) {
        switch (uriMatcher.match(uri)){
            //---get all books---
            case BOOKS:
                return "vnd.android.cursor.dir/vnd.learn2develop.books ";
            //---get a particular book---
            case BOOK_ID:
                return "vnd.android.cursor.item/vnd.learn2develop.books ";
            default:
                throw new IllegalArgumentException("Unsupported URI: " + uri);
        }
    }

    @Override
    public Uri insert(Uri uri, ContentValues values) {
        //---add a new book---
        long rowID = booksDB.insert(
            DATABASE_TABLE,
            "",
            values);

        //---if added successfully---
        if (rowID>0)
        {
            Uri _uri = ContentUris.withAppendedId(CONTENT_URI, rowID);
            getContext().getContentResolver().notifyChange(_uri, null);
            return _uri;
        }
        throw new SQLException("Failed to insert row into " + uri);
    }

    @Override
    public boolean onCreate() {
        Context context = getContext();
        DatabaseHelper dbHelper = new DatabaseHelper(context);
        booksDB = dbHelper.getWritableDatabase();
        return (booksDB == null)? false:true;
    }

    @Override
    public Cursor query(Uri uri, String[] projection, String selection,
            String[] selectionArgs, String sortOrder) {
        SQLiteQueryBuilder sqlBuilder = new SQLiteQueryBuilder();
        sqlBuilder.setTables(DATABASE_TABLE);

        if (uriMatcher.match(uri) == BOOK_ID)
            //---if getting a particular book---
            sqlBuilder.appendWhere(
```

```
                    _ID + " = " + uri.getPathSegments().get(1));

        if (sortOrder==null || sortOrder=="")
            sortOrder = TITLE;

        Cursor c = sqlBuilder.query(
                booksDB,
                projection,
                selection,
                selectionArgs,
                null,
                null,
                sortOrder);

        //---register to watch a content URI for changes---
        c.setNotificationUri(getContext().getContentResolver(), uri);
        return c;
    }

    @Override
    public int update(Uri uri, ContentValues values, String selection,
            String[] selectionArgs) {
        int count = 0;
        switch (uriMatcher.match(uri)){
            case BOOKS:
                count = booksDB.update(
                        DATABASE_TABLE,
                        values,
                        selection,
                        selectionArgs);
                break;
            case BOOK_ID:
                count = booksDB.update(
                        DATABASE_TABLE,
                        values,
                        _ID + " = " + uri.getPathSegments().get(1) +
                        (!TextUtils.isEmpty(selection) ? " AND (" +
                            selection + ')' : ""),
                        selectionArgs);
                break;
            default: throw new IllegalArgumentException("Unknown URI " + uri);
        }
        getContext().getContentResolver().notifyChange(uri, null);
        return count;
    }
}
```

4. Add the following statements in bold to the AndroidManifest.xml file:

```
<?xml version="1.0" encoding="utf-8"?>
<manifest xmlns:android="http://schemas.android.com/apk/res/android"
    package="net.learn2develop.ContentProviders"
    android:versionCode="1"
    android:versionName="1.0">
    <application android:icon="@drawable/icon" android:label="@string/app_name">
```

```
            <activity android:name=".MainActivity"
                      android:label="@string/app_name">
                <intent-filter>
                    <action android:name="android.intent.action.MAIN" />
                    <category android:name="android.intent.category.LAUNCHER" />
                </intent-filter>
            </activity>
            <provider android:name="BooksProvider"
                      android:authorities="net.learn2develop.provider.Books" />
        </application>
        <uses-sdk android:minSdkVersion="9" />
    </manifest>
```

How It Works

In this example, you first created a class named `BooksProvider` that extends the `ContentProvider` base class. The various methods to override in this class are as follows:

➤ `getType()` — Returns the MIME type of the data at the given URI

➤ `onCreate()` — Called when the provider is started

➤ `query()` — Receives a request from a client. The result is returned as a `Cursor` object.

➤ `insert()` — Inserts a new record into the content provider

➤ `delete()` — Deletes an existing record from the content provider

➤ `update()` — Updates an existing record from the content provider

Within your content provider, you are free to choose how you want to store your data — a traditional file system, XML, a database, or even through Web services. For this example, you use the SQLite database approach that was discussed in the previous chapter.

You then defined the following constants within the `BooksProvider` class:

```java
public static final String PROVIDER_NAME =
    "net.learn2develop.provider.Books";

public static final Uri CONTENT_URI =
    Uri.parse("content://"+ PROVIDER_NAME + "/books");

public static final String _ID = "_id";
public static final String TITLE = "title";
public static final String ISBN = "isbn";

private static final int BOOKS = 1;
private static final int BOOK_ID = 2;

private static final UriMatcher uriMatcher;
static{
    uriMatcher = new UriMatcher(UriMatcher.NO_MATCH);
    uriMatcher.addURI(PROVIDER_NAME, "books", BOOKS);
    uriMatcher.addURI(PROVIDER_NAME, "books/#", BOOK_ID);
}
```

Observe in the preceding code that you use an `UriMatcher` object to parse the content URI that is passed to the content provider through a `ContentResolver`. For example, the following content URI represents a request for all books in the content provider:

`content://net.learn2develop.provider.Books/books`

The following represents a request for a particular book with _id 5:

`content://net.learn2develop.provider.MailingList/books/5`

Your content provider uses a SQLite database to store the books. Note that you use the `SQLiteOpenHelper` helper class to help manage your database:

```
private static class DatabaseHelper extends SQLiteOpenHelper
{
    DatabaseHelper(Context context) {
        super(context, DATABASE_NAME, null, DATABASE_VERSION);
    }

    @Override
    public void onCreate(SQLiteDatabase db)
    {
        db.execSQL(DATABASE_CREATE);
    }

    @Override
    public void onUpgrade(SQLiteDatabase db, int oldVersion,
    int newVersion) {
        Log.w("Content provider database",
            "Upgrading database from version " +
            oldVersion + " to " + newVersion +
            ", which will destroy all old data");
        db.execSQL("DROP TABLE IF EXISTS titles");
        onCreate(db);
    }
}
```

Next, you override the `getType()` method to uniquely describe the data type for your content provider. Using the `UriMatcher` object, you return `"vnd.android.cursor.item/vnd.learn2develop.books"` for a single book, and `"vnd.android.cursor.dir/vnd.learn2develop.books"` for multiple books:

```
@Override
public String getType(Uri uri) {
    switch (uriMatcher.match(uri)){
        //---get all books---
        case BOOKS:
            return "vnd.android.cursor.dir/vnd.learn2develop.books ";
        //---get a particular book---
        case BOOK_ID:
            return "vnd.android.cursor.item/vnd.learn2develop.books ";
        default:
            throw new IllegalArgumentException("Unsupported URI: " + uri);
    }
}
```

Next, you override the `onCreate()` method to open a connection to the database when the content provider is started:

```
@Override
public boolean onCreate() {
    Context context = getContext();
    DatabaseHelper dbHelper = new DatabaseHelper(context);
    booksDB = dbHelper.getWritableDatabase();
    return (booksDB == null)? false:true;
}
```

You override the `query()` method to allow clients to query for books:

```
@Override
public Cursor query(Uri uri, String[] projection, String selection,
        String[] selectionArgs, String sortOrder) {
    SQLiteQueryBuilder sqlBuilder = new SQLiteQueryBuilder();
    sqlBuilder.setTables(DATABASE_TABLE);

    if (uriMatcher.match(uri) == BOOK_ID)
        //---if getting a particular book---
        sqlBuilder.appendWhere(
            _ID + " = " + uri.getPathSegments().get(1));

    if (sortOrder==null || sortOrder=="")
        sortOrder = TITLE;

    Cursor c = sqlBuilder.query(
            booksDB,
            projection,
            selection,
            selectionArgs,
            null,
            null,
            sortOrder);

    //---register to watch a content URI for changes---
    c.setNotificationUri(getContext().getContentResolver(), uri);
    return c;
}
```

By default, the result of the query is sorted using the `title` field. The resulting query is returned as a `Cursor` object.

To allow a new book to be inserted into the content provider, override the `insert()` method:

```
@Override
public Uri insert(Uri uri, ContentValues values) {
    //---add a new book---
    long rowID = booksDB.insert(
        DATABASE_TABLE,
        "",
        values);

    //---if added successfully---
    if (rowID>0)
```

```
        {
            Uri _uri = ContentUris.withAppendedId(CONTENT_URI, rowID);
            getContext().getContentResolver().notifyChange(_uri, null);
            return _uri;
        }
        throw new SQLException("Failed to insert row into " + uri);
    }
```

Once the record is inserted successfully, call the `notifyChange()` method of the `ContentResolver`. This will notify registered observers that a row was updated.

To delete a book, override the `delete()` method:

```
public int delete(Uri arg0, String arg1, String[] arg2) {
    // arg0 = uri
    // arg1 = selection
    // arg2 = selectionArgs
    int count=0;
    switch (uriMatcher.match(arg0)){
        case BOOKS:
            count = booksDB.delete(
                    DATABASE_TABLE,
                    arg1,
                    arg2);
            break;
        case BOOK_ID:
            String id = arg0.getPathSegments().get(1);
            count = booksDB.delete(
                    DATABASE_TABLE,
                    _ID + " = " + id +
                    (!TextUtils.isEmpty(arg1) ? " AND (" +
                            arg1 + ')' : ""),
                            arg2);
            break;
        default: throw new IllegalArgumentException("Unknown URI " + arg0);
    }
    getContext().getContentResolver().notifyChange(arg0, null);
    return count;
}
```

Likewise, call the `notifyChange()` method of the `ContentResolver` after the deletion. This will notify registered observers that a row was deleted.

Finally, to update a book, override the `update()` method:

```
@Override
public int update(Uri uri, ContentValues values, String selection,
        String[] selectionArgs) {
    int count = 0;
    switch (uriMatcher.match(uri)){
        case BOOKS:
            count = booksDB.update(
                    DATABASE_TABLE,
                    values,
                    selection,
                    selectionArgs);
```

```
                break;
            case BOOK_ID:
                count = booksDB.update(
                        DATABASE_TABLE,
                        values,
                        _ID + " = " + uri.getPathSegments().get(1) +
                        (!TextUtils.isEmpty(selection) ? " AND (" +
                            selection + ')' : ""),
                        selectionArgs);
                break;
            default: throw new IllegalArgumentException("Unknown URI " + uri);
        }
        getContext().getContentResolver().notifyChange(uri, null);
        return count;
    }
}
```

As with the `insert()` and `delete()` methods, you call the `notifyChange()` method of the `ContentResolver` after the update. This notifies registered observers that a row was updated.

Finally, to register your content provider with Android, modify the `AndroidManifest.xml` file by adding the `<provider>` element.

Using the Content Provider

Now that you have built your new content provider, you can test it from within your Android application. The following Try It Out demonstrates how this can be done.

TRY IT OUT Using the Newly Created Content Provider

1. Using the same project created in the previous section, add the following statements in bold to the `main.xml` file:

```xml
<?xml version="1.0" encoding="utf-8"?>
<LinearLayout xmlns:android="http://schemas.android.com/apk/res/android"
    android:orientation="vertical"
    android:layout_width="fill_parent"
    android:layout_height="fill_parent" >

<TextView
    android:layout_width="fill_parent"
    android:layout_height="wrap_content"
    android:text="ISBN" />

<EditText
    android:id="@+id/txtISBN"
    android:layout_height="wrap_content"
    android:layout_width="fill_parent" />

<TextView
    android:layout_width="fill_parent"
    android:layout_height="wrap_content"
```

```
        android:text="Title" />

<EditText
    android:id="@+id/txtTitle"
    android:layout_height="wrap_content"
    android:layout_width="fill_parent" />

<Button
    android:text="Add title"
    android:id="@+id/btnAdd"
    android:layout_width="fill_parent"
    android:layout_height="wrap_content" />

<Button
    android:text="Retrieve titles"
    android:id="@+id/btnRetrieve"
    android:layout_width="fill_parent"
    android:layout_height="wrap_content" />

</LinearLayout>
```

2. In the `MainActivity.java` file, add the following statements in bold:

```
package net.learn2develop.ContentProviders;

import android.app.Activity;
import android.os.Bundle;

import android.util.Log;
import android.view.View;
import android.widget.Button;
import android.widget.EditText;
import android.widget.Toast;
import android.content.ContentValues;
import android.database.Cursor;
import android.net.Uri;

public class MainActivity extends Activity {
    /** Called when the activity is first created. */
    @Override
    public void onCreate(Bundle savedInstanceState) {
        super.onCreate(savedInstanceState);
        setContentView(R.layout.main);

        Button btnAdd = (Button) findViewById(R.id.btnAdd);
        btnAdd.setOnClickListener(new View.OnClickListener() {
            public void onClick(View v) {
                //---add a book---
                ContentValues values = new ContentValues();
                values.put(BooksProvider.TITLE, ((EditText)
                    findViewById(R.id.txtTitle)).getText().toString());
                values.put(BooksProvider.ISBN, ((EditText)
                    findViewById(R.id.txtISBN)).getText().toString());
                Uri uri = getContentResolver().insert(
                    BooksProvider.CONTENT_URI, values);
```

```
                    Toast.makeText(getBaseContext(),uri.toString(),
                        Toast.LENGTH_LONG).show();
                }
            });

            Button btnRetrieve = (Button) findViewById(R.id.btnRetrieve);
            btnRetrieve.setOnClickListener(new View.OnClickListener() {
                public void onClick(View v) {
                    //---retrieve the titles---
                    Uri allTitles = Uri.parse(
                        "content://net.learn2develop.provider.Books/books");
                    Cursor c = managedQuery(allTitles, null, null, null,
                        "title desc");
                    if (c.moveToFirst()) {
                        do{
                            Log.v("ContentProviders",
                                c.getString(c.getColumnIndex(
                                    BooksProvider._ID)) + ", " +
                                c.getString(c.getColumnIndex(
                                    BooksProvider.TITLE)) + ", " +
                                c.getString(c.getColumnIndex(
                                    BooksProvider.ISBN)));
                        } while (c.moveToNext());
                    }
                }
            });
        }
    }
```

3. Press F11 to debug the application on the Android Emulator.

4. Enter an ISBN and title for a book and click the Add title button. Figure 7-6 shows the Toast class displaying the URI of the book added to the content provider. To retrieve all the titles stored in the content provider, click the Retrieve titles button and observe the values printed in the Logcat window of Eclipse.

How It Works

First, you modified the activity so that users can enter a book's ISBN and title to add to the content provider that you have just created.

To add a book to the content provider, you create a new ContentValues object and then populate it with the various information about a book:

```
                //---add a book---
                ContentValues values = new ContentValues();
                values.put(BooksProvider.TITLE, ((EditText)
                    findViewById(R.id.txtTitle)).getText().toString());
                values.put(BooksProvider.ISBN, ((EditText)
                    findViewById(R.id.txtISBN)).getText().toString());
                Uri uri = getContentResolver().insert(
                    BooksProvider.CONTENT_URI, values);
```

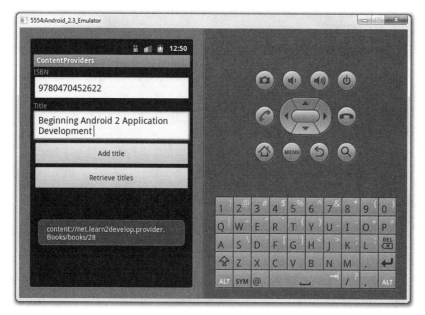

FIGURE 7-6

Notice that because your content provider is in the same package, you can use the BooksProvider.TITLE and the BooksProvider.ISBN constants to refer to the "title" and "isbn" fields, respectively. If you were accessing this content provider from another package, then you would not be able to use these constants. In that case, you need to specify the field name directly, like this:

```
ContentValues values = new ContentValues();
values.put("title", ((EditText)
    findViewById(R.id.txtTitle)).getText().toString());
values.put("isbn", ((EditText)
    findViewById(R.id.txtISBN)).getText().toString());
Uri uri = getContentResolver().insert(
        Uri.parse(
        "content://net.learn2develop.provider.Books/books"),
        values);
Toast.makeText(getBaseContext(),uri.toString(),
    Toast.LENGTH_LONG).show();
```

Also note that for external packages you need to refer to the content URI using the fully qualified content URI:

```
Uri.parse(
        "content://net.learn2develop.provider.Books/books"),
```

To retrieve all the titles in the content provider, you used the following code snippets:

```
Uri allTitles = Uri.parse(
        "content://net.learn2develop.provider.Books/books");
```

```
Cursor c = managedQuery(allTitles, null, null, null,
    "title desc");
if (c.moveToFirst()) {
    do{
        Log.v("ContentProviders",
            c.getString(c.getColumnIndex(
                BooksProvider._ID)) + ", " +
            c.getString(c.getColumnIndex(
                BooksProvider.TITLE)) + ", " +
            c.getString(c.getColumnIndex(
                BooksProvider.ISBN)));
    } while (c.moveToNext());
}
```

The preceding query will return the result sorted in descending order based on the `title` field.

If you want to update a book's detail, call the `update()` method with the content URI indicating the book's ID:

```
ContentValues editedValues = new ContentValues();
editedValues.put(BooksProvider.TITLE, "Android Tips and Tricks");
getContentResolver().update(
    Uri.parse(
        "content://net.learn2develop.provider.Books/books/2"),
    editedValues,
    null,
    null);
```

To delete a book, use the `delete()` method with the content URI indicating the book's ID:

```
getContentResolver().delete(
    Uri.parse("content://net.learn2develop.provider.Books/books/2"),
    null, null);
```

To delete all books, simply omit the book's ID in your content URI:

```
getContentResolver().delete(
    Uri.parse("content://net.learn2develop.provider.Books/books"),
    null, null);
```

SUMMARY

In this chapter, you learned what content providers are and how to use some of the built-in content providers in Android. In particular, you have seen how to use the Contacts content provider. Google's decision to provide content providers enables applications to share data through a standard set of programming interfaces. In addition to the built-in content providers, you can also create your own custom content provider to share data with other packages.

EXERCISES

1. Write the query to retrieve all contacts from the Contacts application that contain the word "jack."

2. Name the methods that you need to override in your own implementation of a content provider.

3. How do you register a content provider in your `AndroidManifest.xml` file?

Answers can be found in Appendix C.

▶ WHAT YOU LEARNED IN THIS CHAPTER

TOPIC	KEY CONCEPTS
Retrieving a managed cursor	Use the `managedQuery()` method.
Two ways to specify a query for a content provider	Use either a query URI or a predefined query string constant.
Retrieving the value of a column in a content provider	Use the `getColumnIndex()` method.
Query URI for accessing a contact's name	`ContactsContract.Contacts.CONTENT_URI`
Query URI for accessing a contact's phone number	`ContactsContract.CommonDataKinds.Phone.CONTENT_URI`
Creating your own content provider	Create a class and extend the `ContentProvider` class.

8

Messaging and Networking

WHAT YOU WILL LEARN IN THIS CHAPTER

➤ How to send SMS messages programmatically from within your application

➤ How to send SMS messages using the built-in Messaging application

➤ How to receive incoming SMS messages

➤ How to send e-mail messages from your application

➤ How to connect to the Web using HTTP

➤ How to consume Web services

Once your basic Android application is up and running, the next interesting thing you can add to it is the capability to communicate with the outside world. You may want your application to send an SMS message to another phone when an event happens (such as when you reach a particular geographical location), or you may wish to access a Web service that provides certain services (such as currency exchange, weather, etc.).

In this chapter, you learn how to send and receive SMS messages programmatically from within your Android application.

You will also learn how to use the HTTP protocol to talk to web servers so that you can download text and binary data. The last part of this chapter shows you how to parse XML files to extract the relevant parts of an XML file — a technique that is useful if you are accessing Web services.

SMS MESSAGING

SMS messaging is one of the main *killer applications* on a mobile phone today — for some users as necessary as the phone itself. Any mobile phone you buy today should have at least SMS messaging capabilities, and nearly all users of any age know how to send and receive such messages. Android comes with a built-in SMS application that enables you to send and receive SMS messages. However, in some cases you might want to integrate SMS capabilities into your own Android application. For example, you might want to write an application that automatically sends a SMS message at regular time intervals. For example, this would be useful if you wanted to track the location of your kids — simply give them an Android device that sends out an SMS message containing its geographical location every 30 minutes. Now you know if they really went to the library after school! (Of course, that would also mean you would have to pay the fees incurred in sending all those SMS messages...)

This section describes how you can programmatically send and receive SMS messages in your Android applications. The good news for Android developers is that you don't need a real device to test SMS messaging: The free Android Emulator provides that capability.

Sending SMS Messages Programmatically

You will first learn how to send SMS messages programmatically from within your application. Using this approach, your application can automatically send an SMS message to a recipient without user intervention. The following Try It Out shows you how.

TRY IT OUT   Sending SMS Messages

codefile SMS.zip available for download at Wrox.com

1.   Using Eclipse, create a new Android project and name it as shown in Figure 8-1.

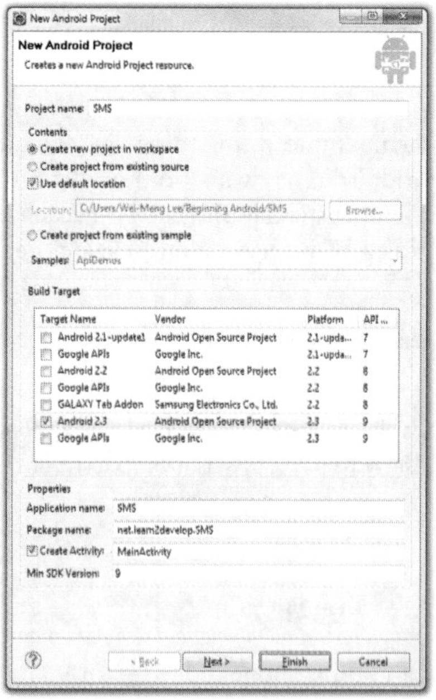

FIGURE 8-1

2. Add the following statements in bold to the `main.xml` file:

```xml
<?xml version="1.0" encoding="utf-8"?>
<LinearLayout xmlns:android="http://schemas.android.com/apk/res/android"
    android:orientation="vertical"
    android:layout_width="fill_parent"
    android:layout_height="fill_parent"
>

<Button
    android:id="@+id/btnSendSMS"
    android:layout_width="fill_parent"
    android:layout_height="wrap_content"
    android:text="Send SMS" />

</LinearLayout>
```

3. In the `AndroidManifest.xml` file, add the following statements in bold:

```xml
<?xml version="1.0" encoding="utf-8"?>
<manifest xmlns:android="http://schemas.android.com/apk/res/android"
      package="net.learn2develop.SMS"
      android:versionCode="1"
      android:versionName="1.0">
    <application android:icon="@drawable/icon" android:label="@string/app_name">
        <activity android:name=".MainActivity"
                  android:label="@string/app_name">
            <intent-filter>
                <action android:name="android.intent.action.MAIN" />
                <category android:name="android.intent.category.LAUNCHER" />
            </intent-filter>
        </activity>
    </application>
    <uses-sdk android:minSdkVersion="8" />
    <uses-permission android:name="android.permission.SEND_SMS"></uses-permission>
</manifest>
```

4. Add the following statements in bold to the `MainActivity.java` file:

```java
package net.learn2develop.SMS;

import android.app.Activity;
import android.os.Bundle;

import android.app.PendingIntent;
import android.content.Intent;
import android.telephony.SmsManager;
import android.view.View;
import android.widget.Button;

public class MainActivity extends Activity {
    Button btnSendSMS;
    /** Called when the activity is first created. */
    @Override
    public void onCreate(Bundle savedInstanceState) {
        super.onCreate(savedInstanceState);
```

```
    setContentView(R.layout.main);

    btnSendSMS = (Button) findViewById(R.id.btnSendSMS);
    btnSendSMS.setOnClickListener(new View.OnClickListener()
    {
        public void onClick(View v)
        {
            sendSMS("5556", "Hello my friends!");

        }
    });
}

//---sends an SMS message to another device---
private void sendSMS(String phoneNumber, String message)
{
    SmsManager sms = SmsManager.getDefault();
    sms.sendTextMessage(phoneNumber, null, message, null, null);
}
}
```

5. Press F11 to debug the application on the Android Emulator. Using the Android SDK and AVD Manager, launch another AVD.

6. On the first Android Emulator, click the Send SMS button to send an SMS message to the second emulator. The left side of Figure 8-2 shows the SMS message received by the second emulator (note the notification bar at the top of the second emulator).

FIGURE 8-2

How It Works

Android uses a permissions-based policy whereby all the permissions needed by an application must be specified in the `AndroidManifest.xml` file. This ensures that when the application is installed, the user knows exactly which access permissions it requires.

Because sending SMS messages incurs additional costs on the user's end, indicating the SMS permissions in the `AndroidManifest.xml` file enables users to decide whether to allow the application to install or not.

To send an SMS message programmatically, you use the `SmsManager` class. Unlike other classes, you do not directly instantiate this class; instead, you call the `getDefault()` static method to obtain a `SmsManager` object. You then send the SMS message using the `sendTextMessage()` method:

```
private void sendSMS(String phoneNumber, String message)
{
    SmsManager sms = SmsManager.getDefault();
    sms.sendTextMessage(phoneNumber, null, message, null, null);
}
```

Following are the five arguments to the `sendTextMessage()` method:

➤   `destinationAddress` — Phone number of the recipient

➤   `scAddress` — Service center address; use null for default SMSC

➤   `text` — Content of the SMS message

➤   `sentIntent` — Pending intent to invoke when the message is sent (discussed in more detail in the next section)

➤   `deliveryIntent` — Pending intent to invoke when the message has been delivered (discussed in more detail in the next section)

Getting Feedback after Sending the Message

In the previous section, you learned how to programmatically send SMS messages using the `SmsManager` class; but how do you know that the message has been sent correctly? To do so, you can create two `PendingIntent` objects to monitor the status of the SMS message-sending process. These two `PendingIntent` objects are passed to the last two arguments of the `sendTextMessage()` method. The following code snippets show how you can monitor the status of the SMS message being sent:

```
//---sends an SMS message to another device---
private void sendSMS(String phoneNumber, String message)
{
    String SENT = "SMS_SENT";
    String DELIVERED = "SMS_DELIVERED";

    PendingIntent sentPI = PendingIntent.getBroadcast(this, 0,
        new Intent(SENT), 0);

    PendingIntent deliveredPI = PendingIntent.getBroadcast(this, 0,
```

```java
        new Intent(DELIVERED), 0);

    //---when the SMS has been sent---
    registerReceiver(new BroadcastReceiver(){
        @Override
        public void onReceive(Context arg0, Intent arg1) {
            switch (getResultCode())
            {
                case Activity.RESULT_OK:
                    Toast.makeText(getBaseContext(), "SMS sent",
                            Toast.LENGTH_SHORT).show();
                    break;
                case SmsManager.RESULT_ERROR_GENERIC_FAILURE:
                    Toast.makeText(getBaseContext(), "Generic failure",
                            Toast.LENGTH_SHORT).show();
                    break;
                case SmsManager.RESULT_ERROR_NO_SERVICE:
                    Toast.makeText(getBaseContext(), "No service",
                            Toast.LENGTH_SHORT).show();
                    break;
                case SmsManager.RESULT_ERROR_NULL_PDU:
                    Toast.makeText(getBaseContext(), "Null PDU",
                            Toast.LENGTH_SHORT).show();
                    break;
                case SmsManager.RESULT_ERROR_RADIO_OFF:
                    Toast.makeText(getBaseContext(), "Radio off",
                            Toast.LENGTH_SHORT).show();
                    break;
            }
        }
    }, new IntentFilter(SENT));

    //---when the SMS has been delivered---
    registerReceiver(new BroadcastReceiver(){
        @Override
        public void onReceive(Context arg0, Intent arg1) {
            switch (getResultCode())
            {
                case Activity.RESULT_OK:
                    Toast.makeText(getBaseContext(), "SMS delivered",
                            Toast.LENGTH_SHORT).show();
                    break;
                case Activity.RESULT_CANCELED:  .
                    Toast.makeText(getBaseContext(), "SMS not delivered",
                            Toast.LENGTH_SHORT).show();
                    break;
            }
        }
    }, new IntentFilter(DELIVERED));

    SmsManager sms = SmsManager.getDefault();
    sms.sendTextMessage(phoneNumber, null, message, sentPI, deliveredPI);
}
```

Here, you created two `PendingIntent` objects. You then registered for two `BroadcastReceivers`. These two `BroadcastReceivers` listen for intents that match "SMS_SENT" and "SMS_DELIVERED" (which are fired by the OS when the message has been sent and delivered, respectively). Within each `BroadcastReceiver` you override the `onReceive()` method and get the current result code.

The two `PendingIntent` objects are passed into the last two arguments of the `sendTextMessage()` method:

```
sms.sendTextMessage(phoneNumber, null, message, sentPI, deliveredPI);
```

In this case, whether a message has been sent correctly or failed to be delivered, you will be notified of its status via the two `PendingIntent` objects.

Sending SMS Messages Using Intent

Using the `SmsManager` class, you can send SMS messages from within your application without the need to involve the built-in Messaging application. However, sometimes it would be easier if you could simply invoke the built-in Messaging application and let it do all the work of sending the message.

To activate the built-in Messaging application from within your application, you can use an Intent object together with the MIME type `"vnd.android-dir/mms-sms"` as shown by the following code snippet:

```
/** Called when the activity is first created. */
@Override
public void onCreate(Bundle savedInstanceState) {
    super.onCreate(savedInstanceState);
    setContentView(R.layout.main);

    btnSendSMS = (Button) findViewById(R.id.btnSendSMS);
    btnSendSMS.setOnClickListener(new View.OnClickListener()
    {
        public void onClick(View v)
        {
            //sendSMS("5556", "Hello my friends!");
            Intent i = new
                Intent(android.content.Intent.ACTION_VIEW);
            i.putExtra("address", "5556; 5558; 5560");

            i.putExtra("sms_body", "Hello my friends!");
            i.setType("vnd.android-dir/mms-sms");
            startActivity(i);
        }
    });
}
```

This will invoke the Messaging application, as shown in Figure 8-3. Note that you can send your SMS to multiple recipients by simply separating each phone number with a semicolon (in the `putExtra()` method).

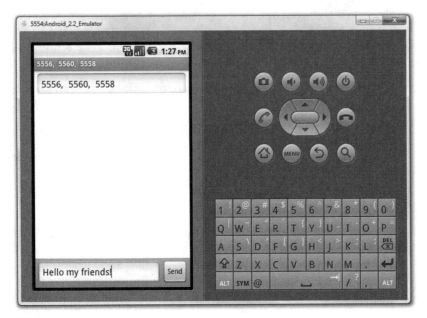

FIGURE 8-3

> **NOTE** *If you use this method to invoke the Messaging application, there is no need to ask for the* SMS_SEND *permission in* AndroidManifest.xml *because your application is ultimately not the one sending the message.*

Receiving SMS Messages

Besides sending SMS messages from your Android applications, you can also receive incoming SMS messages from within your application by using a BroadcastReceiver object. This is useful when you want your application to perform an action when a certain SMS message is received. For example, you might want to track the location of your phone in case it is lost or stolen. In this case, you can write an application that automatically listens for SMS messages containing some secret code. Once that message is received, you can then send an SMS message containing the location's coordinates back to the sender.

The following Try It Out shows how to programmatically listen for incoming SMS messages.

TRY IT OUT Receiving SMS Messages

1. Using the same project created in the previous section, add the following statements in bold to the AndroidManifest.xml file:

```
<?xml version="1.0" encoding="utf-8"?>
<manifest xmlns:android="http://schemas.android.com/apk/res/android"
```

```
            package="net.learn2develop.SMS"
            android:versionCode="1"
            android:versionName="1.0">
    <application android:icon="@drawable/icon" android:label="@string/app_name">
        <activity android:name=".MainActivity"
                  android:label="@string/app_name">
            <intent-filter>
                <action android:name="android.intent.action.MAIN" />
                <category android:name="android.intent.category.LAUNCHER" />
            </intent-filter>
        </activity>
        <receiver android:name=".SMSReceiver">
            <intent-filter>
                <action android:name=
                    "android.provider.Telephony.SMS_RECEIVED" />
            </intent-filter>
        </receiver>
    </application>
    <uses-sdk android:minSdkVersion="8" />
    <uses-permission android:name="android.permission.SEND_SMS"></uses-permission>
    <uses-permission android:name="android.permission.RECEIVE_SMS">
    </uses-permission>
</manifest>
```

2. In the src folder of the project, add a new Class file to the package name and call it SMSReceiver.java (see Figure 8-4).

3. Code the SMSReceiver.java file as follows:

```
package net.learn2develop.SMS;

import android.content.BroadcastReceiver;
import android.content.Context;
import android.content.Intent;
import android.os.Bundle;
import android.telephony.SmsMessage;
import android.widget.Toast;

public class SMSReceiver extends BroadcastReceiver
{
    @Override
    public void onReceive(Context context, Intent intent)
    {
        //---get the SMS message passed in---
        Bundle bundle = intent.getExtras();
        SmsMessage[] msgs = null;
        String str = "";
        if (bundle != null)
        {
            //---retrieve the SMS message received---
            Object[] pdus = (Object[]) bundle.get("pdus");
            msgs = new SmsMessage[pdus.length];
            for (int i=0; i<msgs.length; i++){
                msgs[i] = SmsMessage.createFromPdu((byte[])pdus[i]);
                str += "SMS from " + msgs[i].getOriginatingAddress();
```

FIGURE 8-4

```
            str += " :";
            str += msgs[i].getMessageBody().toString();
            str += "\n";
        }
        //---display the new SMS message---
        Toast.makeText(context, str, Toast.LENGTH_SHORT).show();
    }
  }
}
```

4. Press F11 to debug the application on the Android Emulator.

5. Using the DDMS, send a message to the emulator. Your application should be able to receive the message and display it using the `Toast` class (see Figure 8-5).

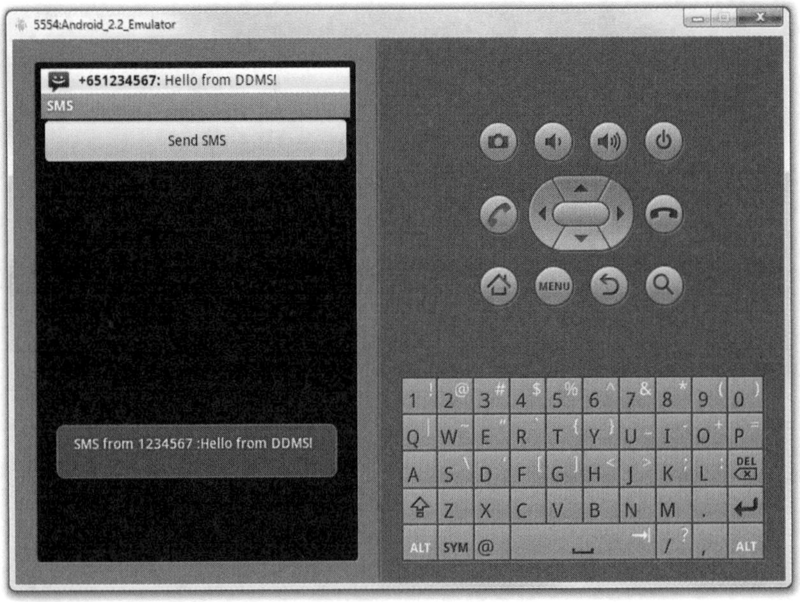

FIGURE 8-5

How It Works

To listen for incoming SMS messages, you create a `BroadcastReceiver` class. The `BroadcastReceiver` class enables your application to receive intents sent by other applications using the `sendBroadcast()` method. Essentially, it enables your application to handle events raised by other applications. When an intent is received, the `onReceive()` method is called; hence, you need to override this.

When an incoming SMS message is received, the `onReceive()` method is fired. The SMS message is contained in the `Intent` object (intent; the second parameter in the `onReceive()` method) via a `Bundle` object. The messages are stored in an `Object` array in the PDU format. To extract each message, you use the static `createFromPdu()` method from the `SmsMessage` class. The SMS message is then displayed using the `Toast` class. The phone number of the sender is obtained via the `getOriginatingAddress()`

method, so if you need to send an autoreply to the sender, this is the method to obtain the sender's phone number.

One interesting characteristic of the BroadcastReceiver is that you can continue to listen for incoming SMS messages even if the application is not running; as long as the application is installed on the device, any incoming SMS messages will be received by the application.

Updating an Activity from a BroadcastReceiver

The previous section described how you can use a BroadcastReceiver class to listen for incoming SMS messages and then use the Toast class to display the received SMS message. Often, you'll want to send the SMS message back to the main activity of your application. For example, you might wish to display the message in a TextView. The following Try It Out demonstrates how you can do this.

TRY IT OUT   Creating a View-Based Application Project

1. Using the same project created in the previous section, add the following lines in bold to the main.xml file:

```xml
<?xml version="1.0" encoding="utf-8"?>
<LinearLayout xmlns:android="http://schemas.android.com/apk/res/android"
    android:orientation="vertical"
    android:layout_width="fill_parent"
    android:layout_height="fill_parent"
>

<Button
    android:id="@+id/btnSendSMS"
    android:layout_width="fill_parent"
    android:layout_height="wrap_content"
    android:text="Send SMS" />

<TextView
    android:id="@+id/textView1"
    android:layout_width="wrap_content"
    android:layout_height="wrap_content" />

</LinearLayout>
```

2. Add the following statements in bold to the SMSReceiver.java file:

```java
package net.learn2develop.SMS;

import android.content.BroadcastReceiver;
import android.content.Context;
import android.content.Intent;
import android.os.Bundle;
import android.telephony.SmsMessage;
import android.widget.Toast;

public class SMSReceiver extends BroadcastReceiver
```

```
{
    @Override
    public void onReceive(Context context, Intent intent)
    {
        //---get the SMS message passed in---
        Bundle bundle = intent.getExtras();
        SmsMessage[] msgs = null;
        String str = "";
        if (bundle != null)
        {
            //---retrieve the SMS message received---
            Object[] pdus = (Object[]) bundle.get("pdus");
            msgs = new SmsMessage[pdus.length];
            for (int i=0; i<msgs.length; i++){
                msgs[i] = SmsMessage.createFromPdu((byte[])pdus[i]);
                str += "SMS from " + msgs[i].getOriginatingAddress();
                str += " :";
                str += msgs[i].getMessageBody().toString();
                str += "\n";
            }
            //---display the new SMS message---
            Toast.makeText(context, str, Toast.LENGTH_SHORT).show();

            //---send a broadcast intent to update the SMS received in the activity---
            Intent broadcastIntent = new Intent();
            broadcastIntent.setAction("SMS_RECEIVED_ACTION");
            broadcastIntent.putExtra("sms", str);
            context.sendBroadcast(broadcastIntent);
        }
    }
}
```

3. Add the following statements in bold to the `MainActivity.java` file:

```
package net.learn2develop.SMS;

import android.app.Activity;
import android.os.Bundle;
import android.app.PendingIntent;
import android.content.Context;
import android.content.Intent;
import android.telephony.SmsManager;
import android.view.View;
import android.widget.Button;
import android.widget.Toast;

import android.content.BroadcastReceiver;
import android.content.IntentFilter;
import android.widget.TextView;

public class MainActivity extends Activity {
    Button btnSendSMS;
    IntentFilter intentFilter;

    private BroadcastReceiver intentReceiver = new BroadcastReceiver() {
```

```java
    @Override
    public void onReceive(Context context, Intent intent) {
        //---display the SMS received in the TextView---
        TextView SMSes = (TextView) findViewById(R.id.textView1);
        SMSes.setText(intent.getExtras().getString("sms"));
    }
};

/** Called when the activity is first created. */
@Override
public void onCreate(Bundle savedInstanceState) {
    super.onCreate(savedInstanceState);
    setContentView(R.layout.main);

    //---intent to filter for SMS messages received---
    intentFilter = new IntentFilter();
    intentFilter.addAction("SMS_RECEIVED_ACTION");

    btnSendSMS = (Button) findViewById(R.id.btnSendSMS);
    btnSendSMS.setOnClickListener(new View.OnClickListener()
    {
        public void onClick(View v)
        {
            //sendSMS("5554", "Hello my friends!");

            Intent i = new
                Intent(android.content.Intent.ACTION_VIEW);
            i.putExtra("address", "5556; 5558; 5560");
            i.putExtra("sms_body", "Hello my friends!");
            i.setType("vnd.android-dir/mms-sms");
            startActivity(i);
        }
    });
}

@Override
protected void onResume() {
    //---register the receiver---
    registerReceiver(intentReceiver, intentFilter);
    super.onResume();
}

@Override
protected void onPause() {
    //---unregister the receiver---
    unregisterReceiver(intentReceiver);
    super.onPause();
}

//---sends an SMS message to another device---
private void sendSMS(String phoneNumber, String message)
{
    //...
}
}
```

4. Press F11 to debug the application on the Android Emulator. Using the DDMS, send an SMS message to the emulator. Figure 8-6 shows the `Toast` class displaying the message received, and the `TextView` showing the message received.

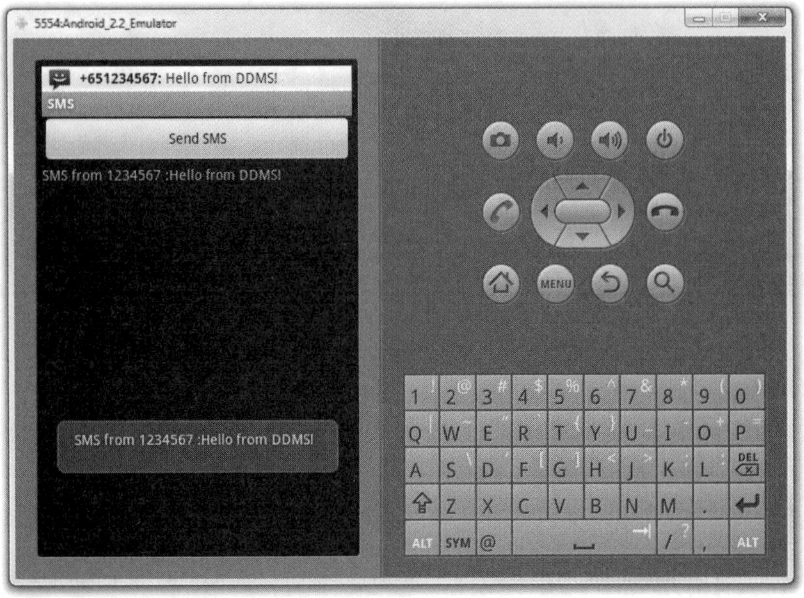

FIGURE 8-6

How It Works

You first added a `TextView` to your activity so that it can be used to display the received SMS message.

Next, you modified the `SMSReceiver` class so that when it receives an SMS message, it will broadcast another `Intent` object so that any applications listening for this intent can be notified (which we will implement in the activity next). The SMS received is also sent out via this intent:

```
//---send a broadcast intent to update the SMS received in the activity---
Intent broadcastIntent = new Intent();
broadcastIntent.setAction("SMS_RECEIVED_ACTION");
broadcastIntent.putExtra("sms", str);
context.sendBroadcast(broadcastIntent);
```

Next, in your activity you created a `BroadcastReceiver` object to listen for broadcast intents:

```
private BroadcastReceiver intentReceiver = new BroadcastReceiver() {
    @Override
    public void onReceive(Context context, Intent intent) {
        //---display the SMS received in the TextView---
        TextView SMSes = (TextView) findViewById(R.id.textView1);
        SMSes.setText(intent.getExtras().getString("sms"));
    }
};
```

When a broadcast intent is received, you update the SMS message in the TextView.

You need to create an IntentFilter object so that you can listen for a particular intent. In this case, the intent is "SMS_RECEIVED_ACTION":

```
@Override
public void onCreate(Bundle savedInstanceState) {
    super.onCreate(savedInstanceState);
    setContentView(R.layout.main);

    //---intent to filter for SMS messages received---
    intentFilter = new IntentFilter();
    intentFilter.addAction("SMS_RECEIVED_ACTION");
    //...
}
```

Finally, you register the BroadcastReceiver in the activity's onResume() event and unregister it in the onPause() event:

```
@Override
protected void onResume() {
    //---register the receiver---
    registerReceiver(intentReceiver, intentFilter);
    super.onResume();
}

@Override
protected void onPause() {
    //---unregister the receiver---
    unregisterReceiver(intentReceiver);
    super.onPause();
}
```

This means that the TextView will display the SMS message only when the message is received while the activity is visible on the screen. If the SMS message is received when the activity is not in the foreground, the TextView will not be updated.

Invoking an Activity from a BroadcastReceiver

The previous example shows how you can pass the SMS message received to be displayed in the activity. However, in many situations your activity may be in the background when the SMS message is received. In this case, it would be useful to be able to bring the activity to the foreground when a message is received. The following Try It Out shows you how.

TRY IT OUT   Invoking an Activity

1.   Using the same project created in the previous section, add the following lines in bold to the MainActivity.java file:

```
/** Called when the activity is first created. */
@Override
```

```java
public void onCreate(Bundle savedInstanceState) {
    super.onCreate(savedInstanceState);
    setContentView(R.layout.main);

    //---intent to filter for SMS messages received---
    intentFilter = new IntentFilter();
    intentFilter.addAction("SMS_RECEIVED_ACTION");

    //---register the receiver---
    registerReceiver(intentReceiver, intentFilter);

    btnSendSMS = (Button) findViewById(R.id.btnSendSMS);
    btnSendSMS.setOnClickListener(new View.OnClickListener()
    {
        public void onClick(View v)
        {
            //sendSMS("5554", "Hello my friends!");
            Intent i = new
                Intent(android.content.Intent.ACTION_VIEW);
            i.putExtra("address", "5556; 5558; 5560");


            i.putExtra("sms_body", "Hello my friends!");
            i.setType("vnd.android-dir/mms-sms");
            startActivity(i);
        }
    });
}

@Override
protected void onResume() {
    //---register the receiver---
    //registerReceiver(intentReceiver, intentFilter);
    super.onResume();
}

@Override
protected void onPause() {
    //---unregister the receiver---
    //unregisterReceiver(intentReceiver);
    super.onPause();
}

@Override
protected void onDestroy() {
    //---unregister the receiver---
    unregisterReceiver(intentReceiver);
    super.onPause();
}
```

2. Add the following statements in bold to the SMSReceiver.java file:

```java
@Override
public void onReceive(Context context, Intent intent)
{
```

```
        //---get the SMS message passed in---
        Bundle bundle = intent.getExtras();
        SmsMessage[] msgs = null;
        String str = "";
        if (bundle != null)
        {
            //---retrieve the SMS message received---
            Object[] pdus = (Object[]) bundle.get("pdus");
            msgs = new SmsMessage[pdus.length];
            for (int i=0; i<msgs.length; i++){
                msgs[i] = SmsMessage.createFromPdu((byte[])pdus[i]);
                str += "SMS from " + msgs[i].getOriginatingAddress();
                str += " :";
                str += msgs[i].getMessageBody().toString();
                str += "\n";
            }
            //---display the new SMS message---
            Toast.makeText(context, str, Toast.LENGTH_SHORT).show();

            //---launch the MainActivity---
            Intent mainActivityIntent = new Intent(context, MainActivity.class);
            mainActivityIntent.setFlags(Intent.FLAG_ACTIVITY_NEW_TASK);
            context.startActivity(mainActivityIntent);

            //---send a broadcast to update the SMS received in the activity---
            Intent broadcastIntent = new Intent();
            broadcastIntent.setAction("SMS_RECEIVED_ACTION");
            broadcastIntent.putExtra("sms", str);
            context.sendBroadcast(broadcastIntent);
        }
    }
```

3. Modify the `main.xml` file as follows:

```
<activity android:name=".MainActivity"
          android:label="@string/app_name"
          android:launchMode="singleTask" >
    <intent-filter>
        <action android:name="android.intent.action.MAIN" />
        <category android:name="android.intent.category.LAUNCHER" />
    </intent-filter>
</activity>
```

4. Press F11 to debug the application on the Android Emulator. When the `MainActivity` is shown, click the Home button to send the activity to the background.

5. Use the DDMS to send an SMS message to the emulator again. This time, note that the activity will be brought to the foreground, displaying the SMS message received.

How It Works

In the `MainActivity` class, you first register the `BroadcastReceiver` in the activity's `onCreate()` event, instead of the `onResume()` event; and instead of unregistering it in the `onPause()` event, you now unregister it in the onDestroy() event. This ensures that even if the activity is in the background, it will still be able to listen for the broadcast intent.

Next, you modify the onReceive() event in the SMSReceiver class by using an intent to bring the activity to the foreground before broadcasting another intent:

```
//---launch the MainActivity---
Intent mainActivityIntent = new Intent(context, MainActivity.class);
mainActivityIntent.setFlags(Intent.FLAG_ACTIVITY_NEW_TASK);
context.startActivity(mainActivityIntent);

//---send a broadcast to update the SMS received in the activity---
Intent broadcastIntent = new Intent();
broadcastIntent.setAction("SMS_RECEIVED_ACTION");
broadcastIntent.putExtra("sms", str);
context.sendBroadcast(broadcastIntent);
```

The startActivity() method launches the activity and brings it to the foreground. Note that you need to set the Intent.FLAG_ACTIVITY_NEW_TASK flag because calling startActivity() from outside of an activity context requires the FLAG_ACTIVITY_NEW_TASK flag.

You also need to set the launchMode attribute of the <activity> element in the AndroidManifest.xml file to singleTask:

```
<activity android:name=".MainActivity"
          android:label="@string/app_name"
          android:launchMode="singleTask" >
```

If you don't set this, multiple instances of the activity will be launched as your application receives SMS messages.

Note that in this example, when the activity is in the background (such as when you click the Home button to show the home screen), the activity is brought to the foreground and its TextView is updated with the SMS received. However, if the activity was killed (such as when you click the Back button to destroy it), the activity is launched again but the TextView is not updated.

Caveats and Warnings

While the ability to send and receive SMS messages makes Android a very compelling platform for developing sophisticated applications, this flexibility comes with a price. A seemingly innocent application may send SMS messages behind the scene without the user knowing, as demonstrated by a recent case of an SMS-based Trojan Android application (http://forum.vodafone.co.nz/topic/5719-android-sms-trojan-warning/). Claiming to be a media player, once installed, the application sends SMS messages to a premium number, resulting in huge phone bills for the user.

While the user needs to explicitly give permission to your application, the request for permission is only shown at installation time. Figure 8-7 shows the request for permission that appears when you try to install the application (as an APK file; Chapter 11 discusses packaging your Android applications in more detail) on the emulator (same as on a real device). If the user clicks the Install button, he or she is considered to have given permission to allow the application to send and receive SMS messages. This is dangerous, as after the application is installed it can send and receive SMS messages without ever prompting the user again.

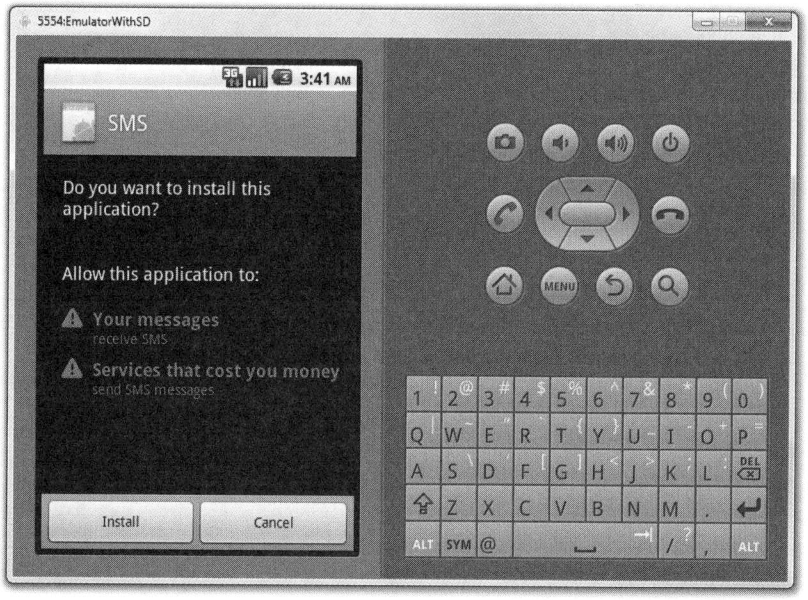

FIGURE 8-7

In addition to this, the application can also "sniff" for incoming SMS messages. For example, based on the techniques you learned from the previous section, you can easily write an application that checks for certain keywords in the SMS message. When an SMS message contains the keyword you are looking for, you can then use the Location Manager (discussed in Chapter 9) to obtain your geographical location and then send the coordinates back to the sender of the SMS message. The sender could then easily track your location. All these tasks can be done easily without the user knowing it! That said, users should try to avoid installing Android applications that come from dubious sources, such as from unknown websites, strangers, etc.

SENDING E-MAIL

Like SMS messaging, Android also supports e-mail. The Gmail/Email application on Android enables you to configure an e-mail account using POP3 or IMAP. Besides sending and receiving e-mails using the Gmail/Email application, you can also send e-mail messages programmatically from within your Android application. The following Try It Out shows you how.

TRY IT OUT   **Sending E-mail Programmatically**

codefile Emails.zip available for download at Wrox.com

1. Using Eclipse, create a new Android project and name it **Emails**.

2. Add the following statements in bold to the main.xml file:

```xml
<?xml version="1.0" encoding="utf-8"?>
<LinearLayout xmlns:android="http://schemas.android.com/apk/res/android"
    android:orientation="vertical"
    android:layout_width="fill_parent"
    android:layout_height="fill_parent"
    >

<Button
    android:id="@+id/btnSendEmail"
    android:layout_width="fill_parent"
    android:layout_height="wrap_content"
    android:text="Send Email" />

</LinearLayout>
```

3. Add the following statements in bold to the MainActivity.java file:

```java
package net.learn2develop.Email;

import android.app.Activity;
import android.os.Bundle;

import android.content.Intent;
import android.net.Uri;
import android.view.View;
import android.widget.Button;

public class MainActivity extends Activity {
    Button btnSendEmail;

    /** Called when the activity is first created. */
    @Override
    public void onCreate(Bundle savedInstanceState) {
        super.onCreate(savedInstanceState);
        setContentView(R.layout.main);

        btnSendEmail = (Button) findViewById(R.id.btnSendEmail);
        btnSendEmail.setOnClickListener(new View.OnClickListener()
        {
            public void onClick(View v)
            {
                String[] to = {"weimenglee@learn2develop.net", "weimenglee@gmail.com"};
                String[] cc = {"course@learn2develop.net"};
                sendEmail(to, cc, "Hello", "Hello my friends!");
            }
        });
```

```
    }

    //---sends an SMS message to another device---
    private void sendEmail(String[] emailAddresses, String[] carbonCopies,
    String subject, String message)
    {
        Intent emailIntent = new Intent(Intent.ACTION_SEND);
        emailIntent.setData(Uri.parse("mailto:"));
        String[] to = emailAddresses;
        String[] cc = carbonCopies;
        emailIntent.putExtra(Intent.EXTRA_EMAIL, to);
        emailIntent.putExtra(Intent.EXTRA_CC, cc);
        emailIntent.putExtra(Intent.EXTRA_SUBJECT, subject);
        emailIntent.putExtra(Intent.EXTRA_TEXT, message);
        emailIntent.setType("message/rfc822");
        startActivity(Intent.createChooser(emailIntent, "Email"));
    }
}
```

4. Press F11 to test the application on a real Android device. Click the Send Email button and you should see the Email application launched in your device, as shown in Figure 8-8.

FIGURE 8-8

How It Works

In this example, you are launching the built-in Email application to send an e-mail message. To do so, you use an Intent object and set the various parameters using the setData(), putExtra(), and setType() methods:

```
Intent emailIntent = new Intent(Intent.ACTION_SEND);
emailIntent.setData(Uri.parse("mailto:"));
String[] to = emailAddresses;
String[] cc = carbonCopies;
emailIntent.putExtra(Intent.EXTRA_EMAIL, to);
emailIntent.putExtra(Intent.EXTRA_CC, cc);
emailIntent.putExtra(Intent.EXTRA_SUBJECT, subject);
emailIntent.putExtra(Intent.EXTRA_TEXT, message);
emailIntent.setType("message/rfc822");
startActivity(Intent.createChooser(emailIntent, "Email"));
```

NETWORKING

The previous sections covered how to get connected to the outside world using SMS and e-mail. Another way to achieve that is to use the HTTP protocol. Using the HTTP protocol, you can perform a wide variety of tasks, such as downloading web pages from a web server, downloading binary data, and so on.

The following Try It Out creates an Android project so that you can use the HTTP protocol to connect to the Web to download all sorts of data.

TRY IT OUT Creating the Project

codefile Networking.zip available for download at Wrox.com

1. Using Eclipse, create a new Android project and name it **Networking**.

2. Add the following statement in bold to the `AndroidManifest.xml` file:

```xml
<?xml version="1.0" encoding="utf-8"?>
<manifest xmlns:android="http://schemas.android.com/apk/res/android"
      package="net.learn2develop.Networking"
      android:versionCode="1"
      android:versionName="1.0">
    <application android:icon="@drawable/icon" android:label="@string/app_name">
        <activity android:name=".MainActivity"
                android:label="@string/app_name">
            <intent-filter>
                <action android:name="android.intent.action.MAIN" />
                <category android:name="android.intent.category.LAUNCHER" />
            </intent-filter>
        </activity>
    </application>
    <uses-sdk android:minSdkVersion="8" />
    <uses-permission android:name="android.permission.INTERNET"></uses-permission>
</manifest>
```

3. Import the following namespaces in the `MainActivity.java` file:

```java
package net.learn2develop.Networking;

import android.app.Activity;
import android.os.Bundle;

import java.io.IOException;
import java.io.InputStream;
import java.io.InputStreamReader;
import java.net.HttpURLConnection;
import java.net.URL;
import java.net.URLConnection;
import android.graphics.Bitmap;
import android.graphics.BitmapFactory;
import android.widget.ImageView;
import android.widget.Toast;

import javax.xml.parsers.DocumentBuilder;
```

```java
import javax.xml.parsers.DocumentBuilderFactory;
import javax.xml.parsers.ParserConfigurationException;

import org.w3c.dom.Document;
import org.w3c.dom.Element;
import org.w3c.dom.Node;
import org.w3c.dom.NodeList;

public class MainActivity extends Activity {
    /** Called when the activity is first created. */
    @Override
    public void onCreate(Bundle savedInstanceState) {
        super.onCreate(savedInstanceState);
        setContentView(R.layout.main);
    }
}
```

4. Define the `OpenHttpConnection()` method in the `MainActivity.java` file:

```java
public class MainActivity extends Activity {

    private InputStream OpenHttpConnection(String urlString)
    throws IOException
    {
        InputStream in = null;
        int response = -1;

        URL url = new URL(urlString);
        URLConnection conn = url.openConnection();

        if (!(conn instanceof HttpURLConnection))
            throw new IOException("Not an HTTP connection");
        try{
            HttpURLConnection httpConn = (HttpURLConnection) conn;
            httpConn.setAllowUserInteraction(false);
            httpConn.setInstanceFollowRedirects(true);
            httpConn.setRequestMethod("GET");
            httpConn.connect();
            response = httpConn.getResponseCode();
            if (response == HttpURLConnection.HTTP_OK) {
                in = httpConn.getInputStream();
            }
        }
        catch (Exception ex)
        {
            throw new IOException("Error connecting");
        }
        return in;
    }

    /** Called when the activity is first created. */
    @Override
    public void onCreate(Bundle savedInstanceState) {
        super.onCreate(savedInstanceState);
        setContentView(R.layout.main);
    }
}
```

How It Works

Because you are using the HTTP protocol to connect to the Web, your application needs the INTERNET permission; hence, the first thing you do is add the permission in the AndroidManifest.xml file.

You then define the OpenHttpConnection() method, which takes a URL string and returns an InputStream object. Using an InputStream object, you can download the data by reading bytes from the stream object. In this method, you made use of the HttpURLConnection object to open an HTTP connection with a remote URL. You set all the various properties of the connection, such as the request method, and so on:

```
HttpURLConnection httpConn = (HttpURLConnection) conn;
httpConn.setAllowUserInteraction(false);
httpConn.setInstanceFollowRedirects(true);
httpConn.setRequestMethod("GET");
```

After you try to establish a connection with the server, you get the HTTP response code from it. If the connection is established (via the response code HTTP_OK), then you proceed to get an InputStream object from the connection:

```
httpConn.connect();
response = httpConn.getResponseCode();
if (response == HttpURLConnection.HTTP_OK) {
    in = httpConn.getInputStream();
}
```

Using the InputStream object, you can then start to download the data from the server.

Downloading Binary Data

One of the common tasks you need to perform is downloading binary data from the Web. For example, you may want to download an image from a server so that you can display it in your application. The following Try It Out shows how this is done.

TRY IT OUT Creating the Project

1. Using the same project created earlier, add the following statements in bold to the main.xml file:

```xml
<?xml version="1.0" encoding="utf-8"?>
<LinearLayout xmlns:android="http://schemas.android.com/apk/res/android"
    android:orientation="vertical"
    android:layout_width="fill_parent"
    android:layout_height="fill_parent"
    >

<ImageView
    android:id="@+id/img"
    android:layout_width="wrap_content"
    android:layout_height="wrap_content"
    android:layout_gravity="center" />

</LinearLayout>
```

2. Add the following statements in bold to the `MainActivity.java` file:

```java
public class MainActivity extends Activity {
    ImageView img;

    private InputStream OpenHttpConnection(String urlString)
    throws IOException
    {
        //...
    }

    private Bitmap DownloadImage(String URL)
    {
        Bitmap bitmap = null;
        InputStream in = null;
        try {
            in = OpenHttpConnection(URL);
            bitmap = BitmapFactory.decodeStream(in);
            in.close();
        } catch (IOException e1) {
            Toast.makeText(this, e1.getLocalizedMessage(),
                Toast.LENGTH_LONG).show();

            e1.printStackTrace();
        }
        return bitmap;
    }

    /** Called when the activity is first created. */
    @Override
    public void onCreate(Bundle savedInstanceState) {
        super.onCreate(savedInstanceState);
        setContentView(R.layout.main);

        //---download an image---
        Bitmap bitmap =
            DownloadImage(
            "http://www.streetcar.org/mim/cable/images/cable-01.jpg");
        img = (ImageView) findViewById(R.id.img);
        img.setImageBitmap(bitmap);
    }
}
```

3. Press F11 to debug the application on the Android Emulator. Figure 8-9 shows the image downloaded from the Web and then displayed in the `ImageView`.

How It Works

The `DownloadImage()` method takes the URL of the image to download and then opens the connection to the server using the `OpenHttpConnection()` method that you have defined earlier. Using the `InputStream` object returned by the connection, the `decodeStream()` method from the `BitmapFactory` class is used to download and decode the data into a `Bitmap` object. The `DownloadImage()` method returns a `Bitmap` object.

FIGURE 8-9

The image is then displayed using an `ImageView` view.

REFERRING TO LOCALHOST FROM YOUR EMULATOR

When working with the Android Emulator, you may frequently need to access data hosted on the local web server using `localhost`. For example, your own Web services is likely to be hosted on your local computer during development time and you want to test it on the same development machine you use to write your Android applications. In such cases, you should use the special IP address of 10.0.2.2 (not 127.0.0.1) to refer to the host computer's loopback interface. From the Android Emulator's perspective, `localhost` (127.0.0.1) refers to its own loopback interface.

Downloading Text Files

Besides downloading binary data, you can also download plain-text files. For example, you might be writing an RSS Reader application and hence need to download RSS XML feeds for processing. The following Try It Out shows how you can download a plain-text file in your application.

TRY IT OUT Downloading Plain-Text Files

1. Using the same project created earlier, add the following statements in bold to the `MainActivity`
`.java` file:

```java
public class MainActivity extends Activity {
    ImageView img;

    private InputStream OpenHttpConnection(String urlString)
    throws IOException
    {
        //...
    }

    private Bitmap DownloadImage(String URL)
    {
        //...
    }

    private String DownloadText(String URL)
    {
        int BUFFER_SIZE = 2000;
        InputStream in = null;
        try {
            in = OpenHttpConnection(URL);
        } catch (IOException e1) {
            Toast.makeText(this, e1.getLocalizedMessage(),
                Toast.LENGTH_LONG).show();

            e1.printStackTrace();
            return "";
        }

        InputStreamReader isr = new InputStreamReader(in);
        int charRead;
        String str = "";
        char[] inputBuffer = new char[BUFFER_SIZE];
        try {
            while ((charRead = isr.read(inputBuffer))>0)
            {
                //---convert the chars to a String---
                String readString =
                    String.copyValueOf(inputBuffer, 0, charRead);
                str += readString;
                inputBuffer = new char[BUFFER_SIZE];
            }
            in.close();
        } catch (IOException e) {
            Toast.makeText(this, e.getLocalizedMessage(),
                Toast.LENGTH_LONG).show();

            e.printStackTrace();
```

```
            return "";
        }
        return str;
    }

    /** Called when the activity is first created. */
    @Override
    public void onCreate(Bundle savedInstanceState) {
        super.onCreate(savedInstanceState);
        setContentView(R.layout.main);

        //---download an image---
        Bitmap bitmap =
            DownloadImage(
            "http://www.streetcar.org/mim/cable/images/cable-01.jpg");
        img = (ImageView) findViewById(R.id.img);
        img.setImageBitmap(bitmap);

        //---download an RSS feed---
        String str = DownloadText(
            "http://www.appleinsider.com/appleinsider.rss");
        Toast.makeText(getBaseContext(), str,
                    Toast.LENGTH_SHORT).show();
    }
}
```

2. Press F11 to debug the application on the Android Emulator. Figure 8-10 shows the RSS feed downloaded and displayed using the Toast class.

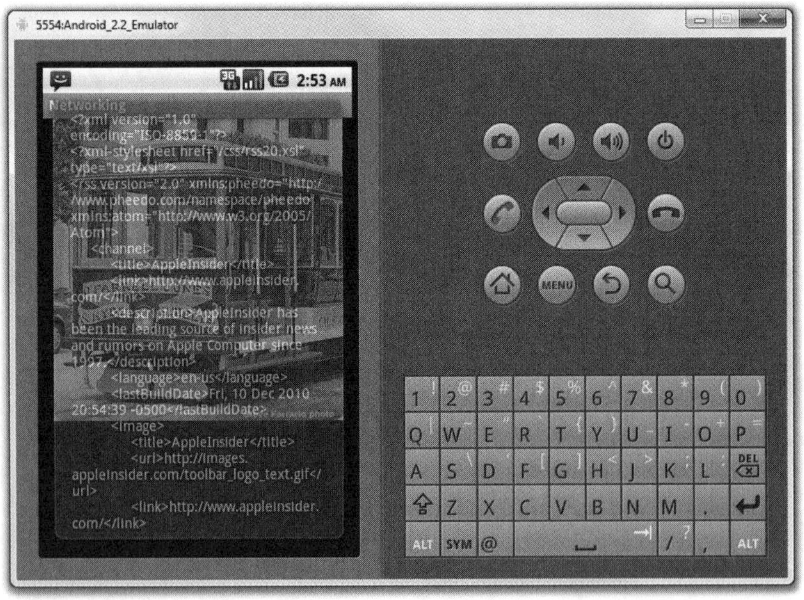

FIGURE 8-10

How It Works

The DownloadText() method takes an URL of the text file to download and then returns the string of the text file downloaded. It basically opens an HTTP connection to the server and then uses an InputStreamReader object to read each character from the stream and save it in a String object.

Accessing Web Services

So far you have seen how to download images and text from the Web. The previous section showed how to download an RSS feed from a server. Very often, you need to download XML files and parse the contents (a good example of this is consuming Web services). Therefore, in this section you learn how to connect to a Web service using the HTTP GET method. Once the Web service returns a result in XML, you will extract the relevant parts and display its content using the Toast class.

For this example, the web method you will be using is from http://services.aonaware.com/DictService/DictService.asmx?op=Define. This web method is from a Dictionary Web service that returns the definitions of a given word.

The web method takes a request in the following format:

```
GET /DictService/DictService.asmx/Define?word=string HTTP/1.1
Host: services.aonaware.com
HTTP/1.1 200 OK
Content-Type: text/xml; charset=utf-8
Content-Length: length
```

It returns a response in the following format:

```
<?xml version="1.0" encoding="utf-8"?>
<WordDefinition xmlns="http://services.aonaware.com/webservices/">
  <Word>string</Word>
  <Definitions>
    <Definition>
      <Word>string</Word>
      <Dictionary>
        <Id>string</Id>
        <Name>string</Name>
      </Dictionary>
      <WordDefinition>string</WordDefinition>
    </Definition>
    <Definition>
      <Word>string</Word>
      <Dictionary>
        <Id>string</Id>
        <Name>string</Name>
      </Dictionary>
      <WordDefinition>string</WordDefinition>
    </Definition>
  </Definitions>
</WordDefinition>
```

Hence, to obtain the definition of a word, you need to establish an HTTP connection to the web method and then parse the XML result that is returned. The following Try It Out shows you how.

TRY IT OUT   Consuming Web Services

1. Using the same project created earlier, add the following statements in bold to the `MainActivity` `.java` file:

```java
public class MainActivity extends Activity {
    ImageView img;

    private InputStream OpenHttpConnection(String urlString)
    throws IOException
    {
        //...
    }

    private Bitmap DownloadImage(String URL)
    {
        //...
    }

    private String DownloadText(String URL)
    {
        //...
    }

    private void WordDefinition(String word) {
        InputStream in = null;
        try {
            in = OpenHttpConnection(
    "http://services.aonaware.com/DictService/DictService.asmx/Define?word=" + word);
            Document doc = null;
            DocumentBuilderFactory dbf =
                DocumentBuilderFactory.newInstance();
            DocumentBuilder db;
            try {
                db = dbf.newDocumentBuilder();
                doc = db.parse(in);
            } catch (ParserConfigurationException e) {
                // TODO Auto-generated catch block
                e.printStackTrace();
            } catch (Exception e) {
                // TODO Auto-generated catch block
                e.printStackTrace();
            }
            doc.getDocumentElement().normalize();

            //---retrieve all the <Definition> nodes---
            NodeList itemNodes =
                doc.getElementsByTagName("Definition");

            String strDefinition = "";
            for (int i = 0; i < definitionElements.getLength(); i++) {
```

```
                    Node itemNode = definitionElements.item(i);
                    if (itemNode.getNodeType() == Node.ELEMENT_NODE)
                    {
                        //---convert the Node into an Element---
                        Element definitionElement = (Element) itemNode;

                        //---get all the <WordDefinition> elements under
                        // the <Definition> element---
                        NodeList wordDefinitionElements =
                            (definitionElement).getElementsByTagName(
                            "WordDefinition");

                        strDefinition = "";
                        for (int j = 0; j < wordDefinitionElements.getLength(); j++) {
                            //---convert a <WordDefinition> Node into an Element---
                            Element wordDefinitionElement =
                                (Element) wordDefinitionElements.item(j);

                            //---get all the child nodes under the
                            // <WordDefinition> element---
                            NodeList textNodes =
                                ((Node) wordDefinitionElement).getChildNodes();

                            strDefinition +=
                                ((Node) textNodes.item(0)).getNodeValue() + ". ";
                        }

                        //---display the title---
                        Toast.makeText(getBaseContext(),strDefinition,
                            Toast.LENGTH_SHORT).show();
                    }
                }
        } catch (IOException e1) {
            Toast.makeText(this, e1.getLocalizedMessage(),
                Toast.LENGTH_LONG).show();
            e1.printStackTrace();
        }
    }

    /** Called when the activity is first created. */
    @Override
    public void onCreate(Bundle savedInstanceState) {
        super.onCreate(savedInstanceState);
        setContentView(R.layout.main);

        //---download an image---
        Bitmap bitmap =
            DownloadImage(
            "http://www.streetcar.org/mim/cable/images/cable-01.jpg");
        img = (ImageView) findViewById(R.id.img);
        img.setImageBitmap(bitmap);

        //---download an RSS feed---
        String str = DownloadText(
```

```
                        "http://www.appleinsider.com/appleinsider.rss");
            Toast.makeText(getBaseContext(), str,
                            Toast.LENGTH_SHORT).show();

            //---access a Web service using GET---
            WordDefinition("Apple");
        }
    }
```

2. Press F11 to debug the application on the Android Emulator. Figure 8-11 shows the result of the Web service call being parsed and then displayed using the Toast class.

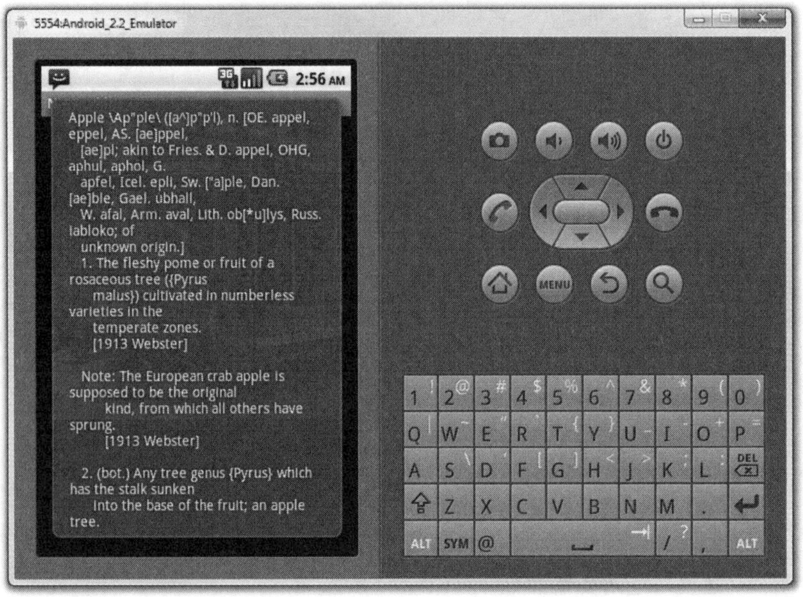

FIGURE 8-11

How It Works

The WordDefinition() method first opens an HTTP connection to the Web service, passing in the word that you are interested in:

```
            in = OpenHttpConnection(
    "http://services.aonaware.com/DictService/DictService.asmx/Define?word=" + word);
```

It then uses the DocumentBuilderFactory and DocumentBuilder objects to obtain a Document (DOM) object from an XML file (which is the XML result returned by the Web service):

```
            Document doc = null;
            DocumentBuilderFactory dbf =
                DocumentBuilderFactory.newInstance();
            DocumentBuilder db;
            try {
```

```
        db = dbf.newDocumentBuilder();
        doc = db.parse(in);
    } catch (ParserConfigurationException e) {
        // TODO Auto-generated catch block
        e.printStackTrace();
    } catch (Exception e) {
        // TODO Auto-generated catch block
        e.printStackTrace();
    }
    doc.getDocumentElement().normalize();
```

Once the `Document` object is obtained, you will find all the elements with the `<Definition>` tag:

```
//---retrieve all the <Definition> nodes---
NodeList itemNodes =
    doc.getElementsByTagName("Definition");
```

Figure 8-12 shows the structure of the XML document returned by the Web service.

```
▼<WordDefinition xmlns:xsi="http://www.w3.org/2001/
  XMLSchema-instance" xmlns:xsd="http://www.w3.org/2001/
  XMLSchema" xmlns="http://services.aonaware.com/
  webservices/">
    <Word>apple</Word>
  ▼<Definitions>
    ▼<Definition>
       <Word>apple</Word>
     ▶<Dictionary>...</Dictionary>
     ▶<WordDefinition>...</WordDefinition>
     </Definition>
    ▼<Definition>
       <Word>apple</Word>
     ▶<Dictionary>...</Dictionary>
     ▶<WordDefinition>...</WordDefinition>
     </Definition>
   ▶<Definition>...</Definition>
   ▶<Definition>...</Definition>
   ▶<Definition>...</Definition>
   </Definitions>
</WordDefinition>
```

FIGURE 8-12

As the definition of a word is contained within the `<WordDefinition>` element, you then proceed to extract all the definitions:

```
String strDefinition = "";
for (int i = 0; i < definitionElements.getLength(); i++) {
    Node itemNode = definitionElements.item(i);
    if (itemNode.getNodeType() == Node.ELEMENT_NODE)
    {
        //---convert the Node into an Element---
        Element definitionElement = (Element) itemNode;

        //---get all the <WordDefinition> elements under
        // the <Definition> element---
        NodeList wordDefinitionElements =
            (definitionElement).getElementsByTagName(
            "WordDefinition");

        strDefinition = "";
        for (int j = 0; j < wordDefinitionElements.getLength(); j++) {
            //---convert a <WordDefinition> Node into an Element---
```

```
                         Element wordDefinitionElement =
                             (Element) wordDefinitionElements.item(j);

                         //---get all the child nodes under the
                         // <WordDefinition> element---
                         NodeList textNodes =
                             ((Node) wordDefinitionElement).getChildNodes();
                         //---get the first node, which contains the text---
                         strDefinition +=
                             ((Node) textNodes.item(0)).getNodeValue() + ". ";
                     }
                     //---display the title---
                     Toast.makeText(getBaseContext(),strDefinition,
                         Toast.LENGTH_SHORT).show();
                 }
             }
         } catch (IOException e1) {
             Toast.makeText(this, e1.getLocalizedMessage(),
                 Toast.LENGTH_LONG).show();
             e1.printStackTrace();
         }
```

The above loops through all the <Definition> elements and then for each <Definition> element it looks for a child element named <WordDefinition>. The text content of the <WordDefinition> element contains the definition of a word. The Toast class displays each word definition that is retrieved.

Performing Asynchronous Calls

So far, all the connections made in the previous few sections are all *synchronous* – that is, the connection to a server will not return until the data is received. In real life, this presents some problems due to network connections being inherently slow. When you connect to a server to download some data, the user interface of your application remains frozen until a response is obtained. In most cases, this is not acceptable. Hence, you need to ensure that the connection to the server is made in an asynchronous fashion.

The easiest way to connect to the server asynchronously is to use the AsyncTask class available in the Android SDK. Using AsyncTask enables you to perform background tasks in a separate thread and then return the result in a UI thread. Using this class enables you to perform background operations without needing to handle complex threading issues.

Using the previous example of downloading an image from the server and then displaying the image in an ImageView, you could wrap the code in an instance of the AsyncTask class, as shown below:

```
public class MainActivity extends Activity {
    ImageView img;

    private class BackgroundTask extends AsyncTask
        <String, Void, Bitmap> {
            protected Bitmap doInBackground(String... url) {
```

```
        //---download an image---
        Bitmap bitmap = DownloadImage(url[0]);
        return bitmap;
    }

    protected void onPostExecute(Bitmap bitmap) {
        ImageView img = (ImageView) findViewById(R.id.img);
        img.setImageBitmap(bitmap);
    }
}

private InputStream OpenHttpConnection(String urlString)
throws IOException
{
    ...
}
```

Basically, you defined a class that extends the AsyncTask class. In this case, there are two methods within the BackgroundTask class — doInBackground() and onPostExecute(). You put all the code that needs to be run asynchronously in the doInBackground() method. When the task is completed, the result is passed back via the onPostExecute() method. The onPostExecute() method is executed on the UI thread, hence it is thread safe to update the ImageView with the bitmap downloaded from the server.

> **NOTE** *You will learn more about the* AsyncTask *class in Chapter 10 which covers developing services in Android.*

To perform the asynchronous tasks, simply create an instance of the BackgroundTask class and call its execute() method:

```
@Override
public void onCreate(Bundle savedInstanceState) {
    super.onCreate(savedInstanceState);
    setContentView(R.layout.main);
        new BackgroundTask().execute(
            "http://www.streetcar.org/mim/cable/images/cable-01.jpg");
}
```

SUMMARY

This chapter described the various ways to communicate with the outside world. You first learned how to send and receive SMS messages. You then learned how to send e-mail messages from within your Android application. Besides SMS and e-mail, another way to communicate with the outside world is through the use of the HTTP protocol. Using the HTTP protocol, you can download data from a web server. One good application of this is to talk to Web services, whereby you need to parse XML files.

EXERCISES

1. Name the two ways in which you can send SMS messages in your Android application.

2. Name the permissions you need to declare in your `AndroidManifest.xml` file for sending and receiving SMS messages.

3. How do you notify an activity from a `BroadcastReceiver`?

4. Name the permissions you need to declare in your `AndroidManifest.xml` file for an HTTP connection.

Answers to Exercises can be found in Appendix C.

▶ **WHAT YOU LEARNED IN THIS CHAPTER**

TOPIC	KEY CONCEPTS
Programmatically send-ing SMS messages	Use the `SmsManager` class.
Getting feedback on messages sent	Use two `PendingIntent` objects in the `sendTextMessage()` method.
Sending SMS messages using Intent	Set the intent type to "`vnd.android-dir/mms-sms`".
Receiving SMS messages	Implement a `BroadcastReceiver` and set it in the `AndroidManifest.xml` file.
Sending e-mail using Intent	Set the intent type to "`message/rfc822`".
Establishing an HTTP connection	Use the `HttpURLConnection` class.
Accessing Web services	Use the `Document`, `DocumentBuilderFactory`, and `DocumentBuilder` classes to parse the XML result returned by the Web service.

9

Location-Based Services

WHAT YOU WILL LEARN IN THIS CHAPTER

➤ How to display Google Maps in your Android application

➤ How to display the zoom controls on the map

➤ How to switch between the different map views

➤ How to add markers to maps

➤ How to get the address location touched on the map

➤ How to perform geocoding and reverse geocoding

➤ How to obtain geographical data using GPS, Cell-ID, and Wi-Fi triangulation

➤ How to monitor for a location

We have all seen the explosive growth of mobile apps in recent years. One category of apps that is very popular is location-based services, commonly known as LBS. LBS apps track your location, and may offer additional services such as locating amenities nearby, as well as offering suggestions for route planning, and so on. Of course, one of the key ingredients in a LBS app is maps, which present a visual representation of your location.

In this chapter, you will learn how to make use of the Google Maps in your Android application, and how to manipulate it programmatically. In addition, you will learn how to obtain your geographical location using the `LocationManager` class available in the Android SDK.

DISPLAYING MAPS

Google Maps is one of the many applications bundled with the Android platform. In addition to simply using the Maps application, you can also embed it into your own applications and make it do some very cool things. This section describes how to use Google Maps in your Android applications and programmatically perform the following:

➤ Change the views of Google Maps.

➤ Obtain the latitude and longitude of locations in Google Maps.

➤ Perform geocoding and reverse geocoding (translating an address to latitude and longitude and vice versa).

➤ Add markers to Google Maps.

Creating the Project

To get started, you need to first create an Android project so that you can display the Google Maps in your activity.

TRY IT OUT   Creating the Project

codefile LBS.zip available for download at Wrox.com

1.   Using Eclipse, create an Android project as shown in Figure 9-1.

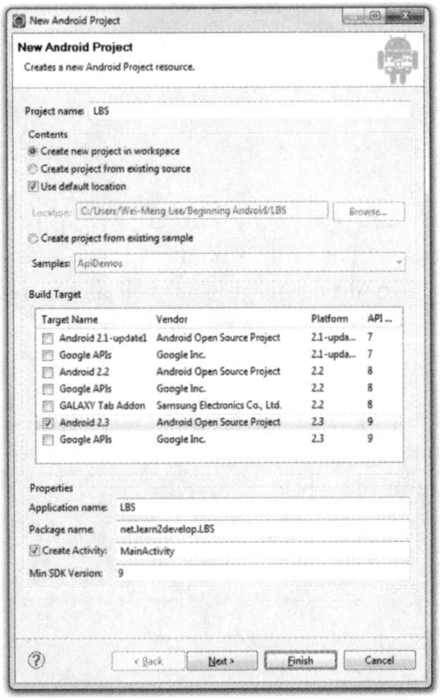

FIGURE 9-1

> **NOTE** *In order to use Google Maps in your Android application, you need to ensure that you check the Google APIs as your build target. Google Maps is not part of the standard Android SDK, so you need to find it in the Google APIs add-on.*

2. Once the project is created, observe the additional JAR file (`maps.jar`) located under the Google APIs folder (see Figure 9-2).

FIGURE 9-2

How It Works

This simple activity created an Android project that uses the Google APIs add-on. The Google APIs add-on includes the standard Android library, with the addition of the Maps library, as packaged within the `maps.jar` file.

Obtaining the Maps API Key

Beginning with the Android SDK release v1.0, you need to apply for a free Google Maps API key before you can integrate Google Maps into your Android application. When you apply for the key, you must also agree to Google's terms of use, so be sure to read them carefully.

To apply for a key, follow the series of steps outlined next.

> **NOTE** *Google provides detailed documentation on applying for a Maps API key at* `http://code.google.com/android/add-ons/google-apis/mapkey.html`.

First, if you are testing the application on the Android Emulator or an Android device directly connected to your development machine, locate the SDK debug certificate located in the default folder (`C:\Users\<username>\.android` for Windows 7 users). You can verify the existence of the debug certificate by going to Eclipse and selecting Window ➪ Preferences. Expand the Android item and select Build (see Figure 9-3). On the right side of the window, you will be able to see the debug certificate's location.

> **NOTE** *For Windows XP users, the default Android folder is*
> `C:\Documents and Settings\<username>\Local Settings\Application Data\Android.`

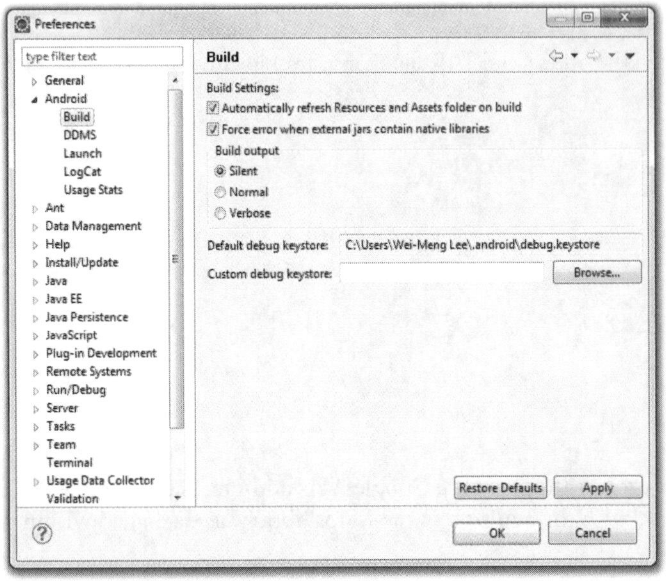

FIGURE 9-3

The filename of the debug keystore is `debug.keystore`. This is the certificate that Eclipse uses to sign your application so that it may be run on the Android Emulator or devices.

Using the debug keystore, you need to extract its MD5 fingerprint using the `Keytool.exe` application included with your JDK installation. This fingerprint is needed to apply for the free Google Maps key. You can usually find the `Keytool.exe` in the `C:\Program Files\Java\<JDK_version_number>\bin` folder.

Issue the following command (see Figure 9-4) to extract the MD5 fingerprint:

```
keytool.exe -list -alias androiddebugkey -keystore
"C:\Users\<username>\.android\debug.keystore" -storepass android
-keypass android
```

FIGURE 9-4

In this example, my MD5 fingerprint is `EF:7A:61:EA:AF:E0:B4:2D:FD:43:5E:1D:26:04:34:BA`.

Copy the MD5 certificate fingerprint and navigate your web browser to: `http://code.google.com/android/maps-api-signup.html`. Follow the instructions on the page to complete the application and obtain the Google Maps key. When you are done, you should see something similar to what is shown in Figure 9-5.

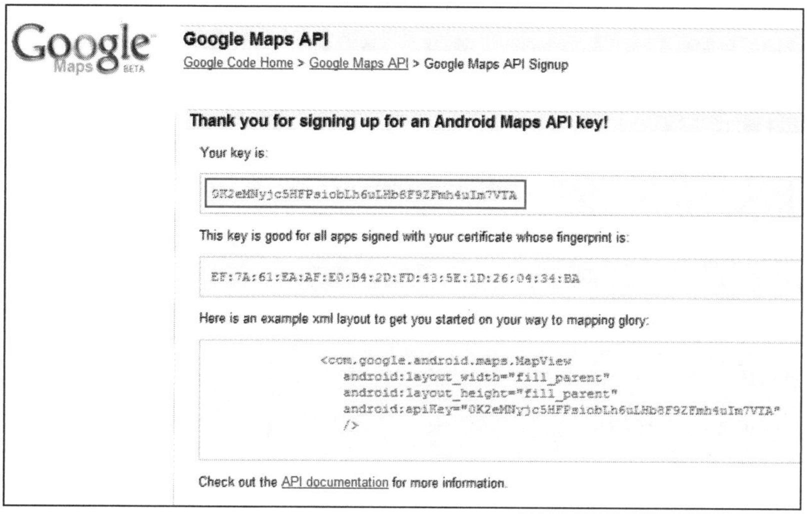

FIGURE 9-5

> **NOTE** *Although you can use the MD5 fingerprint of the debug keystore to obtain the Maps API key for debugging your application on the Android Emulator or devices, the key will not be valid if you try to deploy your Android application as an APK file. Once you are ready to deploy your application to the Android Market (or other methods of distribution), you need to reapply for a Maps API key using the certificate that will be used to sign your application. Chapter 11 discusses this topic in more detail.*

Displaying the Map

You are now ready to display Google Maps in your Android application. This involves two main tasks:

➤ Modify your `AndroidManifest.xml` file by adding both the `<uses-library>` element and the `INTERNET` permission.

➤ Add the `MapView` element to your UI.

The following Try It Out shows you how.

TRY IT OUT   Displaying Google Maps

1. Using the project created in the previous section, add the following lines in bold to the main.xml file (be sure to replace the value of the apiKey attribute with the API key you obtained earlier):

```xml
<?xml version="1.0" encoding="utf-8"?>
<LinearLayout xmlns:android="http://schemas.android.com/apk/res/android"
    android:orientation="vertical"
    android:layout_width="fill_parent"
    android:layout_height="fill_parent"
    >
<com.google.android.maps.MapView
    android:id="@+id/mapView"
    android:layout_width="fill_parent"
    android:layout_height="fill_parent"
    android:enabled="true"
    android:clickable="true"
    android:apiKey="<YOUR KEY>" />
</LinearLayout>
```

2. Add the following lines in bold to the main.xml file:

```xml
<?xml version="1.0" encoding="utf-8"?>
<manifest xmlns:android="http://schemas.android.com/apk/res/android"
    package="net.learn2develop.LBS"
    android:versionCode="1"
    android:versionName="1.0">
<application android:icon="@drawable/icon" android:label="@string/app_name">

    <uses-library android:name="com.google.android.maps" />

        <activity android:name=".MainActivity"
                android:label="@string/app_name">
            <intent-filter>
                <action android:name="android.intent.action.MAIN" />
                <category android:name="android.intent.category.LAUNCHER" />
            </intent-filter>
        </activity>

    </application>
    <uses-sdk android:minSdkVersion="8" />

    <uses-permission android:name="android.permission.INTERNET"></uses-permission>
</manifest>
```

3. Add the following statements in bold to the MainActivity.java file. Note that MainActivity is now extending the MapActivity class.

```java
package net.learn2develop.LBS;

import android.app.Activity;
```

```
import android.os.Bundle;

import com.google.android.maps.MapActivity;

public class MainActivity extends MapActivity {
    /** Called when the activity is first created. */
    @Override
    public void onCreate(Bundle savedInstanceState) {
        super.onCreate(savedInstanceState);
        setContentView(R.layout.main);
    }

    @Override
    protected boolean isRouteDisplayed() {
        // TODO Auto-generated method stub
        return false;
    }
}
```

4. Press F11 to debug the application on the Android Emulator. Figure 9-6 shows Google Maps displaying in the activity of your application.

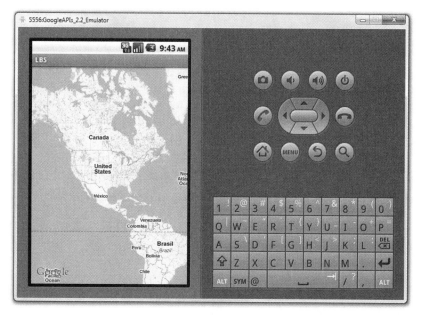

FIGURE 9-6

How It Works

In order to display Google Maps in your application, you first need to have the INTERNET permission in your manifest file. You then add the <com.google.android.maps.MapView> element to your UI file to embed the map within your activity. Very importantly, your activity must now extend the MapActivity class, which itself is an extension of the Activity class. For the MapActivity class, you need to implement one method: isRouteDisplayed(). This method is used for Google's accounting purposes, and you should return `true` for this method if you are displaying routing information on the map. For most simple cases, you can simply return `false`.

CAN'T SEE THE MAP?

If instead of seeing Google Maps displayed you see an empty screen with grids, then most likely you are using the wrong API key in the `main.xml` file. It is also possible that you omitted the `INTERNET` permission in your `AndroidManifest.xml` file. Finally, ensure that you have Internet access on your emulator/devices.

If your program does not run (i.e., it crashes), then you probably forgot to add the following statement to the `AndroidManifest.xml` file:

```
<uses-library android:name="com.google.android.maps" />
```

Note its placement in the `AndroidManifest.xml` file; it should be within the `<Application>` element.

Displaying the Zoom Control

The previous section showed how you can display Google Maps in your Android application. You can pan the map to any desired location and it will be updated on-the-fly. However, on the emulator there is no way to zoom in or out from a particular location (on a real Android device you can pinch the map to zoom it). Thus, in this section, you will learn how you can let users zoom in or out of the map using the built-in zoom controls.

TRY IT OUT   Displaying the Built-In Zoom Controls

1. Using the project created in the previous activity, add in the following statements in bold:

```
package net.learn2develop.LBS;

import android.app.Activity;
import android.os.Bundle;

import com.google.android.maps.MapActivity;

import com.google.android.maps.MapView;

public class MainActivity extends MapActivity {
    MapView mapView;
    /** Called when the activity is first created. */
    @Override
    public void onCreate(Bundle savedInstanceState) {
        super.onCreate(savedInstanceState);
        setContentView(R.layout.main);

        mapView = (MapView) findViewById(R.id.mapView);
```

```
        mapView.setBuiltInZoomControls(true);
    }

    @Override
    protected boolean isRouteDisplayed() {
        // TODO Auto-generated method stub
        return false;
    }
}
```

2. Press F11 to debug the application on the Android Emulator. Observe the built-in zoom controls that appear at the bottom of the map when you click and drag the map (see Figure 9-7). You can click the minus (–) icon to zoom out of the map and the plus (+) icon to zoom into the map.

FIGURE 9-7

How It Works

To display the built-in zoom controls, you first get a reference to the map and then call the setBuiltInZoomControls() method:

```
mapView = (MapView) findViewById(R.id.mapView);
mapView.setBuiltInZoomControls(true);
```

Besides displaying the zoom controls, you can also programmatically zoom in or out of the map using the zoomIn() or zoomOut() method of the MapController class. The following Try It Out shows you how to achieve this.

TRY IT OUT Programmatically Zooming In or Out of the Map

1. Using the project created in the previous activity, add the following statements in bold to the MainActivity.java file:

```
package net.learn2develop.LBS;

import android.app.Activity;
import android.os.Bundle;

import com.google.android.maps.MapActivity;
import com.google.android.maps.MapView;

import android.view.KeyEvent;
import com.google.android.maps.MapController;

public class MainActivity extends MapActivity {
    MapView mapView;
    /** Called when the activity is first created. */
    @Override
    public void onCreate(Bundle savedInstanceState) {
        super.onCreate(savedInstanceState);
```

```
        setContentView(R.layout.main);

        mapView = (MapView) findViewById(R.id.mapView);
        mapView.setBuiltInZoomControls(true);
    }

    public boolean onKeyDown(int keyCode, KeyEvent event)
    {
        MapController mc = mapView.getController();
        switch (keyCode)
        {
            case KeyEvent.KEYCODE_3:
                mc.zoomIn();
                break;
            case KeyEvent.KEYCODE_1:
                mc.zoomOut();
                break;
        }
        return super.onKeyDown(keyCode, event);
    }

    @Override
    protected boolean isRouteDisplayed() {
        // TODO Auto-generated method stub
        return false;
    }
}
```

2. Press F11 to debug the application on the Android Emulator. You can now zoom into the map by pressing the numeric 3 key on the emulator. To zoom out of the map, press the numeric 1 key.

How It Works

To handle key presses on your activity, you handle the `onKeyDown` event:

```
    public boolean onKeyDown(int keyCode, KeyEvent event)
    {
        //...
    }
```

To manage the panning and zooming of the map, you need to obtain an instance of the `MapController` class from the `MapView` object. The `MapController` class contains the `zoomIn()` and `zoomOut()` methods (plus some other methods to control the map) to enable users to zoom in or out of the map, respectively.

Changing Views

By default, Google Maps is displayed in *map view*, which is basically drawings of streets and places of interest. You can also set Google Maps to display in *satellite view* using the `setSatellite()` method of the `MapView` class:

```
    @Override
    public void onCreate(Bundle savedInstanceState) {
```

```
    super.onCreate(savedInstanceState);
    setContentView(R.layout.main);

    mapView = (MapView) findViewById(R.id.mapView);
    mapView.setBuiltInZoomControls(true);
    mapView.setSatellite(true);
}
```

Figure 9-8 shows Google Maps displayed in satellite view.

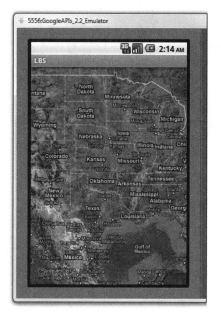

FIGURE 9-8

Besides satellite view, you can also display the map in *street view* (which highlights all the streets on the map) using the setStreetView() method. Figure 9-9 shows the map displaying a location in both street view (left) and satellite view (right).

```
@Override
public void onCreate(Bundle savedInstanceState) {
    super.onCreate(savedInstanceState);
    setContentView(R.layout.main);

    mapView = (MapView) findViewById(R.id.mapView);
    mapView.setBuiltInZoomControls(true);
    mapView.setSatellite(true);
    mapView.setStreetView(true);
}
```

If you want to display traffic conditions on the map, use the setTraffic() method:

```
    mapView.setTraffic(true);
```

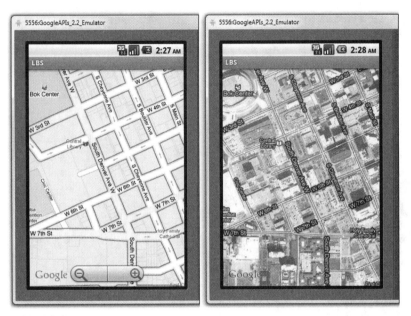

FIGURE 9-9

Figure 9-10 shows the map displaying the current traffic conditions. The different colors reflect the varying traffic conditions. In general, green color equates to smooth traffic of about 50 miles per hour, yellow equates to moderate traffic of about 25-50 miles per hour, and red equates to slow traffic of about less than 25 miles per hour.

Note that the traffic information is only available in major cities in the United States, France, Britain, Australia, and Canada, with new cities and countries frequently added.

Navigating to a Specific Location

By default, Google Maps displays the map of the United States when it is first loaded. However, you can also set Google Maps to display a particular location. In this case, you can use the `animateTo()` method of the `MapController` class.

The following Try It Out shows how you can programmatically animate Google Maps to a particular location.

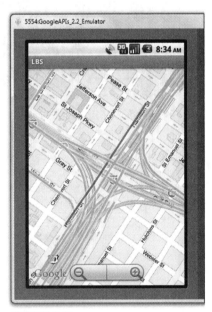

FIGURE 9-10

TRY IT OUT Navigating the Map to Display a Specific Location

1. Using the project created in the previous activity, add the following statements in bold to the `MainActivity.java` file:

```
package net.learn2develop.LBS;

import android.app.Activity;
import android.os.Bundle;
import android.view.KeyEvent;
import com.google.android.maps.MapActivity;
import com.google.android.maps.MapController;
import com.google.android.maps.MapView;

import com.google.android.maps.GeoPoint;

public class MainActivity extends MapActivity {
    MapView mapView;
    MapController mc;
    GeoPoint p;

    /** Called when the activity is first created. */
    @Override
    public void onCreate(Bundle savedInstanceState) {
        super.onCreate(savedInstanceState);
        setContentView(R.layout.main);

        mapView = (MapView) findViewById(R.id.mapView);
        mapView.setBuiltInZoomControls(true);

        //mapView.setSatellite(true);

        mapView.setStreetView(true);


        mc = mapView.getController();
        String coordinates[] = {"1.352566007", "103.78921587"};
        double lat = Double.parseDouble(coordinates[0]);
        double lng = Double.parseDouble(coordinates[1]);

        p = new GeoPoint(
            (int) (lat * 1E6),
            (int) (lng * 1E6));

        mc.animateTo(p);
        mc.setZoom(13);
        mapView.invalidate();
    }

    public boolean onKeyDown(int keyCode, KeyEvent event)
    {
```

```
            MapController mc = mapView.getController();
            switch (keyCode)
            {
                case KeyEvent.KEYCODE_3:
                    mc.zoomIn();
                    break;
                case KeyEvent.KEYCODE_1:
                    mc.zoomOut();
                    break;
            }
            return super.onKeyDown(keyCode, event);
        }

        @Override
        protected boolean isRouteDisplayed() {
            // TODO Auto-generated method stub
            return false;
        }
    }
```

2. Press F11 to debug the application on the Android Emulator. When the map is loaded, observe that it now animates to a particular location in Singapore (see Figure 9-11).

FIGURE 9-11

How It Works

In the preceding code, you first obtain a map controller from the MapView instance and assign it to a MapController object (mc). You then use a GeoPoint object to represent a geographical location. Note that for this class, the latitude and longitude of a location are represented in micro degrees. This means that they are stored as integer values. For a latitude value of 40.747778, for example, you need to multiply it by 1e6 (which is one million) to obtain 40747778.

To navigate the map to a particular location, you can use the `animateTo()` method of the `MapController` class. The `setZoom()` method enables you to specify the zoom level at which the map is displayed (the bigger the number, the more details you see on the map). The `invalidate()` method forces the `MapView` to be redrawn.

Adding Markers

Adding markers to a map to indicate places of interest enables your users to easily locate the places they are looking for. The following Try It Out shows you how to add a marker to Google Maps.

TRY IT OUT **Adding Markers to the Map**

1. Create a GIF image containing a pushpin (see Figure 9-12) and copy it into the `res/drawable-mdpi` folder of the project. For the best effect, make the background of the image transparent so that it does not block parts of the map when the image is added to the map.

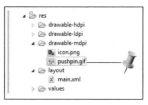

2. Using the project created in the previous activity, add the following statements in bold to the `MainActivity.java` file:

FIGURE 9-12

```
package net.learn2develop.LBS;

import android.app.Activity;

import android.os.Bundle;
import android.view.KeyEvent;

import com.google.android.maps.GeoPoint;
import com.google.android.maps.MapActivity;
import com.google.android.maps.MapController;
import com.google.android.maps.MapView;

import android.graphics.Bitmap;
import android.graphics.BitmapFactory;
import android.graphics.Canvas;
import android.graphics.Point;
import com.google.android.maps.Overlay;
import java.util.List;

public class MainActivity extends MapActivity {
    MapView mapView;
    MapController mc;
    GeoPoint p;

    class MapOverlay extends com.google.android.maps.Overlay
    {
        @Override
```

```java
    public boolean draw(Canvas canvas, MapView mapView,
    boolean shadow, long when)
    {
        super.draw(canvas, mapView, shadow);

        //---translate the GeoPoint to screen pixels---
        Point screenPts = new Point();
        mapView.getProjection().toPixels(p, screenPts);

        //---add the marker---
        Bitmap bmp = BitmapFactory.decodeResource(
            getResources(), R.drawable.pushpin);
        canvas.drawBitmap(bmp, screenPts.x, screenPts.y-50, null);
        return true;
    }
}

/** Called when the activity is first created. */
@Override
public void onCreate(Bundle savedInstanceState) {
    super.onCreate(savedInstanceState);
    setContentView(R.layout.main);

    mapView = (MapView) findViewById(R.id.mapView);
    mapView.setBuiltInZoomControls(true);

    //mapView.setSatellite(true);
    //mapView.setStreetView(true);

    mc = mapView.getController();
    String coordinates[] = {"1.352566007", "103.78921587"};
    double lat = Double.parseDouble(coordinates[0]);
    double lng = Double.parseDouble(coordinates[1]);

    p = new GeoPoint(
        (int) (lat * 1E6),
        (int) (lng * 1E6));

    mc.animateTo(p);
    mc.setZoom(13);

    //---Add a location marker---
    MapOverlay mapOverlay = new MapOverlay();
    List<Overlay> listOfOverlays = mapView.getOverlays();
    listOfOverlays.clear();
    listOfOverlays.add(mapOverlay);

    mapView.invalidate();
}

public boolean onKeyDown(int keyCode, KeyEvent event)
{
    MapController mc = mapView.getController();
    switch (keyCode)
```

```
        {
            case KeyEvent.KEYCODE_3:
                mc.zoomIn();
                break;
            case KeyEvent.KEYCODE_1:
                mc.zoomOut();
                break;
        }
        return super.onKeyDown(keyCode, event);
    }
    @Override
    protected boolean isRouteDisplayed() {
        // TODO Auto-generated method stub
        return false;
    }
}
```

3. Press F11 to debug the application on the Android Emulator. Figure 9-13 shows the marker added to the map.

FIGURE 9-13

How It Works

To add a marker to the map, you first need to define a class that extends the Overlay class:

```
class MapOverlay extends com.google.android.maps.Overlay
{
    @Override
    public boolean draw(Canvas canvas, MapView mapView,
```

```
        boolean shadow, long when)
        {
            //...
        }
    }
```

An overlay represents an individual item that you can draw on the map. You can add as many overlays as you want. In the MapOverlay class, override the draw() method so that you can draw the pushpin image on the map. In particular, note that you need to translate the geographical location (represented by a GeoPoint object, p) into screen coordinates:

```
//---translate the GeoPoint to screen pixels---
Point screenPts = new Point();
mapView.getProjection().toPixels(p, screenPts);
```

Because you want the pointed tip of the pushpin to indicate the position of the location, you need to deduct the height of the image (which is 50 pixels) from the *y* coordinate of the point (see Figure 9-14) and draw the image at that location:

```
//---add the marker---
Bitmap bmp = BitmapFactory.decodeResource(
    getResources(), R.drawable.pushpin);
canvas.drawBitmap(bmp, screenPts.x, screenPts.y-50, null);
```

Point to draw image
`screenPts.x, screenPts.y-50`

`50`

`screenPts.x, screenPts.y`
Location of point

FIGURE 9-14

To add the marker, create an instance of the MapOverlay class and add it to the list of overlays available on the MapView object:

```
//---Add a location marker---
MapOverlay mapOverlay = new MapOverlay();
List<Overlay> listOfOverlays = mapView.getOverlays();
listOfOverlays.clear();
listOfOverlays.add(mapOverlay);
```

Getting the Location That Was Touched

After using Google Maps for a while, you may want to know the latitude and longitude of a location corresponding to the position on the screen that was just touched. Knowing this information is very useful, as you can determine a location's address, a process known as *reverse geocoding* (you will learn how this is done in the next section).

If you have added an overlay to the map, you can override the onTouchEvent() method within the MapOverlay class. This method is fired every time the user touches the map. This method has two parameters: MotionEvent and MapView. Using the MotionEvent parameter, you can determine whether the user has lifted his or her finger from the screen using the getAction() method. In the following code snippet, if the user has touched and then lifted the finger, you display the latitude and longitude of the location touched:

```java
import android.view.MotionEvent;
import android.widget.Toast;
//...

    class MapOverlay extends com.google.android.maps.Overlay
    {
        @Override
        public boolean draw(Canvas canvas, MapView mapView,
        boolean shadow, long when)
        {
            super.draw(canvas, mapView, shadow);

            //---translate the GeoPoint to screen pixels---
            Point screenPts = new Point();
            mapView.getProjection().toPixels(p, screenPts);

            //---add the marker---
            Bitmap bmp = BitmapFactory.decodeResource(
                getResources(), R.drawable.pushpin);
            canvas.drawBitmap(bmp, screenPts.x, screenPts.y-50, null);
            return true;
        }

        @Override
        public boolean onTouchEvent(MotionEvent event, MapView mapView)
        {
            //---when user lifts his finger---
            if (event.getAction() == 1) {
                GeoPoint p = mapView.getProjection().fromPixels(
                    (int) event.getX(),
                    (int) event.getY());
                    Toast.makeText(getBaseContext(),
                        "Location: "+
                        p.getLatitudeE6() / 1E6 + "," +
                        p.getLongitudeE6() /1E6 ,
                        Toast.LENGTH_SHORT).show();
            }
            return false;
        }
    }
```

The getProjection() method returns a projection for converting between screen-pixel coordinates and latitude/longitude coordinates. The fromPixels() method then converts the screen coordinates into a GeoPoint object.

Figure 9-15 shows the map displaying a set of coordinates when the user clicks a location on the map.

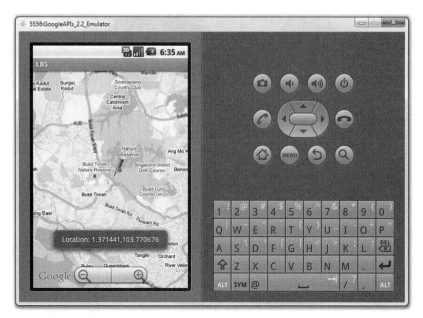

FIGURE 9-15

Geocoding and Reverse Geocoding

As mentioned in the preceding section, if you know the latitude and longitude of a location, you can find out its address using a process known as reverse geocoding. Google Maps in Android supports this via the `Geocoder` class. The following code snippet shows how you can retrieve the address of a location just touched using the `getFromLocation()` method:

```
import android.location.Address;
import android.location.Geocoder;
import java.util.Locale;
import java.io.IOException;
//...

        @Override
        public boolean onTouchEvent(MotionEvent event, MapView mapView)
        {
            //---when user lifts his finger---
            if (event.getAction() == 1) {
                GeoPoint p = mapView.getProjection().fromPixels(
                    (int) event.getX(),
                    (int) event.getY());
                /*
                Toast.makeText(getBaseContext(),
                    "Location: "+
                    p.getLatitudeE6() / 1E6 + "," +
                    p.getLongitudeE6() /1E6 ,
                    Toast.LENGTH_SHORT).show();
```

```
                             */
            Geocoder geoCoder = new Geocoder(
                getBaseContext(), Locale.getDefault());
            try {
                List<Address> addresses = geoCoder.getFromLocation(
                    p.getLatitudeE6()  / 1E6,
                    p.getLongitudeE6() / 1E6, 1);

                String add = "";
                if (addresses.size() > 0)
                {
                    for (int i=0; i<addresses.get(0).getMaxAddressLineIndex();
                        i++)
                        add += addresses.get(0).getAddressLine(i) + "\n";
                }
                Toast.makeText(getBaseContext(), add, Toast.LENGTH_SHORT).show();
            }
            catch (IOException e) {
                e.printStackTrace();
            }
            return true;
        }
        return false;
    }
}
```

The Geocoder object converts the latitude and longitude into an address using the getFromLocation() method. Once the address is obtained, you display it using the Toast class. Figure 9-16 shows the application displaying the address of a location that was touched on the map.

If you know the address of a location but want to know its latitude and longitude, you can do so via geocoding. Again, you can use the Geocoder class for this purpose. The following code shows how you can find the exact location of the Empire State Building by using the getFromLocationName() method:

```
//---geo-coding---
Geocoder geoCoder = new Geocoder(this, Locale.getDefault());
try {
    List<Address> addresses = geoCoder.getFromLocationName(
        "empire state building", 5);

    String add = "";
    if (addresses.size() > 0) {
        p = new GeoPoint(
                (int) (addresses.get(0).getLatitude() * 1E6),
                (int) (addresses.get(0).getLongitude() * 1E6));
        mc.animateTo(p);
        mapView.invalidate();
    }
} catch (IOException e) {
    e.printStackTrace();
}
```

Figure 9-17 shows the map navigating to the location of the Empire State Building.

FIGURE 9-16   **FIGURE 9-17**

GETTING LOCATION DATA

Nowadays, mobile devices are commonly equipped with GPS receivers. Because of the many satellites orbiting the earth, you can use a GPS receiver to find your location easily. However, GPS requires a clear sky to work and hence does not always work indoors or where satellites can't penetrate (such as a tunnel through a mountain).

Another effective way to locate your position is through *cell tower triangulation*. When a mobile phone is switched on, it is constantly in contact with base stations surrounding it. By knowing the identity of cell towers, it is possible to translate this information into a physical location through the use of various databases containing the cell towers' identities and their exact geographical locations. The advantage of cell tower triangulation is that it works indoors, without the need to obtain information from satellites. However, it is not as precise as GPS because its accuracy depends on overlapping signal coverage, which varies quite a bit. Cell tower triangulation works best in densely populated areas where the cell towers are closely located.

A third method of locating your position is to rely on Wi-Fi triangulation. Rather than connect to cell towers, the device connects to a Wi-Fi network and checks the service provider against databases to determine the location serviced by the provider. Of the three methods described here, Wi-Fi triangulation is the least accurate.

On the Android, the SDK provides the LocationManager class to help your device determine the user's physical location. The following Try It Out shows you how this is done in code.

TRY IT OUT   Navigating the Map to a Specific Location Using the Location Manager Class

1.   Using the same project created in the previous section, add the following statements in bold to the MainActivity.java file:

```
package net.learn2develop.LBS;

import android.app.Activity;
```

```java
import android.content.Context;
//...
//...

import android.location.Location;
import android.location.LocationListener;
import android.location.LocationManager;

public class MainActivity extends MapActivity {
    MapView mapView;
    MapController mc;
    GeoPoint p;

    private LocationManager lm;
    private LocationListener locationListener;

    class MapOverlay extends com.google.android.maps.Overlay
    {
        //...
    }

    /** Called when the activity is first created. */
    @Override
    public void onCreate(Bundle savedInstanceState) {
        super.onCreate(savedInstanceState);
        setContentView(R.layout.main);

        mapView = (MapView) findViewById(R.id.mapView);
        mapView.setBuiltInZoomControls(true);

        mc = mapView.getController();

        //---navigate to a point first---
        String coordinates[] = {"1.352566007", "103.78921587"};
        double lat = Double.parseDouble(coordinates[0]);
        double lng = Double.parseDouble(coordinates[1]);
        p = new GeoPoint(
            (int) (lat * 1E6),
            (int) (lng * 1E6));
        mc.animateTo(p);
        mc.setZoom(13);

        //---Add a location marker---
        //...
        //---reverse geo-coding---
        //...

        //---use the LocationManager class to obtain locations data---
        lm = (LocationManager)
            getSystemService(Context.LOCATION_SERVICE);

        locationListener = new MyLocationListener();

        lm.requestLocationUpdates(
                LocationManager.GPS_PROVIDER,
                0,
```

```
                0,
                locationListener);
    }

    private class MyLocationListener implements LocationListener
    {
        @Override
        public void onLocationChanged(Location loc) {
            if (loc != null) {
                Toast.makeText(getBaseContext(),
                    "Location changed : Lat: " + loc.getLatitude() +
                    " Lng: " + loc.getLongitude(),
                    Toast.LENGTH_SHORT).show();
            }

            p = new GeoPoint(
                    (int) (loc.getLatitude() * 1E6),
                    (int) (loc.getLongitude() * 1E6));

            mc.animateTo(p);
            mc.setZoom(18);
        }

        @Override
        public void onProviderDisabled(String provider) {
        }

        @Override
        public void onProviderEnabled(String provider) {
        }

        @Override
        public void onStatusChanged(String provider, int status,
            Bundle extras) {
        }
    }

    public boolean onKeyDown(int keyCode, KeyEvent event)
    {
        //...
    }

    @Override
    protected boolean isRouteDisplayed() {
        // TODO Auto-generated method stub
        return false;
    }
}
```

2. Press F11 to debug the application on the Android Emulator.

3. To simulate GPS data received by the Android Emulator, you use the Location Controls tool (see Figure 9-18) located in the DDMS perspective.

4. Ensure that you have first selected the emulator in the Devices tab. Then, in the Emulator Control tab, locate the Location Controls tool and select the Manual tab. Enter a latitude and longitude and click the Send button.

5. Observe that the map on the emulator now animates to another location (see Figure 9-19). This proves that the application has received the GPS data.

FIGURE 9-18

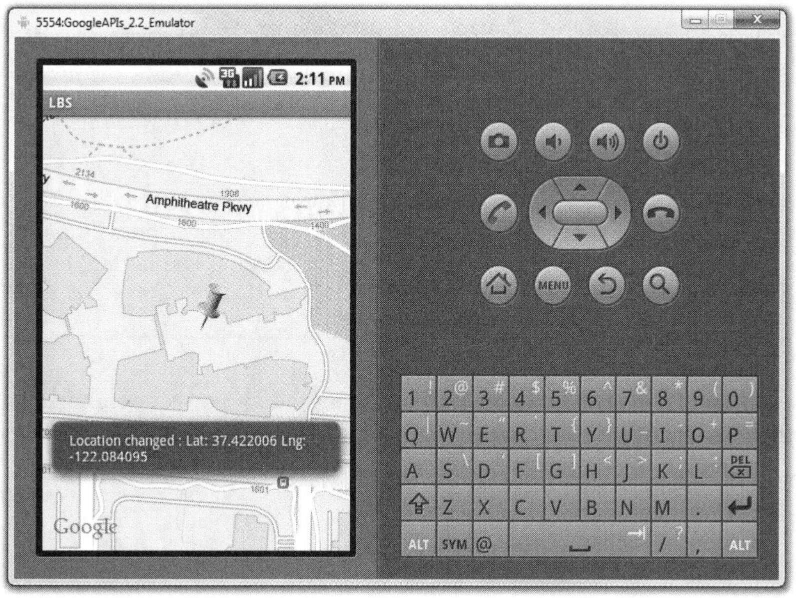

FIGURE 9-19

How It Works

In Android, location-based services are provided by the `LocationManager` class, located in the `android.location` package. Using the `LocationManager` class, your application can obtain periodic updates of the device's geographical locations, as well as fire an intent when it enters the proximity of a certain location.

In the `MainActivity.java` file, you first obtain a reference to the `LocationManager` class using the `getSystemService()` method. To be notified whenever there is a change in location, you need to register a request for location changes so that your program can be notified periodically. This is done via the `requestLocationUpdates()` method:

```
lm.requestLocationUpdates(
        LocationManager.GPS_PROVIDER,
        0,
        0,
        locationListener);
```

This method takes four parameters:

➤ `provider` — The name of the provider with which you register. In this case, you are using GPS to obtain your geographical location data.

➤ `minTime` — The minimum time interval for notifications, in milliseconds

➤ `minDistance` — The minimum distance interval for notifications, in meters

➤ `listener` — An object whose `onLocationChanged()` method will be called for each location update

The `MyLocationListener` class implements the `LocationListener` abstract class. You need to override four methods in this implementation:

➤ `onLocationChanged(Location location)` — Called when the location has changed

➤ `onProviderDisabled(String provider)` — Called when the provider is disabled by the user

➤ `onProviderEnabled(String provider)` — Called when the provider is enabled by the user

➤ `onStatusChanged(String provider, int status, Bundle extras)` — Called when the provider status changes

In this example, you're more interested in what happens when a location changes, so you'll write some code in the `onLocationChanged()` method. Specifically, when a location changes, you will display a small dialog on the screen showing the new location information: latitude and longitude. You show this dialog using the `Toast` class.

If you want to use Cell-ID and Wi-Fi triangulation (important for indoor use) for obtaining your location data, you can use the network location provider, like this:

```
lm.requestLocationUpdates(
        LocationManager.NETWORK_PROVIDER,
        0,
        0,
        locationListener);
```

You can combine both the GPS location provider with the network location provider within your application.

Monitoring a Location

One very cool feature of the `LocationManager` class is its ability to monitor a specific location. This is achieved using the `addProximityAlert()` method. The following code snippet shows how to monitor a particular location so that if the user is within a five-meter radius from that location, your application will fire an intent to launch the web browser:

```
//---use the LocationManager class to obtain locations data---
lm = (LocationManager)
    getSystemService(Context.LOCATION_SERVICE);

//---PendingIntent to launch activity if the user is within some locations---
PendingIntent pendIntent = PendingIntent.getActivity(
    this, 0, new
    Intent(android.content.Intent.ACTION_VIEW,
      Uri.parse("http://www.amazon.com")), 0);

lm.addProximityAlert(37.422006, -122.084095, 5, -1, pendIntent);
```

The `addProximityAlert()` method takes five arguments: latitude, longitude, radius (in meters), expiration (time for the proximity alert to be valid, after which it will be deleted; -1 for no expiration), and the pending intent.

Note that if the Android device's screen goes to sleep, the proximity is also checked once every four minutes in order to preserve the battery life of the device.

SUMMARY

This chapter took a whirlwind tour of the `MapView` object, which displays Google Maps in your Android application. You have learned the various ways in which the map can be manipulated, and you have also seen how you can obtain geographical location data using the various network providers: GPS, Cell-ID, or Wi-Fi triangulation.

EXERCISES

1. If you have embedded the Google Maps API into your Android application but it does not show the map when the application is loaded, what could be the likely reasons?

2. What is the difference between geocoding and reverse geocoding?

3. Name the two location providers that you can use to obtain your location data.

4. What is the method for monitoring a location?

Answers to Exercises can be found in Appendix C.

▶ **WHAT YOU LEARNED IN THIS CHAPTER**

TOPIC	KEY CONCEPTS
Displaying the MapView	```<com.google.android.maps.MapView` ` android:id="@+id/mapView"` ` android:layout_width="fill_parent"` ` android:layout_height="fill_parent"` ` android:enabled="true"` ` android:clickable="true"` ` android:apiKey="0K2eMNyjc5HFPsiobLh6uLHb8F9ZFmh4uIm7VTA" />```
Referencing the Map library	`<uses-library android:name="com.google.android.maps" />`
Displaying the zoom controls	`mapView.setBuiltInZoomControls(true);`
Programmatically zooming in or out of the map	`mc.zoomIn();` `mc.zoomOut();`

Changing views	`mapView.setSatellite(true);`
	`mapView.setStreetView(true);`
	`mapView.setTraffic(true);`

Animating to a particular location	`mc = mapView.getController();`
	`String coordinates[] = {"1.352566007", "103.78921587"};`
	`double lat = Double.parseDouble(coordinates[0]);`
	`double lng = Double.parseDouble(coordinates[1]);`
	`p = new GeoPoint(`
	`    (int) (lat * 1E6),`
	`    (int) (lng * 1E6));`
	` mc.animateTo(p);`

Adding markers	Implement an Overlay class and override the draw() method

Getting the location of the map touched	`GeoPoint p = mapView.getProjection().fromPixels(`
	`    (int) event.getX(),`
	`    (int) event.getY());`

Geocoding and reverse geocoding	Use the Geocoder class

TOPIC	KEY CONCEPTS
| **Obtaining location data** | ```java
private LocationManager lm;

//...

    lm = (LocationManager)
        getSystemService(Context.LOCATION_SERVICE);

    locationListener = new MyLocationListener();

    lm.requestLocationUpdates(
            LocationManager.GPS_PROVIDER,
            0,
            0,
            locationListener);

//...

private class MyLocationListener implements LocationListener
{
    @Override
    public void onLocationChanged(Location loc) {
        if (loc != null) {
        }
    }

    @Override
    public void onProviderDisabled(String provider) {
    }

    @Override
    public void onProviderEnabled(String provider) {
    }

    @Override
    public void onStatusChanged(String provider, int status,
        Bundle extras) {
    }
}
``` |
| **Monitoring a location** | ```java
lm.addProximityAlert(37.422006, -122.084095, 5, -1, pendIntent);
``` |

10

Developing Android Services

WHAT YOU WILL LEARN IN THIS CHAPTER

➤ How to create a service that runs in the background

➤ How to perform long-running tasks in a separate thread

➤ How to perform repeated tasks in a service

➤ How an activity and a service communicate

A service is an application in Android that runs in the background without needing to interact with the user. For example, while using an application, you may want to play some background music at the same time. In this case, the code that is playing the background music has no need to interact with the user, and hence it can be run as a service. Services are also ideal for situations in which there is no need to present a UI to the user. A good example of this scenario is an application that continually logs the geographical coordinates of the device. In this case, you can write a service to do that in the background. In this chapter, you will learn how to create your own services and use them to perform background tasks asynchronously.

CREATING YOUR OWN SERVICES

The best way to understand how a service works is by creating one. The following Try It Out shows you the steps to create a simple service. Subsequent sections will add more functionality to this service. For now, you will learn how to start and stop a service.

TRY IT OUT Creating a Simple Service

codefile Services.zip available for download at Wrox.com

1. Using Eclipse, create a new Android project and name it as shown in Figure 10-1.

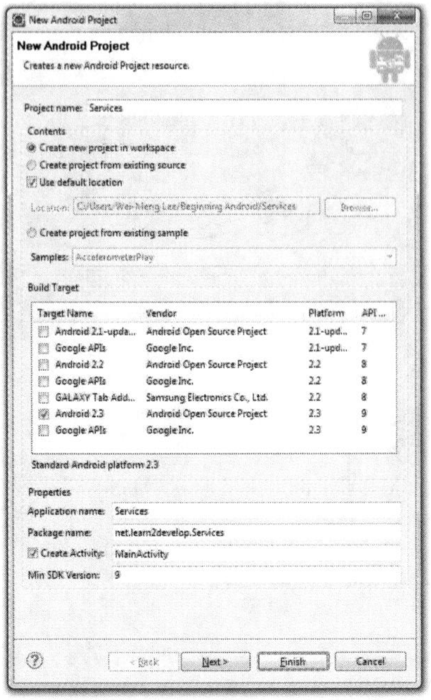

FIGURE 10-1

2. Add a new class file to the project and name it **MyService.java**. Populate it with the following code:

```
package net.learn2develop.Services;

import android.app.Service;
import android.content.Intent;
import android.os.IBinder;
import android.widget.Toast;

public class MyService extends Service {

    @Override
    public IBinder onBind(Intent arg0) {
        return null;
    }

    @Override
    public int onStartCommand(Intent intent, int flags, int startId) {
        // We want this service to continue running until it is explicitly
        // stopped, so return sticky.
        Toast.makeText(this, "Service Started", Toast.LENGTH_LONG).show();
        return START_STICKY;
    }

    @Override
    public void onDestroy() {
        super.onDestroy();
```

```
            Toast.makeText(this, "Service Destroyed", Toast.LENGTH_LONG).show();
    }
}
```

3. In the `AndroidManifest.xml` file, add the following statement in bold:

```xml
<?xml version="1.0" encoding="utf-8"?>
<manifest xmlns:android="http://schemas.android.com/apk/res/android"
      package="net.learn2develop.Services"
      android:versionCode="1"
      android:versionName="1.0">
    <application android:icon="@drawable/icon" android:label="@string/app_name">
        <activity android:name=".MainActivity"
                  android:label="@string/app_name">
            <intent-filter>
                <action android:name="android.intent.action.MAIN" />
                <category android:name="android.intent.category.LAUNCHER" />
            </intent-filter>
        </activity>
        <service android:name=".MyService" />
    </application>
    <uses-sdk android:minSdkVersion="9" />
</manifest>
```

4. In the `main.xml` file, add the following statements in bold:

```xml
<?xml version="1.0" encoding="utf-8"?>
<LinearLayout xmlns:android="http://schemas.android.com/apk/res/android"
    android:orientation="vertical"
    android:layout_width="fill_parent"
    android:layout_height="fill_parent"
    >
<Button android:id="@+id/btnStartService"
    android:layout_width="fill_parent"
    android:layout_height="wrap_content"
    android:text="Start Service" />
<Button android:id="@+id/btnStopService"
    android:layout_width="fill_parent"
    android:layout_height="wrap_content"
    android:text="Stop Service" />
</LinearLayout>
```

5. Add the following statements in bold to the `MainActivity.java` file:

```java
package net.learn2develop.Services;

import android.app.Activity;
import android.os.Bundle;

import android.content.Intent;
import android.view.View;
import android.widget.Button;

public class MainActivity extends Activity {
    /** Called when the activity is first created. */
    @Override
```

```
public void onCreate(Bundle savedInstanceState) {
    super.onCreate(savedInstanceState);
    setContentView(R.layout.main);

    Button btnStart = (Button) findViewById(R.id.btnStartService);
    btnStart.setOnClickListener(new View.OnClickListener() {
        public void onClick(View v) {
            startService(new Intent(getBaseContext(), MyService.class));
        }
    });

    Button btnStop = (Button) findViewById(R.id.btnStopService);
    btnStop.setOnClickListener(new View.OnClickListener() {
        public void onClick(View v) {
            stopService(new Intent(getBaseContext(), MyService.class));
        }
    });
}
}
```

6.   Press F11 to debug the application on the Android Emulator.

7.   Clicking the Start Service button will start the service (see Figure 10-2). To stop the service, click the Stop Service button.

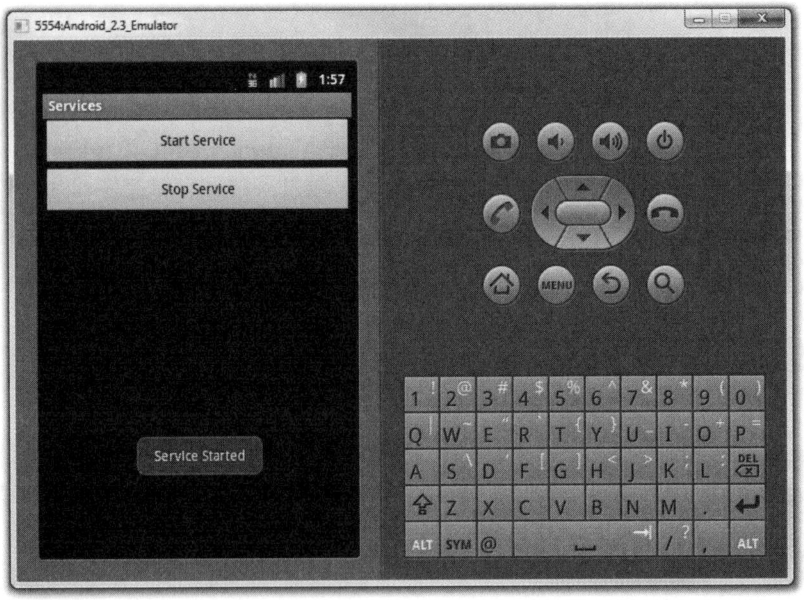

FIGURE 10-2

How It Works

This example demonstrated the simplest service that you can create. The service itself is not doing anything useful, of course, but it serves to illustrate the creation process.

First, you defined a class that extends the `Service` base class. All services extend the `Service` class:

```
public class MyService extends Service {

}
```

Within the `MyService` class, you implemented three methods:

```
@Override
public IBinder onBind(Intent arg0) {...}

@Override
public int onStartCommand(Intent intent, int flags, int startId) {...}

@Override
public void onDestroy() {...}
```

The `onBind()` method enables you to bind an activity to a service. This in turn enables an activity to directly access members and methods inside a service. For now, you simply return a `null` for this method. Later in this chapter you will learn more about binding.

The `onStartCommand()` method is called when you start the service explicitly using the `startService()` method (discussed shortly). This method signifies the start of the service, and you code it to do the things you need to do for your service. In this method, you returned the constant `START_STICKY` so that the service will continue to run until it is explicitly stopped.

The `onDestroy()` method is called when the service is stopped using the `stopService()` method. This is where you clean up the resources used by your service.

All services that you have created must be declared in the `AndroidManifest.xml` file, like this:

```
<service android:name=".MyService" />
```

If you want your service to be available to other applications, you can always add an intent filter with an action name, like this:

```
<service android:name=".MyService">
    <intent-filter>
        <action android:name="net.learn2develop.MyService" />
    </intent-filter>
</service>
```

To start a service, you use the `startService()` method, like this:

```
startService(new Intent(getBaseContext(), MyService.class));
```

If you are calling an external service, then the call to the `startService()` method will look like this:

```
startService(new Intent("net.learn2develop.MyService"));
```

To stop a service, use the `stopService()` method, like this:

```
stopService(new Intent(getBaseContext(), MyService.class));
```

Performing Long-Running Tasks in a Service

Because the service you created in the previous section does not do anything useful, in this section you will modify the service so that it perform a task. In the following Try It Out, you will simulate the service of downloading a file from the Internet.

TRY IT OUT   Making Your Service Useful

1. Using the same project created in the previous section, add the following statements in bold to the MainActivity.java file:

```java
package net.learn2develop.Services;

import android.app.Service;
import android.content.Intent;
import android.os.IBinder;
import android.widget.Toast;

import java.net.MalformedURLException;
import java.net.URL;

public class MyService extends Service {
    @Override
    public IBinder onBind(Intent arg0) {
        return null;
    }

    @Override
    public int onStartCommand(Intent intent, int flags, int startId) {
        // We want this service to continue running until it is explicitly
        // stopped, so return sticky.
        Toast.makeText(this, "Service Started", Toast.LENGTH_LONG).show();

        try {
            int result = DownloadFile(new URL("http://www.amazon.com/somefile.pdf"));
            Toast.makeText(getBaseContext(),
                "Downloaded " + result + " bytes",
                Toast.LENGTH_LONG).show();
        } catch (MalformedURLException e) {
            // TODO Auto-generated catch block
            e.printStackTrace();
        }
        return START_STICKY;
    }

    @Override
    public void onDestroy() {
        super.onDestroy();
        Toast.makeText(this, "Service Destroyed", Toast.LENGTH_LONG).show();
    }

    private int DownloadFile(URL url) {
        try {
            //---simulate taking some time to download a file---
```

```
            Thread.sleep(5000);
        } catch (InterruptedException e) {
            e.printStackTrace();
        }
        //---return an arbitrary number representing
        // the size of the file downloaded---
        return 100;
    }
}
```

2. Press F11 to debug the application on the Android Emulator.

3. Click the Start Service button to start the service to download the file. Observe that the activity will be frozen for a few seconds (see Figure 10-3) before the Toast class displays the "Downloaded 100 bytes" message.

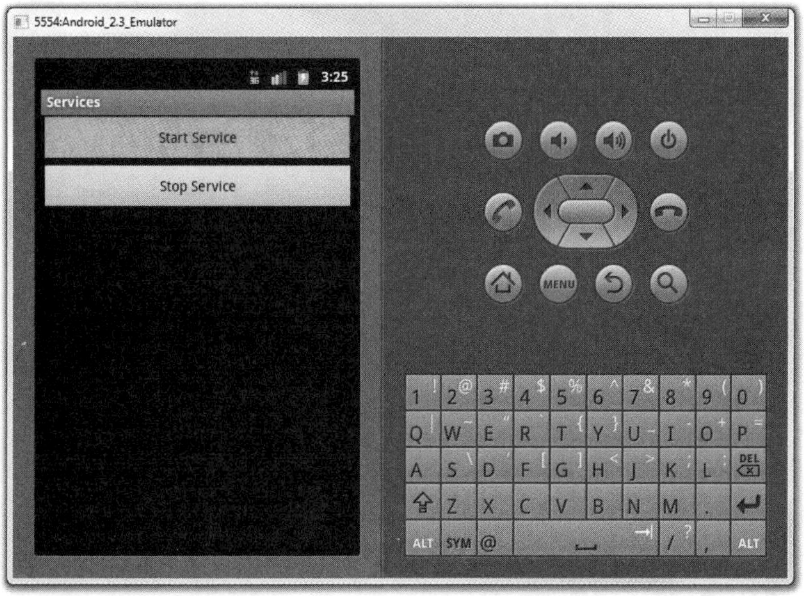

FIGURE 10-3

How It Works

In this example, your service calls the DownloadFile() method to simulate downloading a file from a given URL. This method returns the total number of bytes downloaded (which you have hardcoded as 100). To simulate the delays experienced by the service when downloading the file, you used the Thread .Sleep() method to pause the service for five seconds (5,000 milliseconds).

As you start the service, note that the activity is suspended for about five seconds, which is the time taken for the file to be downloaded from the Internet. During this time, the entire activity is not responsive, proving a very important point: The service runs on the same thread as your activity. In this case, because the service is suspended for five seconds, so is the activity.

Hence, for a long-running service, it is important that you put all long-running code into a separate thread so that it does not tie up the application that calls it. The following Try It Out shows you how.

TRY IT OUT Performing Tasks in a Service Asynchronously

1. Using the same project created in the previous section, add the following statements in bold to the `MyService.java` file:

```java
package net.learn2develop.Services;

import android.app.Service;
import android.content.Intent;
import android.os.IBinder;
import android.util.Log;
import android.widget.Toast;

import java.net.MalformedURLException;
import java.net.URL;

import android.os.AsyncTask;

public class MyService extends Service {
    @Override
    public IBinder onBind(Intent arg0) {
        return null;
    }

    @Override
    public int onStartCommand(Intent intent, int flags, int startId) {
        // We want this service to continue running until it is explicitly
        // stopped, so return sticky.
        Toast.makeText(this, "Service Started", Toast.LENGTH_LONG).show();
        try {
            new DoBackgroundTask().execute(
                    new URL("http://www.amazon.com/somefiles.pdf"),
                    new URL("http://www.wrox.com/somefiles.pdf"),
                    new URL("http://www.google.com/somefiles.pdf"),
                    new URL("http://www.learn2develop.net/somefiles.pdf"));
        } catch (MalformedURLException e) {
            e.printStackTrace();
        }
        return START_STICKY;
    }

    @Override
    public void onDestroy() {
        super.onDestroy();
        Toast.makeText(this, "Service Destroyed", Toast.LENGTH_LONG).show();
    }

    private int DownloadFile(URL url) {
```

```
        try {
            //---simulate taking some time to download a file---
            Thread.sleep(5000);
        } catch (InterruptedException e) {
            e.printStackTrace();
        }
        //---return an arbitrary number representing
        // the size of the file downloaded---
        return 100;
    }

    private class DoBackgroundTask extends AsyncTask<URL, Integer, Long> {
        protected Long doInBackground(URL... urls) {
            int count = urls.length;
            long totalBytesDownloaded = 0;
            for (int i = 0; i < count; i++) {
                totalBytesDownloaded += DownloadFile(urls[i]);
                //---calculate percentage downloaded and
                // report its progress---
                publishProgress((int) (((i+1) / (float) count) * 100));
            }
            return totalBytesDownloaded;
        }

        protected void onProgressUpdate(Integer... progress) {
            Log.d("Downloading files",
                    String.valueOf(progress[0]) + "% downloaded");
            Toast.makeText(getBaseContext(),
                String.valueOf(progress[0]) + "% downloaded",
                Toast.LENGTH_LONG).show();
        }

        protected void onPostExecute(Long result) {
            Toast.makeText(getBaseContext(),
                    "Downloaded " + result + " bytes",
                    Toast.LENGTH_LONG).show();
            stopSelf();
        }
    }
}
```

2. Press F11 to debug the application on the Android Emulator.

3. Click the Start Service button. The Toast class will display a message indicating what percentage of the download is completed (see Figure 10-4). You should see four of them: 25%, 50%, 75%, and 100%.

4. You will also observe the following output in the LogCat window:

```
01-16 02:56:29.051: DEBUG/Downloading files(8844): 25% downloaded
01-16 02:56:34.071: DEBUG/Downloading files(8844): 50% downloaded
01-16 02:56:39.106: DEBUG/Downloading files(8844): 75% downloaded
01-16 02:56:44.173: DEBUG/Downloading files(8844): 100% downloaded
```

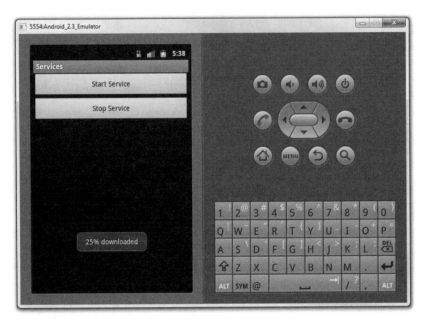

FIGURE 10-4

How It Works

This example illustrates one way in which you can execute a task asynchronously within your service. You do so by creating an inner class that extends the AsyncTask class. The AsyncTask class enables you to perform background execution without needing to manually handle threads and handlers.

The DoBackgroundTask class extends the AsyncTask class by specifying three generic types:

```
private class DoBackgroundTask extends AsyncTask<URL, Integer, Long> {
```

In this case, the three types specified are URL, Integer and Long. These three types specify the data type used by the following three methods that you implement in an AsyncTask class:

➤   doInBackground() — This method takes an array of the first generic type specified earlier. In this case, the type is URL. This method is executed in the background thread and is where you put your long-running code. To report the progress of your task, you call the publishProgress() method, which invokes the next method, onProgressUpdate(), which you implement in an AsyncTask class. The return type of this method takes the third generic type specified earlier, which is Long in this case.

➤   onProgressUpdate() — This method is invoked in the UI thread and is called when you call the publishProgress() method. It takes an array of the second generic type specified earlier. In this case, the type is Integer. Use this method to report the progress of the background task to the user.

➤   onPostExecute() — This method is invoked in the UI thread and is called when the doInBackground() method has finished execution. This method takes an argument of the third generic type specified earlier, which in this case is a Long.

To download multiple files in the background, you created an instance of the `DoBackgroundTask` class and then called its `execute()` method by passing in an array of `URL`s:

```
try {
    new DoBackgroundTask().execute(
            new URL("http://www.amazon.com/somefiles.pdf"),
            new URL("http://www.wrox.com/somefiles.pdf"),
            new URL("http://www.google.com/somefiles.pdf"),
            new URL("http://www.learn2develop.net/somefiles.pdf"));
} catch (MalformedURLException e) {
    // TODO Auto-generated catch block
    e.printStackTrace();
}
```

The preceding causes the service to download the files in the background, and reports the progress as a percentage of files downloaded. More important, the activity remains responsive while the files are downloaded in the background, on a separate thread.

Note that when the background thread has finished execution, you need to manually call the `stopSelf()` method to stop the service:

```
protected void onPostExecute(Long result) {
    Toast.makeText(getBaseContext(),
            "Downloaded " + result + " bytes",
            Toast.LENGTH_LONG).show();
    stopSelf();
}
```

The `stopSelf()` method is the equivalent of calling the `stopService()` method to stop the service.

Performing Repeated Tasks in a Service

Besides performing long-running tasks in a service, you might also perform some repeated tasks in a service. For example, you may write an alarm clock service that runs persistently in the background. In this case, your service may need to periodically execute some code to check whether a prescheduled time has been reached so that an alarm can be sounded. To execute a block of code to be executed at a regular time interval, you can use the `Timer` class within your service. The following Try It Out shows you how.

TRY IT OUT   Running Repeated Tasks Using the Timer Class

1. Using the same project created in the previous section, add the following statements in bold to the `MyService.java` file:

```
package net.learn2develop.Services;

import android.app.Service;
import android.content.Intent;
import android.os.AsyncTask;
import android.os.IBinder;
import android.util.Log;
```

```java
import android.widget.Toast;
import java.net.URL;

import java.util.Timer;
import java.util.TimerTask;

public class MyService extends Service {
    int counter = 0;
    static final int UPDATE_INTERVAL = 1000;
    private Timer timer = new Timer();

    @Override
    public IBinder onBind(Intent arg0) {
        return null;
    }

    @Override
    public int onStartCommand(Intent intent, int flags, int startId) {
        // We want this service to continue running until it is explicitly
        // stopped, so return sticky.
        Toast.makeText(this, "Service Started", Toast.LENGTH_LONG).show();
        doSomethingRepeatedly();
        return START_STICKY;
    }

    private void doSomethingRepeatedly() {
        timer.scheduleAtFixedRate( new TimerTask() {
            public void run() {
                Log.d("MyService", String.valueOf(++counter));
            }
        }, 0, UPDATE_INTERVAL);
    }

    @Override
    public void onDestroy() {
        super.onDestroy();
        if (timer != null){
            timer.cancel();
        }
        Toast.makeText(this, "Service Destroyed", Toast.LENGTH_LONG).show();
    }
}
```

2. Press F11 to debug the application on the Android Emulator.

3. Click the Start Service button.

4. Observe the output displayed in the LogCat window:

```
01-16 15:12:04.364: DEBUG/MyService(495): 1
01-16 15:12:05.384: DEBUG/MyService(495): 2
01-16 15:12:06.386: DEBUG/MyService(495): 3
01-16 15:12:07.389: DEBUG/MyService(495): 4
01-16 15:12:08.364: DEBUG/MyService(495): 5
01-16 15:12:09.427: DEBUG/MyService(495): 6
01-16 15:12:10.374: DEBUG/MyService(495): 7
```

How It Works

In this example, you created a `Timer` object and called its `scheduleAtFixedRate()` method inside the `doSomethingRepeatedly()` method that you have defined:

```
private void doSomethingRepeatedly() {
    timer.scheduleAtFixedRate(new TimerTask() {
        public void run() {
            Log.d("MyService", String.valueOf(++counter));
        }
    }, 0, UPDATE_INTERVAL);
}
```

You passed an instance of the `TimerTask` class to the `scheduleAtFixedRate()` method so that you can execute the block of code within the `run()` method repeatedly. The second parameter to the `scheduleAtFixedRate()` method specifies the amount of time, in milliseconds, before first execution. The third parameter specifies the amount of time, in milliseconds, between subsequent executions.

In the preceding example, you essentially print out the value of the counter every one second (1,000 milliseconds). The service repeatedly prints the value of `counter` until the service is terminated:

```
@Override
public void onDestroy() {
    super.onDestroy();
    if (timer != null){
        timer.cancel();
    }
    Toast.makeText(this, "Service Destroyed", Toast.LENGTH_LONG).show();
}
```

For the `scheduleAtFixedRate()` method, your code is executed at fixed time intervals, regardless of how long each task takes. For example, if the code within your `run()` method takes two seconds to complete, then your second task will start immediately after the first task has ended. Similarly, if your delay is set to three seconds and the task takes two seconds to complete, then the second task will wait for one second before starting.

Executing Asynchronous Tasks on Separate Threads Using IntentService

Earlier in this chapter, you saw how to start a service using the `startService()` method and stop a service using the `stopService()` method. You have also seen how you should execute long-running task on a separate thread — not the same thread as the calling activities. It is important to note that once your service has finished executing a task, it should be stopped as soon as possible so that it does not unnecessarily hold up valuable resources. That's why you use the `stopSelf()` method to stop the service when a task has been completed. Unfortunately, a lot of developers often forgot to terminate the service when it is done performing its task. To easily create a service that runs a task asynchronously and terminates itself when it is done, you can use the `IntentService` class.

The IntentService class is a base class for Service that handles asynchronous requests on demand. It is started just like a normal service and it executes its task within a worker thread and terminates itself when the task is completed.

The following Try It Out demonstrates how to use the IntentService class.

TRY IT OUT **Using the IntentService Class to Auto-Stop a Service**

1. Using the same project created in the previous section, add a new class file named **MyIntentService.java.**

2. Populate the MyIntentService.java file as follows:

```
package net.learn2develop.Services;

import java.net.MalformedURLException;
import java.net.URL;

import android.app.IntentService;
import android.content.Intent;
import android.util.Log;

public class MyIntentService extends IntentService {

    public MyIntentService() {
        super("MyIntentServiceName");
    }

    @Override
    protected void onHandleIntent(Intent intent) {
        try {
            int result =
                DownloadFile(new URL("http://www.amazon.com/somefile.pdf"));
            Log.d("IntentService", "Downloaded " + result + " bytes");
        } catch (MalformedURLException e) {
            e.printStackTrace();
        }
    }

    private int DownloadFile(URL url) {
        try {
            //---simulate taking some time to download a file---
            Thread.sleep(5000);
        } catch (InterruptedException e) {
            // TODO Auto-generated catch block
            e.printStackTrace();
        }
        return 100;
    }
}
```

3. Add the following statement in bold to the AndroidManifest.xml file:

```
<?xml version="1.0" encoding="utf-8"?>
<manifest xmlns:android="http://schemas.android.com/apk/res/android"
      package="net.learn2develop.Services"
      android:versionCode="1"
```

```
        android:versionName="1.0">
    <application android:icon="@drawable/icon" android:label="@string/app_name">
        <activity android:name=".MainActivity"
                android:label="@string/app_name">
            <intent-filter>
                <action android:name="android.intent.action.MAIN" />
                <category android:name="android.intent.category.LAUNCHER" />
            </intent-filter>
        </activity>
        <service android:name=".MyService" />
        <service android:name=".MyIntentService" />
    </application>
    <uses-sdk android:minSdkVersion="9" />
    <uses-permission android:name="android.permission.INTERNET"></uses-permission>
</manifest>
```

4. Add the following statement in bold to the `MainActivity.java` file:

```
public class MainActivity extends Activity {
    /** Called when the activity is first created. */
    @Override
    public void onCreate(Bundle savedInstanceState) {
        super.onCreate(savedInstanceState);
        setContentView(R.layout.main);

        Button btnStart = (Button) findViewById(R.id.btnStartService);
        btnStart.setOnClickListener(new View.OnClickListener() {
            public void onClick(View v) {
                //startService(new Intent(getBaseContext(), MyService.class));
                startService(new Intent(getBaseContext(), MyIntentService.class));
            }
        });

        Button btnStop = (Button) findViewById(R.id.btnStopService);
        btnStop.setOnClickListener(new View.OnClickListener() {
            public void onClick(View v) {
                stopService(new Intent(getBaseContext(), MyService.class));
            }
        });
    }
}
```

5. Press F11 to debug the application on the Android Emulator.

6. Click the Start Service button. After about five seconds, you should observe the following statement in the LogCat window:

```
01-17 03:05:21.244: DEBUG/IntentService(692): Downloaded 100 bytes
```

How It Works

First, you defined the `MyIntentService` class, which extends the `IntentService` class instead of the `Service` class:

```
public class MyIntentService extends IntentService {
    ...
}
```

You needed to implement a constructor for the class and call its superclass with the name of the intent service (setting it with a string):

```
public MyIntentService() {
    super("MyIntentServiceName");
}
```

You then implemented the `onHandleIntent()` method, which is executed on a worker thread:

```
@Override
protected void onHandleIntent(Intent intent) {
    try {
        int result =
            DownloadFile(new URL("http://www.amazon.com/somefile.pdf"));
        Log.d("IntentService", "Downloaded " + result + " bytes");
    } catch (MalformedURLException e) {
        e.printStackTrace();
    }
}
```

The `onHandleIntent()` method is where you place the code that needs to be executed on a separate thread, such as downloading a file from a server. When the code has finished executing, the thread is terminated and the service is stopped automatically.

COMMUNICATING BETWEEN A SERVICE AND AN ACTIVITY

Often a service simply executes in its own thread, independently of the activity that calls it. This doesn't pose any problem if you simply want the service to perform some tasks periodically and the activity does not need to be notified of the status of the service. For example, you may have a service that periodically logs the geographical location of the device to a database. In this case, there is no need for your service to interact with any activities, because its main purpose is to save the coordinates into a database. However, suppose you want to monitor for a particular location. When the service logs an address that is near the location you are monitoring, it might need to communicate that information to the activity. In this case, you would need to devise a way for the service to interact with the activity.

The following Try It Out demonstrates how a service can communicate with an activity using a `BroadcastReceiver`.

TRY IT OUT   Invoking an Activity from a Service

1. Using the same project created in the previous section, add the following statements in bold to the `MyIntentService.java` file:

```
package net.learn2develop.Services;

import java.net.MalformedURLException;
import java.net.URL;
```

```java
import android.app.IntentService;
import android.content.Intent;
import android.util.Log;

public class MyIntentService extends IntentService {
    public MyIntentService() {
        super("MyIntentServiceName");
    }

    @Override
    protected void onHandleIntent(Intent intent) {
        try {
            int result =
                DownloadFile(new URL("http://www.amazon.com/somefile.pdf"));
            Log.d("IntentService", "Downloaded " + result + " bytes");

            //---send a broadcast to inform the activity
            // that the file has been downloaded---
            Intent broadcastIntent = new Intent();
            broadcastIntent.setAction("FILE_DOWNLOADED_ACTION");
            getBaseContext().sendBroadcast(broadcastIntent);
        } catch (MalformedURLException e) {
            e.printStackTrace();
        }
    }

    private int DownloadFile(URL url) {
        try {
            //---simulate taking some time to download a file---
            Thread.sleep(5000);
        } catch (InterruptedException e) {
            e.printStackTrace();
        }
        return 100;
    }
}
```

2. Add the following statements in bold to the `MainActivity.java` file:

```java
package net.learn2develop.Services;

import android.app.Activity;
import android.content.BroadcastReceiver;
import android.content.Context;
import android.content.Intent;
import android.os.Bundle;
import android.view.View;
import android.widget.Button;
import android.widget.Toast;

import android.content.IntentFilter;

public class MainActivity extends Activity {
```

```
    IntentFilter intentFilter;

    /** Called when the activity is first created. */
    @Override
    public void onCreate(Bundle savedInstanceState) {
        super.onCreate(savedInstanceState);
        setContentView(R.layout.main);

        //---intent to filter for file downloaded intent---
        intentFilter = new IntentFilter();
        intentFilter.addAction("FILE_DOWNLOADED_ACTION");

        //---register the receiver---
        registerReceiver(intentReceiver, intentFilter);

        Button btnStart = (Button) findViewById(R.id.btnStartService);
        btnStart.setOnClickListener(new View.OnClickListener() {
            public void onClick(View v) {
                //startService(new Intent(getBaseContext(), MyService.class));
                startService(new Intent(getBaseContext(), MyIntentService.class));
            }
        });

        Button btnStop = (Button) findViewById(R.id.btnStopService);
        btnStop.setOnClickListener(new View.OnClickListener() {
            public void onClick(View v) {
                stopService(new Intent(getBaseContext(), MyService.class));
            }
        });
    }

    private BroadcastReceiver intentReceiver = new BroadcastReceiver() {
        @Override
        public void onReceive(Context context, Intent intent) {
            Toast.makeText(getBaseContext(), "File downloaded!",
                    Toast.LENGTH_LONG).show();
        }
    };
}
```

3. Press F11 to debug the application on the Android Emulator.

4. Click the Start Service button. After about five seconds, the Toast class will display a message indicating that the file has been downloaded (see Figure 10-5).

How It Works

To notify an activity when a service has finished its execution, you broadcast an intent using the sendBroadcast() method:

```
    @Override
    protected void onHandleIntent(Intent intent) {
        try {
            int result =
                DownloadFile(new URL("http://www.amazon.com/somefile.pdf"));
```

```
        Log.d("IntentService", "Downloaded " + result + " bytes");

        //---send a broadcast to inform the activity
        // that the file has been downloaded---
        Intent broadcastIntent = new Intent();
        broadcastIntent.setAction("FILE_DOWNLOADED_ACTION");
        getBaseContext().sendBroadcast(broadcastIntent);
    } catch (MalformedURLException e) {
        e.printStackTrace();
    }
}
```

The action of this intent that you are broadcasting is set to `"FILE_DOWNLOADED_ACTION"`, which means any activity that is listening for this intent will be invoked. Hence, in your `MainActivity.java` file, you listen for this intent using the `registerReceiver()` method from the `IntentFilter` class:

```
@Override
public void onCreate(Bundle savedInstanceState) {
    super.onCreate(savedInstanceState);
    setContentView(R.layout.main);

    //---intent to filter for file downloaded intent---
    intentFilter = new IntentFilter();
    intentFilter.addAction("FILE_DOWNLOADED_ACTION");
    //---register the receiver---
    registerReceiver(intentReceiver, intentFilter);
    ...
    ...
}
```

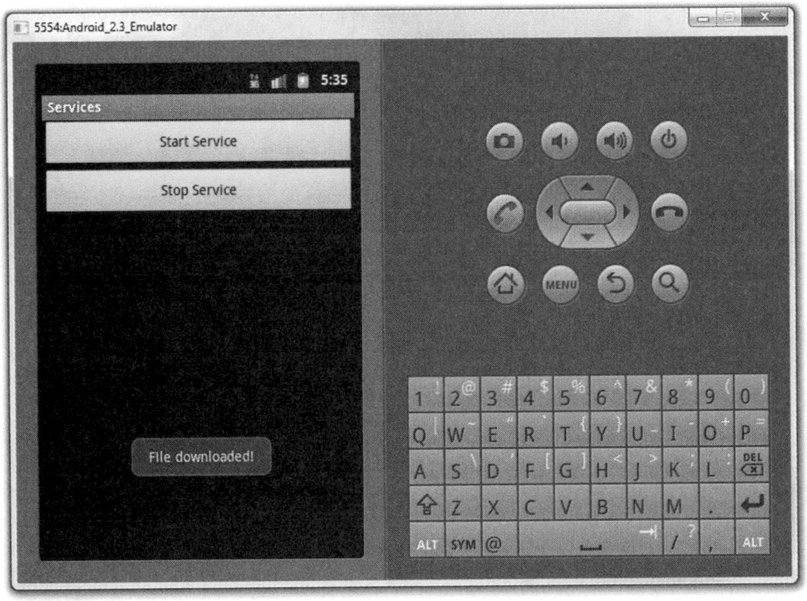

FIGURE 10-5

When the intent is received, it invokes an instance of the `BroadcastReceiver` class that you have defined:

```
    private BroadcastReceiver intentReceiver = new BroadcastReceiver() {
        @Override
        public void onReceive(Context context, Intent intent) {
            Toast.makeText(getBaseContext(), "File downloaded!",
                    Toast.LENGTH_LONG).show();
        }
    };
}
```

> **NOTE** *Chapter 8 discusses the* `BroadcastReceiver` *class in more detail.*

In this case, you displayed the message "File downloaded!" Of course, if you need to pass some data from the service to the activity, you can make use of the `Intent` object. The next section discusses this.

BINDING ACTIVITIES TO SERVICES

So far, you have seen how services are created and how they are called and terminated when they are done with their task. All the services that you have seen are simple — either they start with a counter and increment at regular intervals, or they download a fixed set of files from the Internet. However, real-world services are usually much more sophisticated, requiring the passing of data so that they can do the job correctly for you.

Using the service demonstrated earlier that downloads a set of files, suppose you now want to let the calling activity determine what files to download, instead of hardcoding them in the service. Here is what you need to do.

First, in the calling activity, you create an `Intent` object, specifying the service name:

```
    Button btnStart = (Button) findViewById(R.id.btnStartService);
    btnStart.setOnClickListener(new View.OnClickListener() {
        public void onClick(View v) {
            Intent intent = new Intent(getBaseContext(), MyService.class);
        }
    });
```

You then create an array of URL objects and assign it to the `Intent` object through its `putExtra()` method. Finally, you start the service using the `Intent` object:

```
    Button btnStart = (Button) findViewById(R.id.btnStartService);
    btnStart.setOnClickListener(new View.OnClickListener() {
        public void onClick(View v) {
            Intent intent = new Intent(getBaseContext(), MyService.class);
            try {
                URL[] urls = new URL[] {
```

```
                          new URL("http://www.amazon.com/somefiles.pdf"),
                          new URL("http://www.wrox.com/somefiles.pdf"),
                          new URL("http://www.google.com/somefiles.pdf"),
                          new URL("http://www.learn2develop.net/somefiles.pdf")};
                  intent.putExtra("URLs", urls);
              } catch (MalformedURLException e) {
                  e.printStackTrace();
              }
              startService(intent);
          }
      });
```

Note that the URL array is assigned to the Intent object as an Object array.

On the service's end, you need to extract the data passed in through the Intent object in the onStartCommand() method:

```
@Override
public int onStartCommand(Intent intent, int flags, int startId) {
    // We want this service to continue running until it is explicitly
    // stopped, so return sticky.
    Toast.makeText(this, "Service Started", Toast.LENGTH_LONG).show();

    Object[] objUrls = (Object[]) intent.getExtras().get("URLs");
    URL[] urls = new URL[objUrls.length];
    for (int i=0; i<objUrls.length-1; i++) {
        urls[i] = (URL) objUrls[i];
    }
    new DoBackgroundTask().execute(urls);
    return START_STICKY;
}
```

The preceding first extracts the data using the getExtras() method to return a Bundle object. It then uses the get() method to extract out the URL array as an Object array. Because in Java you cannot directly cast an array from one type to another, you have to create a loop and cast each member of the array individually. Finally, you execute the background task by passing the URL array into the execute() method.

This is one way in which your activity can pass values to the service. As you can see, if you have relatively complex data to pass to the service, you have to do some additional work to ensure that the data is passed correctly. A better way to pass data is to bind the activity directly to the service so that the activity can call any public members and methods on the service directly. The following Try It Out shows you how to bind an activity to a service.

TRY IT OUT   **Accessing Members of a Property Directly through Binding**

1.   Using the same project created earlier, add the following statements in bold to the MyService.java file:

```
package net.learn2develop.Services;

import java.net.URL;
import java.util.Timer;
```

```java
import java.util.TimerTask;

import android.app.Service;
import android.content.Intent;
import android.os.AsyncTask;
import android.util.Log;
import android.widget.Toast;
import android.os.IBinder;

import android.os.Binder;

public class MyService extends Service {
    int counter = 0;
    URL[] urls;

    static final int UPDATE_INTERVAL = 1000;
    private Timer timer = new Timer();

    private final IBinder binder = new MyBinder();

    public class MyBinder extends Binder {
        MyService getService() {
            return MyService.this;
        }
    }

    @Override
    public IBinder onBind(Intent arg0) {
        //return null;
        return binder;
    }

    @Override
    public int onStartCommand(Intent intent, int flags, int startId) {
        // We want this service to continue running until it is explicitly
        // stopped, so return sticky.
        Toast.makeText(this, "Service Started", Toast.LENGTH_LONG).show();
        new DoBackgroundTask().execute(urls);
        return START_STICKY;
    }

    @Override
    public void onDestroy() {
        ...
    }

    private int DownloadFile(URL url) {
        ...
    }

    private class DoBackgroundTask extends AsyncTask<URL, Integer, Long> {
        ...
    }
}
```

2. In the `MainActivity.java` file, add the following statements in bold:

```java
package net.learn2develop.Services;

import java.net.MalformedURLException;
import java.net.URL;

import android.app.Activity;
import android.content.BroadcastReceiver;
import android.content.ComponentName;
import android.content.Context;
import android.content.Intent;
import android.content.IntentFilter;
import android.os.Bundle;
import android.view.View;
import android.widget.Button;
import android.widget.Toast;

import android.os.IBinder;
import android.content.ServiceConnection;

public class MainActivity extends Activity {
    IntentFilter intentFilter;

    private MyService serviceBinder;
    Intent i;

    private ServiceConnection connection = new ServiceConnection() {
        public void onServiceConnected(ComponentName className, IBinder service) {
            //---called when the connection is made---
            serviceBinder = ((MyService.MyBinder)service).getService();
            try {
                URL[] urls = new URL[] {
                    new URL("http://www.amazon.com/somefiles.pdf"),
                    new URL("http://www.wrox.com/somefiles.pdf"),
                    new URL("http://www.google.com/somefiles.pdf"),
                    new URL("http://www.learn2develop.net/somefiles.pdf")};
                    //---assign the URLs to the service through the serviceBinder object---
                    serviceBinder.urls = urls;
                } catch (MalformedURLException e) {
                    e.printStackTrace();
                }
                startService(i);
        }
        public void onServiceDisconnected(ComponentName className) {
            //---called when the service disconnects---
            serviceBinder = null;
        }
    };

    /** Called when the activity is first created. */
    @Override
    public void onCreate(Bundle savedInstanceState) {
        super.onCreate(savedInstanceState);
```

```
        setContentView(R.layout.main);

        //---intent to filter for file downloaded intent---
        intentFilter = new IntentFilter();
        intentFilter.addAction("FILE_DOWNLOADED_ACTION");

        //---register the receiver---
        registerReceiver(intentReceiver, intentFilter);

        Button btnStart = (Button) findViewById(R.id.btnStartService);
        btnStart.setOnClickListener(new View.OnClickListener() {
            public void onClick(View v) {
                i = new Intent(MainActivity.this, MyService.class);
                bindService(i, connection, Context.BIND_AUTO_CREATE);
            }
        });

        Button btnStop = (Button) findViewById(R.id.btnStopService);
        btnStop.setOnClickListener(new View.OnClickListener() {
            public void onClick(View v) {
                stopService(new Intent(getBaseContext(), MyService.class));
            }
        });
    }

    private BroadcastReceiver intentReceiver = new BroadcastReceiver() {
        ...
    };
}
```

3. Press F11 to debug the application. Clicking the Start Service button will start the service as normal.

How It Works

To bind activities to a service, you must first declare an inner class in your service that extends the Binder class:

```
public class MyBinder extends Binder {
    MyService getService() {
        return MyService.this;
    }
}
```

Within this class you implemented the getService() method, which returns an instance of the service.

You then created an instance of the MyBinder class:

```
private final IBinder binder = new MyBinder();
```

You also modified the onBind() method to return the MyBinder instance:

```
@Override
public IBinder onBind(Intent arg0) {
    //return null;
    return binder;
}
```

In the `onStartCommand()` method, you then call the `execute()` method using the `urls` array, which you declared as a public member in your service:

```java
public class MyService extends Service {
    int counter = 0;
    URL[] urls;
...
...
...

    @Override
    public int onStartCommand(Intent intent, int flags, int startId) {
        // We want this service to continue running until it is explicitly
        // stopped, so return sticky.
        Toast.makeText(this, "Service Started", Toast.LENGTH_LONG).show();
        new DoBackgroundTask().execute(urls);
        return START_STICKY;
    }
}
```

This URL array can be set directly from your activity, which you did next.

In the `MainActivity.java` file, you first declared an instance of your service and an `Intent` object:

```java
private MyService serviceBinder;
Intent i;
```

The `serviceBinder` object will be used as a reference to the service, which you accessed directly.

You then created an instance of the `ServiceConnection` class so that you could monitor the state of the service:

```java
private ServiceConnection connection = new ServiceConnection() {
    public void onServiceConnected(ComponentName className, IBinder service) {
        //---called when the connection is made---
        serviceBinder = ((MyService.MyBinder)service).getService();
        try {
            URL[] urls = new URL[] {
                new URL("http://www.amazon.com/somefiles.pdf"),
                new URL("http://www.wrox.com/somefiles.pdf"),
                new URL("http://www.google.com/somefiles.pdf"),
                new URL("http://www.learn2develop.net/somefiles.pdf")};
                //---assign the URLs to the service through the serviceBinder object---
                serviceBinder.urls = urls;
        } catch (MalformedURLException e) {
            e.printStackTrace();
        }
        startService(i);
    }
    public void onServiceDisconnected(ComponentName className) {
        //---called when the service disconnects---
        serviceBinder = null;
    }
};
```

You need to implement two methods: onServiceConnected() and onServiceDisconnected(). The onServiceConnected() method is called when the activity is connected to the service; the onServiceDisconnected() method is called when the service is disconnected from the activity.

In the onServiceConnected() method, when the activity is connected to the service, you obtained an instance of the service by using the getService() method of the service argument and then assigning it to the serviceBinder object. The serviceBinder object is a reference to the service, and all the members and methods in the service can be accessed through this object. Here, you created an URL array and then directly assigned it to the public member in the service:

```
URL[] urls = new URL[] {
    new URL("http://www.amazon.com/somefiles.pdf"),
    new URL("http://www.wrox.com/somefiles.pdf"),
    new URL("http://www.google.com/somefiles.pdf"),
    new URL("http://www.learn2develop.net/somefiles.pdf")};

//---assign the URLs to the service through the serviceBinder object---
serviceBinder.urls = urls;
```

You then started the service using an Intent object:

```
startService(i);
```

Before you can start the service, you have to bind the activity to the service. This you did in the onClick() method of the Start Service button:

```
Button btnStart = (Button) findViewById(R.id.btnStartService);
btnStart.setOnClickListener(new View.OnClickListener() {
    public void onClick(View v) {
        i = new Intent(MainActivity.this, MyService.class);
        bindService(i, connection, Context.BIND_AUTO_CREATE);
    }
});
```

The bindService() method enables your activity to be connected to the service. It takes three arguments: an Intent object, a ServiceConnection object, and a flag to indicate how the service should be bound.

SUMMARY

In this chapter, you learned how to create a service in your Android project to execute long-running tasks. You have seen the many approaches you can use to ensure that the background task is executed in an asynchronous fashion, without tying up the main calling activity. You have also learned how an activity can pass data into a service, and how you can alternatively bind to an activity so that it can access a service more directly.

EXERCISES

1. Why is it important to put long-running code in a service on a separate thread?

2. What is the use of the `IntentService` class?

3. Name the three methods you need to implement in an `AsyncTask` class.

4. How can a service notify an activity of an event happening?

Answers to Exercises can be found in Appendix C.

► WHAT YOU LEARNED IN THIS CHAPTER

TOPIC	KEY CONCEPTS
Creating a service	Create a class and extend the `Service` class.
Implementing the methods in a service	Implement the following methods: `onBind()`, `onStartCommand()`, and `onDestroy()`.
Starting a service	Use the `startService()` method.
Stopping a service	Use the `stopService()` method.
Performing long-running tasks	Use the `AsyncTask` class and implement three methods: `doInBackground()`, `onProgressUpdate()`, and `onPostExecute()`.
Performing repeated tasks	Use the Timer class and call its `scheduleAtFixedRate()` method.
Executing tasks on a separate thread and auto-stopping a service	Use the `IntentService` class.
Communicating between an activity and a service	Use the `Intent` object to pass data into the service. For a service, broadcast an `Intent` to notify an activity.
Binding an activity to a service	Use the `Binder` class in your service and implement the `ServiceConnection` class in your calling activity.

11

Publishing Android Applications

WHAT YOU WILL LEARN IN THIS CHAPTER

➤ How to prepare your application for deployment

➤ How to export your application as an APK file and sign it with a new certificate

➤ How to distribute your Android application

➤ How to publish your application on the Android Market

So far you have seen quite a lot of interesting things you can do with Android. However, in order to get your application running on users' devices, you need a way to deploy it and distribute it. In this chapter, you will learn how to prepare your Android applications for deployment and get them onto your customer's devices. In addition, you will learn how to publish your applications on the Android Market, where you can sell them and make some money!

PREPARING FOR PUBLISHING

Google has made it relatively easy to publish your Android application so that it can be quickly distributed to end users. The steps to publishing your Android application generally involve the following:

1. Export your application as an APK (Android Package) file.

2. Generate your own self-signed certificate and digitally sign your application with it.

3. Deploy the signed application.

4. Use the Android Market for hosting and selling your application.

In the following sections, you will learn how to prepare your application for signing, and then learn about the various ways to deploy your applications.

This chapter uses the LBS project created in Chapter 9 to demonstrate how to deploy an Android application.

Versioning

Beginning with version 1.0 of the Android SDK, the AndroidManifest.xml file of every Android application includes the android:versionCode and android:versionName attributes:

```xml
<?xml version="1.0" encoding="utf-8"?>
<manifest xmlns:android="http://schemas.android.com/apk/res/android"
    package="net.learn2develop.LBS"
    android:versionCode="1"
    android:versionName="1.0">
    <application android:icon="@drawable/icon" android:label="@string/app_name">
    <uses-library android:name="com.google.android.maps" />
        <activity android:name=".MainActivity"
                android:label="@string/app_name">
            <intent-filter>
                <action android:name="android.intent.action.MAIN" />
                <category android:name="android.intent.category.LAUNCHER" />
            </intent-filter>
        </activity>
    </application>
    <uses-sdk android:minSdkVersion="7" />
    <uses-permission android:name="android.permission.INTERNET" />
<uses-permission android:name="android.permission.ACCESS_FINE_LOCATION" />
<uses-permission android:name="android.permission.ACCESS_COARSE_LOCATION" />
</manifest>
```

The android:versionCode attribute represents the version number of your application. For every revision you make to the application, you should increment this value by 1 so that you can programmatically differentiate the newest version from the previous one. This value is never used by the Android system, but is useful for developers as a means to obtain the version number of an application. However, the android:versionCode attribute is used by Android Market to determine if there is a newer version of your application available.

You can programmatically retrieve the value of the android:versionCode attribute by using the getPackageInfo() method from the PackageManager class, like this:

```java
PackageManager pm = getPackageManager();
try {
    //---get the package info---
    PackageInfo pi =
        pm.getPackageInfo("net.learn2develop.LBS", 0);
    //---display the versioncode---
    Toast.makeText(getBaseContext(),
        "VersionCode: " +Integer.toString(pi.versionCode),
        Toast.LENGTH_SHORT).show();
```

```
        } catch (NameNotFoundException e) {
            // TODO Auto-generated catch block
            e.printStackTrace();
        }
```

The `android:versionName` attribute contains versioning information that is visible to the users. It should contain values in the format: *<major>.<minor>.<point>*. If your application undergoes a major upgrade, you should increase the *<major>* by 1. For small incremental updates, you can either increase the *<minor>* or *<point>* by 1. For example, a new application may have a version name of "1.0.0". For a small incremental update, you might change to "1.1.0" or "1.0.1". For the next major update, you might change it "2.0.0".

If you are planning to publish your application on the Android Market (`www.android.com/market/`), the `AndroidManifest.xml` file must have the following attributes:

➤   `android:versionCode` (within the `<manifest>` element)

➤   `android:versionName` (within the `<manifest>` element)

➤   `android:icon` (within the `<application>` element)

➤   `android:label` (within the `<application>` element)

The `android:label` attribute specifies the name of your application. This name will be displayed in the Settings ➪ Applications ➪ Manage Applications section of your Android device. For the LBS project, we'll give the application the name "Where Am I":

```xml
<?xml version="1.0" encoding="utf-8"?>
<manifest xmlns:android="http://schemas.android.com/apk/res/android"
    package="net.learn2develop.LBS"
    android:versionCode="1"
    android:versionName="1.0">
    <application android:icon="@drawable/icon" android:label="Where Am I">
    <uses-library android:name="com.google.android.maps" />
        <activity android:name=".MainActivity"
                android:label="@string/app_name">
            <intent-filter>
                <action android:name="android.intent.action.MAIN" />
                <category android:name="android.intent.category.LAUNCHER" />
            </intent-filter>
        </activity>
    </application>
    <uses-sdk android:minSdkVersion="7" />
    <uses-permission android:name="android.permission.INTERNET" />
<uses-permission android:name="android.permission.ACCESS_FINE_LOCATION" />
<uses-permission android:name="android.permission.ACCESS_COARSE_LOCATION" />
</manifest>
```

In addition, if your application needs a minimum version of the SDK, you can specify it in the `AndroidManifest.xml` file using the `<uses-sdk>` element:

```xml
<?xml version="1.0" encoding="utf-8"?>
<manifest xmlns:android="http://schemas.android.com/apk/res/android"
```

```
            package="net.learn2develop.LBS"
            android:versionCode="1"
            android:versionName="1.0">
      <application android:icon="@drawable/icon" android:label="Where Am I">
      <uses-library android:name="com.google.android.maps" />

         <activity android:name=".MainActivity"
                 android:label="@string/app_name">
           <intent-filter>
               <action android:name="android.intent.action.MAIN" />
               <category android:name="android.intent.category.LAUNCHER" />
           </intent-filter>
         </activity>
      </application>
      <uses-sdk android:minSdkVersion="7" />
      <uses-permission android:name="android.permission.INTERNET" />
      <uses-permission android:name="android.permission.ACCESS_FINE_LOCATION" />
      <uses-permission android:name="android.permission.ACCESS_COARSE_LOCATION" />
   </manifest>
```

In the preceding example, the application requires a minimum of SDK version 7, which is Android 2.1. In general, it is always good to set this version number to the lowest one that your application can support. This ensures that a wider range of users will be able to run your application. Although the latest version of Android at the time of writing is 2.3, a lot of devices are still running Android 2.1 and 2.2.

Digitally Signing Your Android Applications

All Android applications must be digitally signed before they are allowed to be deployed onto a device (or emulator). Unlike some mobile platforms, you need not purchase digital certificates from a certificate authority (CA) to sign your applications. Instead, you can generate your own self-signed certificate and use it to sign your Android applications.

When you use Eclipse to develop your Android application and then press F11 to deploy it to an emulator, Eclipse automatically signs it for you. You can verify this by going to Windows ➪ Preferences in Eclipse, expanding the Android item, and selecting Build (see Figure 11-1). Eclipse uses a default debug keystore (appropriately named "debug.keystore") to sign your application. A keystore is commonly known as a *digital certificate.*

If you are publishing an Android application, you must sign it with your own certificate. Applications signed with the debug certificate cannot be published. While you can manually generate your own certificates using the keytool.exe utility provided by the Java SDK, Eclipse has made it easy for you by including a wizard that walks you through the steps to generate a certificate. It will also sign your application with the generated certificate (which you can also sign manually using the jarsigner.exe tool from the Java SDK).

The following Try It Out demonstrates how to use Eclipse to export an Android application and sign it with a newly generated certificate.

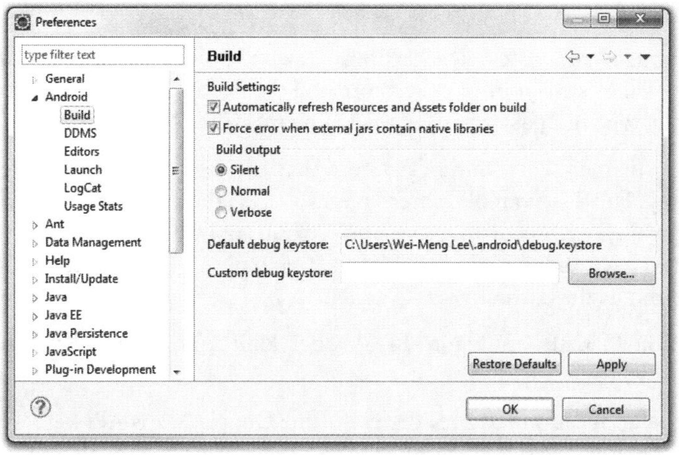

FIGURE 11-1

TRY IT OUT Exporting and Signing an Android Application

1. Using Eclipse, open the LBS projected created in Chapter 9.

2. Select the LBS project in Eclipse and then select File ⇨ Export….

3. In the Export dialog, expand the Android item and select Export Android Application (see Figure 11-2). Click Next.

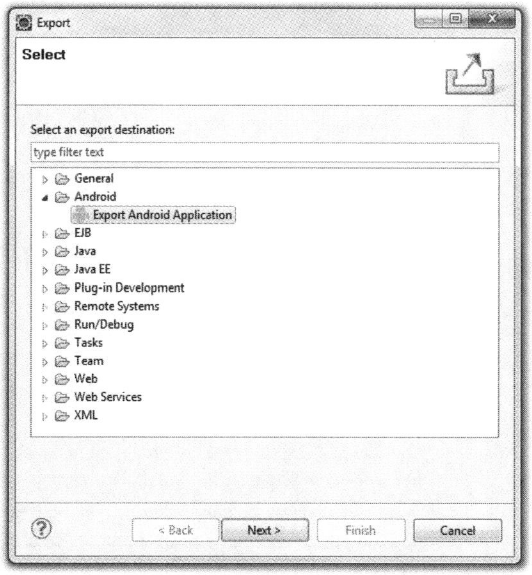

FIGURE 11-2

4. The LBS project should now be displayed (see Figure 11-3). Click Next.

5. Select the "Create new keystore" option to create a new certificate (keystore) for signing your application (see Figure 11-4). Enter a path to save your new keystore and then enter a password to protect the keystore. For this example, type in "**password**" as the password. Click Next.

6. Provide an alias for the private key (name it **DistributionKeyStoreAlias**; see Figure 11-5) and enter a password to protect the private key. For this example, enter "**password**" as the password. You also need to enter a validity period for the key. According to Google, your application must be signed with a cryptographic private key whose validity period ends after 22 October 2033. Hence, enter a number that is greater than 2033 minus the current year. Click Next.

7. Enter a path to store the destination APK file (see Figure 11-6). Click Finish. The APK file will now be generated.

8. Recall from Chapter 9 that the LBS application requires the use of the Google Maps API key, which you applied by using your debug.keystore's MD5 fingerprint. This means that the Google Maps API key is essentially tied to the debug.keystore used to sign your application. Because you are now generating your new keystore to sign your application for deployment, you need to apply for the Google Maps API key again, using the new keystore's MD5 fingerprint. To do so, go to the command prompt and enter the following command (the location of your keytool.exe utility might differ slightly and you would need to replace the path of the keystore with the path you selected earlier in step 5; see also Figure 11-7):

```
C:\Program Files\Java\jre6\bin>keytool.exe -list -alias DistributionKeyStoreAlias
-keystore "C:\Users\Wei-Meng Lee\Desktop\DistributionKeyStore" -storepass password
-keypass password
```

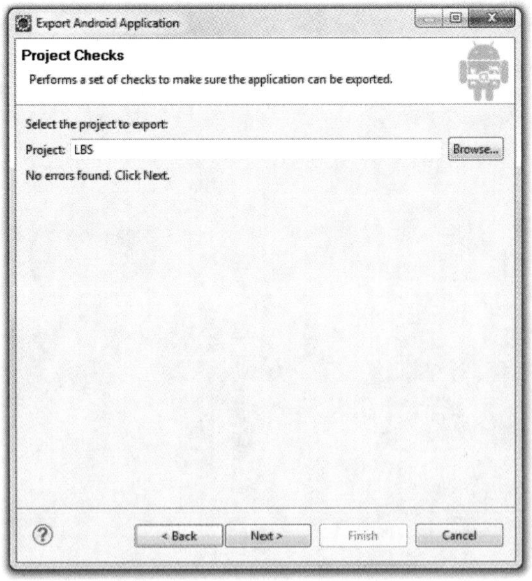

FIGURE 11-3

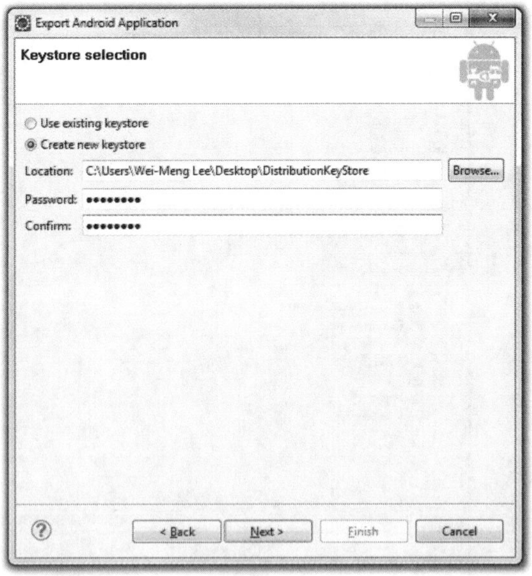

FIGURE 11-4

FIGURE 11-5

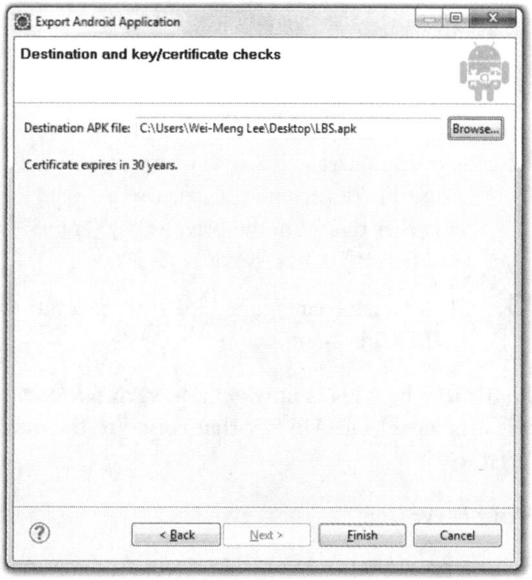

FIGURE 11-6

9. Using the MD5 fingerprint obtained from the previous step, go to `http://code.google.com/android/add-ons/google-apis/maps-api-signup.html` and sign up for a new Maps API key.

10. Enter the new Maps API key in the `main.xml` file:

```xml
<?xml version="1.0" encoding="utf-8"?>
<LinearLayout xmlns:android="http://schemas.android.com/apk/res/android"
    android:orientation="vertical"
    android:layout_width="fill_parent"
    android:layout_height="fill_parent"
    >
<com.google.android.maps.MapView
    android:id="@+id/mapView"
    android:layout_width="fill_parent"
    android:layout_height="fill_parent"
    android:enabled="true"
    android:clickable="true"
    android:apiKey="<Your Key Here>" />
</LinearLayout>
```

FIGURE 11-7

11. With the new Maps API key entered in the `main.xml` file, you now need to export the application once more and re-sign it. Repeat steps 2 through 4. When you are asked to select a keystore, select the "Use existing keystore" option (see Figure 11-8) and enter the password you used earlier to protect your keystore (in this case, "`password`"). Click Next.

12. Select the "Use existing key" option (see Figure 11-9) and enter the password you set earlier to secure the private key (enter "`password`"). Click Next.

13. Click Finish (see Figure 11-10) to generate the APK file again.

That's it! The APK is now generated and it contains the new Map API key that is tied to the new keystore.

How It Works

Eclipse provides the Export Android Application option, which helps you to both export your Android application as an APK file and generate a new keystore to sign the APK file. For applications that use the Maps API key, note that the Maps API key must be associated with the new keystore that you use to sign your APK file.

FIGURE 11-8

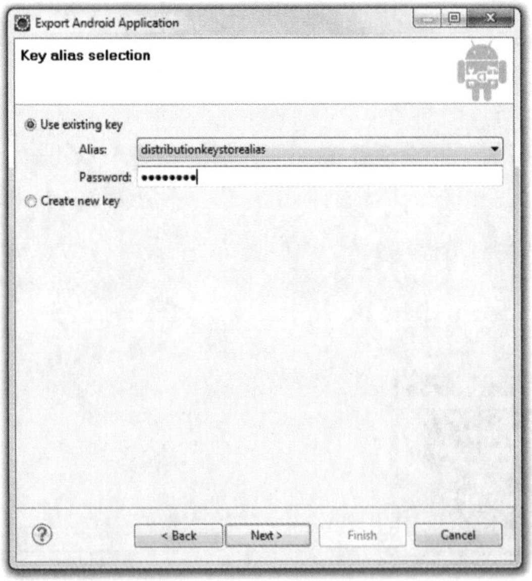

FIGURE 11-9

FIGURE 11-10

DEPLOYING APK FILES

Once you have signed your APK files, you need a way to get them onto your users' devices. The following sections describe the various ways to deploy your APK files. Three methods are covered:

➤ Deploying manually using the `adb.exe` tool

➤ Hosting the application on a web server

➤ Publishing through the Android Market

Besides the above methods, you can install your applications on users' devices through e-mails, SD card, etc. As long as you can transfer the APK file onto the user's device, you can install the application.

Using the adb.exe Tool

Once your Android application is signed, you can deploy it to emulators and devices using the `adb.exe` (Android Debug Bridge) tool (located in the `platform-tools` folder of the Android SDK).

Using the command prompt in Windows, navigate to the "`<Android_SDK>\platform-tools`" folder. To install the application to an emulator/device (assuming the emulator is currently up and running or a device is currently connected), issue the following command:

```
adb install "C:\Users\Wei-Meng Lee\Desktop\LBS.apk"
```

EXPLORING THE ADB.EXE TOOL

The `adb.exe` tool is a very versatile tool that enables you to control Android devices (and emulators) connected to your computer.

By default, when you use the `adb` command, it assumes that currently there is only one connected device/emulator. If you have more than one device connected, the `adb` command returns an error message:

```
error: more than one device and emulator
```

You can view the devices currently connected to your computer by using the `devices` option with `adb`, like this:

```
D:\Android 2.3\android-sdk-windows\platform-tools>adb devices
List of devices attached
HT07YPY09335    device
emulator-5554   device
emulator-5556   device
```

As the preceding example shows, this returns the list of devices currently attached. To issue a command for a particular device, you need to indicate the device using the `-s` option, like this:

```
adb -s emulator-5556 install LBS.apk
```

continues

(continued)

If you try to install an APK file onto a device that already has the APK file, it will display the following error message:

```
Failure [INSTALL_FAILED_ALREADY_EXISTS]
```

Figure 11-11 shows an APK file successfully installed onto a real device.

FIGURE 11-11

When you inspect the Launcher on the Android device/emulator, you will be able to see the LBS icon (on the left of Figure 11-12). If you select Settings⇨ Applications⇨ Manage Applications on your Android device/emulator, you will see the "Where Am I" application (on the right in Figure 11-12).

FIGURE 11-12

Besides using the `adb.exe` tool to install applications, you can also use it to remove an installed application. To do so, you can use the `shell` option to remove an application from its installed folder:

```
adb shell rm /data/app/net.learn2develop.LBS.apk
```

Another way to deploy an application is to use the DDMS tool in Eclipse (see Figure 11-13). With an emulator (or device) selected, use the File Explorer in DDMS to go to the `/data/app` folder and use the "Push a file onto the device" button to copy the APK file onto the device.

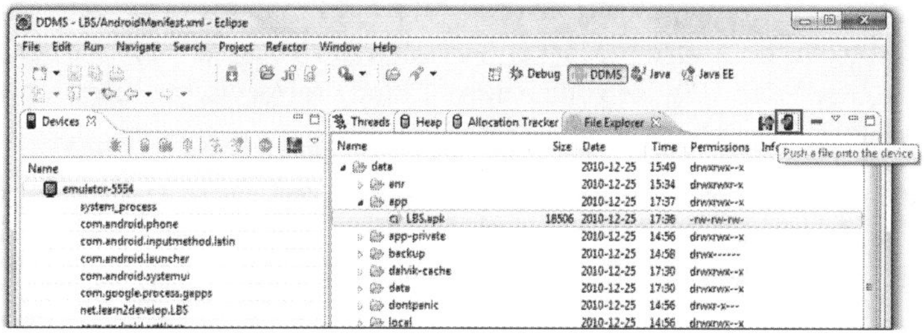

FIGURE 11-13

Using a Web Server

If you wish to host your application on your own, you can use a web server to do that. This is ideal if you have your own web hosting services and want to provide the application free of charge to your users (or you can restrict access to certain groups of people).

> **NOTE** *Even if you restrict your application to a certain group of people, there is nothing to stop users from redistributing your application to other users after they have downloaded your APK file.*

To demonstrate this, I will use the Internet Information Server (IIS) on my Windows 7 computer. Copy the signed `LBS.apk` file to `c:\inetpub\wwwroot\`. In addition, create a new HTML file named `Install.html` with the following content:

```
<html>
<title>Where Am I application</title>
<body>
Download the Where Am I application <a href="LBS.apk">here</a>
</body>
</html>
```

> **NOTE** *If you are unsure how to set up the IIS on your Windows 7 computer, check out the following link:* `http://technet.microsoft.com/en-us/library/cc725762.aspx`*.*

On your web server, you may need to register a new MIME type for the APK file. The MIME type for the .apk extension is `application/vnd.android.package-archive`.

> **NOTE** *To install APK files over the Web, you need an SD card installed on your emulator or device. This is because the downloaded APK files will be saved to the* `download` *folder created on the SD card.*

By default, for online installation of Android applications, the Android Emulator or device only allows applications to be installed from the Android Market (www.android.com/market/). Hence, for installation over a web server, you need to configure your Android Emulator/device to accept applications from non-Market sources.

From the Application settings menu, check the "Unknown sources" item (see Figure 11-14). You will be prompted with a warning message. Click OK. Checking this item will allow the Emulator/device to install applications from other non-Market sources (such as from a web server).

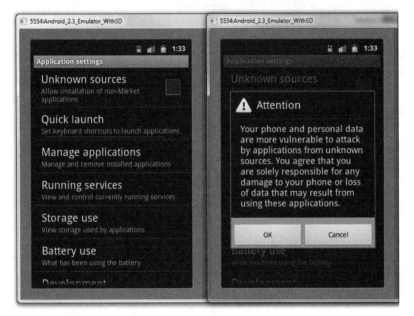

FIGURE 11-14

To install the LBS.apk application from the IIS web server running on your computer, launch the Browser application on the Android Emulator/device and navigate to the URL pointing to the APK file. To refer to the computer running the emulator, you should use the special IP address of 10.0.2.2. Alternatively, you can also use the IP address of the host computer. Figure 11-15 shows the Install .html file loaded on the web browser. Clicking the "here" link will download the APK file onto your device. Drag the notification bar down to reveal the download status.

To install the downloaded application, simply tap on it and it will show the permission(s) required by this application (see Figure 11-16).

Click the Install button to proceed with the installation. When the application is installed, you can launch it by clicking the Open button (see Figure 11-17).

Besides using a web server, you can also e-mail your application to users as an attachment; when the users receive the e-mail they can download the attachment and install the application directly onto their device.

FIGURE 11-15

FIGURE 11-16

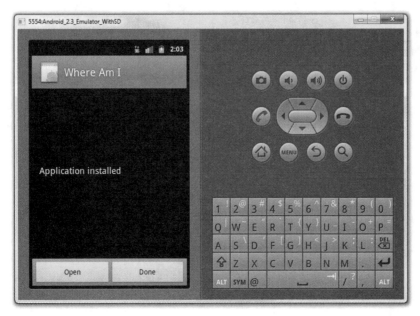

FIGURE 11-17

Publishing on the Android Market

So far, you have learned how to package your Android application and distribute it in various ways — via web server, the `adb.exe` file, e-mail, SD card, and so on.

However, these methods do not provide a way for users to discover your applications easily. A better way is to host your application on the Android Market, a Google-hosted service that makes it very easy for users to discover and download (i.e., purchase) applications for their Android devices. Users simply need to launch the Market application on their Android device in order to discover a wide range of applications that they can install on their devices.

In this section, you will learn how to publish your Android application on the Android Market. I will walk you through each of the steps involved, including the various items you need to prepare for your application for submission to the Android Market.

Creating a Developer Profile

The first step toward publishing on the Android Market is to create a developer profile at `http://market .android.com/publish/Home`. For this, you need a Google account (such as your Gmail account). Once you have logged in to the Android Market, you first create your developer profile (see Figure 11-18). Click Continue after entering the required information.

For publishing on the Android Market, you need to pay a one-time registration fee, currently U.S.$25. Click the Google Checkout button (see Figure 11-19) to be redirected to a page where you can pay the registration fee. After paying, click the Continue link.

Next, you need to agree to the Android Market Developer Distribution Agreement. Check the "I agree" checkbox and click the "I agree. Continue" link (see Figure 11-20).

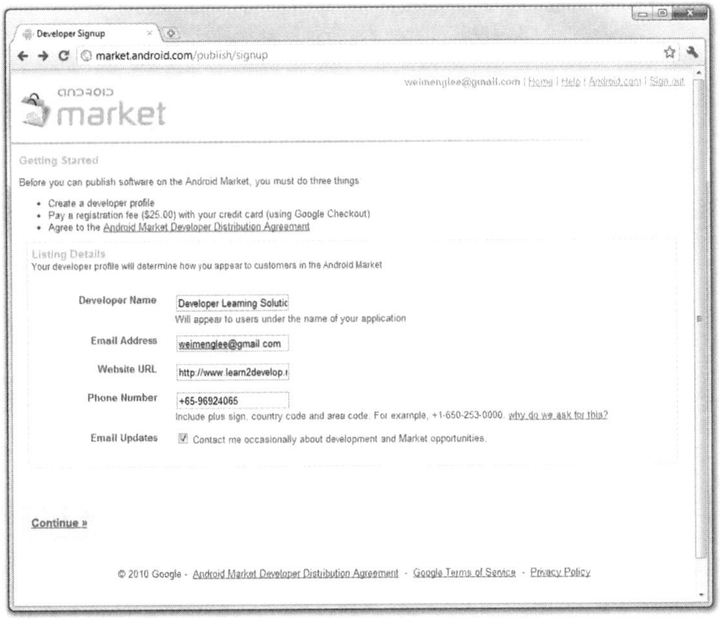

FIGURE 11-18

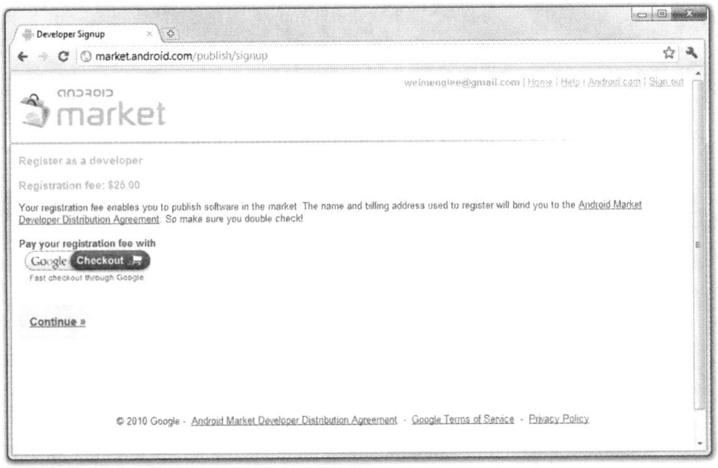

FIGURE 11-19

Submitting Your Apps

Once you have set up your profile, you are ready to submit your application to the Android Market. If you intend to charge for your application, click the Setup Merchant Account link located at the bottom of the screen. Here you enter additional information such as bank account and tax ID.

For free applications, click the Upload Application link, shown in Figure 11-21.

FIGURE 11-20

FIGURE 11-21

You will be asked to supply some details for your application. Figure 11-22 shows the first set of details you need to provide. Among the information needed, the following are compulsory:

➤ The application in APK format

➤ At least two screenshots. You can use the DDMS perspective in Eclipse to capture screenshots of your application running on the Emulator or real device.

➤ A high-resolution application icon. This size of this image must be 512×512 pixels.

The other information details are optional, and you can always supply them later.

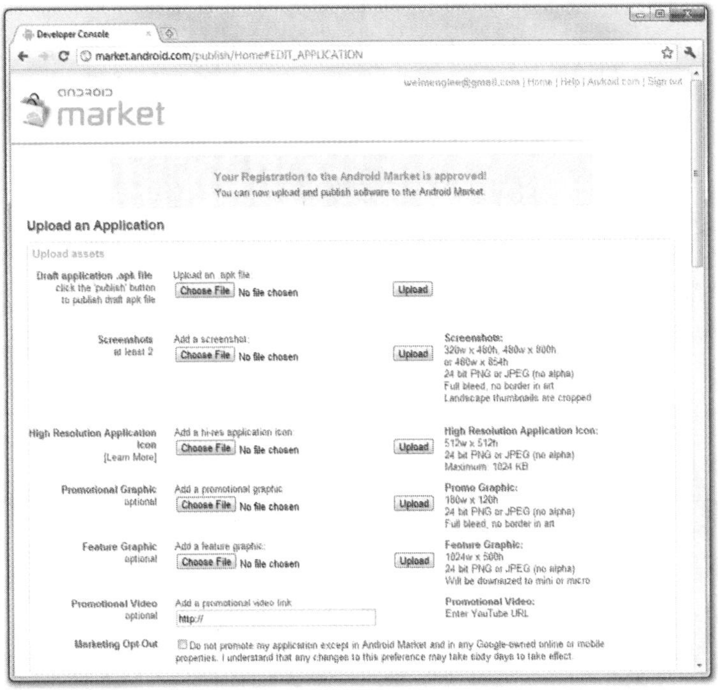

FIGURE 11-22

Figure 11-23 shows that I have uploaded the LBS.apk file to the Android Market site. In particular, note that based on the APK file that you have uploaded, the user will be warned about any specific permissions required, and your application's features will be used to filter search results. For example, because my application requires GPS access, it will not appear in the search result list if a user searches for my application on a device that does not have a GPS receiver.

The next set of information you need to supply, shown in Figure 11-24, includes the title of your application, its description, as well as recent changes' details (useful for application updates). You can also select the application type and the category in which it will appear in the Android Market.

On the last dialog, you indicate whether your application employs copy protection, and specify a content rating. You also supply your website URL and your contact information (see Figure 11-25).

When you have given your consent to the two guidelines and agreements, click Publish to publish your application on the Android Market.

FIGURE 11-23

FIGURE 11-24

That's it! Your application is now available on the Android Market. You will be able to monitor any comments submitted about your application (see Figure 11-26), as well as bug reports and total number of downloads.

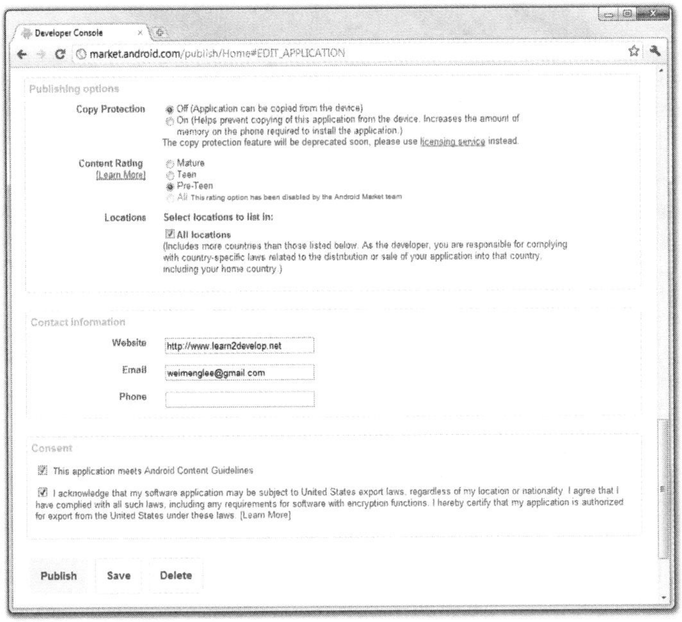

FIGURE 11-25

FIGURE 11-26

Good luck! All you need to do now is wait for the good news; and hopefully you can laugh your way to the bank soon!

SUMMARY

In this chapter, you have seen how you can export your Android application as an APK file and then digitally sign it with a keystore created by yourself. You then learned about the various ways you can distribute your application, and the advantages of each method. Finally, you walked through the steps required to publish on the Android Market, which makes it possible for you to sell your application and reach out to a wider audience. Hopefully, this exposure enables you to sell a lot of copies and thereby make some decent money!

EXERCISES

1. How do you specify the minimum version of Android required by your application?

2. How do you generate a self-sign certificate for signing your Android application?

3. How do you configure your Android device to accept applications from non-Market sources?

Answers to Exercises can be found in Appendix C.

▶ **WHAT YOU LEARNED IN THIS CHAPTER**

TOPIC	KEY CONCEPTS
Checklist for publishing your apps	To publish an application on the Android Market, an application must have the four required attributes in the `AndroidManifest.xml` file: `android:versionCode`, `android:versionName`, `android:icon`, and `android:label`.
Applications must be signed	All applications to be distributed must be signed with a self-signed certificate. The debug keystore is not valid for distribution.
Exporting an application and signing it	Use the Export feature of Eclipse to export the application as an APK file and then sign it with a self-signed certificate.
Deploying APK files	You can deploy using various means – web server, e-mail, `adb.exe`, DDMS, etc.
Publishing your application on the Android Market	Apply for the Android Market with a one-time fee of US$25 and you will be able to sell and host your apps on the Android Market.

A

Using Eclipse for Android Development

Although Google supports the development of Android applications using IDEs such as IntelliJ, or basic editors like Emacs, Google's recommendation is to use the Eclipse IDE together with the ADT Plugin. Doing so makes developing Android applications much easier and more productive. This appendix describes some of the neat features available in Eclipse that can make your development life much easier.

> **NOTE** *If you have not downloaded Eclipse yet, please start with Chapter 1, where you will learn how to obtain Eclipse and configure it to work with the Android SDK. This appendix assumes that you have already set up your Eclipse environment for Android development.*

GETTING AROUND IN ECLIPSE

Eclipse is a highly extensible multi-language software development environment that supports application development of all sorts. Using Eclipse, you could write and test your applications using a wide variety of languages, such as Java, C, C++, PHP, Ruby, and so on. Because of its extensibility, new users of Eclipse often feel inundated with the IDE. Hence, the following sections aim to make you more at home with Eclipse when you develop your Android applications.

Workspaces

Eclipse adopts the concept of a *workspace*. A workspace is a folder that you have chosen to store all your projects.

When you first start Eclipse, you are prompted to select a workspace (see Figure A-1).

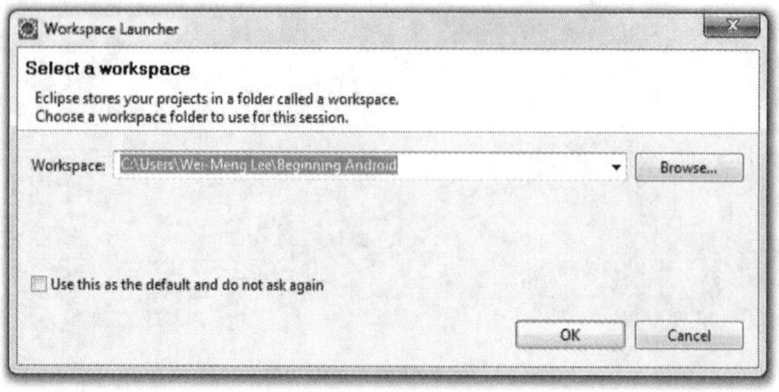

FIGURE A-1

When Eclipse has finished launching the projects located in your workspace, it will display several panes in the IDE (see Figure A-2).

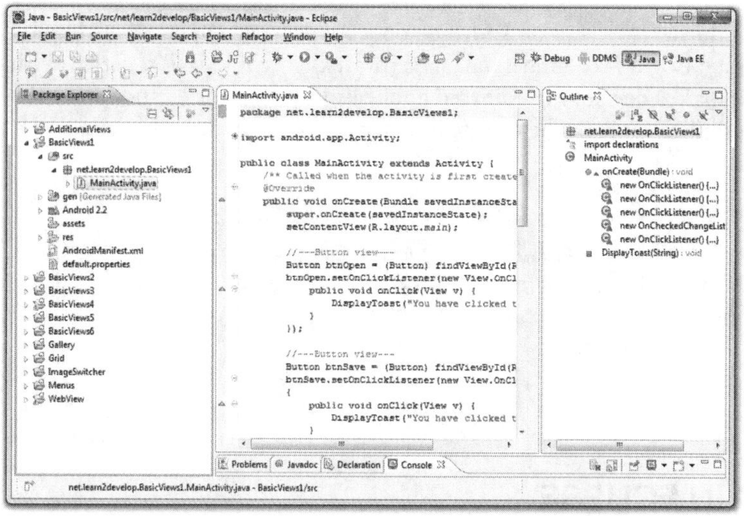

FIGURE A-2

The following sections highlight some of the more important panes that you need to know about when developing Android applications.

Package Explorer

The Package Explorer, shown in Figure A-3, lists all the projects currently in your workspace. To edit a particular item in your project, you can double-click on it and the file will be displayed in the respective editor.

You can also right-click on each item displayed in the Package Explorer to display context sensitive menu(s) related to the selected item. For example, if you wish to add a new .java file to the project, you can right-click on the package name in the Package Explorer and then select New ➪ Class (see Figure A-4).

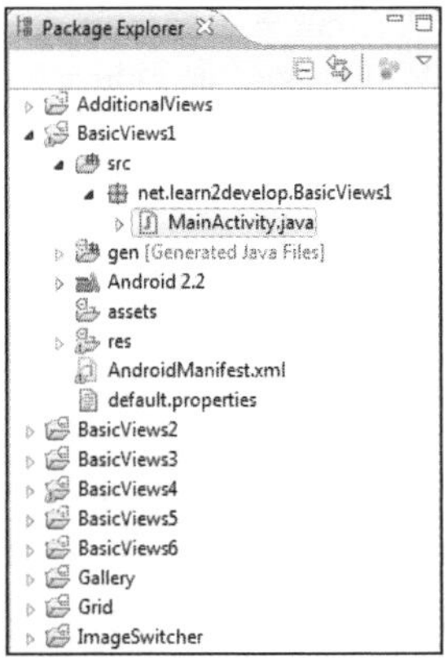

FIGURE A-3

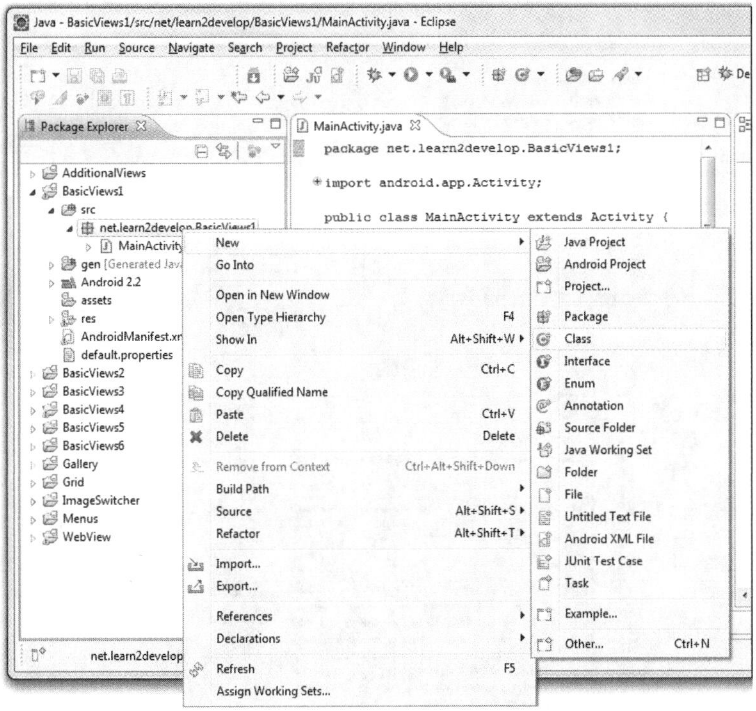

FIGURE A-4

Using Projects from Other Workspaces

There may be times when you have several workspaces created to store different projects. If you need to access the project in another workspace, there are generally two ways to go about doing so. First, you can switch to the desired workspace by selecting File ⇨ Switch Workspace (see Figure A-5). Specify the new workspace to work on and then restart Eclipse.

The second method is to import the project from another workspace into the current one. To do so, select File ➪ Import… and then select General ➪ Existing Projects into Workspace (see Figure A-6).

In the Select root directory textbox, enter the path of the workspace containing the project(s) you want to import and tick the project(s) you want to import (see Figure A-7). To import the selected project(s), click Finish.

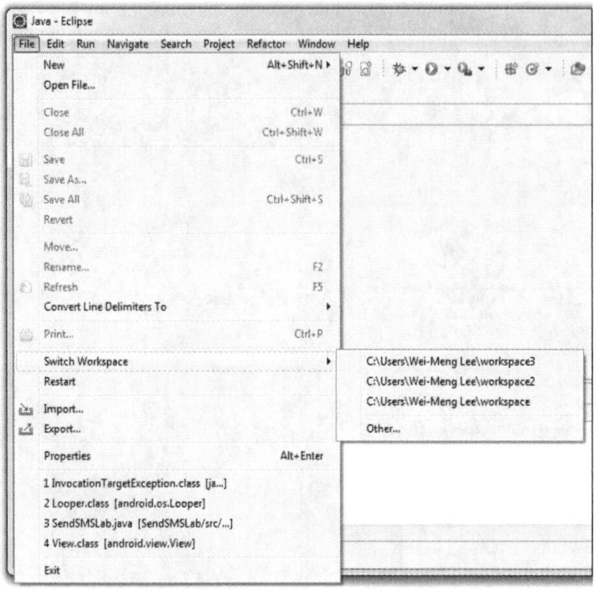

FIGURE A-5

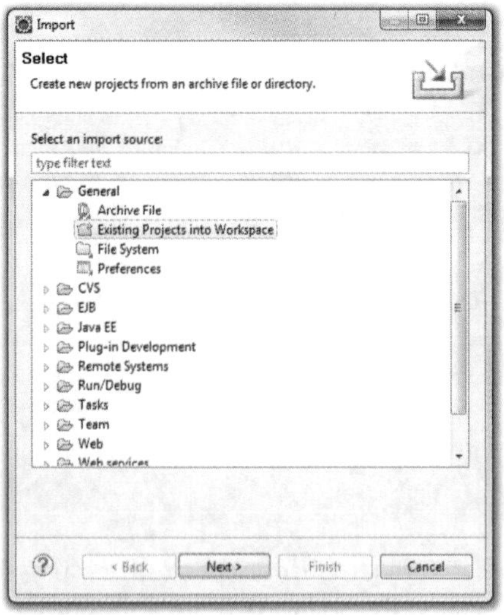

FIGURE A-6

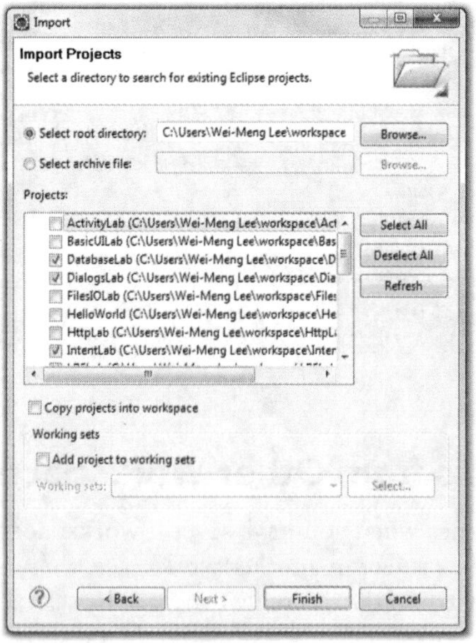

FIGURE A-7

Note that even when you import a project from another workspace into the current workspace, the physical location of the imported project remains unchanged. That is, it will still be located in its original directory. To have a copy of the project in the current workspace, check the "Copy projects into workspace" option.

Editors

Depending on the type of items you have double-clicked in the Package Explorer, Eclipse will open the appropriate editor for you to edit the file. For example, if you double-click on a .java file, the text editor for editing the source file will be opened (see Figure A-8).

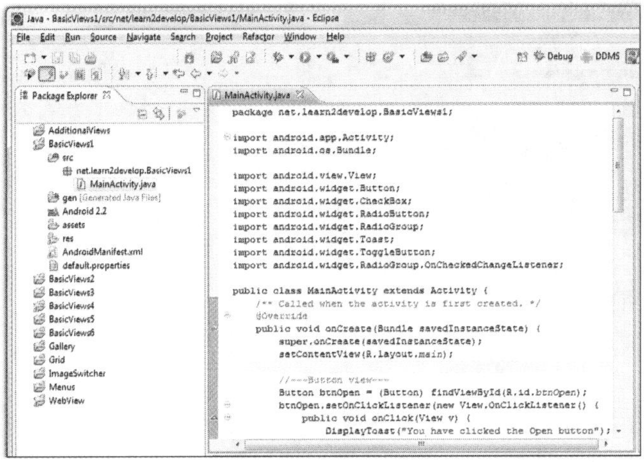

FIGURE A-8

If you double-click on the icon.png file in the res/drawable-mdpi folder, the Windows Photo Viewer application will be invoked to display the image (see Figure A-9).

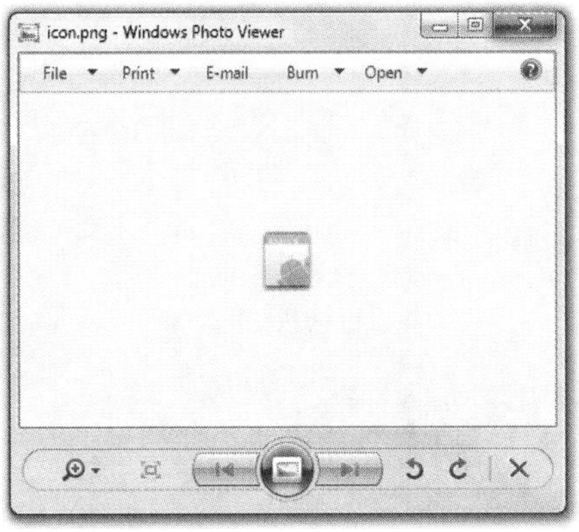

FIGURE A-9

If you double-click on the `main.xml` file in the `res/layout` folder, Eclipse will display the UI editor, where you can graphically view and build the layout of your UI (see Figure A-10).

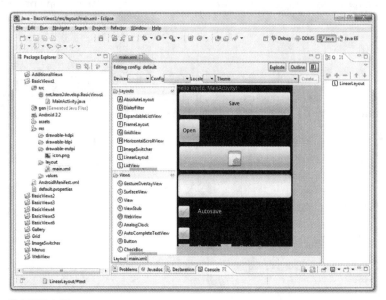

FIGURE A-10

To edit the UI manually using XML, you can switch to XML view by clicking on the main.xml tab located at the bottom of the screen (see Figure A-11).

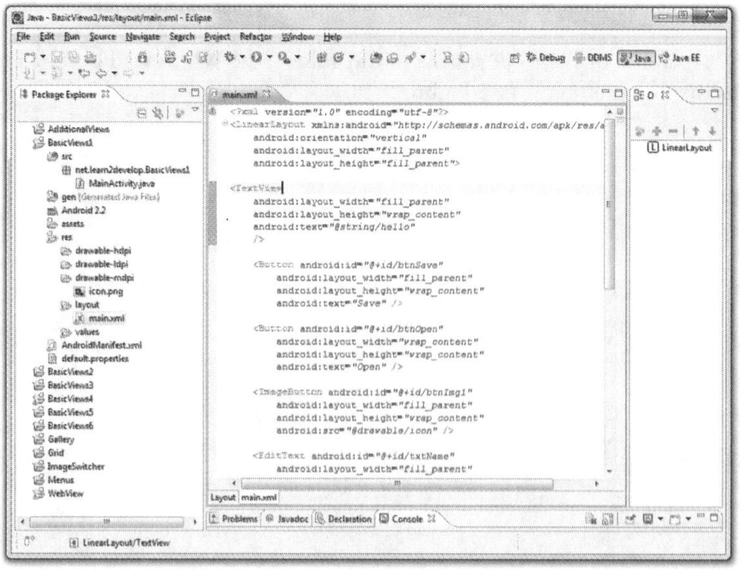

FIGURE A-11

Perspectives

In Eclipse, a *perspective* is a visual container for a set of views and editors. When you edit your project in Eclipse, you are in the Java perspective (see Figure A-12).

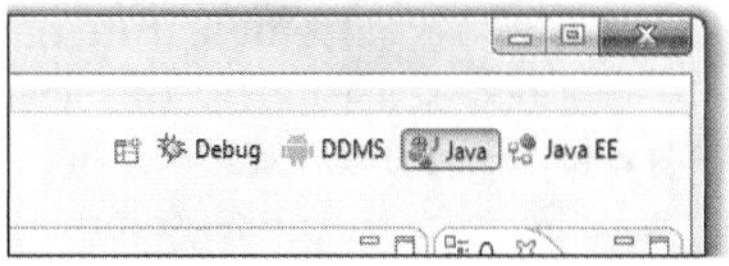

The Java EE perspective is used for developing enterprise Java applications, and it includes other modules that are relevant to it.

FIGURE A-12

You can switch to other perspectives by clicking on the perspective name. If the perspective name is not shown, you can click the Open Perspective button and add a new perspective (see Figure A-13).

The DDMS perspective contains the tools for communicating with Android emulators and devices. This is covered in more detail in Appendix B. The Debug perspective contains panes used for debugging your Android applications. You will learn more about this later in this appendix.

FIGURE A-13

Auto Import of Namespaces

The various classes in the Android library are organized into namespaces. As such, when you use a particular class from a namespace, you need to import the appropriate namespaces, like this:

```
import android.app.Activity;
import android.os.Bundle;
```

Because the number of classes in the Android Library is very large, remembering the correct namespace for each class is not an easy task. Fortunately, Eclipse can help find the correct namespace for you, enabling you to import it with just a click.

Figure A-14 shows that I have declared an object of type Button. Because I did not import the correct namespace for the Button class, Eclipse signals an error beneath the statement. When you move the mouse over the Button class, Eclipse displays a list of suggested fixes. In this case, I need to import the android .widget.Button namespace. Clicking the "Import 'Button' (android.widget)" link will add the import statement at the top of the file.

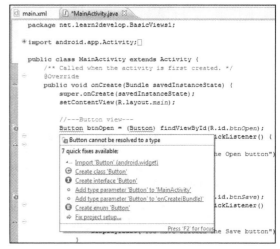

FIGURE A-14

Alternatively, you can also use the following key combination: Control+Shift+o. This key combination will cause Eclipse to automatically import all the namespaces required by your class.

Code Completion

Another very useful feature of Eclipse is the support for code completion. Code completion displays a context-sensitive list of relevant classes, objects, methods, and property names as you type in the code editor. For example, Figure A-15 shows code-completion in action. As I type the word "`fin`," I can activate the code-completion feature by pressing Ctrl+Space. This will bring up a list of names that begin with "`fin`."

To select the required name, simply double-click on it or use your cursor to highlight it and press the Enter key.

Code completion also works when you type a "." after an object/class name. Figure A-16 shows an example.

FIGURE A-15

FIGURE A-16

Refactoring

Refactoring is a very useful feature that most modern IDEs support. Eclipse supports a whole slew of refactoring features that make application development efficient.

In Eclipse, when you position the cursor at a particular object/variable, the editor will highlight all occurrences of the selected object in the current source (see Figure A-17).

FIGURE A-17

This feature is very useful for identifying where a particular object is used in your code. To change the name of an object, simply right-click on it and select Refactor ➪ Rename... (see Figure A-18).

After entering a new name for the object, all occurrences of the object will be changed dynamically (see Figure A-19).

A detailed discussion of refactoring is beyond the scope of this book. For more information on refactoring in Eclipse, refer to `www.ibm.com/developerworks/library/os-ecref/`.

```
public class MainActivity extends Activity {
    /** Called when the activity is first created. */
    @Override
    public void onCreate(Bundle savedInstanceState) {
        super.onCreate(savedInstanceState);
        setContentVie
```

			Rename...	Alt+Shift+R
Undo Typing	Ctrl+Z		Move...	Alt+Shift+V
Revert File				
Save	Ctrl+S		Change Method Signature...	Alt+Shift+C
			Extract Method...	Alt+Shift+M
Open Declaration	F3		Extract Local Variable...	Alt+Shift+L
Open Type Hierarchy	F4		Extract Constant...	
Open Call Hierarchy	Ctrl+Alt+H		Inline...	Alt+Shift+I
Show in Breadcrumb	Alt+Shift+B		Convert Local Variable to Field...	
Quick Outline	Ctrl+O		Extract Interface...	
Quick Type Hierarchy	Ctrl+T		Extract Superclass...	
Show In	Alt+Shift+W ▸		Use Supertype Where Possible...	
Cut	Ctrl+X		Pull Up...	
Copy	Ctrl+C		Push Down...	
Copy Qualified Name				
Paste	Ctrl+V		Extract Class...	
			Introduce Parameter Object...	
Quick Fix	Ctrl+1		Introduce Parameter...	
Source	Alt+Shift+S ▸			
Refactor	Alt+Shift+T ▸		Generalize Declared Type...	
Surround With	Alt+Shift+Z ▸			
Local History	▸			

FIGURE A-18

```
//---Button view---
Button btnOpen = (Button) findViewById(R.id.btnOpen);
btnOpen.setOnClickListener(new View.OnClickListener() {
    pu   Enter new name, press Enter to refactor ▼
            DisplayToast("You have clicked the Open button");
    }
});
```

FIGURE A-19

DEBUGGING

Eclipse supports debugging your application on both the Android Emulators as well as on real Android devices. When you press F11 in Eclipse, Eclipse will first determine whether an Android Emulator instance is already running or a real device is connected. If at least one emulator (or device) is running, Eclipse will deploy the application onto the running emulator or the connected device. If there is no emulator running and no connected device, Eclipse will automatically launch an instance of the Android Emulator and deploy the application onto it.

If you have more than one emulator or device connected, Eclipse will prompt you to select the target emulator/device on which to deploy the application (see Figure A-20). Select the target device you want to use and click OK.

If you want to launch a new emulator instance to test the application, select Window ➪ Android SDK and AVD Manager to launch the AVD manager.

Setting Breakpoints

Setting breakpoints is a good way to temporarily pause the execution of the application and then examine the content of variables and objects.

To set a breakpoint, double-click on the leftmost column in the code editor. Figure A-21 shows a breakpoint set on a particular statement.

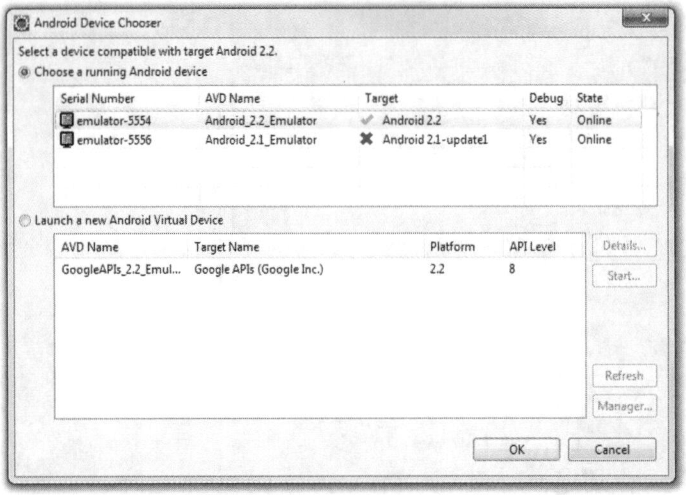

FIGURE A-20

When the application is running and the first breakpoint is reached, Eclipse will display a Confirm Perspective Switch dialog. Basically, it wants to switch to the Debug perspective. To prevent this window from appearing again, check the "Remember my decision" checkbox at the bottom and click Yes.

FIGURE A-21

Eclipse now highlights the breakpoint (see Figure A-22).

At this point, you can right-click on any selected object/variable and view its content using the various options (Watch, Inspect, and Display) shown in Figure A-23.

Figure A-24 shows the Inspect option displaying the content of the `str` variable.

There are several options at this point to continue the execution:

➤ **Step Into** — Press F5 to step into the next method call/statement.

➤ **Step Over** — Press F6 to step over the next method call without entering it.

➤ **Step Return** — Press F7 to return from a method that has been stepped into.

➤ **Resume Execution** — Press F8 to resume the execution.

Exceptions

As you develop in Android, you will encounter numerous run-time exceptions that prevent your program from continuing. Examples of run-time exceptions include the following:

➤ Null reference exception (accessing an object which is null)

➤ Failure to specify the required permissions required by your application

➤ Arithmetic operation exceptions

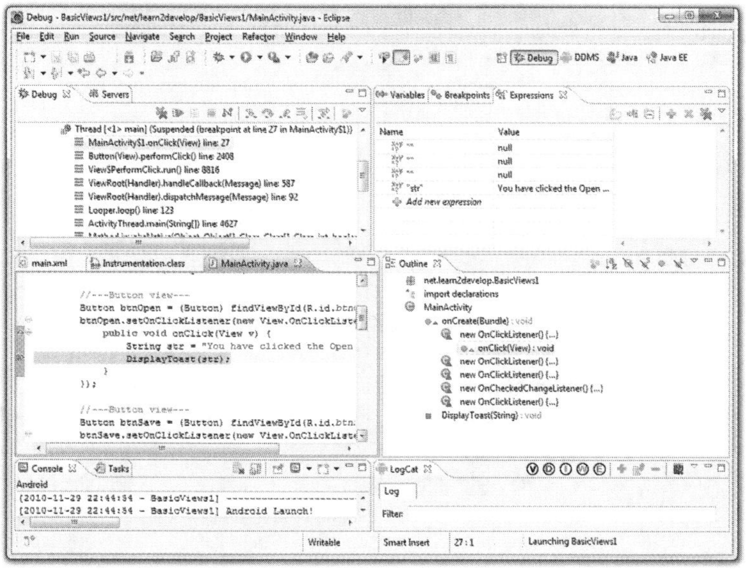

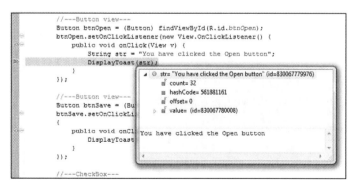

FIGURE A-22

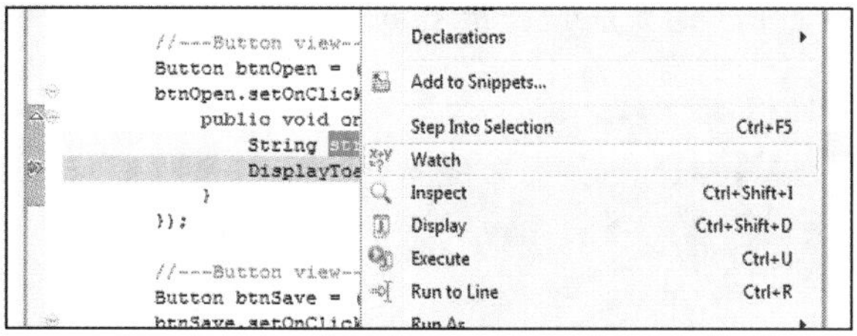

FIGURE A-23

FIGURE A-24

Figure A-25 shows the current state of an application when an exception occurred. In this example, I am trying to send an SMS message from my application and it crashes when the SMS message is about to be sent.

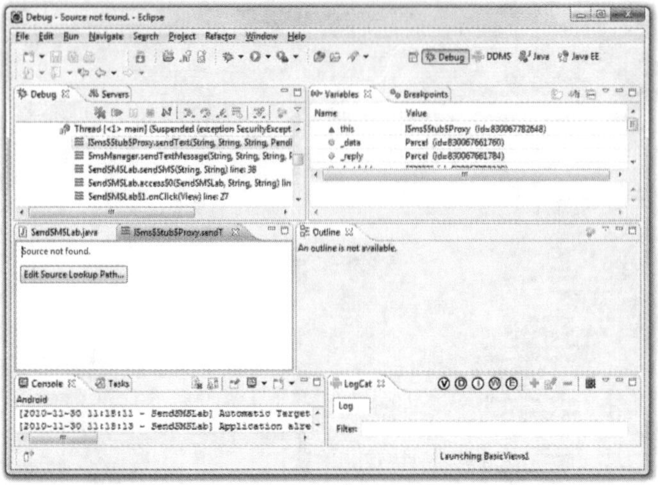

FIGURE A-25

The various windows do not really identify the cause of the exception. To find out more, press F6 in Eclipse so that it can step over the current statement. The Variables window, shown in Figure A-26, indicates the cause of the exception. In this case, the SEND_SMS permission is missing.

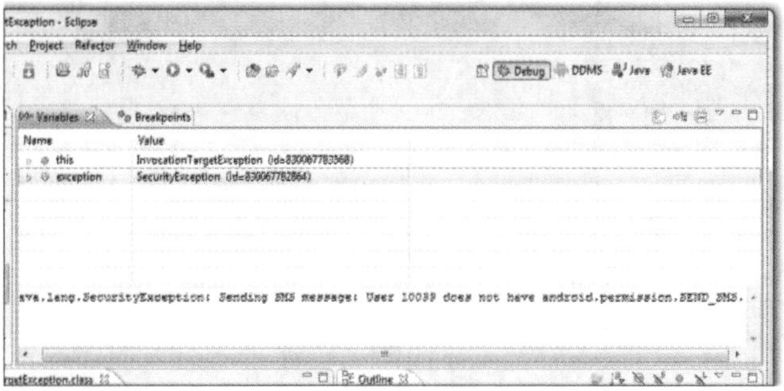

FIGURE A-26

To remedy this, all you need to do is to add the following permission statement in the AndroidManifest.xml file:

```
<uses-permission
    android:name="android.permission.SEND_SMS"/>
```

B

Using the Android Emulator

The Android Emulator ships with the Android SDK and is an invaluable tool to help test your application without requiring you to purchase a real device. While you should thoroughly test your applications on real devices before you deploy them, the emulator mimics most of the capabilities of real devices. It is a very handy tool that you should make use of during the development stage of your project. This appendix provides some common tips and tricks for mastering the Android Emulator.

USES OF THE ANDROID EMULATOR

As discussed in Chapter 1, you can use the Android Emulator to emulate the different Android configurations by creating Android Virtual Devices (AVDs).

You launch the Android Emulator by directly starting the AVD you have created in the Android SDK and AVD Manager window (see Figure B-1). Simply select the AVD and click the Start button. You have the option to scale the emulator to a particular size and monitor DPI.

Alternatively, when you run an Android project in Eclipse, the Android Emulator is automatically invoked to test your application. You can customize the Android Emulator for each of your Android projects in Eclipse. To do so, simply select Run ➪ Run Configurations. Select the project name listed under Android Application on the left (see Figure B-2), and on the right you will see the Target tab. You can choose which AVD to use for testing your application, as well as emulate different scenarios, such as network speed and network latency.

INSTALLING CUSTOM AVDS

Sometimes device manufacturers provide their own AVDs that you can use to emulate your applications running on their devices. A good example is Samsung, which provides the Samsung Galaxy Tab add-on (`http://innovator.samsungmobile.com/galaxyTab.do`) for emulating their Samsung Galaxy Tab tablet. To install the Samsung Galaxy Tab add-on, first launch the Android SDK and AVD Manager in Eclipse, and then select the Available Packages option on the left side of the dialog (see Figure B-3).

FIGURE B-1

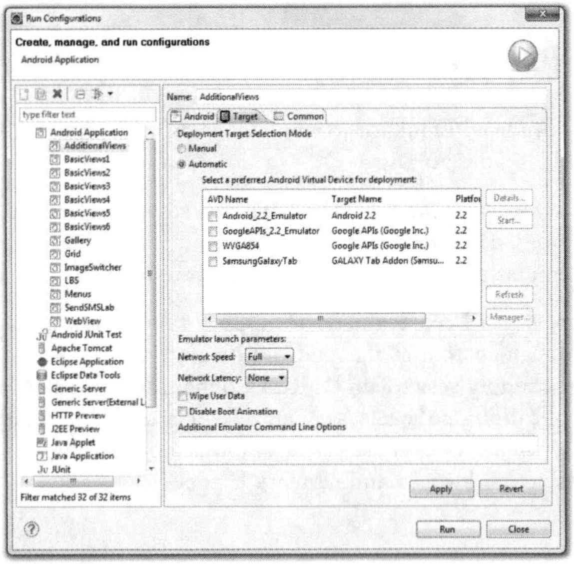

FIGURE B-2

At the bottom of the screen, click the Add Add-on Site... button and enter the following URL:
`http://innovator.samsungmobile.com/android/repository/srepository.xml` (see Figure B-4).
Click OK.

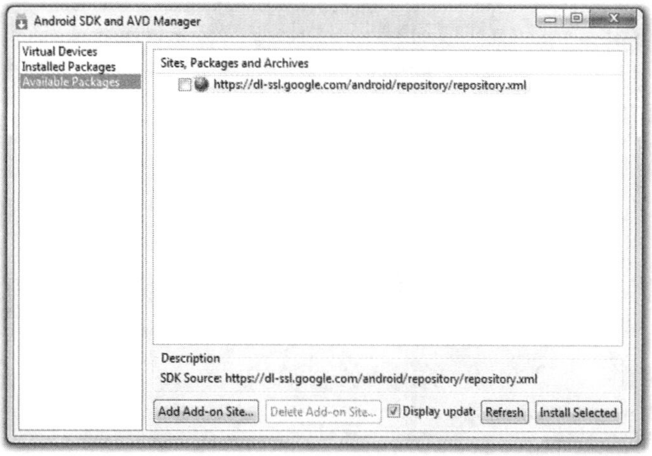

FIGURE B-3

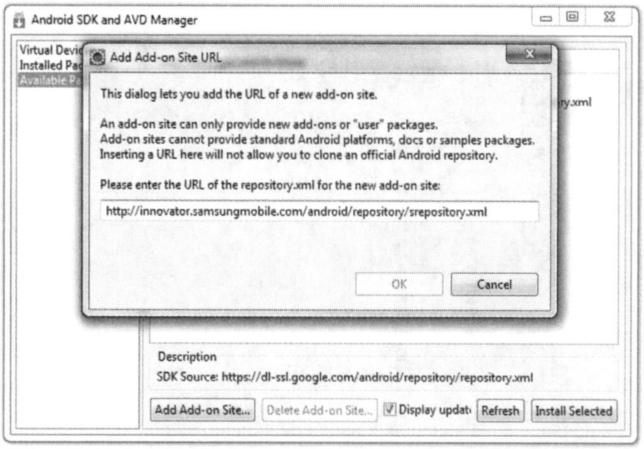

FIGURE B-4

You should now see the additional package available (see Figure B-5). Check the package and click Install Selected.

In the dialog that pops up, click "Accept" to accept the licensing agreement and then click Install to download and install the package.

After the downloaded package is installed, you can create a new AVD based on the newly downloaded package. Select the Virtual Devices item in the Androids SDK and AVD Manager window and click the New button.

Name the new AVD as shown in Figure B-6. Click the Create AVD button to create the AVD.

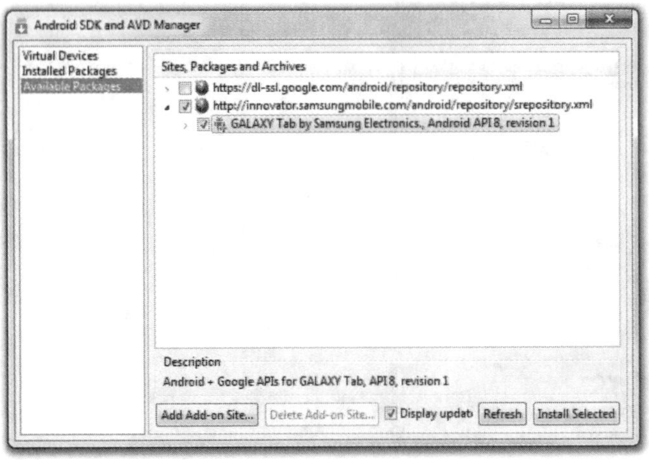

FIGURE B-5

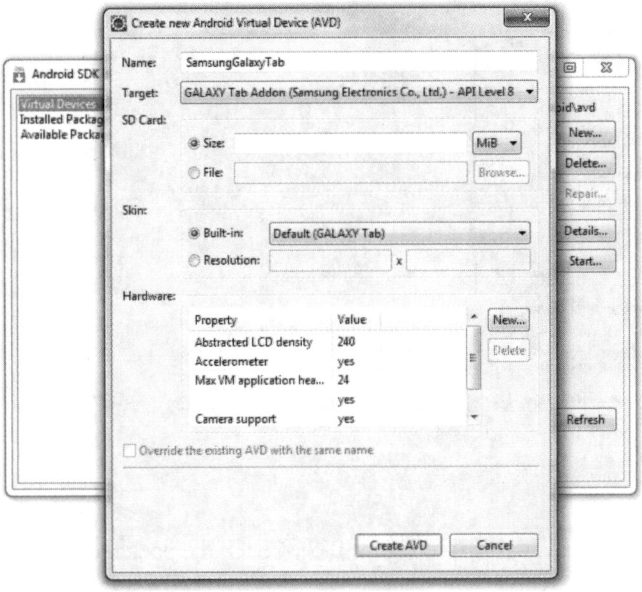

FIGURE B-6

To launch the SamsungGalaxyTab AVD, select it and click the Start… button. The Launch Options dialog, shown in Figure B-7, will appear.

Check the "Scale display to real size" option if you want to resize the emulator. This is very useful if you are running the emulator on a small monitor (such as on a notebook computer). Specify a screen size and click the Launch button to start the emulator. Figure B-8 shows the Samsung Galaxy Tab emulator.

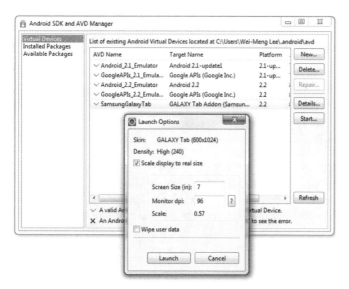

FIGURE B-7

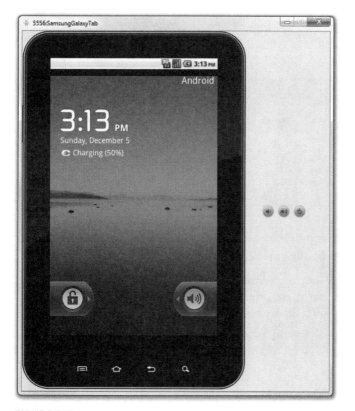

FIGURE B-8

EMULATING REAL DEVICES

Besides using the Android Emulator to test the different configurations of Android, you can also make use of the emulator to emulate real devices, using the system images provided by device manufacturers.

For example, HTC provides images for their devices running Android 1.5 and 1.6 (`http://developer .htc.com/google-io-device.html#s3`). You can download a device's system image and then use the Android Emulator to emulate it using the system image. Here is how this can be done (in theory, this should work for any version of Android).

> **NOTE** *If you use HTC's image, you should be able to boot up the emulator without problems. However, the network cannot be enabled. Some kind souls have uploaded a modified image that works properly. You can try downloading it at* `www.4shared.com/get/x6pZm3-W/system.html`*.*

First, using the Android SDK and AVD Manager, create a new AVD. In the case of HTC, create an AVD using Android 1.6 as the platform. The AVD will be located in the `C:\Users\<username>\ .android\avd\<avd_name>.avd` folder. As shown in Figure B-9, a newly created AVD contains only two files in the folder.

Using the downloaded system image, copy the `system.img` file into the AVD folder, as shown in Figure B-10.

FIGURE B-9   **FIGURE B-10**

Launch the AVD and you should see it booting up (see Figure B-11).

You can proceed to sign in using your Google account (see Figure B-12). When prompted to slide open the keyboard, press Ctrl+F11 to change the orientation of the emulator. This action tricks the emulator into believing that you are sliding the keyboard open.

Once you have successfully signed in, you will be able to explore the Android Market on your emulator (see Figure B-13)!

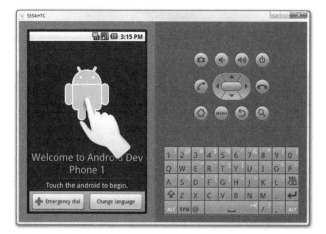

FIGURE B-11

FIGURE B-12

SD CARD EMULATION

When you create a new AVD, you can emulate the existence of an SD card (see Figure B-14). Simply enter the size of the SD card that you want to emulate (in the figure, it is 200MiB).

FIGURE B-13

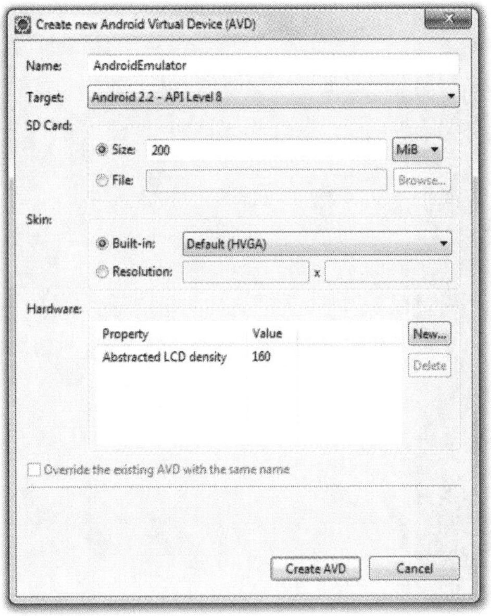

FIGURE B-14

Alternatively, you can simulate the presence of an SD card in the Android Emulator by creating a disk image first and then attaching it to the AVD. The mksdcard.exe utility (also located in the tools folder of the Android SDK) enables you to create an ISO disk image. The following command creates an ISO image that is 2GB in size (see also Figure B-15):

```
mksdcard 2048M sdcard.iso
```

FIGURE B-15

Once the image is created, you can specify the location of the ISO file, as shown in Figure B-16.

FIGURE B-16

EMULATING DEVICES WITH DIFFERENT SCREEN SIZES

Besides emulating an SD card, you can also emulate devices with different screen sizes. Figure B-17 indicates that the AVD is emulating the WVGA854 skin, which has a resolution of 480×854 pixels. Note that the LCD density is 240, which means that this screen has a pixel density of 240 pixels per inch.

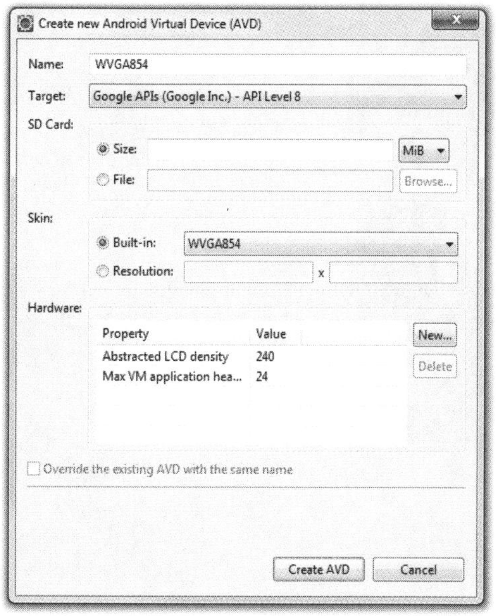

FIGURE B-17

For each target that you select, a list of skins is available. The Android SDK supports the following screen resolutions:

- ➤ **QVGA** — 240×320
- ➤ **WQVGA400** — 240×400
- ➤ **WQVGA432** — 240×432
- ➤ **HVGA** — 320×480
- ➤ **WVGA800** — 480×800
- ➤ **WVGA854** — 480×854

Figure B-18 shows the Android Emulator using the WVGA854 skin.

FIGURE B-18

EMULATING PHYSICAL CAPABILITIES

In addition to emulating devices of different screen sizes, you also have the option to emulate different hardware capabilities. When creating a new AVD, clicking the New button will display a dialog for choosing the type of hardware that you want to emulate (see Figure B-19).

For example, if you want to emulate an Android device with no touch screen, select the "Touch-screen support" property and click OK. Back in the AVD dialog, change the value of the property from yes to no (see Figure B-20).

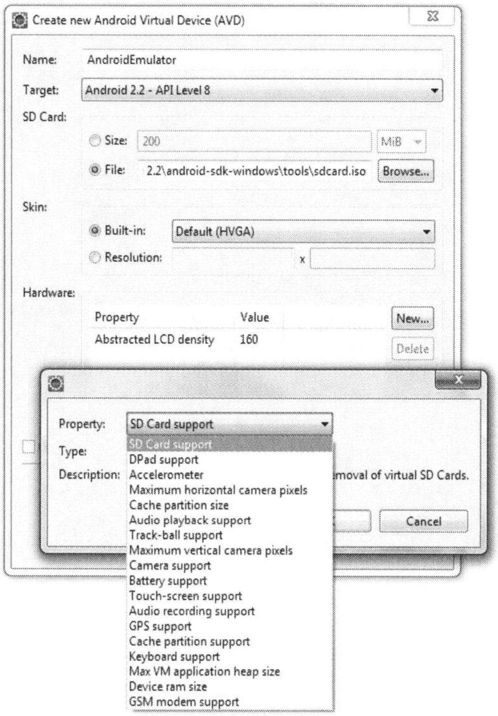

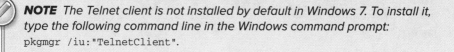

FIGURE B-19 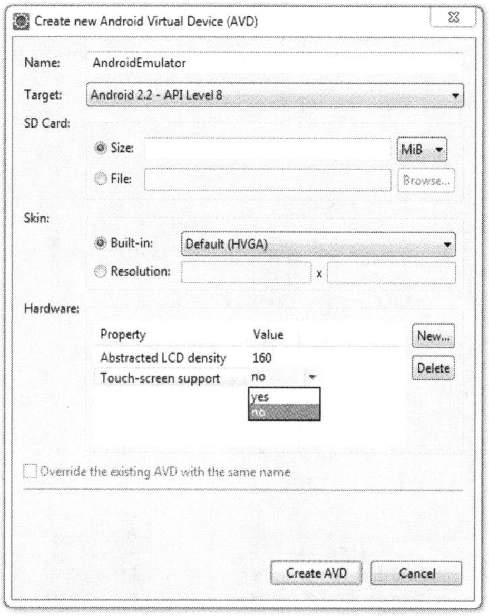   **FIGURE B-20**

This will create an AVD with no touch-screen support (i.e., users won't be able to use their mouse to click on the screen).

You can also simulate location data using the Android Emulator. Chapter 9 discusses this in more details.

One useful tip to make your development more productive is to keep your Android Emulator running during development — avoid closing and restarting it. Because the emulator takes time to boot up, it is much better to leave it running when you are debugging your applications.

SENDING SMS MESSAGES TO THE EMULATOR

You can emulate sending SMS messages to the Android Emulator using either the Dalvik Debug Monitor Service (DDMS) tool available in Eclipse, or the Telnet client.

> **NOTE** *The Telnet client is not installed by default in Windows 7. To install it, type the following command line in the Windows command prompt:*
> `pkgmgr /iu:"TelnetClient".`

KEYBOARD SHORTCUTS

The Android Emulator supports several keyboard shortcuts that enable you to mimic the behavior of a real handset. The following list shows the list of shortcuts that you can use with the emulator:

➤ **Esc** — Back

➤ **Home** — Main screen

➤ **F2** — Toggles context-sensitive menu

➤ **F3** — Call Log

➤ **F4** — Lock

➤ **F5** — Search

➤ **F8** — Toggles data network (3G)

➤ **Ctrl+F5** — Ringer volume up

➤ **Ctrl+F6** — Ringer volume down

➤ **Ctrl+F11/Ctrl+F12** — Toggle orientation

For example, by pressing Ctrl+F11, you can change the orientation of the emulator to landscape mode (see Figure B-21).

FIGURE B-21

Take a look at how this is done in Telnet. First, ensure that the Android Emulator is running. In order to Telnet to the emulator, you need to know the port number of the emulator. You can obtain this by looking at the title bar of the Android Emulator window. It normally starts with 5554, with each subsequent emulator having a port number incremented by two, such as 5556, 5558, and so on. Assuming that you currently have one Android Emulator running, you can Telnet to it using the following command:

```
C:\telnet localhost 5554
```

To send an SMS message to the emulator, use the following command:

```
sms send +651234567 Hello my friend!
```

The syntax of the sms send command is as follows:

```
sms send <phone_number> <message>
```

Figure B-22 shows the emulator receiving the sent SMS message.

Besides using Telnet for sending SMS messages, you can also use the DDMS perspective in Eclipse. If the DDMS perspective is not visible within Eclipse, you can display it by clicking the Open Perspective button (see Figure B-23) and selecting Other.

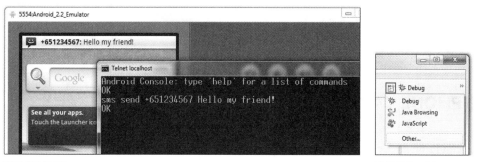

FIGURE B-22   **FIGURE B-23**

Select the DDMS perspective (see Figure B-24) and click OK.

Once the DDMS perspective is displayed, you will see the Devices tab (see Figure B-25), which shows the list of emulators currently running. Select the emulator instance to which you want to send the SMS message, and under the Emulator Control tab you will see the Telephony Actions section. In the Incoming number field, enter an arbitrary phone number and check the SMS radio button. Enter a message and click the Send button.

The selected emulator will now receive the incoming SMS message.

If you have multiple AVDs running at the same time, you can send SMS messages between each AVD by using the port number of the emulator as the phone number. For example, if you have an emulator running on port number 5554 and another on 5556, their phone numbers will be 5554 and 5556, respectively.

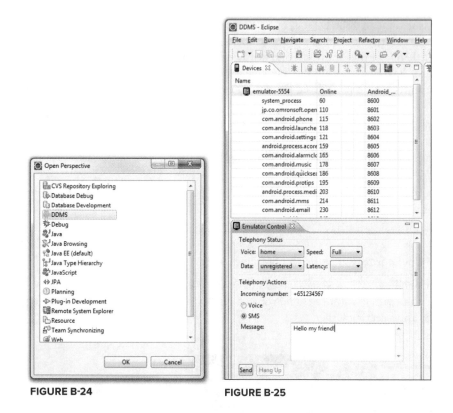

FIGURE B-24   FIGURE B-25

MAKING PHONE CALLS

Besides sending SMS messages to the emulator, you can also use the Telnet client to make a phone call to the emulator. To do so, simply use the following commands.

To Telnet to the emulator, use this command:

```
C:\telnet localhost 5554
```

To make a phone call to the emulator, use this command:

```
gsm call +651234567
```

The syntax of the gsm send command is as follows:

```
gsm call <phone_number>
```

Figure B-26 shows the emulator receiving an incoming call.

Likewise, you can also use the DDMS perspective to make a phone call to the emulator. Figure B-27 shows how to make a phone call using the Telephony Actions section.

As with sending SMS, you can also make phone calls between AVDs by using their port numbers as phone numbers.

FIGURE B-26

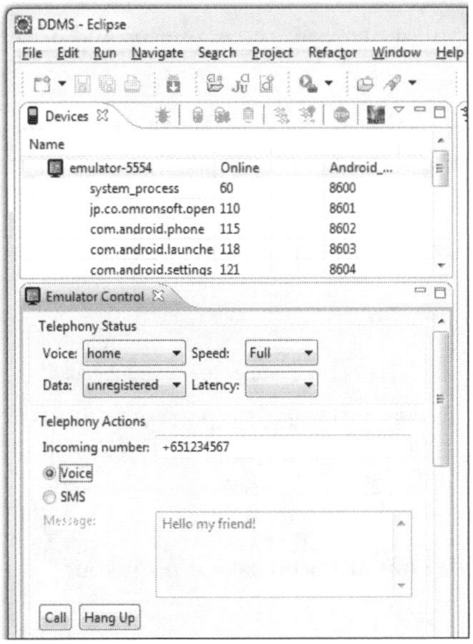

FIGURE B-27

TRANSFERRING FILES INTO AND OUT OF THE EMULATOR

Occasionally, you may need to transfer files into or out of the emulator. The easiest way is to use the DDMS perspective. From the DDMS perspective, select the emulator (or device if you have a real Android device connected to your computer) and click the File Explorer tab to examine its file systems (see Figure B-28).

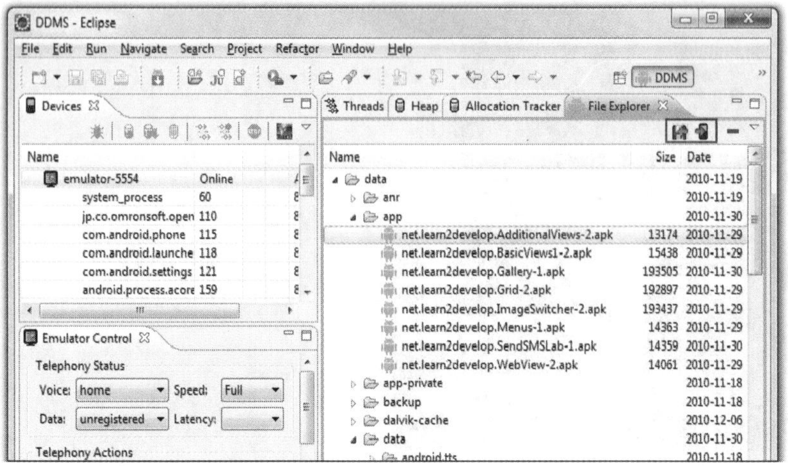

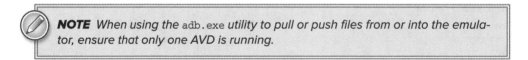

FIGURE B-28

The two buttons shown in Figure B-28 enable you to both pull a file from the emulator and push a file into the emulator.

Alternatively, you can also use the `adb.exe` utility shipped with the Android SDK to push or pull files to and from the emulator. This utility, like `emulator.exe`, is located in the *<Android_SDK_Folder>*`\tools\` folder.

To copy a file from the connected emulator/device onto the computer, use the following command:

```
adb.exe pull /data/app/<filename> c:\
```

> **NOTE** *When using the* `adb.exe` *utility to pull or push files from or into the emulator, ensure that only one AVD is running.*

Figure B-29 shows how you can extract an APK file from the emulator and save it onto your computer.

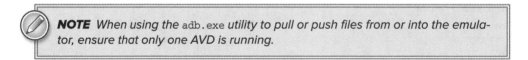

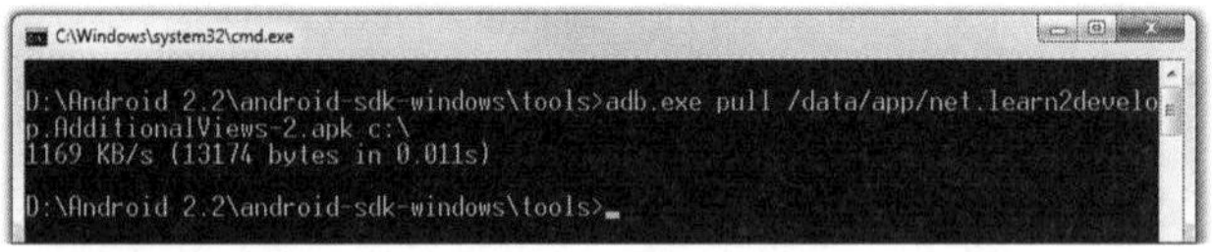

FIGURE B-29

To copy a file into the connected emulator/device, use the following command:

```
adb.exe push NOTICE.txt /data/app
```

The preceding command copies the `NOTICE.txt` file located in the current directory and saves it onto the emulator's `/data/app` folder (see Figure B-30).

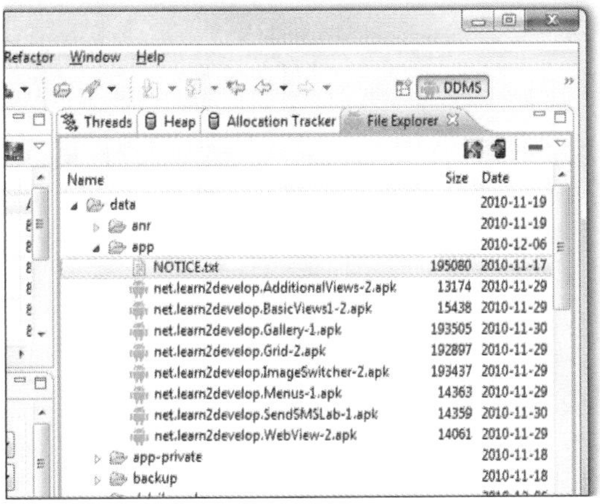

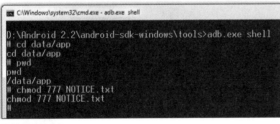

FIGURE B-30

If you need to modify the permissions of the files in the emulator, you can use the `adb.exe` utility together with the shell option, like this:

```
adb.exe shell
```

Figure B-31 shows how you can change the permissions of the `NOTICE.txt` file by using the `chmod` command.

```
D:\Android 2.2\android-sdk-windows\tools>adb.exe shell
# cd data/app
cd data/app
# pwd
pwd
/data/app
# chmod 777 NOTICE.txt
chmod 777 NOTICE.txt
#
```

FIGURE B-31

Using the `adb.exe` utility, you can issue Unix commands against your Android Emulator.

RESETTING THE EMULATOR

All applications and files that you have deployed to the Android Emulator are stored in a file named `userdata-qemu.img` located in the `C:\Users\<username>\.android\avd\<avd_name>.avd` folder. For example, I have an AVD named Android_2.2_Emulator; hence, the `userdata-qemu.img` file is located in the `C:\Users\Wei-Meng Lee\.android\avd\Android_2.2_Emulator.avd` folder.

If you want to restore the emulator to its original state (to reset it, that is), simply delete the `userdata-qemu.img` file.

Answers to Exercises

This appendix includes the answers to the end of chapter exercises.

CHAPTER 1 ANSWERS

1. An AVD is an Android Virtual Device. It represents an Android Emulator, which emulates a particular configuration of an actual Android device.

2. The `android:versionCode` attribute is used to programmatically check if an application can be upgraded. It should contain a running number (an updated application should be set to a higher number than the older version). The `android:versionName` attribute is used mainly for displaying to the user. It is a string, such as "1.0.1".

3. The `strings.xml` file is used to store all string constants in your application. This enables you to easily localize your application by simply replacing the strings and then recompiling your application.

CHAPTER 2 ANSWERS

1. The Android OS will display a dialog from which users can choose which activity they want to use.

2.
```
Intent i = new
    Intent(android.content.Intent.ACTION_VIEW,
       Uri.parse("http://www.amazon.com"));
startActivity(i);
```

3. In an intent filter, you can specify the following: action, data, type, and category.

4. The `Toast` class is used to display alerts to the user and disappears after a few seconds. The `NotificationManager` class is used to display notifications on the device's status bar. The alert displayed by the `NotificationManager` class is persistent and can only be dismissed by the user when selected.

CHAPTER 3 ANSWERS

1. The `dp` unit is density independent and 160dp is equivalent to one inch. The `px` unit corresponds to an actual pixel on screen. You should always use the `dp` unit because it enables your activity to scale properly when run on devices of varying screen size.

2. With the advent of devices with different screen sizes, using the `AbsoluteLayout` makes it difficult for your application to have a consistent look and feel across devices.

3. The `onPause()` event is fired whenever an activity is killed or sent to the background. The `onSaveInstanceState()` event is like the `onPause()` event, except that it is not always called, such as when the user presses the Back button to kill the activity.

4. The three events are `onPause()`, `onSaveInstanceState()`, and `onRetainNonConfigurationInstance()`.

CHAPTER 4 ANSWERS

1. You should check the `isChecked()` method of each `RadioButton` to determine if it has been checked.

2. You can use the `getResources()` method.

3. The code snippet to obtain the current date is as follows:

```
//---get the current date---
Calendar today = Calendar.getInstance();
yr = today.get(Calendar.YEAR);
month = today.get(Calendar.MONTH);
day = today.get(Calendar.DAY_OF_MONTH);
showDialog(DATE_DIALOG_ID);
```

CHAPTER 5 ANSWERS

1. The `ImageSwitcher` enables images to be displayed with animation. You can animate the image when it is being displayed, as well as when it is being replaced by another image.

2. The two methods are `onCreateOptionsMenu()` and `onOptionsItemSelected()`.

3. The two methods are `onCreateContextMenu()` and `onContextItemSelected()`.

4. To prevent launching the device's web browser, you need to implement the `WebViewClient` class and override the `shouldOverrideUrlLoading()` method.

CHAPTER 6 ANSWERS

1. The former allows the data to be shared among all the activities in an application, whereas the latter is accessible only to the activity that created it.

2. The method name is `getExternalStorageDirectory()`.

3. The permission is `WRITE_EXTERNAL_STORAGE`.

CHAPTER 7 ANSWERS

1. The code is as follows:

```
Cursor c = managedQuery(
    allContacts,
    projection,
    ContactsContract.Contacts.DISPLAY_NAME + " LIKE ?",
    new String[] {"%jack%"} ,
    ContactsContract.Contacts.DISPLAY_NAME + " ASC");
```

2. The methods are `getType()`, `onCreate()`, `query()`, `insert()`, `delete()`, and `update()`.

3. The code is as follows:

```
<provider android:name="BooksProvider"
          android:authorities="net.learn2develop.provider.Books" />
```

CHAPTER 8 ANSWERS

1. You can either programmatically send a SMS message from within your Android application or invoke the built-in Messaging application to send it on your application's behalf.

2. The two permissions are `SEND_SMS` and `RECEIVE_SMS`.

3. The Broadcast receiver should fire a new intent to be received by the activity. The activity should implement another `BroadcastReceiver` to listen for this new intent.

4. The permission is `INTERNET`.

CHAPTER 9 ANSWERS

1. The likely reasons are as follows:

➤ No Internet connection

➤ Incorrect placement of the `<uses-library>` element in the `AndroidManifest.xml` file

➤ Missing `INTERNET` permission in the `AndroidManifest.xml` file

2. Geocoding is the act of converting an address into its coordinates (latitude and longitude). Reverse geocoding converts a pair of location coordinates into an address.

3. The two providers are as follows:

> ➤ `LocationManager.GPS_PROVIDER`

> ➤ `LocationManager.NETWORK_PROVIDER`

4. The method is `addProximityAlert()`.

CHAPTER 10 ANSWERS

1. This is because a service runs on the same process as the calling activity. If a service is long-running, you need to run it on a separate thread so that it does not block the activity.

2. The `IntentService` class is similar to the `Service` class, except that it runs the tasks in a separate thread and automatically stops the service when the task has finished execution.

3. The three methods are `doInBackground()`, `onProgressUpdate()`, and `onPostExecute()`.

4. The service can broadcast an intent, and the activity can register an intent using an `IntentFilter` class.

CHAPTER 11 ANSWERS

1. You specify the minimum Android version required using the `minSdkVersion` attribute in the `AndroidManifest.xml` file.

2. You can either use the keytool.exe utility from the Java SDK, or use Eclipse's Export feature to generate a certificate.

3. Go to the Settings application and select the Applications item. Check the "Unknown sources" item.

INDEX

Symbols

. (period), APK naming
convention, 16
- (minus sign), TimePicker, 144
+ (plus sign), TimePicker, 144

A

abd.exe, 367–369, 408
AbsoluteLayout, 82, 87–89, 412
ACTION_PICK, 63
actions
  <intent-filter>, 70, 411
  intents, 61
ACTION_VIEW, 62, 70
activities, 22, 27–42
  AndroidManifest.xml, 28
  applications, 47
  BroadcastReceiver, 273–280
  categories, 71–73
  debugging, 31
  dialog windows, 34–38
  EditText, 54, 55
  hiding title, 33–34
  intents, 43–78
  life cycle, 30–32
  orientation, 104–108, 110–111
  progress dialog, 39–42
  services
    binding, 350–356
    communication, 346–350
  styles, 32–33
  themes, 32–33

ViewGroups, 82–83
Views, 82–83
Activities, 32
Activity, 27–29
  Context, 38
  events, 28
  ListActivity, 158
  MainActivity, 180
  managedQuery(), 242
  MapActivity, 307
  methods, 114–119
  onCreate(), 82
  onCreateDialog(), 34, 36
  onKeyDown(), 117
  setContentView(), 82
  setRequestOrientation(),
    110–111
<activity>, 33, 110–111
Activity.findViewById(),
  132, 134
adb, 367
add(), 188
addCategory(), 72
addProximityAlert(), 327
ADT. *See* Android Development
  Tools
AlertDialog, 37
alias, 364
AnalogClock, 194
anchoring
  orientation, 98–100
  RelativeLayout, 98
Android 2.3, 22
Android Debug Bridge, 367–369

Android Development Tools
  (ADT), 7–11
Android Device Chooser, 21
Android Emulator, 403–407
  APK, 408
  AVDs, 393–397
  debugging, 36, 46, 52, 55, 69,
    76, 116, 143, 144, 146,
    148, 150, 157, 159, 162,
    164, 174, 175, 180, 184,
    189, 192, 196, 206–207,
    212, 241, 266, 272, 276,
    279, 287, 290, 294, 307,
    309, 310, 314, 317, 324,
    334, 337, 345, 393–409
  devices, 398–399
  file transfer, 407–409
  localhost, 288
  orientation, 106
  permissions, 409
  Phone button, 32
  phone calls, 406–407
  physical capabilities, 402–403
  resetting, 409
  screens, 401–402
  SD, 399–401
  shortcut keys, 404
  SMS messaging, 403–406
  testing, 18–19, 214
Android Hierarchy Viewer, 8
Android library, 387
Android Market, 6
  AndroidManifest.xml, 361
  applications, 359, 372–378
  developer profile, 372–373

Android Packages (APK), 7, 16
  Android Emulator, 408
  application publishing, 359
  deploying files, 367–378
  MIME, 369
  SD, 369
Android runtime, 4
Android SDK, 7, 303
Android Virtual Devices (AVDs),
    11–14, 411
  Android Emulator, 393–397
  AVD Manager, 21, 266
  customization, 393–397
  testing, 21
android.content.Intent
    .ACTION_VIEW, 61
android:icon, 361
android:id, 108
android.intent.action.VIEW, 70
android.intent.category.
    LAUNCHER, 24
android.jar, 22
android:label, 361
android_layout_x, 88
android_layout_y, 88
android.location, 326
AndroidManifest.xml, 22, 251–252
  activities, 28
  <activity>, 33, 110–111
  Android Market, 361
  <application>, 308
  <category>, 71
  content providers, 241
  <intent-filter>, 65–71
  IntentService, 344–345
  INTERNET, 305, 413
  MyBrowserActivity, 70
  networking, 284
  permissions, 267, 270, 286
  services, 333, 335
  SMS messaging, 265, 270–271
  SMS_SEND, 270
  <uses-sdk>, 361

versions, 23, 360
  WRITE_EXTERNAL_STORAGE, 216
android:minSdkVersion, 24
android:orientation, 86
android.permission.CALL_PHONE,
    62
android:screenOrientation,
    110–111
android:theme, 33
android:versionCode, 360, 361,
    411
android:versionName, 360, 361
android.view.ViewGroup, 82
animateTo(), 312, 315
anonymous class, 120
Apache License, 2
API key, 303–305
apiKey, 306
APK. See Android Packages
.apk, 369
<application>, 308, 361
applications, 4
  activities, 47
  anatomy, 22–25
  Android Market, 359, 372–378
  built-in
    intents, 56–65
    SMS messaging, 269
  creating, 14–22
  databases, 231–233
  DDMS, 368
  digital certificates, 359, 362–366
  Export Android Application,
    363–366
  framework, 4
  Gmail/Email, 281
  icons, 375
  launcher, 20
  Manage applications, 48
  market, 4
  permissions, 280–281
  publishing, 359–379
  versions, 360–362
  web servers, 369–372

Application name, 21
app_name, 24
architecture, 3–4
arguments, 61, 77
ArrayAdapter, 143, 165
assets, 22, 199, 231
asynchronous calls, 296–297
asynchronous services, 338–341,
    343–346
AsyncTask, 296–297, 340
attributes
  Button, 99
  RelativeLayout, 92
AutoCompleteTextView, 141–144
  ArrayAdapter, 143
  debugging, 143
  EditText, 141
  MainActivity.java, 142
  setThreshold(), 144
  simple_dropdown_item_line, 143
Available Packages, 12
AVD Manager, 21, 266
AVDs. See Android Virtual
    Devices

B

Back button, 32, 164
BackgroundTask, 297
Barnes and Noble, 4
BaseAdapter, 176, 181
binary data downloads, 286–288
  debugging, 287
  MainActivity.java, 287
  main.xml, 286
Binder, 354
bindService(), 356
Bitmap, 287
BitmapFactory, 287
BooksProvider.java, 248–251
boolean, 118
breakpoints, 389–390
BroadcastReceiver, 269, 350
  activities, 273–280

intents, 276
MainActivity, 279–280
MainActivity.java, 277–278
main.xml, 279
onDestroy(), 280
onPause(), 277, 279–280
onResume(), 277, 279–280
sendBroadcast(), 272
SMSReceiver.java, 278–279
Browser, 237
Browser.BOOKMARKS_URI, 243
Browser.SEARCHES_URI, 243
browser.xml, 68
Builder, 37
built-in applications
intents, 56–65
SMS messaging, 269
built-in zoom controls, 196
debugging, 309, 310
Google Maps, 308–310
MainActivity.java, 309–310
multi-touch, 197
onKeyDown, 310
Bundle
getExtras(), 56, 351
Intent, 56
key/value pairs, 56
onReceive(), 272
onSaveInstanceState, 108–109
putExtras(), 56
Button, 85, 113, 127–135
android_layout_x, 88
android_layout_y, 88
attributes, 99
DatePicker, 152
events, 117
FrameLayout, 93–94
id, 132
layout_width, 130
LinearLayout, 95–96
main.xml, 98–99
setOnCreateContextMenu
Listener(), 192
TimePicker, 146
byte stream, 213

C

CA. *See* certificate authority
callbacks
onCreateDialog(), 37
setOnClickListener(), 134
showDialog(), 37
CallLog, 237
CallLog.CONTENT_URI, 243
cancel(), 78
categories
activities, 71–73
Intent, 65
<intent-filter>, 70, 411
<category>, 71–73
cell tower triangulation, 322
certificate authority (CA), 362
character array, 213
CheckBox, 127–135
chmod, 409
classes
Android library, 387
anonymous, 120
MainActivity.java, 46
Notification, 77
Clear defaults button, 48
<com.google.android.maps
.MapView>, 307
commit(), 208
component name, 64
configuration change, orientation,
108–109
Confirm Perspective Switch
dialog, 390
connectivity, 3
constructors
Intent, 61
Notification, 77
Contacts, 238, 242, 243
contacts, 221
ContactsContract.Contacts
.CONTENT_URI, 243
ContactsContract.Contacts
.DISPLAY_NAME, 245

ContactsContract.Contacts
.HAS_PHONE_NUMBER, 246
ContactsContract
.Contacts._ID, 245
Content, 242
content providers, 237–262
AndroidManifest.xml, 241
creating, 247–260
data sharing, 237–238
debugging, 241
MainActivity(), 257–258
MainActivity.java, 240
main.xml, 239–240, 256–257
queries, 238
ContentProvider, 247
ContentResolver, 253, 255
ContentUris, 243
ContentValues, 223
Context, 38
Toast, 38
Context menu, 185, 190–193
debugging, 192
MainActivity.java, 191–192
CopyDB(), 232–233
counter, 343
Create Activity, 21
createFromPdu(), 272
CreateMenu()
Menu, 188
onCreateContextMenu(), 192
Options menu, 189
cursor, 242
Cursor, 244
moveToFirst(), 226
queries, 223, 254
customization
AVDs, 393–397
ListView, 159–161
ProgressBar, 139–141

D

Dalvik Debug Monitor Service
(DDMS), 8
Android Emulator, 403–407

Dalvik Debug Monitor
    Service *(continued)*
  applications, 368
  databases, 233
  internal storage, 214
  Location Controls, 324
  perspectives, 387
  screenshots, 375
  SMS messaging, 272, 276, 279
Dalvik virtual machine, 4
data
  <intent-filter>, 70, 411
  intents, 61
  path, 238
  persistence, 203–235
    databases, 218–233
    files, 209–218
  sharing, 237–238
  types
    ContentValues, 223
    getType(), 253
    Intent, 64–65
    <intent-filter>, 411
data, 54
/data/app, 368, 408
databases
  applications, 231–233
  data persistence, 218–233
  DDMS, 233
  methods, 222–223
  pre-creating, 230–233
Database Browser, 230
DATABASE_CREATE, 221
databases, 224
DATABASE_VERSION, 222, 230
DatePicker, 149–156
  Button, 152
  debugging, 150
  dialog windows, 153–156
  MainActivity.java, 150–151,
    153–155
  onDateSet(), 156
DatePickerDialog, 156
day, 156

DBAdapter, 218–223
  deleteContact(), 228–229
  getAllContacts(), 225–226
  getContact(), 226–227
  onCreate(), 221–222
  onUpgrade(), 221–222
  SQLiteOpenHelper, 221
  updateContact(), 227–228
DDMS. *See* Dalvik Debug Monitor
  Service
debugging. *See also* Dalvik Debug
  Monitor Service
  activities, 31
  Android Debug Bridge, 367–369
  Android Device Chooser, 21
  Android Emulator, 36, 46, 52, 55,
    69, 76, 116, 137, 143, 144,
    146, 148, 150, 157, 159, 162,
    164, 174, 175, 180, 184, 189,
    192, 196, 206–207, 212, 241,
    266, 272, 276, 279, 287, 290,
    294, 307, 309, 310, 314, 317,
    324, 334, 337, 345, 393–409
  Android SDK, 303
  AutoCompleteTextView, 143
  binary data downloads, 287
  built-in zoom controls, 309, 310
  certificate, 303–304
  content providers, 241
  Context menu, 192
  DatePicker, 150
  Eclipse, 389
  Gallery, 174
  getSharedPreferences(),
    206–207
  Google Maps, 307, 314, 317
  GridView, 184
  ImageSwitcher, 180
  ImageView, 175
  IntentService, 345
  internal storage, 212
  ListView, 157, 159
  Location Manager, 324
  Options menu, 189

perspectives, 387
ProgressBar, 137
services, 334, 337
SMS messaging, 266, 272,
    276, 279
SpinnerView, 164
strings.xml, 162
text file downloads, 290
TimePicker, 144, 146, 148
views, 128–129
Web services, 294
WebView, 196
debug.keystore, 304, 364–365
decodeStream(),
    BitmapFactory, 287
<Definition>, 295–296
delete(), 413
  content providers, 252, 255
deleteContact(), 228–229
deliveryIntent, 267
Dell, 4
density-independent pixel. *See* dp
Desire HD, 4
destinationAddress, 267
developer profile, 372–373
devices, 4–5
  Android Emulator, 398–399
devices, 367
Devices tab, 325
dialog windows
  activities, 34–38
  DatePicker, 153–156
  showDialog(), 148
  TimePicker, 147–149
Dictionary Web service, 291
digital certificates
  applications, 359, 362–366
  keytool.exe, 362
DigitalClock, 194
Display, 110
Display Notification button, 76
DisplayContact(), 226
DistributionKeyStoreAlias, 364
DoBackgroundTask, 341

Document, 294–295
DocumentBuilder, 294
DocumentBuilderFactory, 294
doInBackground(), 297, 340, 414
doSomethingRepeatedly(), 343
doSomeWork()
  progressStatus, 141
  run(), 138
download, 369
downloads
  binary data, 286–288
  text file, 288–291
  XML, 291
DownloadFile(), 337
DownloadImage(), 287
DownloadText(), 291
dp, 85, 412
drawable, 23
drawable-<resolution>, 22

E

Eclipse, 381–392
  Android Device Chooser, 21
  breakpoints, 389–390
  code completion, 388
  debugging, 389
  editors, 385–386
  exceptions, 390–392
  IDE for Java EE Developers, 6–7
  Package Explorer, 382–383
  perspectives, 387
  refactoring, 388–389
  R.java, 24
  workspaces, 381–382
eclipse.exe, 7
Editor, 207
editors, Eclipse, 385–386
EditText, 127–135
  activities, 54, 55
  AutoCompleteTextView, 141
  events, 117
  internal storage, 212
  LinearLayout, 95–96

onFocusChange(), 120–121
orientation, 106, 108
SeekBar, 207
setHint(), 56
e-mail, 281–283
  Intent, 283
  MainActivity.java, 282–283
  main.xml, 282
  putExtra(), 283
  setData(), 283
  setType(), 283
Emulator Control tab, 325
emulator.exe, 408
e-reader devices, 4–5
events
  Activity, 28
  Button, 117
  EditText, 117
  handlers, 120
  views, 119–121, 133–135
exceptions, 390–392
execute(), 341, 351
  onStartCommand(), 355
Export Android Application, 363–366
Export dialog, 363
external storage, 214–216

F

features, 3
files
  data persistence, 209–218
  transfer, 407–409
File Explorer tab, 407
FILE_DOWNLOAD_ACTION, 349
FileInputStream, 213
FileOutputStream, 213
fill_parent, 84, 130
filtering. See also <intent-filter>
  IntentFilter, 349, 414
  ListView, 160
  setTextFilterEnabled(), 160
finish(), 53

Flash support, 3
flush(), 213
FrameLayout, 82, 93–95
fromPixels(), 319

G

Galaxy Tab, 4
Gallery, 170–176
  debugging, 174
  MainActivity.java, 172–174
  main.xml, 171, 176
gen, 22
Geocoder, 320–321
geocoding, 320–322, 413
GeoPoint, 314, 318, 319
GET, 291
get(), 351
getAction(), 319
getActivity(), 77
getAllContacts(), 225–226
getBaseContext(), 38
getContact(), 226–227
getCurrentHour(), 146–147
getCurrentMinute(), 146
getData(), 54
getDayOfMonth(), 153
getDefault(), 267
getDefaultDisplay(), 110
getExternalStorageDirectory(), 215, 413
getExtras(), 56, 351
getFromLocation(), 320–321
getFromLocationName(), 321
getIntent(), 56
getListView(), 160
getMonth(), 153
getOriginatingAddress(), 272–273
getPackageInfo(), 360–361
getPreferences(), 208–209
getProjection(), 319
getResources(), 162, 412
getService(), 354, 356

getSharedPreferences(), 204–208
  debugging, 206–207
  MainActivity.java, 205–206
  main.xml, 204–205
getString(), 56
getSystemService(), 326
getType(), 413
  content providers, 253
  data types, 253
  MIME, 252
getYear(), 153
Gmail/Email application, 281
GONE, 138
Google Maps, 13, 302–322
  Android SDK, 303
  API key, 303–305
  built-in zoom controls, 308–310
  debugging, 307, 314, 317
  displaying, 305–308
  geocoding, 320–322
  INTERNET, 307
  MainActivity.java, 306–307,
    313–317
  main.xml, 306
  markers, 315–318
  navigation, 312–315
  reverse geocoding, 318, 320–322
  views, 310–312
Google TV, 4
GridView, 181–185
groupId, 188

H

hardware support, 3
helper methods, 186–188
hint text, 55
Home button, 19, 32
horizontal, 132
HTC, 4, 398
HTML, 198–199
HTTP, 284–286
  GET, 291
  WordDefinition(), 294

http://, 70
HTTP_OK, 286
HttpURLConnection, 286

I

icon.png, 23, 385
icons
  android:icon, 361
  applications, 375
id, 238
  Button, 132
IDE. See integrated development
    environment
IIS. See Internet Information
    Server
ImageAdapter
  BaseAdapter, 176, 181
  GridView, 184–185
  ImageView, 181
ImageButton, 127–135
ImageSwitcher, 177–181, 412
  debugging, 180
  MainActivity.java, 178–180
  main.xml, 177
  makeView(), 180
  onCreate(), 181
  View, 181
  ViewFactory, 180
ImageView, 170–176
  AsyncTask, 296
  debugging, 175
  FrameLayout, 93
  GridView, 181
  ImageAdapter, 181
  MainActivity.java, 175
  main.xml, 171, 176
import, namespaces, 387
InputStream, 233, 286
InputStreamReader, 213, 291
insert(), 252, 254–255, 413
insertContact(), 224
Install button, 281, 370

integrated development
    environment (IDE), 6
Intent, 64–65
  addCategory(), 72
  arguments, 61
  bindService(), 356
  Bundle, 56
  categories, 65
  constructors, 61
  data types, 64–65
  e-mail, 283
  key/value pairs, 77
  MainActivity.java, 355
  NotificationView, 76
  Object, 351
  onStartCommand(), 351
  passing data, 54–56
  request code, 53
  setData(), 53, 64
  SMS messaging, 272, 276
  startActivityForResult(), 63
  URL, 350–351
intents
  actions, 61
  activities, 43–78
  BroadcastReceiver, 276
  built-in applications, 56–65
  data, 61
  notifications, 73–78
  resolution, 48–49, 64
  results, 50–54
  SMS messaging, 269–270
    TextView, 277
IntentFilter, 349, 414
<intent-filter>, 24, 411
  actions, 70
  AndroidManifest.xml, 65–71
  categories, 70
  data, 70
  intent resolution, 48–49
  services, 335
Intent.FLAG_ACTIVITY
    _NEW_TASK, 280
IntentService, 343–346, 414

internal storage
  DDMS, 214
  debugging, 212
  EditText, 212
  MainActivity.java, 210–212
  main.xml, 209
  save, 209–214
INTERNET
  AndroidManifest.xml, 305, 413
  Google Maps, 307
  permissions, 286, 413
Internet Information
    Server (IIS), 369
Internet TVs, 4–5
invalidate(), 315
INVISIBLE, 138
isChecked(), 135, 412
isRouteDisplayed(), 307
itemId, 188

J

JAR, 303
.java, 22, 385
Java EE, 6–7, 387
Java SE Development Kit (JDK), 7
java.io, 209
JDK. *See* Java SE Development Kit

K

KeyEvent.KEYCODE_DPAD_CENTER, 47
keystores, 304, 363–364
keytool.exe, 304–305
  digital certificates, 362
key/value pairs
  Bundle, 56
  ContentValues, 223
  Intent, 77
keywords, 281

L

label view. *See* TextView

landscape orientation, 97,
    102–103, 104
Launch my Browser button, 69
Launch Options dialog, 396
layout, 101–102
Layout view, 17
layout_alignLeft, 92
layout_alignParentBottom, 99
layout_alignParentLeft, 92, 99
layout_alignParentRight, 99
layout_alignParentTop, 92, 99
layout_alignRight, 92
layout_below, 92
layout_centerHorizontal, 92, 99
layout_centerVertical, 99
layout_gravity, 84, 85–86
layout_height, 83, 131
layout-land, 102–103
layout_marginBottom, 83
layout_marginLeft, 83
layout_marginRight, 83
layout_marginTop, 83
LayoutParams, 112, 113
layout_weight, 84, 85–86
layout_width, 83
  Button, 130
  fill_parent, 130
  RadioButton, 132
  wrap_content, 84, 130, 132
layout_x, 84
layout_y, 84
LBS. *See* location-based services
LG, 4
libraries, 4, 305, 387, 413
LinearLayout, 82, 83–87, 112–114
  Button, 95–96
  EditText, 95–96
  layout_gravity, 85–86
  LayoutParams, 113
  layout_weight, 85–86
  main.xml, 83
  ScrollView, 95–96
  <LinearLayout>, 83, 130
Linux kernel, 4

list views, 156–165
ListActivity, 158, 160
listener, 326
ListView, 156–162, 242
  customization, 159–161
  debugging, 157, 159
  filtering, 160
  getListView(), 160
  ListActivity, 158
  MainActivity.java, 157, 159
  main.xml, 158
  onListItemClick(), 158
  ScrollView, 95
  setChoiceMode(), 160
  simple_list_item_1, 158
Load button, 215–216
loadDataWithBaseURL(), 198–199
loadUrl(), 196, 199
localhost, 288
Location Controls, 324
Location Manager, 281, 322–327
  debugging, 324
  MainActivity.java, 322–324
location-based services (LBS),
    301–329
  Google Maps, 13, 302–322
  location data, 322–327
LocationListener, 326
LocationManager, 326, 327
LocationManager
  .GPS_PROVIDER, 414
LocationManager.NETWORK_
    PROVIDER, 414
LogCat, 31, 32, 230
  orientation, 106
  PrintContacts(), 245
  services, 339, 342
  Start Service button, 345

M

MainActivity, 22
  Activity, 180
  BroadcastReceiver, 279–280

MainActivity *(continued)*
　ListActivity, 158
　onKeyDown(), 117
　String, 143
MainActivity(), 257–258
MainActivity.java, 22, 30, 35, 45,
　　67–68
　AutoCompleteTextView, 142
　binary data downloads, 287
　BroadcastReceiver, 277–278
　built-in zoom controls, 309–310
　class, 46
　content providers, 240
　Context menu, 191–192
　DatePicker, 150–151, 153–155
　e-mail, 282–283
　Gallery, 172–174
　getSharedPreferences(),
　　205–206
　Google Maps, 306–307,
　　313–317
　GridView, 182–184
　ImageSwitcher, 178–180
　Intent, 355
　IntentService, 345
　internal storage, 210–212
　ListView, 157, 159
　Location Manager, 322–324
　LocationManager, 326
　networking, 284–285
　onKeyDown, 47
　OpenHttpConnection(), 285
　Options menu, 188–189
　orientation, 105–106
　ProgressBar, 136–137, 139–140
　services, 333–334, 336–337
　SMS messaging, 265–266, 274–275
　SpinnerView, 163–164
　startActivityForResult(), 51
　strings.xml, 162
　text file downloads, 289–290
　TimePicker, 145–148
　Web services, 292–294
　WebView, 195–196

main.xml, 17, 18, 22, 23, 46,
　　66–67, 87–88
　AutoCompleteTextView, 141–142
　binary data downloads, 286
　BroadcastReceiver, 279
　Button, 98–99
　content providers, 239–240,
　　256–257
　copy, 44
　e-mail, 282
　FrameLayout, 93
　Gallery, 171, 176
　getSharedPreferences(),
　　204–205
　Google Maps, 306
　GridView, 182
　ImageSwitcher, 177
　ImageView, 171, 176
　internal storage, 209
　layout, 101–102
　layout-land, 102–103
　LinearLayout, 83
　ListView, 158
　ProgressBar, 136, 139
　<ProgressBar>, 138
　RelativeLayout, 91–92
　res/layout, 81–82, 126,
　　127–128, 136, 141–142,
　　144, 163, 386
　R.layout.main, 25
　ScrollView, 95–96
　services, 333
　setContentView(), 25
　SMS messaging, 265, 273
　SpinnerView, 163
　startActivityForResult(), 50
　TableLayout, 89–90
　<TextView>, 126
　TimePicker, 144
　UI, 112
　WebView, 195
Make Calls button, 59
makeView(), 180

Manage applications, 48
managed cursor, 242
managedQuery()
　Activity, 242
　ORDER BY, 247
　projections, 246
　WHERE, 246
<manifest>, 361
Manual tab, 325
MapActivity, 307
MapController, 310
　animateTo(), 312, 315
　MapView, 314
MapOverlay, 318, 319
maps.jar, 303
MapView, 310
　invalidate(), 315
　MapController, 314
　MapOverlay, 318
　onTouchEvent(), 319
　setSatellite(), 310–311
　UI, 305
markers, 315–318
MD5
　debug.keystore, 364–365
　Keytool.exe, 304–305
measurement units, 85
media support, 3
MediaStore, 238
MediaStore.Images.Media
　　.EXTERNAL_CONTENT_URI, 243
MediaStore.Images.Media
　　.INTERNAL_CONTENT_URI, 243
Menu
　CreateMenu(), 188
　setQuertyMode(), 193
menus
　helper methods, 186–188
　views, 185–193
MENU button, 189, 190
MenuChoice(), 188, 189, 193
MenuItem, 188
messaging. *See* SMS messaging

methods
  Activity, 114–119
  add(), 188
  databases, 222–223
MIME, 369
  getType(), 252
  setType(), 64–65
  SMS messaging, 269
Min SDK Version, 21
minDistance, 326
minSdkVersion, 414
minTime, 326
mksdcard.exe, 400
MMS, 3
MODE_PRIVATE, 207, 213
MODE_WORLD_WRITEABLE, 213
month, 156
MotionEvent, 319
moveToFirst(), 226
MP4 players, 4–5
multi-tasking, 3
multi-touch, 3
  built-in zoom controls, 197
MyBrowserActivity, 70, 72
MyBrowserActivity.java, 65, 68–69
MyDB, 221, 224
MyLocationListener, 326

N

Name, 56
namespaces, 387
navigation, 312–315
netbooks, 4–5
net.learn2develop.MyBrowser, 70
networking, 284–297
  AndroidManifest.xml, 284
  asynchronous calls, 296–297
  binary data downloads, 286–288
  HTTP, 284–286
  MainActivity.java, 284–285
  text file downloads, 288–291
  Web services, 291–296

NOOKcolor, 4
NOTICE.txt, 409
NotifcationManager, 73–78
Notification, 77
notifications
  intents, 73–78
  UI, 114–121
notification bar. *See* status bar
NotificationManager, 77, 412
NotificationView, 76, 78
NotificationView.java, 73
notification.xml, 73
notify(), 78
notifyChange(), 255

O

Object, 351
onBind(), 335, 354
onCheckedChanged(), 135
onClick()
  Load button, 215–216
  Save button, 214
  SD, 214
  Start Service button, 356
  views, 135
onContextItemSelected(), 193
onCreate(), 25, 28, 413
  Activity, 82
  content providers, 252, 254
  DBAdapter, 221–222
  ImageSwitcher, 181
  onRestoreInstanceState(), 108
  orientation, 97, 111
  setContentView(), 158
  setListAdapter(), 158
  UI, 29, 82
  views, 134
onCreateContextMenu(), 192
onCreateDialog(), 34, 36
  callbacks, 37
  showDialog(), 148
onCreateOptionsMenu(), 189, 412

onDateSet(), 156
onDestroy(), 28, 32
  BroadcastReceiver, 280
  stopService(), 335
onFocusChange(), 120–121
onHandleIntent(), 346
onKeyDown(), 114
  Activity, 117
  boolean, 118
  built-in zoom controls, 310
  MainActivity, 117
  MainActivity.java, 47
onKeyUp, 114
onListItemClick(), 158
onLocationChanged(), 326
onMenuItemSelected, 114
onMenuOpened, 114
onNothingSelected(), 164
onOptionsItemSelected(), 189, 412
onPause(), 28, 412
  BroadcastReceiver, 277, 279–280
  orientation, 106, 108
onPostExecute(), 297, 340, 414
onProgressUpdate(), 340, 414
onProviderDisabled(), 326
onProviderEnabled(), 326
onReceive(), 269
  Bundle, 272
  SMSReceiver, 280
onRestart(), 28, 32
onRestoreInstanceState(), 108
onResume(), 28, 32
  BroadcastReceiver, 277, 279–280
onRetainNonConfiguration
    Instance(), 109, 412
onSaveInstanceState(), 412
  Bundle, 108–109
  orientation, 108
onServiceConnected(), 356
onServiceDisconnected(), 356
onStart(), 28, 32
onStartCommand(), 335
  execute(), 355
  Intent, 351

onStatusChanged(), 326
onStop(), 28
onTimeSet(), 149
onTouchEvent(), 319
onUpgrade(), 221–222
Open button, 370
openFileOutput(), 213
OpenHttpConnection()
    DownloadImage(), 287
    InputStream, 286
    MainActivity.java, 285
Optimus One, 4
Options menu, 185, 188–190
    CreateMenu(), 189
    debugging, 189
    MainActivity.java, 188–189
order, 188
ORDER BY, 247
orientation, 86
    activities, 104–108, 110–111
    anchoring, 98–100
    Android Emulator, 106
    configuration change, 108–109
    EditText, 106, 108
    landscape, 97, 102–103, 104
    LogCat, 106
    MainActivity.java, 105–106
    managing changes, 104–108
    onCreate(), 97, 111
    onPause(), 106, 108
    onSaveInstanceState(), 108
    persisting state, 108–109
    portrait, 97, 103
    resizing and repositioning,
        101–104
    res/layout, 101
    UI, 97–111
    WindowManager, 109
    XML, 104
orientation, 132
OutputStream, 233
Overlay, 317–318

P

Package Explorer, 16, 382–383
Package name, 21
PackageManager, 360–361
parse(), 61
Paste, 44
PDU, 272
PendingIntent, 267, 269
    getActivity(), 77
People of Lava, 4
permissions
    Android Emulator, 409
    AndroidManifest.xml, 267,
        270, 286
    android.permission
        .CALL_PHONE, 62
    applications, 280–281
    Install button, 281
    INTERNET, 286, 413
persisting state, 108–109
perspectives, 387
Phone application, 59
Phone button, 32
phone calls, 406–407
physical capabilities, 402–403
picker views, 144–156
pictures, 169–185
pixel. See px
placeholder text, 55
point. See pt
portrait, 111
portrait orientation, 97, 103
predefined constants, 243–246
PrintContacts(), 245
private keys, 364
progress dialog, 39–42
ProgressBar, 135–141
    customization, 139–141
    debugging, 137
    MainActivity.java, 136–137,
        139–140
    setMax, 141

    style, 141
    Visibility, 138
<ProgressBar>, 138
ProgressDialog, 41
progressStatus, 141
Project name, 21
projections, 246
provider, 326
pt, 85
publishing applications, 359–379
Push a file onto the device
        button, 368
put(), 223
putBoolean(), 207
putExtra(), 269, 350
    e-mail, 283
PutExtras(), 56
putFloat(), 208
putInt(), 208
putLong(), 207
putString(), 207
px, 85, 401

Q

queries. See also managedQuery()
    Contacts, 243
    content providers, 238
    Cursor, 223, 254
    strings, 238
        predefined constants, 243–246
    title, 254
query(), 413
    content providers, 252, 254

R

RadioButton, 127–135
    horizontal, 132
    isChecked(), 135
    layout_width, 132
    onCheckedChanged(), 135
    orientation, 132

RadioGroup, 131
  setOnCheckedChange
    Listener(), 135
RadioGroup, 127–135
  RadioButton, 131
  setOnCheckedChange
    Listener(), 135
read(), 213
RECEIVE_SMS, 413
refactoring, 388–389
registerReceiver, 349
RelativeLayout, 82, 91–92
  anchoring, 98
  attributes, 92
  FrameLayout, 93
<RelativeLayout>, 98–99
Remember Password checkbox, 90
request code, 53
requestLocationUpdates(), 326
requestWindowFeature(), 33
res, 22
Research In Motion (RIM), 1
res/layout, 25, 44
  main.xml, 81–82, 126, 127–128,
    136, 141–142, 144, 163, 386
  notification.xml, 73
  orientation, 101
  UI, 28
Resolver getContentResolver(), 242
res/raw, 217–218
results, 50–54
RESULT_CANCELLED, 53
RESULT_OK, 53
res/values, 23
  strings.xml, 161, 163
reverse geocoding, 318, 320–322
RIM. See Research In Motion
R.java, 18, 22, 24
R.layout.main, 25
RSS Reader, 288
run(), 343
  doSomeWork(), 138

Runnable, 138
runtime, 4

S

-s, 367
Samsung, 4
satellite view, 310–311
save
  external storage, 214–216
  internal storage, 209–214
  onSaveInstanceState(),
    108–109, 412
  user preferences, 203–209
Save button, 214
scAddress, 267
scale-independent pixel. See sp
Scandinavia Android TV, 4
scheduleAtFixedRate(), 343
screens. See also orientation
  Android Emulator, 401–402
screenshots, 375
ScrollView, 82, 95–97
  FrameLayout, 95
  LinearLayout, 95–96
  ListView, 95
  main.xml, 95–96
SD. See secure digital
secure digital (SD), 12, 214–216
  Android Emulator, 399–401
  APK, 369
  onClick(), 214
SeekBar, 207
self-signed certificates, 359, 362
Send button, 325
Send Email button, 283
sendBroadcast(), 348–349
  BroadcastReceiver, 272
SEND_SMS, 413
sendTextMessage(), 267
sensor, 111
sentIntent, 267
Service, 335, 344, 414

service, 356
services, 331–356
  activities
    binding, 350–356
    communication, 346–350
  AndroidManifest.xml, 333, 335
  asynchronous, 338–341
    IntentService, 343–346
  debugging, 334, 337
  <intent-filter>, 335
  LogCat, 339, 342
  long-running tasks, 336–341
  MainActivity.java, 333–334,
    336–337
  main.xml, 333
  repeated tasks, 341–343
serviceBinder, 355, 356
ServiceConnection, 355
  bindService(), 356
setAlphabeticShortcut(), 188
setBuiltInZoomControls(),
  196, 309
setChoiceMode(), 160
setContentView()
  Activity, 82
  main.xml, 25
  onCreate(), 158
  UI, 112
setData(), 62
  e-mail, 283
  Intent, 53, 64
SetHint(), 56
setIs24HourView(), 146
setLatestEventInfo(), 78
setListAdapter(), 158
setMax, 141
setMultiChoiceItems(), 38
setNegativeButton(), 38
setOnCheckedChangeListener(), 135
setOnClickListener(), 134
setOnCreateContextMenu
    Listener(), 191, 192
setPositiveButton(), 38

setProgress(), 141
setQueryMode(), 193
setRequestOrientation(), 110–111
setResult(), 53
setSatellite(), 310–311
setStreetView(), 311–312
setTextFilterEnabled(), 160
setThreshold(), 144
Settings, 238
   Manage applications, 48
Settings.CONTENT_URI, 243
setTraffic(), 311–312
setType()
   e-mail, 283
   MIME, 64–65
setZoom(), 315
shared preferences, 203
   XML, 208
SharedPreferences, 203–209
shortcut keys
   Android Emulator, 404
   setAlphabeticShortcut(), 188
   setQueryMode(), 193
shouldOverrideUrlLoading(), 412
Show Map button, 59
showDialog(), 37
   callbacks, 37
   dialog windows, 148
   onCreateDialog(), 148
SimpleCursorAdapter, 242
simple_dropdown_item_line, 143
simple_list_item_1, 158
smartphones, 4–5
SMS messaging, 3, 263–281, 413
   Android Emulator, 403–406
   AndroidManifest.xml, 265,
      270–271
   AVD Manager, 266
   built-in applications, 269
   DDMS, 272, 276, 279
   debugging, 266, 272, 276, 279
   feedback, 267–269
   Intent, 272, 276

intents, 269–270
   TextView, 277
   keywords, 281
   MainActivity.java, 265–266,
      274–275
   main.xml, 265, 273
   MIME, 269
   receiving, 270–280
   sending programmatically,
      264–267
   TextView, 273, 276, 277
   Toast, 272
SMS_DELIVERED, 269
SmsManager, 267
SMSReceiver, 280
SMSReceiver.java, 273–274
   BroadcastReceiver, 278–279
   src, 271
SMS_SEND, 270
SMS_SENT, 269
Sony, 4
sp, 85
SpinnerView, 162–165
   debugging, 164
   MainActivity.java, 163–164
   main.xml, 163
   strings.xml, 163
SQLite, 3, 218
   Database Browser, 230
SQLiteOpenHelper, 253
   DBAdapter, 221
src, 22
   ImageButton, 131
   NotificationView.java, 73
   SMSReceiver.java, 271
standard prefix, 238
Start Service button, 342
   LogCat, 345
   onClick(), 356
   Toast, 337, 339, 348
startActivity(), 47, 48, 70
   Intent.FLAG_ACTIVITY_NEW_
      TASK, 280

startActivityForResult(),
     50–54, 70
   Intent, 63
   MainActivity.java, 51
   main.xml, 50
startService(), 335, 343
START_STICKY, 335
static resources, 217–218
status bar, 73–78
   Display Notification button, 76
   NotificationView, 76
   ticket text, 77
Stop Service button, 334
stopSelf(), 341, 343
stopService(), 341, 343
   onDestroy(), 335
storage, 3
   external, 214–216
   internal, 209–214
Streak, 4
street view, 311–312
String, 213
   InputStreamReader, 291
   MainActivity, 143
@string, 23
strings.xml, 23, 161–162, 411
   app_name, 24
   debugging, 162
   getResources(), 162
   MainActivity.java, 162
   res/values, 163
   SpinnerView, 163
style, 141
styles, 32–33
Switch Workspace, 383–385

T

TableLayout, 82, 89–91
<TableRow>, 89
tablets, 4–5
Telephony Actions, 406
Telnet, 403, 405

testing. *See also* debugging
   Android Emulator, 18–19, 214
   AVDs, 21
tethering, 3
text, 267
text file downloads, 288–291
   debugging, 290
   MainActivity.java, 289–290
textfile.txt, 217–218
TextView, 85, 113, 126
   Context, 38
   SimpleCursorAdapter, 242
   SMS messaging, 273, 276
     intents, 277
   <TextView>, 90
<TextView>, 83
   fill_parent, 84
   main.xml, 126
   TextView, 90
themes, 32–33
Thread, 138
Thread.Sleep(), 337
ticket text, 77
TimePicker, 144–149
   Button, 146
   debugging, 144, 146, 148
   dialog windows, 147–149
   MainActivity.java, 145–148
   onTimeSet(), 149
   UI, 146
TimePickerDialog, 149
Timer, 343
TimerTask, 343
title, 188
   queries, 254
Toast, 36, 174, 188, 412
   Context, 38
   Geocoder, 321
   SMS messaging, 272
   Start Service button, 337, 339, 348
ToggleButton, 127–135
tools, 400

U

UI. *See* user interface
update(), 413
   content providers, 252, 255–256
updateContact(), 227–228
URI, 238
Uri, 61
UriMatcher, 253
URL
   Intent, 350–351
   Object, 351
urls, 355
user interface (UI), 81–123
   AbsoluteLayout, 88
   creating programmatically, 111–114
   main.xml, 17, 22, 23, 46, 87–88, 112
   MapView, 305
   notifications, 114–121
   onCreate(), 29, 82
   orientation, 97–111
   res/layout, 28
   setContentView(), 112
   TimePicker, 146
   views, 125–168
   XML, 82, 386
user preferences, 203–209
user-data-qemu.img, 409
<uses-library>, 305, 413
<uses-sdk>, 24, 361

V

values, 22
versions, 2
   AndroidManifest.xml, 23, 360
   android:minSdkVersion, 24
   android:versionCode, 360, 361, 411
   android:versionName, 360, 361
   applications, 360–362

DATABASE_VERSION, 222, 230
Min SDK Version, 21
minSdkVersion, 414
View, 181
views. *See also specific views*
   activities, 82–83
   debugging, 128–129
   events, 119–121, 133–135
   Google Maps, 310–312
   list, 156–165
   menus, 185–193
   onClick(), 135
   onCreate(), 134
   picker, 144–156
   pictures, 169–185
   UI, 125–168
ViewFactory, 180
View.findViewById(), 132
ViewGroups, 82–83
Visibility, 138
vnd.android-dir/mms-sms, 269

W

Web Browser button, 59
web servers, 369–372
Web services
   debugging, 294
   MainActivity.java, 292–294
   networking, 291–296
WebSettings, 196
WebView, 194–200
   debugging, 196
   HTML, 198–199
   loadUrl(), 196, 199
   MainActivity.java, 195–196
   main.xml, 195
WebViewClient, 412
WHERE, 246
while, 141
Wi-Fi triangulation, 322
Window.FEATURE_NO_TITLE, 33
WindowManager, 109

withAppendedId(), 243
WordDefinition(), 294
<WordDefinition>, 295–296
workspaces
    Eclipse, 381–382
    Switch Workspace, 383–385
wrap_content
    layout_height, 131
    layout_width, 84, 130, 132
write(), 213

WRITE_EXTERNAL_STORAGE, 413
    AndroidManifest.xml, 216

X

XML
    downloads, 291
    orientation, 104
    shared preferences, 208
    UI, 82, 386

Y

yr, 156

Z

zoom. *See* built-in zoom controls
zoomIn(), 309, 310
zoomOut(), 309, 310